DOCTRINES OF DECEPTION

The Conspiracy to Systematically Erase Biblical Christianity

MICHAEL DOLAN

HIGH BRIDGE BOOKS
HOUSTON

Doctrines of Deception
By Michael Dolan

Printed in the United States of America
ISBN (Paperback): 978-1-946615-47-3

High Bridge Books titles may be purchased in bulk for educational, business, fundraising, or sales promotional use. For information please contact High Bridge Books via www.HighBridgeBooks.com/contact.

Published in Houston, Texas by High Bridge Books.

Contents

INTRODUCTION

The year was 1992. I had just separated from 11 years and three months of Active-Duty Air Force. I found difficulty going from a Technical Sergeant position—which carried good pay, authority, and a sense of achievement—to being a civilian and having nine jobs my first year out. In my heart, I knew God was real; my parents took my brothers and me to church when we were young. However, I didn't have a personal relationship with the Savior, Jesus Christ. There is a difference in knowing about someone and knowing someone. Spiritually, that is where I was. I read my Bible from time to time, and I had questions—things didn't make sense. So I made an appointment with a friend's pastor in our small military town of Warner Robins, Georgia.

When I walked into Pastor Webb's office, I don't recall what questions I had. I knew I was looking for answers, and I remember his patience in guiding me through what the Bible had to say about salvation in Christ Jesus. After we exchanged greetings and some basic focus questions, Pastor Webb asked me to open my Bible and read selected verses out loud. Those verses are what some Christians call the Roman Road, Bible verses that pertain to salvation through Jesus Christ.

Pastor Webb asked if I understood what I read. He informed me that I only had to ask Jesus to come into my life and be my Lord and Savior, and that is what I did that day in the pastor's office. Understanding salvation through God's Word was like having a veil lifted off my mind. My view of life was expanded to include the spiritual dimension. There was more; there was another view on life than I was led to believe.

Now I wanted to know and understand what the Bible had to say so I could apply it to the world around me, a world that seemed upside down at times. Wanting more than blind acceptance and more than surface-level understanding, I began to read my Bible daily, searching for more than what the Apostle Paul calls the milk of the text. I was interested in the meat and potatoes. The Scriptures about salvation made sense, so I thought to myself, *What about the rest*?

I applied the same in-depth study attitude that allowed me to be very successful in my Air Force career. I have a passion for wanting to know how things work, for understanding the mechanics beyond the top layer. In the case of my Bible studies, I wanted information that would fill in the blanks. The best way to describe it is I knew something wasn't right and I couldn't put my finger on it. Today, I realize that *something* which was missing was the truth, truth that affected my worldview.

I had several jobs my first year out. When I became a Christian, I was working as a carpenter for a privately owned home building supply store, building the exterior door assemblies, some plain, some fancy. Each day at lunchtime, when my coworkers went to lunch, I would remain in the shop. I stayed to eat my packed lunch and listen to Dr. David Jeremiah's radio broadcast called *Turning Point*. At that time, Dr. Jeremiah was in the middle of an expositional study on the Book of Daniel. I purchased his book *The Handwriting on the Wall: Secrets from the Prophecies of Daniel* and followed along in the study.

I was fascinated with the details and the points of origin that expositional type reading provided: the historical background and relevant cultural facts. I couldn't get enough. It is like having the light turned on when you have been stumbling around in the dark. That type of instruction had me hooked. I had questions, and this type of studying had answers if I was willing to pursue them. I purchased Dr. Jeremiah's books and the books of other authors over the years.

About a week or two after my visit with Pastor Webb, my 12-year-old daughter came to me one evening while I was reading my Bible. She said, "Dad, I want what you have." She wanted to know about Jesus and the Bible. I was a new Christian myself, so all I did is repeat what I learned from my visit with Pastor Webb. I opened my Bible and shared the same Scriptures that Pastor Webb shared with me and led my daughter to salvation through Jesus Christ that night, and we were baptized together in Pastor Webb's church. As a father, it is one of my warmest memories.

Over the past 27 years, I continued my search for answers and experienced the common challenges life had to offer. I experienced a job change, night school, divorce, church life, and so on. My studies led me to a handful of expositional teachers. It wasn't enough to say I was a Christian I wanted to understand where the world I lived in was going. For me, knowledge can be a shield. If I believed I was right, based on honest and sincere research, I wouldn't back down. Now I wasn't belligerent or a bully about what I learned. I enjoyed a healthy discussion that had depth. There were times when I took a stand, and the facts proved me wrong. At that point, I would apologize if I pushed too far.

However, my willingness to take a stand when, in my heart, I believed I was right was important. Of course, this only made me more determined to verify what I was learning before I opened my mouth. I once heard a preacher say we don't get to choose what part of the Bible we prefer; the whole Bible applies. If I was expected to believe the gospel message, then I should also trust the biblical prophecies as well. It was an all-or-nothing scenario.

Being prior military, I knew being caught off guard by the enemy wasn't an option, so I had a strong drive to understand God's prophecies. There are connecting threads that go back and forth through the Bible, and it can be an eye-opening experience filled with joy when you make the connection. I wanted to see and understand them. I found that it doesn't take long to see there are opposing forces, both human and spiritual, that want to remove my freedom and yours!

Not everyone shared my enthusiasm for the truth and answers. It became apparent that the topic made some people uncomfortable. The feel-good messages of the Bible were okay to share, but the realities of our enemies and God's prophetic judgments were not. Not everyone wants their worldview disturbed. So I learned quickly that the audience for such topics was small. At times, it was challenging to come across exciting research or have a deeper understanding of the biblical text. My standard response is to want to talk about it.

It is acceptable to go to our job and show excitement about a football game's results from the night before—game results that add no tangible benefits to our lives. It's entertainment. It's okay to go to church on Sunday and hear the preacher's message that usually doesn't ruffle too many feathers. However, intruding in other people's perceived reality was generally met with resistance and personal defense mechanisms. As the years passed, it became clear to me that I wanted to teach my findings, my research. Being a handyman, the topics I shared varied at times between the Bible and home repairs. But the majority fell on my passion with the mysteries of the Bible.

Before YouTube, learning involved books, TV shows, or on-the-job training. Some people learn better by a hands-on approach, but I learn well with books and then application. This approach may be a result of my military training, which involved the use of tech manuals. Tech manuals reduce human error; the instructions were detailed and specific. Equipment needed to be reliable and mission ready. Pardon my sounding like a geek, but books, especially the Bible, cross time barriers and give a blessing to the reader. You can pick up a book from a different generation, a different century, and learn from someone you could never have met and receive a blessing that expands your worldview.

In my heart, I knew that all my studies into the biblical text would have been a waste of time if I took them to my grave without sharing them. What would the benefit be? I already had salvation through the Lord Jesus. An analogy I heard once compared the Sea of Galilee to the Dead Sea. The Sea of Galilee has water flowing into it and water flowing out. It takes in, and it gives out. It is a sea full of life. The Dead Sea also has water flowing into it, but there is no water flowing out of it. It takes in and gives nothing out. There is no life in the Dead Sea, hence the name.

The thought of becoming like the Christians in the last stage of the Christian church before Jesus returns scared me—like the church of Laodicea in Revelation 3. Those Christians were rich with the knowledge of the gospel message and salvation. But because life was good and they lacked for nothing, they sat on their understanding of salvation, not caring about their neighbors who were lost. The Bible tells of the harsh admonishment they received from the Lord.

Research is far more rewarding when shared with others. About a year and a half ago, I took an early retirement package to protect my pension. About five months after leaving my job, my son's friend, Stephen, asked if I knew what I wanted to do now that I had left the phone company. I said I was not sure—the idea was still fresh, and Stephen asked if I ever thought about writing a book.

I enjoyed learning and sharing information; I helped facilitate in my church's Divorce Care Ministry for nine years. I thought, *Well, God has given me the time and resources to take a break from a job*. The more I thought about it, the more it made sense not to let the opportunity pass by. If God was the motivator behind Stephen's prompt and I ignored it, God would find somebody else, and I could be forfeiting a blessing. I had finished college a few years back, so I figured a book is just a very long essay.

Once I got started, the subject matter just began to fall into alignment. The material I had studied over the years found their proper place in the book. As I wrote, a message began to form, and what started as a simple idea to share information became a responsibility to get a message out. Ezekiel 33 tells the story of the watchman on the wall. A watchman sounds the alarm by blowing his horn, warning if there is an impending danger. The horn I am using to sound the alarm is this book. I wrote the *Doctrines of Deception* to inform and warn others. It is my hope and prayer that I have supported my research well enough to cause the reader to want the truth. It is an informative story of how humanity, the mass population, the majority, have been targeted and manipulated for centuries, all for control and to serve the wishes of a small group of people, the minority. This manipulation involves lies, propaganda, and false biblical teaching that has deceived many. To ignore the completion of this book now would only haunt me, knowing I didn't warn my neighbors when I had the chance. I can't bury my head in the sand or hide in some bunker waiting for the prophetic end. My hope is the reader will find valuable insight and blessing in the information within the pages of this book.

1

TRUTH EQUALS REALITY

In today's world of increasing relativism and diminishing truth, it has become of grave importance to know the origin of our worldviews—the root of what we believe to be the truth. Like a math formula, our worldview contains several variables or parts. The families in which we were raised help shape our reality, our traditions, and our education. These inputs establish the reference point we use to function in society.

Our ability to trust and to distrust others is not by instinct. We develop intuition over time and use it to determine our environment's threat level. Daily, we take in large amounts of data; some of this information is simply a part of moving about our day, stop lights, road signs, weather reports, and so on. Others are in the form of acceptable propaganda and advertisements used to sway our decisions to make purchases. Distributed among this information, as tares among wheat, are billboards, newscasts, and television programming that can chip away at our faith, our beliefs, and our morality. They reshape our culture far from its roots established when the Puritans and Pilgrims landed on our shores centuries ago. These inputs are a form of hypnosis, which impacts our worldview.

The purpose and focus of this chapter are to identify the need to protect our minds and, subsequently, the minds of our children. Developing this habit will defend against the deception that is blinding the masses—to promote the task of verifying your "why," the reason you consider something to be true. The process of knowing the why behind your beliefs is not to create doubt about all that you know but to hold on to that which is good and to purge that which is false. You are protecting one of your most valuable gifts, your mind. Where we are ignorant and blind, the enemy can deceive us.

What Is Truth?

"What is truth?"[1] Pilate asked the Lord Jesus Christ this famed question at His trial. Each of us, at some point, are confronted with this question. Is there a justifiable need to determine the origin of what you know and believe to be the truth? The pursuit of the answer will require sacrifice, the spending of time and effort, but it may just be the most crucial search you will ever complete.

What we believe to be the truth forms our worldview. This view can be dynamic or static. It becomes active as we learn and become more informed about the world around us. It is static when we stop growing intellectually. Each of us has core beliefs, ideas, and understandings, which we consider our point of reference to navigate through life. These foundations are the root of our perceived reality. If this is true, then the origin of our core beliefs, ideas, and understandings are the central focus of our search. The question is, do you know the background of your viewpoints? Not only does it shape your reality, but it has a direct effect on the clarity of the lens through which we see the world.

Some people believe truth is found in the structure of science, while others believe it is found in spirituality. Today, science and religion are considered two separate fields of study. That wasn't always the case. Johannes Kepler (1571–1630), a

[1] John 18:38, KJV.

German mathematician, astronomer, and astrologer, had this to say about investigating the world around you:

> The chief aim of all investigation of the external world should be to discover *the rational order and harmony* which has been imposed on it by God.[2] (Emphasis added)

Truth is defined as:

> Conformity to fact or reality; exact accordance with that which is, or has been or shall be.[3]

Reality is defined as:

> Actual being or existence of anything; truth; fact; in distinction from mere appearance.[4]

Truth and reality are tightly woven together; in principle, if a person cannot function within reality, the truth of what is, then they are considered insane. There are varying degrees of insanity, some of which are a danger to society and others that go unnoticed.

Placing the definitions of "truth" and "reality" in logical form offers the possibility that a person who believes the opposite of truth (a lie) is not living in reality. Therefore, they experience some level of insanity, be it large or small. This deviation from reality is due to the belief of a lie or partial truth. The affective damage to a person's life depends on where and to what degree the falsehood is applied. Because we live in a fallen world, we all operate with some form of skewed reality—this is a simple

---

[2] Johannes Kepler, "Kepler's Quote," The Staddon Family, 02/17/2019, https://www.staddonfamily.com/2010/07/01/keplers-quote/.

[3] Webster, *Truth*, http://webstersdictionary1828.com/Dictionary/truth.

[4] Webster, *Reality*, http://webstersdictionary1828.com/Dictionary/reality.

fact. The term for this condition is "Common Insanity," where one operates on less-than-accurate information. This information may have been distributed out of ignorance or with ill intent.

> Common Insanity: A sickness we all suffer from. We have bought into the lies of the world, the flesh and the devil and therefore we live as if the lie is true, denying reality.[5]

The label of insane, regardless of the degree, leaves a negative taste. Insanity is inserted in the text to make the point that each of us has received information that is out of alignment with reality. We could discover as we pull back the veil of deception that a portion of our worldview is not what it has been portrayed to be. Searching for answers can bring you face to face with confrontation—do you continue believing the lie, or do you make a change; do you remain static or be dynamic?

I found the following two quotes by Churchill and Humpal both humorous and worthy of sharing for their wisdom and simplicity in identifying a human characteristic.

> Most people, sometime in their lives, stumble across truth. Most jump up, brush themselves off, and hurry about their business as if nothing had happened. (Sir Winston Churchill)

> When a man who is honestly mistaken hears the truth, he will either quit being mistaken or cease being honest. (Richard Humpal)

Our minds are in a continuous state of recording at the subconscious level. Daily, we are receiving information, data, and stimuli by way of our five senses. These inputs arrive in a variety

---

[5] *The Truth Project,* 1, "Veritology: What is Truth?" Dr. Dale Tackett, Focus on the Family (Cold Water Media, 2006) DVD.

of forms—they may be formal education, traditions, our own experiences, or the experience of others (wisdom).

Our daily inputs are a blend of what is right and what is false, analogous to the parable of the tares and the wheat.[6] Again, our worldview, our reality, has been skewed and distorted by lies, false doctrines. These acts can be committed out of innocent ignorance or with the intent of spreading propaganda in its darkest form. As you and I go about our daily lives, we try to protect our minds. Knowing what is real and what is false realigns our worldview with reality (the truth of what is). In 2006, Focus on the Family produced a DVD series called *The Truth Project,* which is a study of worldviews. The series gave descriptions for *Formal* and *Personal* worldview.

> *Formal Worldview*: A comprehensive set of truth claims that purports to paint a picture of reality.
>
> *Personal Worldview*: The set of individual truth claims that you have embraced so deeply that you believe they reflect what is really real, and therefore they drive what you think, how you act, and what you feel.[7]

We share our worldview basically at two separate levels of personal disclosure. One level is for the general public. This level has restraint and filtration to provide safety from rejection and ridicule. The second type of exposure is revealed only within our sphere of trusted individuals; this view is unfettered. Why do we have different levels of disclosure? Currently, we have the freedom to express ourselves, and the recipient of our thoughts is

---

[6] Matthew 13:24-23.

[7] *The Truth Project,* 2, "Philosophy and Ethics: Says Who?" Dr. Dale Tackett, Focus on the Family (Cold Water Media, 2006) DVD.

free to disagree; some do it with maturity, while others are hostile.

This hostility is on the rise and is intentional. Today public debates are primed with the political left's subversive mobs and rioters. These aggressors are bused in and use pre-planned tactics. Saul D. Alinsky was a successful organizer, activist, and influential writer. His book, *Rules for Radicals,* is what guides the political left when confronting groups or individuals who stand for conservative rights and Christianity. Note Alinsky's instructions:

> The fourth rule is: Make the enemy live up to their own book of rules. You can kill them with this, for they can no more obey their own rules than the Christian church can live up to Christianity.
>
> The fourth rule carries within it the fifth rule: Ridicule is man's most potent weapon. It is almost impossible to counterattack ridicule. Also it infuriates the opposition, who then react to your advantage.[8]

So we developed a need to protect ourselves at many different levels. This cognitive process is learned to meet a survival need. We are not born with this distrust. Compare this apprehension to the trust of a toddler or small child.

A Culture of Distrust

Searching for the truth generates the following question—is there an agenda to deliberately suppress the truth, to keep the masses ignorant of real-world history? Instead of fact, we are fed a daily ration of orchestrated doctrine and propaganda.

---

[8] Saul D. Alinsky, *Rules for Radicals: A Practical Primer for Realistic Radicals,* (New York, Random House, 1971), 128.

Maintaining control over the masses is the primary goal. Questioning a culture's instituted beliefs (true or false), established norms, and implying a deceptive agenda to hide the truth moves a person into that fringe area of conspiracy theories. Regarding conspiracy theories, an issue is only a theory when there are no supporting facts or evidence. Evolution is one such theory. In general, people can handle the topic of conspiracy as long as it does not invade their reality. As long as it doesn't burst their mental bubble. People are aware that conspiracies exist and the effects of being caught up in their undertow.

I will go ahead and push pause here. You may be thinking, *Okay, great, another book about conspiracies, about not trusting the government, about not trusting the establishment.* Before jumping to this conclusion, let's consider the conditioning of the human ability to openly trust. The human brain is programmable. How has the world culture toward the topic of trust influenced the subconscious mind of the masses? I heard a phrase years ago—*"What you do speaks so loud that what you say I cannot hear."*

Daily, we dedicate a portion of our lives, our time, to the management of our security. Our home exterior doors and windows have at least one lock. Some homes have alarm systems installed, and around our homes, we fence in our property's perimeter. We protect the automobiles we drive in the same way. In public schools, our children have lockers with combination locks. Job sites have padlocks on toolboxes and other storage containers. Financial institutions offer checking-accounts that require authorization by our individually unique signature. We have fraud protection on our credit cards, and our debit cards require access pin codes.

Our cyber activities are increasingly becoming a large part of our day, whether through our work or our home activities, and require authentication processes. Just about every device we use—computers, tablets, cell phones, etc., are password protected. Passwords even protect our home Wi-Fi connections to prevent anyone within the signal range from connecting to our home network or internet service provider. If you exclude the possible crook parked outside within the range of your home network, only your neighbors are left—the same people we are expected to trust in our time of need! In the area of physical protection, the request for a concealed weapons permit is continually increasing.

It is an accepted norm in today's culture to complete these precautionary steps of authentication. If you do not, then you are potentially exposing yourself to theft and deceit in the form of fraud. All this security activity reduces the threat from other human beings who cannot be trusted. These actions are not taking place because our culture promotes a sense of safety and trust; the truth is quite the contrary. We live in a world of regulated distrust and deceit. We have heard the phrase "innocent until proven guilty"; well, an underlying current flows through society: "Do not trust until proven trustworthy." This attitude is an unspoken norm. Do these daily activities affect our personal worldview about openly trusting others on a subconscious level? I believe the answer is yes.

Why does a person receive ridicule and rejection for claiming that our children's public schools have become centers of indoctrination, or that counterfeit Christianity is a means to spread deceptive doctrines, or that propaganda is used to steer the masses? Is it because it puts a crack in the snow globe people call their reality or shatters what they have left of the fairytales they remember as a child?

Multiple parts of our lives are protected from fraud by some form of authentication. Are we expected to ignore the theft of our minds? Shouldn't we authenticate what is claimed to be the truth? For the mature and experienced, the evaluation of our personal safety has become automatic. We analyze our environment within seconds upon entering a room. We subconsciously sense whether we are comfortable or uncomfortable. We automatically complete this analysis by one of our most valuable mental faculties, our intuition.

INTUITION

The book titled *Gift of Fear*, by Gavin De Becker, contains a chapter where he discusses the importance of what he calls our *sixth sense*, our *intuition*. Noah Webster defines intuition as follows:

> INTUI'TION ... A looking on; a sight or view; but restricted to mental view or perception. Particularly and appropriately, the act by which the mind perceives the agreement or disagreement of two ideas, or the truth of things, immediately, or the moment they are presented, without the intervention of other ideas, or without reasoning and deduction.[9]

Our subconscious mind records all our experiences; this is our intuition's database. In a split second, when we are in a potentially dangerous situation, we receive thoughts in the form of a gut feeling. This cognitive process is our intuition comparing all our stored experiences with our current circumstance. The final step in this process is to send its derived message, telling us how to respond, perhaps telling us that something is not right. The message may initiate a sense of danger. As De Becker explains in his book, many a victim will ignore their intuition, ignore the alarm, and suffer the consequences, some deadly. De Becker gives this brief description of intuition:

> What Robert Thompson and many others want to dismiss as a coincidence or a gut feeling is in fact a cognitive process, faster than we recognize and far different from the familiar step-by-step thinking we rely on so willingly. We think conscious thought is somehow better, when in fact, intuition is soaring

[9] Noah Webster, *Intuition*, http://webstersdictionary1828.com/Dictionary/intuition.

> flight compared to the plodding of logic. Nature's greatest accomplishment, the human brain, is never more efficient or invested than when its host is at risk. Then, intuition is catapulted to another level entirely, a height at which it can accurately be called graceful, even miraculous. Intuition is the journey from A to Z without stopping at any other letter along the way. It is knowing without knowing why.[10]

It seems every generation of parents must experience the repeated debate between themselves and their teenage children. Our children want to go out with their friends and have a good time. We know they are not fully aware of the threats that potentially exist. Parents, by design, lean on the side of caution and begin our third-degree investigation—where are you going, who are you going with, what time does it start and finish, who else is going to be there, etc. We do this because, based on experience accrued over time, our intuition informs us that things are not always what they appear to be. Others may have a less-than-honorable agenda that is not safe for our child.

We live in a culture of earned trust, where it is both acceptable and prudent to take safety measures to subconsciously authenticate individuals and evaluate our immediate circumstances by way of our intuition. Why is it considered a paranoid act to apply these same cognitive processes to other areas of our life to validate and authenticate the history lessons we received and authenticate the doctrines we receive from administrators of religious dogma. We are designed to learn and grow, which is one of the joys of being human. We actively and voluntarily seek new experiences, new forms of input. However, we also receive new input and programming that is comparable to hypnosis.

---

[10] Gavin De Becker, *The Gift of Fear* (New York: Dell Publishing, 1997), 25.

HYPNOSIS

Our continuous intake of information starts not far from the cradle and ends with the grave. As long as you or I accept blindly what the mainstream media pumps out as truth without scrutiny, we are susceptible to the power of the lie. At that point, the propaganda has potential power over us. You can look at these uncensored inputs as a form of hypnosis. Wikipedia defines hypnosis as follows:

> Hypnosis is a state of human consciousness involving focused attention and *reduced peripheral awareness* and an *enhanced capacity to respond to suggestion*. The term may also refer to an art, skill, or act of inducing hypnosis.[11] (Emphasis added)

Hypnosis is the power of suggestion, and it is worth understanding its effects. The following chapter gives a better understanding of the subject of *Propaganda* and the power of suggestion. In 1960, Dr. Maxwell Maltz wrote a book called *Psycho-Cybernetics*. Dr. Maltz was a plastic surgeon who performed surgery to remove horrific scars from his patients. What followed caught his attention. Some patients still saw themselves as scared and ugly; *the impact* of *those scars transferred from the patient's exterior to their interior*! The power of belief, regardless of what was real, led Dr. Maltz to investigate how the brain functions with truth and perception. He explored the mechanics of how the brain perceived external information—the relationship between perceived truth and actual truth, reality. Dr. Maltz had this to say about hypnosis:

---

[11] "Hypnosis," Wikipedia: The Free Encyclopedia, August 31, 2018, https://en.wikipedia.org/wiki/Hypnosis.

> The important thing for you to remember is that it does not matter in the least how you got the idea or where it came from. You may never have met a professional hypnotist. You may have never been formally hypnotized. But if you have accepted an idea—from yourself, your teachers, your parents, friends, advertisements—or from any other source, and further, if you are firmly convinced that idea is true, it has the same power over you as the hypnotist's words have over the hypnotized subject.[12]

> It is no exaggeration to say that every human being is hypnotized to some extent, either by ideas he has uncritically accepted from others, or ideas he has repeated to himself or convinced himself are true.[13]

Dr. Ravi Zacharias' writings are referenced several times. From the rear cover of his book, *Deliver Us From Evil: Restoring the Soul in a Disintegrating Culture,* is the following:

> Ravi Zacharias, president of Atlanta–based Ravi Zacharias International Ministries, was born in India. He immigrated to Canada in 1966 and studied at Trinity Evangelical Divinity School in Deerfield, IL, and Cambridge University England.... He has lectured in more than fifty countries, and his weekly radio program, "Let My People Think," is broadcast on more than 550 stations around the world.[14]

---

[12] Maxwell Maltz, *Psycho-Cybernetics* (New York: Pocket Books, 1960), 49-50.

[13] Ibid., 53.

[14] Ravi Zacharias, *Deliver Us From Evil: Restoring the Soul in a Disintegrating Culture,* (Nashville, Tennessee: Thomas Nelson, 1997), rear cover.

Dr. Ravi Zacharias on the unshielded mind:

> We are unavoidably beguiled, in this so-called post-modern world, to an unprecedented degree. The constant bombardment of images shapes the perceptions of a whole generation and results in altered beliefs and lifestyles that make even the aberrant seem normal. The double-edged tragedy is not only that we are in such an environment but any warning that we are being molded possibly for the worse is contemptuously mocked as insane.[15]

Men and women who are caught by the increasing pace of daily living (rat race) have been forced to sacrifice time. It takes time to sort through the vast quantities of information directed our way every day. If it is not instant or immediate, then "I don't have time" or "I'll just *Google* it." We accept the default or predetermined meaning. The benefit of validating your beliefs, your whys, and your worldview may prevent you or your loved ones from falling prey to deception.

Because words mean different things to different people, definitions are added with the text as we progress to reduce assumptions between the reader's understanding and the author's intent. Noah Webster's *1828 American Dictionary of the English Language* will be the source for definitions when possible. Noah Webster printed his dictionary approximately 50 years after the signing of the Declaration of Independence. This was before the revisionists were in full swing of changing the meaning of words to be *politically correct*. The pursuit of the correct version of history will require time and effort that goes beyond public education.

---

[15] Ravi Zacharias, *Deliver Us From Evil: Restoring the Soul in a Disintegrating Culture,* (Nashville, Tennessee: Thomas Nelson, 1997), 20.

Bible references, when relevant, will parallel definitions. The goal is to have a worldview that matches reality. For some people, this will require a more in-depth study of God's Word combined with further research.

> If I can change your historical context, I can change the way you view the present; this is the power of historical revisionism[16]

> He who controls the past controls the future.[17]

There are roughly two schools of thought for the formation of world history—the *Accidental Theory* and the *Conspiratorial Theory*. The *Accidental Theory* views all events, wars, world depressions, rise and fall of nations, economic collapses, political plots, etc. as pure chance or just fate. *All the sheep are sheep*. The *Conspiratorial Theory* views the same events taking place because some people or groups with influential power and resources want them to happen. These powers are hidden and meet in secret and plan the course of nations. Here we have a small group of people, the *minority,* controlling a large group of people, the *majority*. The *Conspiratorial Theory is where not all the sheep are sheep. Some are wolves in sheep's clothing*.

Life in America offers its citizens freedoms we may not find in other countries. Freedom of speech and assembly—which is diminishing—and the right to bear arms. We exercise these freedoms, knowing that certain aspects of our culture are out of our control. Changes can be voted in and out whether we like it or not. Within stable cultures, some reference points are considered unchanging. They act as guideposts as we travel through life. These are known as absolutes.

---

[16] *The Truth Project,* 7, "Sociology: The Divine Imprint," Dr. Dale Tackett, Focus on the Family (Cold Water Media, 2006) DVD.

[17] Ibid.

ABSOLUTES

Do absolutes exist? If you are a Christian, yes, there are because God is absolute. All countries have foundational blocks that support their society, their way of life. Here in America, there is an agenda to tear down the foundational block of believing in absolute truth.

> AB'SOLUTE, ... 1. Literally, in a general sense, free, independent of anything extraneous. Hence, 2. Complete in itself; positive; as an *absolute* declaration. 3. Unconditional, as an *absolute* promise. 4. Existing independent of any other cause, as God is *absolute*[18]

Below is a current look at *absolute truth vs. relativism.* The article from the website allaboutphilosophy.org was short and to the point and, therefore, worth inserting in its original form.

> Absolute Truth – Inflexible Reality
> "Absolute truth" is defined as inflexible reality: fixed, invariable, unalterable facts. For example, it is a fixed, invariable, unalterable fact that there are absolutely no square circles and there are absolutely no round squares.
>
> Absolute Truth vs. Relativism
> While absolute truth is a logical necessity, there are some religious orientations (atheistic humanists, for example) who argue against the existence of absolute truth. Humanism's exclusion of God necessitates moral relativism. Humanist John Dewey (1859-1952),

---

[18] Noah Webster, *American Dictionary of the English Language* (Chesapeake, Virginia: The Foundation for American Christian Education, 2010), http://webstersdictionary1828.com/Dictionary/Absolute.

co-author and signer of the Humanist Manifesto 1 (1933), declared, "There is no God and there is no soul. Hence, there are no needs for the props of traditional religion. With dogma and creed excluded, then immutable truth is also dead and buried. There is no room for fixed, natural law or moral absolutes." Humanists believe one should do, as one feels is right.

Absolute Truth – A Logical Necessity

"There are no absolutes." First, the relativist is declaring there are absolutely no absolutes. That is an absolute statement. The statement is logically contradictory. If the statement is true, there is, in fact, an absolute—there are absolutely no absolutes.

"Truth is relative." Again, this is an absolute statement implying truth is absolutely relative. Besides positing an absolute, suppose the statement was true and "truth is relative." Everything including that statement would be relative. If a statement is relative, it is not always true. If "truth is relative" is not always true, sometimes truth is not relative. This means there are absolutes, which means the above statement is false. When you follow the logic, relativist arguments will always contradict themselves.

"Who knows what the truth is, right?" In the same sentence the speaker declares that no one knows what the truth is, then he turns around and asks those who are listening to affirm the truth of his statement.

"No one knows what the truth is." The speaker obviously believes his statement is true.[19]

---

[19] "Absolute Truth," All About Philosophy, August 15, 2018, https://www.allaboutphilosophy.org/absolute-truth.htm.

Absolute Truth – Morality

Morality is a facet of absolute truth. Thus, relativists often declare, "It's wrong for you to impose your morals on me." By declaring something is wrong, the relativist is contradicting himself by imposing his morals upon you.

You might hear, "There is no right, there is no wrong!" You must ask, is that statement right or wrong?

If you catch a relativist in the act of doing something they know is absolutely wrong, and you try to point it out to them, they may respond in anger, "Truth is relative! There's no right and there's no wrong! We should be able to do whatever we want!" If that is a true statement and there is no right and there is no wrong, and everyone should be able to do whatever they want, then why have they become angry? What basis do they have for their anger? You can't be appalled by an injustice, or anything else for that matter, unless an absolute has somehow been violated.

Relativists often argue, "Everybody can believe whatever they want!" It makes us wonder, why are they arguing? We find it amusing that relativists are the ones who want to argue about relativism.

If you attempt to tell a relativist the difference between right and wrong, you will no doubt hear, "None of that is true! We make our own reality!" If that's true, and we all create our own reality, then our statement of moral accountability is merely a figment of the relativist's imagination. If a relativist has

> a problem with a statement of absolute morality, the relativist should take the issue up with himself.[20]

Without absolutes, there would be no foundation for a person to establish their thinking or worldview. It would be difficult to stay on course when buffeted by life's storms if your mental compass didn't have a "True North," a reliable point of reference.

Is it necessary to have faith in what you believe? Fair question. To have confidence in our actions, actions that spring from our beliefs, we do need faith that what we believe is real. Doubting our beliefs or having weak faith creates instability. A Christian does not want his or her views based on what we consider relativism. From the book of James:

> But let him ask in faith, nothing wavering. For he that wavereth is like a wave of the sea driven with the wind and tossed. For let not that man think that he shall receive any thing of the Lord. A double minded man is unstable in all his ways. [21]

Individually, people will put their faith or trust in their abilities, bank accounts, spouse, education, and any number of things that are not God. In Hebrews 11, we find this much-read verse.

> Now faith is the substance of things hoped for, the evidence of things not seen.[22]

---

[20] "Absolute Truth," All About Philosophy, August 15, 2018, https://www.allaboutphilosophy.org/absolute-truth-2.htm.

[21] James 1:6-8, KJV.

[22] Hebrews 11:1, KJV.

Noah Webster's Reference:

FAITH...

1. Belief; the assent of the mind to the truth of what is declared by another, resting on his authority and veracity, without other evidence; the judgment that what another states or testifies is the truth. I have strong faith or no faith in the testimony of a witness, or in what a historian narrates.
2. The assent of the mind to the truth of a proposition advanced by another; belief, or probable evidence of any kind.
3. In theology, the assent of the mind or understanding to the truth of what God has revealed. Simple belief of the Scriptures, of the being and perfections of God, and of the existence, character and doctrines of Christ, founded on the testimony of the sacred writers, is called historical or speculative faith; a faith little distinguished from the belief of the existence and achievements of Alexander or of Cesar.
4. Evangelical, justifying, or saving faith is the assent of the mind to the truth of divine revelation, on the authority of God's testimony, accompanied with a cordial assent of the will or approbation of the heart; an entire confidence or trust in God's character and declarations, and in the character and doctrines of Christ, with an unreserved surrender of the will to his guidance, and dependence on his merits for salvation. In other words, that firm belief of God's testimony, and of the truth of the gospel, which influences the will, and

leads to an entire reliance on Christ for salvation.[23]

BELIE'F ...

1. A persuasion of the truth, or an assent of mind to the truth of a declaration, proposition, or alleged fact, on the ground of evidence, distinct from personal knowledge; as the belief of the gospel; belief of a witness. belief may also by founded on internal impressions, or arguments and reasons furnished by our own minds; as the belief of our senses; a train of reasoning may result in belief, belief is opposed to knowledge and science.
2. In theology, faith, or a firm persuasion of the truths of religion.[24]

Faith is a critical part of our mental programming; it is a factor in *what we accept and what we reject*—our point of reference. A few years ago, I helped facilitate my church's Divorce Care Ministry. In week one of 13 classes, we introduced the attendees to an analogy to help determine their central focal point. *What you focus on becomes your reality.* Picture a satellite orbiting the Earth. A satellite's orbit remains stable as long as the Earth is stable. Removing the Earth or radically changing its shape will have a direct effect on the satellite's ability to maintain a steady, consistent orbit. In the class, we ask the attendees to evaluate what they have been orbiting around, where they have placed their trust and faith for their life's security or well-being. The goal was for the attendees to identify who or what they were orbiting around.

The central focal point must be someone who doesn't change. Each of us must have a stable reference point for our

---

[23] Webster, *Faith*, http://webstersdictionary1828.com/Dictionary/faith.

[24] Webster, *Belief*, http://webstersdictionary1828.com/Dictionary/belief.

thinking. The human mind needs a reference point by which it can make decisions. This example illustrates the importance of accuracy in what we consider the truth. In the class, we explain that the only stable being to have as your center is God. He is unchanging and always faithful.

As Christians, we are guilty of idolatry if we place our faith in anything other than God. We have all fallen short of this directive. For those who are stubborn, me included, it may take a lifetime of learning to get it right. For the reader who lives in Western culture, there is a small book by author Timothy Keller titled *Counterfeit Gods.*[25] It is an insightful read to see how our Western culture has created counterfeit gods in our lives. A small excerpt from Keller's introduction may prompt you to want to know more.

> The biblical concept of idolatry is an extremely sophisticated idea, integration intellectual, psychological, social, cultural, and spiritual categories. There are personal idols, such as romantic love and family; or money, power, and achievement; or access to particular social circles; or the emotional dependence of others on you; or health, fitness, and physical beauty. Many look to these things for hope, meaning, and fulfillment that only God can provide.[26]

For the Christian, God is both absolute and the source of truth. Consider combining two other words that have been defined, *absolute* and *reality*. Could a claim be made for *absolute reality*? This could easily be another study with many rabbit holes to search out, but to add food for thought, let us consider a

---

[25] ISBN 978-0-525-95136-0.

[26] Timothy Keller, *Counterfeit Gods: The Empty Promises of Money, Sex, and Power, and the Only Hope that Matters* (New York: Penguin Group, 2009), xix.

statement by the Apostle Paul in 2 Corinthians, which I thought alluded to such a thing.

> For our light affliction, which is but for a moment, worketh for us a far more exceeding and eternal weight of glory; While we look not at the things which are seen, but at the things which are not seen: *for the things which are seen are temporal; but the things which are not seen are eternal.*[27] (Emphasis added)

WISDOM

Like "truth" and "reality," the word "wisdom" is often used. In the Bible, wisdom is highly valued above earthly treasures.

> Wisdom is the principal thing; therefore get wisdom: and with all thy getting *get understanding.*[28] (Emphasis added)

> How much better is it to get wisdom than gold! and to *get understanding* rather to be chosen than silver![29] (Emphasis added)

> But let patience have her perfect work, that ye may be perfect and entire, wanting nothing. If any of you lack wisdom, let him ask of God, that giveth to all men liberally, and upbraideth not; and it shall be given him.[30]

---

[27] 2 Corinthians 4:17-18, KJV.

[28] Proverb 4:7, KJV.

[29] Proverb 16:16, KJV.

[30] James 1:4-5, KJV.

In Webster's Dictionary, we find "wisdom" defined as follows:

> 1. The right use or exercise of knowledge; the choice of laudable ends, and of the best means to accomplish them. This is wisdom in act, effect, or practice. If wisdom is to be considered as a faculty of the mind, it is the faculty of discerning or judging what is most just, proper and useful, and if it is to be considered as an acquirement, it is the knowledge and use of what is best, most just, most proper, most conducive to prosperity or happiness. wisdom in the first sense, or practical wisdom is nearly *synonymous with discretion.* It differs somewhat from prudence, in this respect; prudence is the exercise of sound judgment in avoiding evils; *wisdom is the exercise of sound judgment either in avoiding evils or attempting good.* Prudence then is a species, of which wisdom is the genus. (Emphasis added)
>
> WISDOM gained by experience, is of inestimable value.[31]

Wisdom is learning from the experience of others. Education is similar to wisdom; in fact, education is gained from the experience of others. While we do learn from those who have come before us, we also learn from our own experiences. We should evaluate both types of input and stimuli for accuracy.

[31] Webster, *Wisdom,* http://webstersdictionary1828.com/Dictionary/wisdom.

INCOMING DATA

We are bombarded daily with both visual and audible propaganda through billboards, signs, television, radio, cell phones, etc. Today, checking cell phones has become a compulsive habit, especially for our youth. We have all seen patients in a hospital coming down the hall with their IV bag on a pole. These patients are receiving a *steady dose* and are *always connected*. Cell phones are like a propaganda IV bag.

Electronic devices have their benefits. Rarely will a person leave their mobile devices at home. People are not in an endless state of being educated by the steady stream of input they receive from their devices. The truth is most of our daily data from media devices is not helpful. Consciously or unconsciously, we are receiving stimuli that should be filtered and inspected. This action is like the process a computer performs when running a security scan for viruses and malware. People will purchase antivirus software to protect their computers (electronic brain), but do you protect your mind with the same intensity? Years ago, there was a phrase related to the computer programming environment, *garbage in garbage out*. The simple point is boundaries are required to protect our minds and the minds of our children. If there are no boundaries, then there is no first line of defense.

> Keep thy heart with all diligence; for out of it are the issues of life.[32]

Dr. Ravi Zacharias on the need for protective barriers:

> Immersed in this mix of change and decay, can we at least understand the scope of the conflict? Can we appeal to our collective conscience while a few still remain who realize that there must be fences in life,

[32] Proverb 4:23, KJV.

> else predators, with unrestrained and insatiable passions, will break down every wall of protection and relentlessly plunder everything we treasure?[33]

We all receive information from the time we are born until the time we pass into eternity. We are born with our minds being pretty much a blank hard drive, like a new computer sitting on a warehouse shelf. The manufacturer receives an order, and then the computer is programmed with the desired software. Humanity, unlike creatures in the animal kingdom, is not born with a set of built-in instincts (software) to know danger right from birth. A baby gazelle does not need a class in *Lions 101* to know that the hungry lion is not its friend.

When we are born, we have software operating the subconscious level to keep our internal organs and associated body systems automatically functioning. But on a conscious level, we only know to cry out loud if there is an unmet need. From that point forward, we are receiving input (updates) in the form of external stimuli from the world around us. This information comes to us from a myriad of sources—our education, formal and informal, traditions, and the opinions of well-meaning friends and family. This input includes hateful things that have been said to us, etc. These inputs again shape our view of the world around us, what we consider safe or unsafe. Obtaining a quality education is essential. For a society to function both peacefully and efficiently, encouraging our children to become educated is a worthy goal. Public school is a blend of education and indoctrination. Consider this statement from the chapter on propaganda.

> The normal school should provide for the training of the educator to make him realize that his is a twofold

---

[33] Zacharias, *Deliver Us From Evil*, 21.

> job: education as a teacher and education as a propagandist.[34]

Being a typical 1970s teenager in high school, I didn't place the appropriate value on my education. My school years of K through 12 were through the public-school system. That is not a complaint; I have fond memories of some excellent teachers who had a heart for the students in their care. From high school, I went directly into the United States Air Force to take advantage of the training opportunities and look for a fresh start. That was in the days before an "online" anything, especially college. When I wasn't on deployment, I attended night school. The goal of obtaining a higher education was drilled into my head if I wanted to improve my standard of living. Peeking into the book of wisdom, Proverbs, we find,

> In all labour there is profit: but the talk of the lips
> tendeth only to penury.[35]

There is value in working hard toward a goal; through continuous studying while in the Air Force, I was able to progress in rank quickly. My view of the public-school system is double-sided. On one side, there is the benefit of gaining higher education, and on the opposing flank, public schools are part of the propaganda conduit to program the minds of our young. The public school system is not a private institution. It is a state-run institute, and like any government-managed department, it has a hierarchy. Government hierarchies decide which courses and ideologies are acceptable. John Dewey (1859 –1952) is considered the architect behind our modern education. Here's a repeating of Dewey's quote about having God in the schools:

---

[34] Edward L. Bernays, *Propaganda* (New York: Liveright Publishing Corp., 1928), 122.

[35] Proverb 14:23, KJV.

> Faith in the prayer-hearing God is an unproved and outmoded faith. There is no God and there is no soul. Hence, there are no needs for the props of traditional religion. With dogma and creed excluded, then immutable truth is also dead and buried. There is no room for fixed, natural law or moral absolutes.[36]

This is what God has to say:

> The fool hath said in his heart, There is no God.[37]

> My people are destroyed for lack of knowledge: because thou hast rejected knowledge … [38]

Antony Sutton is an author and professor. His credentials include a research fellowship at the Hoover Institute and tenure at Stanford University, and he taught economics at California State University. He received his education from the universities of London, Gottingen, and California. Mr. Sutton earned a D. Sc. Degree from the University of Southampton, England. He has this to add about John Dewey.

> Dewey was an ardent statist, and a believer in the Hegelian idea that the child exists to be trained to serve the State. This requires suppression of individualist tendencies and a careful spoon-feeding of approved knowledge. This "dumbing down" of American education is not easily apparent unless you have studied in both foreign and domestic U.S.

---

[36] Ronald Nash, *The Closing of the American Heart: What's Really Wrong with America's Schools* (United States of America: Probe Books), 91.

[37] Psalm 14:1, KJV.

[38] Hosea 4:6, KJV.

> universities—then the contrast becomes crystal clear. This dumbing down is now receiving attention.[39]

Family traditions are an authoritative source of informal education and can be either helpful or harmful. Children who experience strong emotional ties to family life lessons can experience a significant impact on their belief systems. This impact can become embedded deep within their subconscious. The emotions and the lesson determine whether it becomes a curse or a blessing. Showing a child the value of doing yard work around their home benefits the child. The advantage is the knowledge that the home they live in will require labor if they want to keep it beautiful and in good repair. It is not necessary to show the impact an abusive home life has on children. Our society allows us to see those results every time we turn on the evening news.

My teenage years were during the 1970s, and at that time in Buffalo, New York, if you were at least 12 years old, you could have a newspaper route. To my mother's credit, she made it clear in a house of five boys that if you want to spend money, you will have to earn it. When each of us became 12 years old, we signed up at the local grocery store to have a newspaper route. I was excited. And like the postman, we delivered in all kinds of weather. In addition to a newspaper route, winters in Buffalo provided the opportunity to earn money shoveling snow for those who did not want to deal with it. These minor details of my teenage years show that traditions can have a positive impact on a person's character.

Our character develops from our education, experience, and the wisdom of others in our lives. There is a book for men, written by Dr. Aubrey Andelin, titled *Man of Steel and Velvet.*[40] The

---

[39] Antony Sutton, *America's Secret Establishment, An introduction to The Order of Skull and Bones,* (Billings, Montana: Liberty House Press, 1983), 14.

[40] ISBN: 0-911094-15-6.

book is no longer in print, but you can still find copies sold by booksellers. I highly recommend it to young men as often as I can. A section of the book discusses *character,* and Dr. Andelin wrote the following:

> The supreme quality of manhood is the strength of a noble character. A man may have the strength of masculinity that adds substance to his life, but it will never be of maximum worth unless refined by a sterling character.[41]

The following verse parallels this wisdom:

> Train up a child in the way he should go: and when he is old, he will not depart from it.[42]

Education (doctrine) and traditions have their place in the building of society. But there is an opposing side to truth and what is right and wholesome for a culture. As the old radio program with Paul Harvey was famous for broadcasting:

> Hello Americans, I'm Paul Harvey. You know what the news is—in a minute, you're going to hear the rest of the story.[43]

DOCTRINE

For our youth, we would prefer truth over lies and positive nurturing input, but the chance always exists for information that

---

[41] Dr. Aubrey Andelin, *Man of Steel and Velvet: A Guide to Masculine Development* (Pierce City, Missouri: Pacific Press Santa Barbara, 1972), 133.

[42] Proverb 22:6, KJV.

[43] "Paul Harvey," Wikiquote, August 15, 2018, https://en.wikiquote.org/wiki/Paul_Harvey.

hinders a person to make its way in as well. Now we confront a fundamental term, "doctrine." As with the previous words, for clarity, let us establish the definition from *Webster's Dictionary*:

> DOCTRINE, *noun* [Latin, to teach.]
>
> 1. *In a general sense, whatever is taught.* Hence, a principle or position in any science; whatever is laid down as true by an instructor or master. The doctrines of the gospel are the principles or truths taught by Christ and his apostles. The doctrines of Plato are the principles which he taught. *Hence a doctrine may be true or false; it may be a mere tenet or opinion.*
> 2. The act of teaching. He taught them many things by parables, and said to them in his *doctrine Mark 4:2*
> 3. Learning; knowledge. Whom shall he make to understand doctrine? *Isaiah 28:9*
> 4. The truths of the gospel in general. That they may adorn the *doctrine* of God our Savior in all things. *Titus 2:1*
> 5. Instruction and confirmation in the truths of the gospel. *2 Timothy 3:10.*[44] (Emphasis added)

Johnathan Edwards (1703–1758) was an American preacher, philosopher, and Protestant theologian—a Puritan who held to Reformed theology. A quote from his works published in 1808, relating to doctrine follows:

---

[44] Webster, *Doctrine*, http://webstersdictionary1828.com/Dictionary/Doctrine.

> Of all kinds of knowledge that we can ever obtain, the knowledge of God, and the knowledge of ourselves, are the most important.[45]

It is essential to note the definition of the word "doctrine" applies to more than just religious applications. It means instruction or teaching of any kind. You may be familiar with the subject of false doctrine. It is easier to identify the counterfeit when you have made yourself familiar with the original. We have briefly reviewed the definitions of truth, reality, wisdom, and doctrine. The opposite of the truth is a lie. Today, to avoid being offensive, rather than say the news media is lying to us, they'll call it "fake news." All right, what is a lie? Using Webster's definition,

1. A criminal falsehood; a falsehood uttered for the purpose of deception; an intentional violation of truth. Fiction, or a false statement or representation, not intended to deceive, mislead or injure, as in fables, parables and the like, is not a lie … It is willful deceit that makes a lie. A man may act a lie as by pointing his finger in a wrong direction, when a traveler inquires of him his road….
2. A fiction; in a ludicrous sense….
3. False doctrine. 1 John 2:1….
4. An idolatrous picture of God, or a false god. Romans 1:25….
5. That which deceives and disappoints confidence…. To give the lie to charge with falsehood. A man's actions may give the lie to his words.

[45] Edwards, Johnathan (1808). A careful and strict inquiry into the modern prevailing notions of the freedom of will … . Albany, NY: Backus & Whiting, Author's Preface.

LIE, *verb intransitive*

1. To utter falsehood with an intention to deceive, or with an immoral design.
   Thou hast not lied to men, but to God. Acts 5:3.
2. To exhibit a false representation; to say or do that which deceives another, when he has a right to know the truth, or when morality requires a just representation.[46]

Do lies have an origin or a beginning? The Bible provides an answer, where Jesus Christ states the following:

> Ye are of your father the devil, and the lusts of your father ye will do. He was a murderer from the beginning, and abode not in the truth, because there is no truth in him. When he speaketh a lie, he speaketh of his own: *for he is a liar, and the father of it.*[47] (Emphasis added)

Belief in a lie can have devastating effects on an individual or a nation. Details about this type of devastation are discussed in a later chapter. Belief in a lie can start a chain reaction in a person's thought process and bring them to a false conclusion. This process has been known to lead people astray (off course). Let us follow the chain of events. People's actions originate from their thoughts. If our thinking is affected by our beliefs, and those beliefs come from lies, then our efforts can potentially cause harm.

The word "myth" can be associated with lies due to the lack of support to verify it as truth. Note this short quote from John F. Kennedy, our 35th President:

---

[46] Webster, *Lie*, http://webstersdictionary1828.com/Dictionary/lie.

[47] John 8:44, KJV.

> The great enemy of the truth is very often not the lie—deliberate, contrived, and dishonest—but the myth—persistent, persuasive, and unrealistic.[48]

The devil's weapon of choice in spiritual warfare is to plant lies (seeds) into our subconscious mind to create false beliefs. And he has been very successful from the beginning. The devil plants these seeds to harvest some form of destruction in our lives. It is not a pleasant thought but a reality of spiritual warfare. Of course, you would have to believe in a spiritual realm to even consider such things. The lies that attack us could be about the love God has for each of us[49]. We may have talents and abilities that we don't believe are possible. The devil's lies could be any number of deceptive statements we consider to be true. The point is they are lies, and we act on what we believe and think to be true. Our actions don't just happen without an associated thought triggering that action; our responses are not random. Because the human brain can process information at lightning speed, some of our activities appear to be spontaneous. As a result, we do not act randomly; we operate from information stored either at our conscious or subconscious level. Even though it may seem that we responded almost immediately, our actions are steered by what we know and believe.

> For as he thinketh in his heart, so is he: Eat and drink, saith he to thee; but his heart is not with thee.[50]

---

[48] John F. Kennedy, "Commencement Address at Yale University," June 11, 1962, as quoted by the American Presidency Project, accessed May 27, 2019, https://www.presidency.ucsb.edu/documents/commencement-address-yale-university.

[49] John 3:16, KJV. For God so loved the world, that he gave his only begotten Son, that whosoever believeth in him should not perish, but have everlasting life.

[50] Proverb 23:7, KJV.

An enjoyable little book was written in 1903 by James Allen titled *As a Man Thinketh.*[51] Mr. Allen goes into the "cause and effect" of what our thoughts produce. In biblical terms, *for whatsoever a man soweth, that shall he also reap.*[52]

> A man is literally what he thinks, his character being the complete sum of all his thoughts. As the plant springs from, and could not be without the seed, so every act of a man springs from the hidden seeds of thought, and could not have appeared without them. This applies equally to those acts called "spontaneous" and "unpremeditated" as to those which are deliberately executed.[53]

Dr. Ravi Zacharias on thought and action:

> Behind an act is a thought or a belief, and those thoughts unleashed in antisocial behavior make the headlines. Yet seldom are these thoughts and beliefs scrutinized. When that is done we, like Oscar Wilde, may find out that though we may play with sinister ideas in our imaginations and artistic escapes, we cannot do the same with life.[54]

What's the big deal? Is all this analysis of truth, lies, information, and sources of origin that important? The enemy seems to think so. Humanity's enemy in the spiritual realm is the devil and his associates. In the earthly realm, it is people who are his willing vessels (pawns) or unwilling vessels (victims). The devil

---

[51] ISBN: 0-8802-9785-9.

[52] Galatians 6:7, KJV.

[53] James Allen, *Motivational Classics: As A Man Thinketh* (Mechanicsburg, Pennsylvania: Executive Books, 2007), 91.

[54] Ravi Zacharias, *Deliver Us From Evil,* xv.

makes good use of twisting the truth and spreading false information. The devil cannot compete with the "Truth."

In Matthew 4, we see the account of what happened after Jesus spent 40 days fasting in the wilderness. Satan (the devil) shows up to tempt the Lord into misusing His divine power to satisfy worldly needs. Three times, Satan tries to seduce Jesus by twisting the truth of what God has said, just as he did with Eve. Jesus responds to each temptation with the truth of God's Word. Because Satan failed, he leaves. Satan's alternative to failing to contend with God's Word is to have men and women misinterpret the Scriptures. If we believe a lie or false doctrine, then he has a foot in the door of our lives, by the creation of strongholds.

> Wherefore putting away lying, speak every man truth with his neighbour: for we are members one of another. Be ye angry, and sin not: let not the sun go down upon your wrath: *Neither give place to the devil.*[55] (Emphasis added)

> All Scripture is given by inspiration of God, and is profitable for doctrine, for reproof, for correction, for instruction in righteousness:[56]

STRONGHOLDS

From that point, lies are used to establish what the Bible calls "strongholds."

Noah Webster defines stronghold in this way;

---

[55] Ephesians 4:25-27, KJV.

[56] 2 Timothy 3:16, KJV.

> STRONG-HOLD, *noun* [strong and hold.] A fastness; a fort; a fortified place; a place of security.[57]

A stronghold is a place the enemy establishes to do battle and feel secure *in our territory* (our subconscious mind). History has shown many times over that lies and false information have caused considerable damage, even started wars between individuals and nations alike. If lies can tear down and create chaos, then, logically, knowledge of the truth should have the opposite effect.

> And ye shall know the truth, and the truth shall make you free.[58]

> The thief cometh not, but for to steal, and to kill, and to destroy: I am come that they might have life, and that they might have it more abundantly.[59]

Knowing the truth and applying it are two separate events when it comes to making personal changes. Isn't it interesting how quickly we are willing to help change/correct another person's ways? From our outside perspective, we can see their error! This assessment is mutual in close relationships such as with friends, families, and spouses. The Bible admonishes us to change/correct ourselves first:

> And why beholdest thou the mote that is in thy brother's eye, but considerest not the beam that is in thine own eye? Or how wilt thou say to thy brother, Let me pull out the mote out of thine eye; and,

---

[57] Webster, *Strong-hold*, http://webstersdictionary1828.com/Dictionary/Strong-hold

[58] John 8:32, KJV.

[59] John 10:10, KJV.

> behold, a beam is in thine own eye? Thou hypocrite, first cast out the beam out of thine own eye; and then shalt thou see clearly to cast out the mote out of thy brother's eye.[60]

If we were honest with ourselves, then we are likely aware of how difficult it is to change ourselves even when our discrepancy is known. Change can be challenging. Strongholds can offer a bulwark of resistance when we attempt to alter the way we think, act, and see the world around us. Our brain develops familiar, repetitive ways of responding to life's issues. Our *limbic system* handles these processes—the portion of the brain responsible for our thinking and movement. We begin to create default or habitual responses. From Dr. Bessel A. van der Kolk's book *The Body Keeps Score: Mind and Body in the Healing of Trauma,* note the process in building these pathways:

> The limbic system is shaped in response to experience, in partnership with the infant's own genetic makeup and inborn temperament. (As all parents of more than one child quickly notice, babies differ from birth in the intensity and nature of their reactions to similar events.) Whatever happens to a baby contributes to the emotional and perceptual map of the world that its developing brain creates. As my colleague Bruce Perry explains it, the brain is formed in a "use-dependent manner." This is another way of describing *neuroplasticity,* the relatively recent discovery that neurons that "fire together, *wire together.*" When a circuit fires repeatedly, it can become a default setting—*the response most likely to occur.* If you feel safe and loved, your brain becomes specialized in exploration, play, and cooperation; if you are

[60] Matthew 7:3-5, KJV.

> frightened and unwanted, it specializes in managing feelings of fear and abandonment.[61] (Emphasis added)

How many times have you heard an individual say a phrase like this: "That's just the way I'm wired"? The Apostle Paul, in Romans 12, offers these instructions for us to create new pathways in our thinking:

> And be *not conformed to this world*: but be ye *transformed* by the *renewing of your mind*, that ye may prove what is that good, and acceptable, and perfect, will of God.[62] (Emphasis added)

I have a dear friend, a sister in Christ, who is a licensed family therapist. She explained that through *neuroplasticity*, it could take up to three years to remap our mind. Could this be what the Apostle Paul was expressing in Galatians 1:

> But when it pleased God, who separated me from my mother's womb, and called me by his grace, To reveal his Son in me, that I might preach him among the heathen; immediately I conferred not with flesh and blood: Neither went I up to Jerusalem to them which were apostles before me; but I went into Arabia, and returned again unto Damascus. *Then after three years* I went up to Jerusalem to see Peter, and abode with him fifteen days.[63] (Emphasis added)

---

[61] Bessel A. Van der Kolk, MD., *The Body Keeps Score: Brain, Mind and Body in the Healing of Trauma* (New York, Viking Press, 2014), 56.

[62] Romans 12:2, KJV.

[63] Galatians 1: 15-18, KJV.

From the website *Reading Acts*, writer Phillip J. Long offers this view about the Apostle Paul's three-year trip:

> Sometimes this period is described as a spiritual retreat into the desert, to work out the implications of his encounter with Jesus. I think that it is certain that Paul begins working through what "Jesus as Messiah" means, and what his role as the 'light to the Gentiles" should be. He likely spent a great deal of time reading the Scripture developing the material that he will use later in Antioch, then on the missionary journeys. But this period is not a monastic retreat! Paul is preaching Jesus and being faithful to his calling as the light to the Gentiles.[64]

Strongholds can offer substantial resistance to positive change. Neuroplasticity, the building of new habits and ways of responding, is a means to overcome difficulties with change. For some, a shift in their worldview and thinking doesn't take place until specific strongholds have been torn down.

> For though we walk in the flesh, we do not war after the flesh: (For the weapons of our warfare are not carnal, but mighty through God to the pulling down of strong holds Casting down imaginations, and every high thing that exalteth itself against the knowledge of God, and bringing into captivity every thought to the obedience of Christ; [65]

Lies in the form of strongholds war against the Truth. Jesus Christ makes known His reason for being born and entering our

---

[64] Phillip J. Long, "Why Did Paul Go to Arabia?" Reading Acts, September 8, 2017, https://readingacts.com/2017/09/08/why-did-paul-go-to-arabia/

[65] 2 Corinthians 10:3-5, KJV.

world. This mission is made clear in the exchange between Jesus and Pilate in John 18:

> Pilate therefore said unto him, Art thou a king then? Jesus answered, Thou sayest that I am a king. *To this end was I born,* and for this cause came I into the world, that *I should bear witness unto the truth.* Every one that is of the truth heareth my voice.[66] (Emphasis added)

> He that committeth sin is of the devil; for the devil sinneth from the beginning. For this purpose the Son of God was manifested, *that he might destroy the works of the devil.* [67] (Emphasis added)

We have compared and discussed the terms of truth, reality, absolutes, faith, wisdom, doctrine, lies, and strongholds. It would take all our energy daily if we had to verify consciously every little thing for its trustworthiness. We have learned to operate at a cultural level of trust or faith. A child develops the habit of who and what to trust early in life. We apply this habit of blind trust in the same way a blanket is used to cover a large area.

Blanket Faith

In Christian circles, there is always talk of having faith. Do you have faith? You only need faith. The object of our faith identifies where we have put our trust and security. Every day, we make use of faith that is not spiritual; it is functional. Our society functions on what I call *blanket faith.* We apply a great deal of blind trust or confidence as we go about our day. When visiting a

[66] John 18:37 KJV.

[67] 1 John 3:8, KJV.

restaurant to have a meal, you use blanket faith that the meal won't make you sick, that the salt and pepper shakers have salt and pepper in them and not poison.

This line of reasoning may sound humorous or even absurd to bring into the text, but it is to establish its existence. When shopping at the grocery store, you trust that the products and produce you purchase are safe and healthy for consumption. We are trusting the food manufacturers and government agencies like the Food and Drug Administration who regulate them. The everyday consumer is not aware of the actual process to take food from the farm to the market, from start to finish.

This topic is not about creating fear; it is about recognizing that citizens of society have accepted or developed certain subconscious and automatic habits. We are not born with these habits—*what and whom to trust with little to no scrutiny* must be taught or *programmed in from a young age*. Most adults drive to and from their destinations—to jobs, stores, social gatherings, etc. We exhibit a certain amount of faith in other drivers on the road, hoping they know the rules for safe driving.

I think you see the point. Societies require a sense of trust and faith *instilled in the minds* of the people *regardless of the reality surrounding that society*. When safety and security levels drop below a detectable threshold, acts of fear and panic become apparent, which can create civil unrest. A simple example of public concern is when the news stations announce the potential for a winter storm. People will panic about food and clear their local grocery store's shelves. Trust in the source of food, transportation, civil authorities, public communications, and water treatment facilities is critical to maintaining order in a society.

Our faith and trust in the foods we purchase have changed; it has diminished. Today's prudent shopper wants to know the ingredients in the foods they buy. Are there genetically modified organisms, antibiotics, or hormones, and are the foods free of pesticides? We no longer trust that all foods are healthy for consumption. Driving today has become more dangerous; there was a time when the impaired driver was the primary concern in the cause of vehicle accidents. Today's driver is equipped with some form of electronic communication and navigational aids, which have become a source of driver distractions that have caused a rise in automobile accidents. The circumstances of our environment are always changing.

We can talk openly about any of the above in a public setting. We can question the confidence and faith we have in these industries without ridicule. It is culturally acceptable. If it is acceptable to examine what we put in our stomachs, shouldn't it also be fair to question what we allow into our minds? Or are we supposed to trust and use blanket faith on what we hear on the news, the history taught in our schools, or what our public officials tell us? There is dishonesty, corruption, and fraud in our government agencies, large conglomerates that operate within the food industry, and religious organizations posing as shepherds of Christ's flock. Is it foolish to think these same entities which have lied to the public in one area are capable of dishonesty in other areas of our lives? It is prudent to question what these organizations have confessed to be true.

Only you can decide for yourself if there is a justifiable need to reevaluate all or a portion of what you have accepted without question to be trustworthy. The knowledge we possess comes from multiple sources. We may have received education and indoctrination from the state-run school systems or received informal learning from our families and established traditions. The list goes on.

Is there deceit around every corner? Of course not. That is not the message here. However, as a whole, the general population is kept busy providing for their families, they are overly entertained, and spiritual complacency has crept in. This complacency has weakened our mental guards. In the Bible, we are warned several times by Jesus Christ and the apostles to be wary of the deceptions of the devil. It would be prudent to take those warnings seriously. The Scriptures tell us that the devil deceives the *whole world.*

> And the great dragon was cast out, that old serpent, called the devil, and Satan, which deceiveth the whole world: he was cast out into the earth, and his angels were cast out with him.[68]

You may ask yourself how that is possible. With today's technology, we know it is possible to broadcast news, true or false, all over the world in real-time. But that is today in our modern age of technology—what about before the Industrial Revolution. Could such a mechanism used in the past spread false doctrine and deceive the masses? Yes, and it is still in operation today. The name for that mechanism is propaganda, which will be the subject of the next chapter.

---

[68] Revelation 12:9, KJV.

2

Pieces of Clay

Propaganda! What is it? Is it a machine, a tool, a process, or an invisible weapon? How does it work, can I see it, can I touch it, and how does it affect me? To get started, we will look at some definitions of propaganda and a significant milestone in its history. From there, we will move into a little but extremely informative book written in 1928 by Edward L. Bernays with the same name, *Propaganda*. The propaganda mechanism has many tentacles, and they are far-reaching. Like the roots of a tree, they only need a crack to start the drive for depth into our subconscious mind. Also, we will look at the mechanics and their use in history as it relates to a small group of people (the minority) controlling a large group of people (the majority).

Most people have heard the word propaganda, either via the news or through their workplace. Most of the time, a negative atmosphere surrounds it. So what is it, and how does it work? The Cambridge Dictionary online provides this definition:

> … information, ideas, opinions, or images, often only giving one part of an argument, that are broadcast, published, or in some other way spread with the intention of influencing people's opinions:[1]

[1] "Propaganda," Cambridge Dictionary, September 15, 2018, https://dictionary.cambridge.org/dictionary/english/propaganda.

The American Historical Association gives more of the origin for propaganda:

> The term "propaganda" apparently first came into common use in Europe as a result of the missionary activities of the Catholic church. In 1622 Pope Gregory XV created in Rome the Congregation for the Propagation of the Faith. This was a commission of cardinals charged with spreading the faith and regulating church affairs in heathen lands. A *College of Propaganda was set up* under Pope Urban VIII to train priests for the missions.[2] (Emphasis added)

The College of Propaganda formed centuries ago in 1627; it is essential not to dismiss this historical fact. How effective is the use of propaganda today after close to 400 years of study, fine-tuning, and application? Propaganda is a machine, a tool, and a process of manipulation that is, at times, invisible to its recipient(s). In today's world, it most definitely is a weapon of psychological warfare. The battlefield for humanity is the mind, and to the potters of deception, you are their *piece of clay*! The first chapter of Bernays' book is titled *Organizing Chaos*. The purpose of propaganda is clearly stated at the very beginning:

> THE *conscious* and *intelligent manipulation* of the organized habits and opinions of the masses is an important element in democratic society. Those who manipulate this *unseen mechanism* of society constitute an *invisible government* which is the true *ruling power* of our country. *We are governed, our minds are molded, our tastes formed, our ideas suggested, largely by*

[2] "The Story of Propaganda," American Historical Association, September 15, 2018, https://www.historians.org/about-aha-and-membership/aha-history-and-archives/gi-roundtable-series/pamphlets/em-2-what-is-propaganda-(1944)/the-story-of-propaganda.

> *men we have never heard of.* This is a logical result of the way in which our democratic society is organized. Vast numbers of human beings must cooperate in this manner if they are to live together as a smoothly functioning society.
>
> Whatever attitude one chooses to take toward this condition, it remains a fact that in almost every act of our daily lives, whether in the sphere of politics or business, in our social conduct or our ethical thinking, *we are dominated by the relatively small number of persons*—a trifling fraction of our hundred and twenty million—who understand the mental processes and social patterns of the masses. It is they who pull the wires which *control the public mind,* who harness old social forces and contrive new ways to *bind* and *guide the world.*[3] (Emphasis added)

These statements should disturb you. If they do not, then please reread them. As discussed in chapter one, it is of great importance to determine why you believe what you believe to be accurate. Are the governing powers successfully conducting a mass programming technique on an unsuspecting public? Have our choices been based on our analysis, or have we been manipulated? The reader must understand the power of propaganda and its use throughout our society. I inserted multiple excerpts from Bernays' work, which will show the scope of the propaganda mechanism's reach. With the passing of 400 years, the propaganda mechanism has grown into a Titan. If you and I cannot slay this beast, then, as in any time of war, it is profitable to know as much as possible about your enemy's tactics.

We experience the election process every two to four years, depending on whether the elections are for the House of Representatives or the Presidency. We vote on a limited number of

[3] Bernays, *Propaganda*, 9-10.

candidates. We elect these officials, believing they will have our best interest in mind as they carry out their public service. Honest businesses use propaganda. It is useful to all societies. The intention behind its deployment is what makes the difference. When it comes to our freedom to vote, how successful has propaganda been in the political arena?

> No serious sociologist any longer believes that the voice of the people expresses any divine or specially wise and lofty idea. The voice of the people expresses the mind of the people, and that mind is made up for it by the group leaders in whom it believes and by those persons who understand the manipulation of public opinion. It is composed of inherited prejudices and symbols and clichés and verbal formulas supplied to them by the leaders.[4]

> Good government can be sold to a community just as any other commodity can be sold. I often wonder whether the politicians of the future, who are responsible for maintaining the prestige and effectiveness of their party, will not endeavor to train politicians who are at the same time propagandists. The political leader must be a *creator of circumstances*, not only a creature of mechanical processes of stereotyping and rubber stamping.[5] (Emphasis added)

The method of creating circumstances is related to the use of a process known as the Hegelian dialectic. Examples of the Hegelian dialectic are listed in the ending pages of this chapter.

When you are shopping, you don't have the time or resources to conduct a product study to determine which product

---

[4] Ibid., 92.

[5] Ibid., 105-106.

is best. It is not difficult to see how inefficient that process would be.

> *In theory,* every citizen makes up his mind on public questions and matters of private conduct. In practice, if all men had to study for themselves the abstruse economic, political, and ethical data involved in every question, they would find it impossible to come to a conclusion about anything. [6] (Emphasis added)

A business doesn't open its doors to make a sale just once to a consumer but wants customer's loyalty as a repeat shopper.

> Mass production is only profitable if its rhythm can be maintained—that is, if it can continue to sell its product in steady or increasing quantity.[7]

For the sake of time management, we offload this responsibility to a third party; we use blanket faith. This third party performs quality control and public safety checks on what we consume. So we have blindly trusted government agencies like *The Food and Drug Administration* and independent groups like *Consumer Reports*. We read articles and findings published in magazines. We consume food daily to maintain our health. If you don't receive nutrition, you die—That is a fact of life.

Putting aside the need for perishable foods, we are consistently urged to upgrade and buy new. Many of our homes, cars, and cell phones meet our needs, yet Americans are in considerable debt. America's personal and corporate debt is no accident. Americans learned the habit of debt. I am old enough to say that my grandparents were children through the Great Depression of

---

[6] Ibid., 10.

[7] Ibid., 63.

the 1930s. They understood loss and hunger. They learned the value of living modest lives by not living beyond their means. If they could not pay cash for the extras (nice to have, but not required), they did without until their hard work and savings allowed them to make the purchase. That is called delayed gratification, but most of our youth today are ignorant of this principle!

> The rich ruleth over the poor, and the borrower is servant to the lender.[8]

> There is consequently a vast and *continuous effort* going on to capture our minds in the interest of some policy or commodity or idea. [9]

The keyword is continuous. We are showered daily with ads, opinions, and prompts to consume and purchase more than we need.

> Some of the phenomena of this process are criticized—the *manipulation of news,* the *inflation of personality,* and the general ballyhoo by which politicians and commercial products and social ideas are brought to the consciousness of the masses. The instruments by which public opinion is organized and focused may be *misused.* But such organization and focusing are necessary to orderly life.[10]

At the end of chapter one, Bernays gives the purpose of his book. He openly explains that propaganda is a form of mind control.

---

[8] Proverb 22:7, KJV.

[9] Bernays, *Propaganda,* 11.

[10] Ibid., 12.

> It is the purpose of this book to explain the structure of the mechanism which *controls the public mind,* and *to tell how it is manipulated* by the special pleader who seeks to create public acceptance for a *particular idea* or commodity.[11] (Emphasis added)

When humanity was free to move beyond the Dark Ages into the age of Gutenberg's printing press, the masses were able to be educated; they developed independence in thought. Later, public education and the locomotive were significant catalysts for man to be free in both his thinking and action. The ruling class (the minority) didn't like their power being threatened or taken away and given to the ordinary people (the sheep). Well, they didn't go down without a fight. This time the battle was more devious than open opposition.

> The minority has discovered a powerful help in influencing majorities. It has been found possible so to mold the mind of the masses that they will throw their newly gained strength in the desired direction.[12]

> Universal literacy was supposed to educate the common man to control his environment. Once he could read and write he would have a mind fit to rule. So ran the democratic doctrine. But instead of a mind, universal literacy has given him rubber stamps, rubber stamps inked with advertising slogans, with editorials, with published scientific data, with the trivialities of the tabloids and the platitudes of history, *but quite innocent of original thought*. Each man's rubber stamps are the duplicates of millions of

[11] Ibid., 18.

[12] Ibid., 19.

> others, so that when those millions are exposed to the same stimuli, *all receive identical imprints*. It may seem an exaggeration to say that the American public gets most of its ideas in this wholesale fashion. The mechanism by which ideas are disseminated on a large scale is propaganda, in the broad sense of an organized effort to *spread a particular belief or doctrine*.
>
> Truth is mighty and must prevail, and if anybody of men believe that they have discovered a valuable truth, it is not merely their privilege but their duty to disseminate that truth. If they realize, as they quickly must, that this spreading of the truth can be done upon a large scale and effectively only by organized effort, they will make use of the press and the platform as the best means to give it wide circulation. Propaganda *becomes vicious and reprehensive only when its authors consciously and deliberately disseminate what they know to be lies*, or when they aim at effects which they know to be prejudicial to the common good.[13] (Emphasis added)

As we can see, propaganda can be used to spread the truth. Publishing a book to reach as many people as possible is an everyday use of propaganda. What becomes important is the intent and motivation behind the disseminated information. The sad, but realistic, part is propaganda can be used to accomplish evil acts as well. Propaganda began to take hold of Europe during the 17th century. Bernays wrote his book in 1928, where he uses the phrase "modern propaganda."

> Modern propaganda is a consistent, enduring effort to create or shape events to influence the relations of the public to an enterprise, idea or group. This

---

[13] Ibid., 22.

> practice of *creating circumstances and of creating pictures in the minds of millions* of persons is very common. Virtually no important undertaking is now carried on without it.[14] (Emphasis added)

Move forward close to 100 years. Technology today has advanced its use of green screens, computer-generated graphics, and high-definition television. It is becoming more challenging to determine if what we see on TV is real or fiction. The evolution of the propaganda machine is dominant today. The mainstream media can create what today is called "fake news." If a person openly accepts what he or she sees on the television screen without questioning its validity, then they are in a position to be deceived and manipulated. To the unsuspecting viewer, Hollywood productions are only entertainment. Truthfully, the Hollywood industry is a powerful social conditioning tool—a tool that our unseen rulers use to shape the public mind and manipulate the masses into accepting the governing bodies' next template.

> The American motion picture is *the greatest unconscious carrier* of propaganda in the world to-day. It is a great distributor for ideas and opinions. The motion picture can standardize the ideas and habits of a nation.[15] (Emphasis added)

The subjects of Hegelian dialectic, fake news, and false flags are intertwined with propaganda. The governing authorities use many tools of deceit—first, the Hegelian dialectic. A disturbing difference is the Hegelian dialectic uses conflict to change the world. This process results in war, bloodshed, and the needless death of millions to achieve a one-world government. As with

[14] Ibid., 25.

[15] Ibid., 156.

propaganda, once you have an understanding of how it works, you will recognize it in action behind the scenes. Humanity has been at war since the fall in the garden. However, you would think in this modern age we should be able to achieve a peace that lasts for more than a few years. The sad truth is the governing powers instigate wars and support both sides. Professor Antony Sutton gives a fine description of the Hegelian dialectic.

> The operational history of The Order can only be understood within a framework of the Hegelian dialectic process. Quite simply this is the notion that conflict creates history. From this axiom it follows that controlled conflict can create a predetermined history.
>
> For example: When the Trilateral Commission discusses "managed conflict," as it does extensively in its literature, the Commission implies the managed use of conflict for long run predetermined ends—not for the mere random exercise of manipulative control to solve a problem. [16]
>
> The synthesis sought by the Establishment is called the New World Order. Without controlled conflict this New World Order will not come about. Random individual actions of persons in society would not lead to this synthesis, it's artificial, therefore it has to be created. And this is being done with the calculated, managed, use of conflict. And all the while this synthesis is being sought, there is no profit in playing the involved parties against one another. This explains why the International bankers backed the Nazis, the Soviet Union, North Korea, North Vietnam,

[16] Antony Sutton, *America's Secret Establishment, An Introduction to The Order of Skull and Bones*, (Billings, Montana: Liberty House Press, 1983), 115.

ad nauseum, against the United States. The "conflict" built profits while pushing the world ever closer to One World Government. The process continues today.[17]

President Woodrow Wilson made the revealing statement: "Some of the biggest men in the U.S. in the fields of commerce and manufacturing know that there is a power so organized, so subtle, so complete, so pervasive that they had better not speak above their breath when they speak in condemnation of it."[18]

How the dialectic process works:

> In Hegelian philosophy the conflict of political "right" and political "left," or thesis and antithesis in Hegelian terms, is essential to the forward movement of history and historical change itself. Conflict between thesis and antithesis brings about a synthesis, i.e., a new historical situation.[19]
>
> There is no question that the so-called establishment in the U.S. uses "managed conflict." The practice of "managing" crises to bring about a favorable outcome, that is, favorable to the elite, is freely admitted in the literature of, for example, The Trilateral Commission. Furthermore, there is no question that decisions of war and peace are made by a few in the elite and not by the many in the voting process through a political referendum. This volume explores some

[17] Ibid., 115.

[18] Ibid., 117.

[19] Ibid.

> major conflict decisions made by the few in The Order and the way in which right-left situations have been deliberately created and then placed in a conflict mode to bring about a synthesis.
>
> From this system of Hegelian philosophy comes the historical dialectic, i.e., that all historical events emerge from a conflict between opposing forces. These emerging events are above and different from the conflicting events. Any idea or implementation of an idea may be seen as THESIS. This thesis will encourage emergence of opposing forces, known as ANTITHESIS. The final outcome will be neither thesis nor antithesis, but a synthesis of the two forces in conflict.
>
> Karl Marx, in Das Kapital, posed capitalism as thesis and communism as antithesis. [20]

The elite treats the masses like cattle; they look upon the world populations as dumb animals. Wars are also used to cull the herd. We will also see in the coming chapters that war is used to eliminate large groups of people (genocide) who oppose the governing powers, both political and religious. Sutton continues with a description of how the so-called elite views the masses.

> The clash of opposites must in the Hegelian system bring about a society neither capitalist nor communist. Moreover, in the Hegelian scheme of events, this new synthesis will reflect the concept of the State as God and the individual as totally subordinate to an all powerful State.
>
> What then is the function of a Parliament or a Congress for Hegelians? These institutions are merely to allow individuals to feel that opinions

[20] Ibid.

> have some value and to allow a government to take advantage of whatever wisdom the "peasant" may accidentally demonstrate.
>
> As Hegel puts it: "By virtue of this participation, subjective liberty and conceit, with their general opinion, (individuals) can show themselves palpably efficacious and enjoy the satisfaction of feeling themselves to count for something."[21]

That stings a little now, doesn't it? The Hegelian dialectic is introduced early in this book to give the reader the foreknowledge to see it play out in the coming chapters. This process may not be taught in all schools, especially when it is being used with such wicked intentions.

> College textbooks present war and revolution as more or less accidental results of conflicting forces. The decay of political negotiation into physical conflict comes about, according to these books, after valiant efforts to avoid war. Unfortunately, this is nonsense. War is always a deliberate creative act by individuals.
>
> Revolution is always recorded as a spontaneous event by the politically or economically deprived against an autocratic state. Never in Western textbooks will you find the evidence that revolutions need finance and the source of the finance in many cases traces back to Wall Street. [22]
>
> In this memorandum we will present the concept that world history, certainly since about 1917,

---

[21] Ibid., 120.

[22] Ibid., 122.

> reflects deliberately created conflict with the objective of bringing about a synthesis, a New World Order.[23]

Fake news is a new name for an old propaganda tool. While still on active-duty Air Force, I attended a college course for American Diplomacy and learned about a late 19th-century term known as yellow journalism. America was drawn into the Spanish-American War through yellow journalism (manufactured news) to create what is known as a false flag. What is yellow journalism, and what is a false flag?

> Formerly the rulers were the leaders. They laid out the course of history, by the simple process of doing what they wanted. And if nowadays the successors of the rulers, those whose position or ability gives them power, can no longer do what they want without the approval of the masses, they find in propaganda a tool which is increasingly powerful in gaining that approval. Therefore, propaganda is here to stay.[24]

YELLOW JOURNALISM/ FALSE FLAGS

Let's take a more in-depth look into yellow journalism and false flags. This deception is an old strategy with a new name, fake news.

> **U.S. Diplomacy and Yellow Journalism, 1895–1898**
> Yellow journalism was a style of newspaper reporting that emphasized sensationalism over facts.

---

[23] Ibid., 125.

[24] Ibid., 27.

During its heyday in the late 19th century it was one of many factors that helped push the United States and Spain into war in Cuba and the Philippines, leading to the acquisition of overseas territory by the United States....

The peak of yellow journalism, in terms of both intensity and influence, came in early 1898, when a U.S. battleship, the Maine, sunk in Havana harbor. The naval vessel had been sent there not long before in a display of U.S. power and, in conjunction with the planned visit of a Spanish ship to New York, an effort to defuse growing tensions between the United States and Spain. On the night of February 15, an explosion tore through the ship's hull, and the Maine went down. Sober observers and an initial report by the colonial government of Cuba concluded that the explosion had occurred on board, but Hearst and Pulitzer, who had for several years been selling papers by fanning anti-Spanish public opinion in the United States, published rumors of plots to sink the ship. When a U.S. naval investigation later stated that the explosion had come from a mine in the harbor, the proponents of yellow journalism seized upon it and called for war. By early May, the Spanish-American War had begun.[25]

The whole point of yellow journalism was to produce exciting, sensational stories, even if the truth had to be stretched or a story had to be made up. These stories would boost sales, something very important in this period, when newspapers and magazines were battling for circulation numbers. In

25 "U.S. Diplomacy and Yellow Journalism, 1895-1898," Office of The Historian, https://history.state.gov/milestones/1866-1898/yellow-journalism.

> regard to the situation in Cuba in the mid-1890s, yellow journalism sought to exploit the atrocities in Cuba to sell more magazines and newspapers. The papers depicted Spanish behavior as exaggeratedly bad, and political cartoons depicted "Spain" as a nearly subhuman and brutal monster, while "Cuba" was usually depicted as a pretty white girl being pushed around by the Spanish monster. Once US opinions were inflamed over Cuba, Hearst in particular tried to do everything he could to whip the public into such a frenzy that a war would start. Once the country was at war, Hearst had little doubt his papers would have no end of interesting and sensational articles to publish.[26]

That explains what yellow journalism is. It is what we call fake news today. First, we will look at the definition of a false flag and then actual uses of false flags.

> A false flag is a covert operation *designed to deceive*; the *deception* creates the appearance of a particular party, group, or nation being responsible for some activity, disguising the actual source of responsibility.
>
> The term "false flag" originally referred to pirate ships that flew flags of countries as a disguise to prevent their victims from fleeing or preparing for battle. Sometimes the flag would remain and the blame for the attack laid incorrectly on another country. The term today extends beyond naval encounters to include countries that *organize attacks on themselves*

---

[26] "The Spanish American War (1898-1901) Summary," Spark Notes, September 16, 2018, http://www.sparknotes.com/history/american/spanishamerican/section2/.

> and make the attacks *appear to be by enemy nations or terrorists*, thus giving the nation that was supposedly attacked a pretext for domestic repression and foreign *military aggression*.
>
> Operations carried out during peacetime by civilian organizations, as well as covert government agencies, can (by extension) also be called false flag operations if they seek to *hide the real organization* behind an operation.[27] (Emphasis added)

Where have false flags been used on the American public? From the website RT Question More, the freelance writer Danielle Ryan provides just a few examples of where the United States Government has initiated false flags.

> False flags are real—the US has a long history of lying to start wars: Use of the term 'false flag' is often met with raised eyebrows and accusations of conspiracism. But false flags are a very real and very present feature of geopolitics—and denying that is simply denying reality.
>
> Last week, the United States, along with the United Kingdom and France, bombed Syrian government targets, ostensibly in retaliation for an alleged chemical attack which was carried out one week before in the city of Douma.
>
> The story we're told is simple: Syrian President Bashar Assad is an evil maniac who uses poison gas on his citizens for the sheer entertainment value. As neocon think tank the Atlantic Council put it last week, when Assad gasses people, he is simply "indulging an addiction"—an addiction which he seems to have only recently acquired, given the fact

[27] "False Flag," Wikipedia, 9/16/2018, https://en.wikipedia.org/wiki/False_flag.

that before Syria's war began, American journalists were busy praising the "educated" and "informed" Assad and marveling at the "phenomenal" levels of peace and religious diversity within Syria.

One of the best questions to ask when something like this happens, is: Who benefits? Very clearly in this case, Assad has not benefited at all, but the rebel groups fighting against him have.

Whatever the truth about this alleged chemical attack, the notion of false flag events being used to prompt military action should not be met with such skepticism. The US has a long history of using lies (or 'fake news' you might call it) as a pretext for war. It is important to look at recent events in Syria within that context.

Perhaps the most famous of all examples was the heart-wrenching testimony to Congress of a 15-year-old Kuwaiti girl, identified only as Nayirah, which was used to sell the first Gulf War to the American people in October 1990.

Nayirah was revealed to be the daughter of Kuwait's ambassador to the United States, and actually hadn't seen the "atrocities" she described take place; the PR firm Hill & Knowlton, which had been hired by the Kuwait government to devise a PR campaign to increase American public support for a war against Iraq, had heavily promoted her testimony....

Operation Northwoods

In the 1960s, American military leaders *devised plans to bomb US cities* and blame Cuban leader Fidel

> Castro in order to manufacture public and international support for a war.[28] (Emphasis added)

Please understand that I have sympathy for the families and friends who have lost loved ones in the 9/11 attack. Therefore, given the history of our government, seen or unseen, is it that hard to believe they would conceive to sacrifice 2,997 lives as collateral damage to gain tighter control over 325.7 million people through the Patriot Act? If they were willing to drop bombs on U.S. cities in the 1960s during *Operation Northwoods,* then they would be willing to do it in 2001. These acts are a perfect example of the Hegelian dialectic. Humanity is manipulated and doomed to repeat the errors of the past, due to its ignorance of actual history.

> **Gulf of Tonkin**
> Top US officials also distorted the facts in the lead-up to the Vietnam War and the media dutifully reported the official narrative as absolute fact, helping launch perhaps the most disastrous war in America's history.
>
> On August 2, 1964, North Vietnamese torpedo boats attack the USS 'Maddox' while it was on "routine patrol" in international waters in the Gulf of Tonkin. Two days later, the US Navy reported a second "unprovoked" attack on the 'Maddox' and the USS 'Turner Joy'—a second destroyer which had been sent in after the first attack. President Lyndon B. Johnson told the American people on TV that

---

[28] "False flags are real—US has a long history of lying to start wars," RT Question More, 4/16/2018, https://www.rt.com/op-ed/424298-false-flag-syria-attack/.

> "repeated acts of violence" against the US ships must be met with a strong response.[29]

Bernays' book consistently indicates that the minority indeed controls the majority. People get a sense of this agenda; in fact, we hear the murmuring of people around us, the murmuring that comes when some new law or regulation infringes on our rights. Some new laws chisel away at our freedom. What is important is if the public can become aware of the tactics of how propaganda works, then perhaps there is a chance for them to unplug from the "matrix."

> There are invisible rulers who control the destinies of millions. It is not generally realized to what extent the words and actions of our most influential public men are *dictated by shrewd persons operating behind the scenes*. Nor, what is still more important, the extent to which our thoughts and habits are modified by authorities. In some departments of our daily life, in which we imagine ourselves free agents, we are ruled by dictators exercising great power. A man buying a suit of clothes imagines that he is choosing, according to his taste and his personality, the kind of garment which he prefers. In reality, he may be obeying the orders of an anonymous gentleman tailor in London.[30] (Emphasis added)

> Governments, whether they are monarchical, constitutional, democratic or communist, depend upon acquiescent public opinion for the success of their efforts and, in fact, government is only government by virtue of public acquiescence. Industries, public

---

[29] Ibid.

[30] Bernays, *Propaganda*, 35.

> utilities, educational movements, indeed all groups representing any concept or product, whether they are majority or minority ideas, succeed only because of approving public opinion. Public opinion is the unacknowledged partner in all broad efforts.[31]

> The whole basis of successful propaganda is to have an objective and then to endeavor to arrive at it through an exact knowledge of the public and modifying circumstances to manipulate and sway that public.[32]

Who are these unseen powers, these movers and shakers who pull the puppet strings of our society? In the next chapter, we'll look at the topic of American education and the intentional tearing down of our public schools. Having an American education was once very highly valued and considered a blessing if you had such an opportunity. There are many agents responsible for the derailment of American education. This derailment goes beyond legislation, like the *No Child Left Behind Act of 2001,* which reduced American educational standards.

---

[31] Ibid., 38.

[32] Ibid., 112.

3

EDUCATION

What has happened to the quality of American education? America's public-school system started with high scholastic and biblical standards. What caused the decline in those standards, and why did our education system fall so far from its entry point in history? This plummet did not happen overnight, and it is still spiraling downward. Is this downward spiral fate, or is it intentional? Is it accidental or conspiratorial?

As with Truth, is there an agenda to deliberately restructure the moral fabric of our society through our youth, turning their public education into state indoctrination? Voices from history claim it is a deliberate act and a slow progressive plan of change. In this case, the change is designed to weaken America from within. State-run schools will not provide an accurate depiction of historical truth.

Every generation has authors who produce books written independently of government tailoring and censorship. With this knowledge source, we can educate ourselves above and beyond what is offered by state-run schools. These materials tell a different story when compared to mainstream media and its propaganda. The challenge for the reader who wishes to educate themselves is determining which party is telling the truth and which is lying. With so much information available at our fingertips, discernment is needed to filter through the refuse and disinformation to find what is legitimate and valid. The blessing is, for now, that information is still allowed to flow freely. Documents, books, and images are available; we have public libraries, bookstores, booksellers, and the internet. Anyone who wishes to investigate on their own can do so just as a detective seeks and gathers evidence to build a case—evidence that either supports or rejects the existence of a crime. Is the tearing down of the American education system a crime? Are our school-age children victims of a criminal act? Proving the existence of an active agenda to undermine the quality education of our youth will answer that question. The dumbing down of children is to accomplish control; sheep are much easier to herd than lions.

You or I, with little effort, can identify the guilty parties behind these evil acts. People have been writing and speaking out for years. Authors and witnesses who have spoken out about these crimes fall on deaf ears within today's court system. Steve Feazel and Dr. Carol Swain have much to say about the theft of our children's minds in their book titled *Abduction*. They make a note of the political power the National Education Association has in Washington, DC:

> The public-school system today serves as an indoctrination camp for liberals. It gets worse at the college level. The National Education Association (NEA), which is the public teachers' union, takes liberal positions on issues and endorses liberal candidates for political office. When these candidates win, you can bet they will not support any laws or actions that will go against the NEA. The NEA has become a special-interest group for liberal politicians who, in turn, protect it from needed education reform and policies that would require accountability for schools. There are many metropolitan school systems in which less than 50 percent of students who reach high school ever graduate. We have school systems that are making a failing grade but do not want

> the nation to see the report card. All the while, the teachers and administrators think they know best what your children should learn about history, the origin of life, faith, sex, and a host of other subjects and issues that will shape their values.[1]

Many people, through the years, have made valid attempts to warn their neighbors, their fellow citizens. In Ezekiel 33, we find the story of the watchman on the wall, whose duty was to sound the alarm and blow the horn when he saw impending danger. People both in American history and other countries have sounded the alarm, but as in Ezekiel 33, people of every generation will choose to ignore the warning, and their blood (consequences) is on their heads. The watchman performed his duty.

Propagating these warnings loud enough and fast enough is an arduous process compared to the power and speed of mainstream media outlets. The truth can and will, at times, be in direct opposition or contrast to the propaganda that has been playing like a broken record to the public for years. The average citizen has difficulty accepting any proposed truth that conflicts with their perceived reality, which is not the reality of what is. These manufactured realities, for some, may have existed for decades. They have difficulty matching it to their current programming, their current paradigm. Vladimir Lenin was a Communist Revolutionist, and he made the following short but powerful statement:

> *A lie told often enough becomes the truth.*[2]

---

[1] Steve Feazel, Dr. Carol M. Swain, *Abduction: How Liberalism Steals Our Children's Hearts and Minds* (Meadville, Pennsylvania: Christian Faith Publishing, Inc., 2016), 89.

[2] "Vladimir Lenin Quotes," Brainy Quotes, 8/10/2019, https://www.brainyquote.com/quotes/vladimir_lenin_132031.

America is under attack. While we find this to be an unpleasant thought, it is true. However, unlike conventional warfare, our enemy is working from within our borders. It is easier to deny the existence of clandestine organizations that have been working for generations than to accept the reality of our situation. While we may not always see the faces of these individuals and groups, we can most definitely see the fruit of their labor.

American history shows significant milestones of change, turning points, which have moved our nation and culture further and further away from the established biblical principles laid down for us by our Early American settlers. We hear the phrase, "The dumbing down of America," the dumbing down of our children who are our future citizens and leadership, both vital resources to the survival of any society!

While shocking at times, we can see the moral values of America's culture eroding at an alarming rate. What has changed to produce this new society? These indicators are visible for those who wish to see; have you noticed the decline in simple manners and courtesies between strangers—acts like opening a door for women and the elderly or a stranger stopping to help a shopper load a bulky item into their car. These acts can be as blatant as our youth protesting and rioting in the streets because they believe they are entitled to luxuries without earning them.

Researching for the cause, the origin of this reversal will generate moments of serendipity—moments where you will come across new avenues of relevant information that confirm and corroborate historical events, which, in turn, validate answers to questions. These new avenues and sources come in the form of books, articles, videos, etc. While we may never get all our questions answered, a wealth of information is available to those who are willing to hunt for it. The phrase "ignorance is bliss" seems to oppose searching for answers. While the axiom has some merit, the trade-off can be costly. King Solomon said in the book of Ecclesiastes:

> For in much wisdom is much grief: and he that increaseth knowledge increaseth sorrow. [3]

The trade-off is ignorance can lead to destruction. The prophet Hosea gives this much-repeated warning:

> My people are destroyed for lack of knowledge: because thou hast rejected knowledge ... [4]

Each of us must find our balancing point between the two extremes.

Men and women motivated by a sense of duty have strewn history's path with the spirit of grave importance to speak out, to offer knowledge and identification of our nation's assailants. Our nation's morality is increasingly becoming twisted. Where we once relied on moral absolutes such as biblical principles to act as guideposts to provide boundaries for our culture, we now see the acceptance of relativism forcing these absolutes out.

Sound moral absolutes provide error correction for a culture as it navigates its way through the sea of perpetual change. Today's Liberal Left promotes relativism as the preferred guideposts for change. Disregarding the proven biblical principles that have protected cultures for centuries is intentional. For the new morality to take hold, a catalyst would be needed.

History's dictators, tyrants, and those of wicked intentions have repeatedly targeted the youth of a nation to advance a change that is contrary to the existing culture. One recent example would be the implementation of the Common Core curriculum into our public schools. Steve Feazel and Dr. Carol Swain identify the agenda of the Liberal Left and its use of the public school system to bring about the indoctrination of this new

---

[3] Ecclesiastes 1:18, KJV.

[4] Hosea 4:6, KJV.

morality into the minds of our children. In their book *Abduction,* we find the following:

> Young people, especially teens and preteens, are the focal point of a cultural war raging in America. The prizes at stake in this struggle are the hearts and minds of our children. As it has for decades, the liberal Left is doing all it can to make certain that the worldview being adopted by our young people is the one that benefits liberal political candidates and liberal ideology. In *Abduction,* Steve Feazel and Dr. Carol Swain expose how Liberalism, aka the New Morality, uses culture in sinister ways to deceive young people into accepting a secular worldview that rejects traditional values and shuns the Christian faith.[5]

> A child is taught values at home and heads off to school and public life only to have his or her values attacked from sources that years ago would have affirmed those values. The New Morality is aggressive, active, resourceful, cunning, manipulative, deceitful, and very effective in its objectives. Our children are especially vulnerable to the onslaught, as they are exposed to the New Morality through various media, secular teachings at school, and peer pressure. Families witness a transformation of values in their children and wonder what happened. Parents end up not recognizing their own sons and daughters. Some families have seen severe rebellion. Others have seen

[5] Steve Feazel, Dr. Carol M. Swain, *Abduction: How Liberalism Steals Our Children's Hearts and Minds* (Meadville, Pennsylvania: Christian Faith Publishing, Inc., 2016), 13.

> tragedy as children have entered a dangerous subculture only to be lost forever. [6]

For the governing bodies to accomplish cultural changes, social controls would be needed. One such regulator was the removal of biblical teaching from our public schools—the same instruction which cultivated our traditional values of morality. Not only are the minds of our children a target, but instructing them in the knowledge of truth is targeted as well. Without knowledge of the truth, how could they identify a lie when faced with it? The following is from the book *Abduction*:

> Historical truth is a problem for the New Morality because it offers clear evidence that our nation was born in harmony with Christian morality. The solution is easy for the New Morality. If you don't like the way history is presented, then just rewrite it. The New Morality has its regiment of revisionists in active service. Their accounts of history should be closely questioned, but instead it has become the source of history lessons in public schools. It has been said that the first casualty of war is truth. In the cultural war, truth is more than just a casualty or collateral damage; it is a prime target. The revisionists have taken deadly aim on American history. The New Morality's cause is weakened if people know the truth about American history and believe it strongly enough to make sure it is passed on to succeeding generations.[7]

This process in moral decay isn't fast. However, we can trace the collapse back to its origin. The methods used are not new;

---

[6] Feazel, Swain, *Abduction*, 22.

[7] Ibid., 83.

history records these same tactics and the culprits who were responsible for the downfall of European nations through the centuries. The biblical instruction, which contains the absolutes of God, are targeted for removal—removal of the moral compass. To see the magnitude of change that has been accomplished up to this point, we will need to step back in time.

Did America (before the American Revolution) start as a country that was predominately settled and pioneered by Bible-believing Protestant Christians? The answer is yes, and there is sufficient historical evidence to remove doubt. These were the men and women who established and influenced our public schools, established universities, and laid the moral foundation for civic rules (the Mayflower Compact) that formed the Early American culture.

> As the original version of the Mayflower Compact was lost, the oldest known source in which the text of the document (provided below) can be found is *Mourt's Relation* (1622), an account of Plymouth's settlement written by Edward Winslow and William Bradford.
>
> *In the name of God, Amen. We whose names are underwritten, the loyal subjects of our dread sovereign lord King James, by the grace of God, of Great Britain, France, and Ireland King, Defender of the Faith, etc.*
>
> *Having undertaken, for the glory of God, and advancement of the Christian faith, and honor of our king and country, a voyage to plant the first colony in the northern parts of Virginia, do by these presents solemnly and mutually in the presence of God and one of another, covenant, and combine ourselves together into a civil body politic, for our better ordering and preservation, and furtherance of the ends aforesaid; and by virtue hereof to enact, constitute, and frame such just and equal laws, ordinances, acts, constitutions, offices from time to time,*

> *as shall be thought most meet and convenient for the general good of the colony: unto which we promise all due submission and obedience. In witness whereof we have hereunder subscribed our names; Cape Cod, the 11th of November, in the year of the reign of our sovereign lord King James, of England, France and Ireland eighteenth and of Scotland fifty-fourth, Anno Domini 1620.*[8]

Many Protestant Christians in the past came to the New World to escape persecution. The Pilgrims arrived in 1620, and the Puritans then followed in 1630. These men and women were the Christians who had the foremost influence on the morals and education of early America. We know from history that the Pilgrims were a small group of people, around 100, who left England through the Netherlands and became the second successful English settlement in North America. History records them as being one of the primary developers of Early American culture.

> The Pilgrims or Pilgrim Fathers were early European settlers of the Plymouth Colony in present-day Plymouth, Massachusetts, United States.... The colony was established in 1620 and became the second successful English settlement in North America (after the founding of Jamestown, Virginia in 1607). The Pilgrims' story became a central theme of the history and culture of the United States.[9]

When it comes to our children knowing the truth of who the Pilgrims were, note what Psychology Professor Paul Vitz has to say about public-school textbooks:

---

[8] "Mayflower Compact," Encyclopedia Britannica, 11/14/18, https://www.britannica.com/topic/Mayflower-Compact.

[9] "Pilgrims (Plymouth Colony)," Wikipedia, 11/14/18, https://en.wikipedia.org/wiki/Pilgrims_(Plymouth_Colony).

> Paul Vitz, a New York University psychology professor, has made a study of public-school textbooks. He researched sixty widely used social studies textbooks and did not discover one that communicated the spirituality of the Pilgrims. About his study, he wrote, "Are public school textbooks biased? Are they censored? The answer is yes, and the nature of the bias is clear: Religion, traditional family values, and many conservative positions have been reliably excluded from children's textbooks."[10]

The Puritans wanted to cleanse the church of England of its liturgy and ceremonial practices that could not be supported by Scripture. The Bible was their authority in every part of their lives.

Today, we see the purging of God from our society. Biblical Scripture is the source of Early American cultural and moral values. But our public education no longer teaches these historical facts. Many of the signers of the Declaration of Independence understood the importance of sound biblical teaching. Note the following from Gouverneur Morris and Benjamin Franklin, penmen and signers of the Constitution.

> [F]or avoiding the extremes of despotism or anarchy … the only ground of hope must be on the morals of the people. I believe that religion is the only solid base of morals and that morals are the only possible support of free governments. [T]herefore education should teach the precepts of religion and the duties of man towards God. (Gouverneur Morris)

[10] Paul Vitz, *Censorship: Evidence of Bias in Our Children's Textbooks* (Ann Arbor, Michigan: Servant Books, 1986), 14.

A Bible and a newspaper in every house, a good school in every district—all studied and appreciated as they merit—are the principal support of virtue, morality, and civil liberty. (Benjamin Franklin)

If this biblical requirement is necessary, then how can we possibly expect our children to duplicate those moral values and behavior if they are not being taught in school and not being taught in the home? Has the removal of biblical education from our public schools and, subsequently, our homes created a moral decline? Consider the following 50-year window of change, a comparison of disciplinary problems in public schools between 1940 and 1990.

1940	1990
Talking out of turn	Drug abuse
Chewing gum	Alcohol abuse
Making noise	Pregnancy
Running in the halls	Suicide
Cutting in line	Rape
Dress code infractions	Robbery
Littering	Assault[11]

Shift in Morality

Ask yourself what mental stimulus and doctrine, or lack thereof, has caused such a drastic behavioral difference in our youth since 1990. Today, we see the violence escalating to the use of firearms in the hands of undisciplined youth. Children's minds

[11] Os Hillman, "Did You Know that Education in America Was Once Very Christian?" Crosswalk, 26 June 2013, https://www.crosswalk.com/family/homeschool/high-school/did-you-know-that-education-in-america-was-once-very-christian.html.

arrive as a clean slate, born to us empty and hungry to be filled; it is our responsibility to instruct them.

> Train up a child in the way he should go: and when he is old, he will not depart from it.[12]

Our culture is in upheaval. Relativism and the "New Morality" are ripping sound biblical instruction from our culture. This void leaves our youth standing on *shifting sands*. From Dr. Zacharias:

> But when one probes deeper into these felt realities what stands out is the lack of clear cultural scaffolding on which to build one's values, or a distinctive identity from which a cultural ethos may be drawn.[13]

Without a biblical foundation, our children are left to accept the liberal norms. The argument centers around morality. Let's look at some definitions of morality—First, Noah Webster's definition and then the views of authors Feazel and Swain.

Webster:

> MORAL'ITY, noun, The doctrine or system of moral duties, or the duties of men in their social character; ethics....
>
> 1. The practice of the moral duties; virtue. We often admire the politeness of men whose morality we question.
> 2. The quality of an action which renders it good; the conformity of an act to the divine law, or to the principles of rectitude. This conformity implies that the act must be performed by a free agent,

---

[12] Proverbs 22:6, KJV.

[13] Ravi Zacharias, *Deliver Us From Evil*, 5.

> and from a motive of obedience to the divine will.[14]

Feazel and Dr. Swain:

> Our present-day enemy is the New Morality. It needs to be thoroughly examined so we know what it is, where it came from, what it aims to accomplish, and what will happen if it succeeds. We can begin by defining and clarifying our terms.
>
> Morality is an ethical system based on philosophy that makes distinctions between right and wrong, and good and bad. People often proclaim, "You can't legislate morality." This is a false statement, because governments legislate morality all the time. Otherwise, we would not have laws banning prostitution, incest, murder, polygamy, and theft.[15]

The New Morality rejects the idea of absolute right and wrong. According to this belief, which is aligned with liberal political thought, morality is relative, depending on the individuals and cultures involved. Every act and decision must be judged in light of the context and circumstances in which each takes place. It is connected with postmodernism, which argues against an objective reality. In this system, all moral views are relative, and there is no overarching narrative to explain life. Rather, there is a series of narratives, called metanarratives, that form the basis of our reality. The New Morality emerges most prominently from secular humanism and material naturalist worldviews. Material naturalists, such as the late

---

[14] Webster's, *Morality*, http://webstersdictionary1828.com/Dictionary/morality.

[15] Feazel, Swain, *Abduction*, 25-26.

> Bertrand Russell, view human beings as "accidental collocations" of atoms. Its adherents place their faith in science. Scientism permeates academia and has held great sway over some of our US Supreme Court justices and national leaders who preach tolerance as the highest virtue as long as it doesn't pertain to Christianity.[16]

America's public-school system has the minds of our children for approximately eight hours a day. However, another form of indoctrination is more depraved and immoral, overwriting any traditional values parents may have taught their children. The music our children listen too, sometimes for hours at a time, has a substantial amount of influence and establishes a foothold in a child's worldview.

"What is taught" is a general definition of doctrine. Do the lyrics from songs have a teaching effect? Can they program the mind and affect a person's thinking? The more we engage each of our five senses in our learning process, the better our memory retention becomes. How many childhood songs can you recall because the lyrics are stuck in your head? While we don't expect our children to listen to classical music only, much of today's pop music and rock-n-roll lyrics is not morally sound or preferred as wholesome input.

What is a song but an artist's expression of an opinion, an emotion, or a propaganda message blended with musical notes? These words influence the listener's worldview when we consider that our worldview is determined by our experiences, whether these experiences be firsthand or perceived, added to our mind as software is to a computer. Authors Steve Feazel and Dr. Carol Swain have the following to say about the effect the music industry has on the indoctrination of our children.

---

[16] Ibid., 26.

Today, like never before, some choose to change the moral behavior of our children by putting degrading songs in their brains and then laugh all the way to the bank.[17]

Music aimed at teenagers glamorizes promiscuous sex, drug and alcohol use, rape, and even murder. It usually doesn't show the negative repercussions these lifestyle choices produce.[18]

The First Amendment is used as a loophole to pollute the minds of our youth and as a license to trash any positive moral character development that the youth might have.[19]

Society has a right to constrain activity that puts itself at risk. Is this not the logic behind our drug laws? Could not the same logic apply to music that results in high-risk behavior by those who listen to it? There are people who, when they practice their religion, like to handle snakes. Some states have passed laws to make such practice illegal, because it compromises people's welfare. For their own protection, these people are subject to restrictions on their freedom of expression. They have been censored, and the ACLU isn't running to their aid. We wonder how Mr. Goldberg (Danny Goldberg is President and Owner of Gold Village Entertainment) would explain the way a teen could make a good connection with something when hearing lyrics in a rap song that advocates

---

[17] Ibid., 124.

[18] Ibid., 126.

[19] Ibid., 126.

> raping a fifteen-year-old girl. Maybe he could explain the positive value that comes from a song by The Offspring titled "Beheaded," in which the group sings to listeners about cutting their parents' heads off, or from the song by DMX that describes having sex with a corpse.[8][20]

While legislation may claim to regulate morality, it may not change the mindset of an individual at any given moment; it does impose consequences for following through with immoral thinking and breaking the law.

Dr. Zacharias on allowing a secular government to establish a country's moral law:

> Political differences have taken such a turn because, to the pluralistically minded in a secular culture where shame has already been excised, the power to create and enforce moral relativism has been placed into the hands of government. Political power is a strange place to entrust morality because proverbially politics is not synonymous with moral uprightness. The very institution that is distrusted by most has now become the shaper of the soul.[21]

Laws are passed to deter the individual citizen from committing sinful acts, but America's marketplace gets a free pass! Again, let's reference Feazel and Dr. Swain's work on the abduction of our children's minds:

> The problem with today's gutter-inspired music is that kids don't just hear it; they also see it. Cable TV

---

[20] Ibid., 128.

[21] Ravi Zacharias, *Deliver Us From Evil*, 78.

> channels are not subject to the same federal scrutiny as television broadcast channels.
>
> Bob Pittman, a former MTV chairman, said, "If you can get their emotions going, forget logic: we've got' em."
>
> Pittman also said. "At MTV, we don't shoot for the fourteen-year-olds; we own them," MTV's target is the junior-high kid, and the network is proud of it.
>
> What Hollywood had been prevented from delivering to your fourteen-year-old through movies, MTV takes directly to the child via the protected pipeline of cable TV.[22]

We must teach our children ethics; they will not fully mature on their own. The Early American settlers understood this and provided sound biblical instruction for their children. America, at one time, adhered to rigid moral standards, which come from God's written Word—what is known to be absolute—because He, God, is sovereign. Today in America, our moral standards are voted in and out by men and women wearing black robes.

Our country's ethical standards were once based on absolutes. Now we see the shift to moral relativism, which allows for moral standards to fluctuate, to be inconsistent. What may be unacceptable a month, a year, or a century ago can now change simply by legislation. Moral values have become the flavor of the month. That is the value of having absolutes. What God considered immoral a thousand years ago, he still finds immoral today—murder, abortion, homosexuality, etc. Godly absolutes provide stability. One of the signs that appear before the fall of a nation is a rise in immorality. Allowing our country's moral standards to be based on relativism is a slippery slope that only leads to decay.

---

[22] Ibid.,134.

Early Americans believed that biblical education and the study of God's Word was a priority and essential to the *character* development of their children. The year was 1690.

> *The New England Primer* was first published between 1688 and 1690 by English printer Benjamin Harris, who had come to Boston in 1686 to escape the brief Catholic ascendancy under James II.... It became the most successful educational textbook published in the colonial and early days of United States history.... Each lesson had questions about the Bible and the Ten Commandments. In fact, most of the entire book taught Bible verses at the same time it taught students how to read.... The ninety-page work contained selections from the King James Bible as well as other original selections. It embodied the dominant Puritan attitude and worldview of the day. Among the topics discussed were respect for parental figures, sin, and salvation.... The primer remained in print well into the nineteenth century and was even used until the twentieth. A reported two million copies were sold in the 1700s. No copies of editions before 1727 are known to have survived; earlier editions are known only from publishers' and booksellers' advertisements.[23]

---

[23] Os Hillman, "Did You Know that Education in America Was Once Very Christian?" Crosswalk, 26 June 2013, https://www.crosswalk.com/family/homeschool/high-school/did-you-know-that-education-in-america-was-once-very-christian.html.

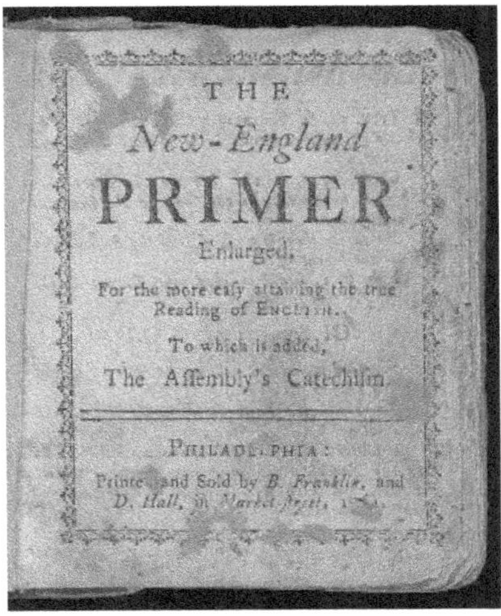
[24]

The United States has no shortage of universities. Our country's first universities had beliefs and creeds based on God's written Word, the Bible.

> The motto that Harvard University adopted in 1692 was *Veritas Christo et Ecclesiae,* which translated from Latin means "Truth for Christ and the church." It was later changed to simply say: "Truth (*Veritas*)." Certainly, they have removed the true source of truth.[25]

The Puritans established Harvard University. Early records reveal that Harvard's rules and precepts, as stated in 1636, were:

---

[24] "New-England Primer Enlarged printed and sold by Benjamin Franklin," Wikimedia Commons, 11/18/18, https://commons.wikimedia.org/w/index.php?curid=14634426.

[25] Os Hillman, "Did You Know that Education in America Was Once Very Christian?" Crosswalk, 26 June 2013, https://www.crosswalk.com/family/homeschool/high-school/did-you-know-that-education-in-america-was-once-very-christian.html.

> Let every student be plainly instructed, and earnestly pressed to consider well, the main end of his life and studies is, to know God and Jesus Christ which is eternal life (John 17:3) and therefore lay Christ at the bottom, as the only foundation of all sound knowledge and learning.[26]

Princeton's Founding Statement 1746 was as follows:

> Cursed is all learning that is contrary to the Cross of Christ.[27]

Columbia University stated:

> Columbia University was founded in 1754 as King's College by royal charter of King George II of England. The motto of the university is, *"In lumine Tuo videbimus lument,"* which means, "By Your light we shall see light" (based on Psalm 36:9). It is the oldest institution of higher learning in the state of New York and the fifth oldest in the United States.[28]
>
> Among the earliest students and trustees of King's College were John Jay, the first chief justice of the United States; Alexander Hamilton, the first secretary of the treasury; Gouverneur Morris, the author of the final draft of the US Constitution; and Robert

---

[26] Josiah Quincy, LL. D., *History of Harvard University* (Boston: Crosby, Nichols, Lee & Co., 1860), 515.

[27] Mark A. Belies & Stephen K. McDowell, *America's Providential History* (Charlottesville: Providence Foundation, 1989), 111.

[28] Os Hillman, "Did You Know that Education in America Was Once Very Christian?" Crosswalk, 26 June 2013, https://www.crosswalk.com/family/homeschool/high-school/did-you-know-that-education-in-america-was-once-very-christian.html.

R. Livingston, a member of the five-man committee that drafted the Declaration of Independence.[29]

THE PATH TO IGNORANCE

American writer Horace Greeley (1811-1872) established the *New York Tribune* in 1841 and developed a reputation as the greatest newspaper editor of his day. Greeley stated, *"It is impossible to enslave, mentally or socially, a Bible-reading people. The principles of the Bible are the ground-work of human freedom.*[30]

In 1852 the Fifth Annual Report of the Board of National Popular Education stated, "God will have men and nations governed; and they must be governed by one of the two instruments—AN OPEN BIBLE, with its hallowed influences, or A STANDING ARMY WITH BRISTLING BAYONETS. One is the product of God's wisdom, the other, of man's folly; and that nation or people that dare discard, or will not yield to the moral power of the one, must submit to the brute force of the other. Herein do we discover the secret of our ability to govern ourselves. Just so long, and no longer, than we preserve the open Bible in our schools, shall we be capable of self-government.[31]

---

[29] Ibid.

[30] Tryon Edwards, D.D., *A Dictionary of Thoughts*, 1908 (Cassell Publishing Company), 301.

[31] George B Cheever, D.D., *Right of the Bible in Our Public Schools*, 1859 (New York: Robert Carter & Brothers), 280.

> In 1985 two-hundred and sixty-one billion dollars was spent on education. That was more than twice what was spent in 1980 and over ten times the amount spent in 1970. The cost per student jumped from two-hundred and ninety-four dollars in 1956 to two-thousand nine-hundred dollars in 1982 and '83. Even allowing for inflation that's a jump of almost one-thousand percent. While expenditures and personnel have increased dramatically, the quality of education has declined. S.A.T. scores dropped consistently from 1963 to 1980 and beyond. And since then even educators' expectations for S.A.T. scores have been lowered. Twenty percent of all graduating high school students in 2007 were functionally illiterate. As a nation we are producing an increasing number of functionally illiterate adults.... This is in great contrast to early America. At the time of our independence John Adams wrote that to find an *"American who cannot read and write, is as rare an appearance as a Jacobite, or a Roman Catholic, i.e., as rare as a comet or an earthquake."*[32]

The above segments, from the article "God and America," are of the view that America started as Christian settlements, and the Protestant Bible was the foundation. That was between the time of the Pilgrims/Puritans and the time of the Revolutionary War. America began as a predominately Protestant nation. The most significant opposition to Protestant's biblical education is the Church of Rome. History documents that the power of the Roman Catholic Church was undermining America long before the rise of secularism. After the Revolutionary War, the Church

---

[32] Brother Terry, "God and America: Political and Religious Foundations of The United States of America,,"9/22/18, http://www.angelfire.com/la2/prophet1/america.html.

of Rome, a foreign political power, infiltrated America and the *Declaration of Independence* removed the existing protection put in place by Early America's founders. The Vatican, a foreign power, has been allowed to influence our nation's governing powers.

> It is important to remember that in 1776 Protestants comprised more than 99% of the population of the new nation, while Catholics comprised less than 1% of the total population. The Roman Catholic church now wields more political power in the U.S., either directly or by proxy, than any other religious organization. This is very significant because the history of this church reveals a far more sinister organization than what is portrayed by her promoters. With a history of over 1000 years of persecuting "heretics" by way of the Crusades, the "Holy Catholic Inquisitions," the "Holy Wars," etc. (murdering millions of people who simply refused to accept Papal dogma or acknowledge the pope as supreme ruler of Christendom and king of the earth), it would be suicidal to view the Church of Rome as anything but a most dangerous politico-religious sect (it is no coincidence that the United Nations, a corrupt international organization whose agenda is a one-world police state, has granted to the Roman Catholic church a privileged position held by no other religion). It is also important to remember that the term "Protestant" was originally used in a derogatory sense. The Romish Communion *departed from* "the faith which was once delivered to the saints,"—the true Catholic faith. When the Reformers, through the grace of God, *restored* the true faith, the Papists "nicknamed" the Reformed Catholics "Protestants." This appellation, though originating in Papal contempt, has, in process of time, become honorable and glorious,

inasmuch as it patently indicates a protest against the[33] "lying traditions of men, and the cunningly-devised fables of Rome."[34]

The following proclamations made in an address of Congress to the people of England, dated at Philadelphia, September 5th, 1774, are not the declarations of a party of a sect, or of a church, but the solemn and sincere deliverances of the first American Congress. In this address to the people of Great Britain, the American Congress of 1774 stated one of their grievances with the British Parliament was that,[35] by another act the dominion of Canada is to be so extended, modeled, and governed, as that by being disunited from us, detached from our interests, by civil as well as religious prejudices, that by their numbers swelling with Catholic emigrants from Europe, and by their devotion to Administration, so friendly to their religion, they might become formidable to us, and on occasion, be fit instruments in the hands of power, to reduce the ancient free Protestant Colonies, to the same state of slavery with themselves.[36]

---

[33] Brother Terry, "God and America: Political and Religious Foundations of The United States of America,"9/22/18, http://www.angelfire.com/la2/prophet1/america.html.

[34] John Heron Macguire, The Catholic handbook: or, Every Protestant his own controversialists,1860 (Seeley & Co … .), 7.

[35] Brother Terry, "God and America: Political and Religious Foundations of The United States of America,"9/22/18, http://www.angelfire.com/la2/prophet1/america.html.

[36] Charles Thomson, *Journals of the Continental Congress 1774-1789* (Washington: Washington Printing Office), 87-88.

> Nor can we suppress our astonishment, that a British Parliament should ever consent to establish in that country a religion that has deluged your Island in blood, and dispersed impiety, bigotry, persecution, murder, and rebellion, through every part of the world.[37]

Several prominent Americans opposed the Catholic Church. The opposition with the Church of Rome was two-fold. First, it was a foreign power permitted to exercise its agenda on American soil, and second, Rome was trying to dictate how we train our children. Rome's goal was to deliberately hinder Protestant Christianity from being taught in public education. The intentional disruption of Bible teaching to the public through education started long before the forming of the United States of America.

The invention of the printing press opened the door to the masses being able to read and learn what the Scriptures have to say without any twisting of meaning. The Catholic Church believes that only its trained priesthood is permitted to give an accurate interpretation of God's Word. It was no longer possible to prevent the masses from reading the Bible. A new plan to attack the Protestant's ability to learn the truth would be necessary. The Catholic Church would infiltrate the institutions of education themselves and shape the minds of the young. To accomplish this, the Jesuits became the school Masters of the universities and colleges of Europe. The process of "learning against learning" had begun.

---

[37] "London Magazine, Or, Gentleman's Monthly Intelligencer, Volume 43," Google Books, 11/25/18 https://books.google.com/books?id=SiEo-AAAAYAAJ&pg=PA631&dq=The+London+magazine+Nor+can+we+suppress+our+astonishment&hl=en&ei=VyaYTcSIMMW4tgeApLDoCw&sa=X&oi=book_result&ct=result&sqi=2%20-%20v=onepage&q&f=false#v=onepage&q=The%20London%20magazine%20Nor%20can%20we%20suppress%20our%20astonishment&f=false.

Just as Leo X's corruption had ignited Luther, Clement VII's shrewdness determined how the church would deal with the proliferation of Bibles. Clement was personally advised by the cagey Niccolò Machiavelli, inventor of modern political science, and Cardinal Thomas Wolsey, Chancellor of England. Machiavelli and Wolsey opined that both printing and Protestantism could be turned to Rome' s advantage by employing movable type to produce a literature that would confuse, diminish, and ultimately marginalize the Bible. Cardinal Wolsey, who would later found Christ Church College at Oxford, characterized the project as "to put learning against learning."

Against the Bible's learning, which demonstrated how man could have eternal life simply by believing in the facts of Christ's death and resurrection, would be put the learning of the Gnostics. Gnosticism held out the hope that man could achieve everlasting life by doing good works himself. To put it succinctly, Bible-learning was Christ-centered; Gnostic learning was man-centered.

An enormous trove of Gnostic learning had been brought from the eastern Mediterranean by agents of Clement VII's great-grandfather, Cosimo d'Medici. Suppressed since the Emperor Justinian had piously shut down the pagan colleges of Athens back in 529, these celebrated mystical, scientific, and philosophical scrolls and manuscripts flattered humanity. They taught that human intelligence was competent to determine truth from falsehood without guidance or assistance from any god. Since, as Protagoras put it, "man is the measure of all things," man could control all the living powers of the universe. If elected and initiated into the secret

> knowledge, or gnosis, man could master the cabalah – the "royal science" of names, numbers, and symbols – to create his very own divinity.[38]

The Church of Rome has millions of members spread throughout the world. While the information in this book is meant to expose Catholicism's hierarchy, the Vatican, the inner circle, and the Society of Jesus (the Jesuits), this leaves millions of Catholic Church laity who are innocent of their church hierarchy's crimes. This chapter contains quotes from Samuel Morse, Horace Greely, Judge Joseph Story, Reverend Charles Hodge, Ex-Priest Bernard Fresenborg, Paul C. Vitz, John Jay, Justin Dewey Fulton, and Richard Harcourt. Martin Luther, the famous Protestant Reformer, saw almost prophetically 500 years ago what would happen to the education system.

> Martin Luther, seeing that learning against learning was the future of Christianity, voiced an "Appeal to the Ruling Classes" (1520), in which he wrote, rather prophetically: Though our children live in the midst of a Christian world, they faint and perish in misery because they lack the gospel in which we should be training and exercising them all the time. I advise no one to place his child where the Scriptures do not reign paramount. Schools will become wide-open gates of hell if they do not diligently engrave the Holy Scriptures on young hearts. Every institution where men are not increasingly occupied with the word of God must become corrupt.[39]

---

[38] F. Tupper Saussy, *Rulers of Evil: Useful Knowledge About Governing Bodies* (Reno, Nevada: Ospray Bookmakers, 1999), 23.

[39] Saussy, *Rulers of Evil*, 24. (https://web.stanford.edu/~jsabol/certainty/readings/Luther-ChristianNobility.pdf).

Samuel Morse (April 27, 1791–April 2, 1872)

Samuel Morse is best known for his invention of the telegraph. Those in the field of electrical communications are familiar with the term Morse Code. Samuel Morse had strong political views and was a leader in the anti-Catholic movement. As we will see, his mistrust was not without merit. He wrote *Foreign Conspiracy Against the Liberties of the United States,* where he indicated that the Church of Rome was a threat to the American way of life.

> We cannot be too often reminded of the *double* character of the enemy who has gained foothold upon our shores; for although Popery is a religious sect, and on this ground claims toleration side by side with other religious sects, yet Popery is also a *political,* a *despotic system,* which we must repel as altogether incompatible with the existence of freedom. I repeat it, Popery is a *political,* a *despotic system,* which must be resisted by all true patriots.

Is it asked, how can we separate the characters thus combined in one individual? How can we repel the *politics* of a Papist without infringing upon his *religious* right? I answer that this is a difficulty for Papists, not for Protestants to solve. If Papists have made their *religion* and *despotism* identical, that is not our fault. Our religion, *the Protestant religion*, and *Liberty*, are identical, and liberty keeps no terms with despotism.[40]

[41]

Horace Greely (February 3, 1811–November 29, 1872)

Horace Greely was the founder and editor of the New York Tribune. He had been a congressman for New York's sixth district and a presidential candidate in the elections of 1872. He was considered eccentric. Horace Greely's biography is a story of persistence and accomplishment. While he started from poor

[40] Samuel F.B. Morse, *Foreign Conspiracy Against the Liberties of the United States* (New York, 1841), 112.

[41] Horace Greeley, New Castle Historical Society, https://www.newcastlehs.org/horace-greeley-1869-age-58/.

beginnings, he became an influential contributor to 19th century America. The phrase "Go West, young man" was created by Horace Greely's initiation of the Homestead Act, where settlers who showed improvement on land could purchase land at low rates.

> The great body of those who seek to drive the Bible out of our schools will not be satisfied after they have driven it out, but will insist on breaking our common-school system into sectarian fragments.... Hence, if we give up the Bible, we only weaken our common-school system ... while we fail to conciliate its enemies and only excite them to new and inadmissible exactions.[42]

43

Judge Joseph Story (September 18, 1779–September 10, 1845)

[42] Cardinal Gibbons, Bishop Keane, Edwin D. Mead, Honorable John Jay, *Denominational Schools* (Boston: Committee of One Hundred, 1890), 48.

[43] Judge Joseph Story, Encyclopedia Britannica, 03/06/2019, https://www.britannica.com/biography/Joseph-Story/media/567679/14549.

An American lawyer who served on the Supreme Court from 1812–1845, Justice Story helped modify American law. Historians are in consensus that Judge Story moved American law in a conservative direction.

> A preliminary and significant step in the war upon our common-school system was taken a few years since, when it was complained of by some Roman Catholic ecclesiastics connected with the mission to America as being sectarian in its character, for the reason that there was allowed the reading of passages from the Holy Scriptures in a version deemed by their church as erroneous and heretical.[44]

> The latest judicial decision in regard to the Bible in the public schools is that of Judge Bennett, of Wisconsin, in the case of Weiss vs. School Board of Edgerton. The action was brought by Roman Catholic parents for a peremptory writ of mandamus directing the board to cause the reading of King James's version of the Bible in the public schools to be discontinued. The reading was not compulsory, nor the plaintiffs' children required to be present at the reading. The exclusion was demanded on the ground that the reading was 'sectarian instruction,' and an unconstitutional interference with the rights of conscience.[45]

---

[44] Ibid., 47.

[45] Ibid., 49.

[46]

Reverend Charles Hodge (December 27, 1797–June 19, 1878)

Rev. Hodge was a Presbyterian theologian who served as the first principal of Princeton Theological Seminary from 1851 to 1878.

> This country is a Christian and Protestant country, granting universal toleration; i.e., allowing men of all religions to live within our borders... and to conduct their religious services according to their own convictions of duty.[47]

[46] Charles Hodge, Wikipedia: The Free Encyclopedia, 03/06/2019, https://en.wikipedia.org/wiki/Charles_Hodge#/media/File:PORTRAIT_OF_CHARLES_HODGE,_Rembrandt_Peale.jpg.

[47] Rufus W. Clark, *Question of The Hour: The Bible and The School Fund*, 1870 (Boston: Lee and Shepard), 14-15.

[48]

Justin Dewey Fulton (March 1, 1828–April 16, 1901)

Not much personal information is available about Justin Dewey Fulton. However, if you want to know about a writer, read his work. He has published several books to bring attention to the activities of the Church of Rome and their manipulation of America. He is best known for his book *Washington in the Lap of Rome*. The following is from his book *The Roman Catholic Element in American History*:

> In 1840 the Catholics, led by Archbishop Hughes, again took the field. They did not come seeking charities, but by one fell stroke to sweep our school system from the board. They did not complain of oppression, nor of being deprived of any rights enjoyed by others, but demanded at the outset, what they claim as theirs, of the school-fund. They found fault with certain reading-books, in general, *with the free use of the Bible, in particular.*
>
> As a compromise the Bible was banished from the leading public schools of the city. Everything that

[48] Justin Dewey Fulton, Find A Grave, 03/06/2019, https://www.findagrave.com/memorial/73467006/justin-dewey-fulton.

could be done to place all upon a common level was performed. But this, instead of satisfying the exacting spirits who had demanded the change, was made, by a most glaring inconsistency, the occasion of a new and more plausible attack. *The schools were denounced as 'Anti-christian, heathen, and godless.'* [49] (Emphasis added)

50

Richard Harcourt (March 17, 1849–November 29, 1932)

Richard Harcourt was a Canadian lawyer, judge, and politician. His background in public service shows several positions relating to the public school system. He was a principal of Cayuga High School, inspector of schools for Haldimand County from 1871 to 1876, and inspector of schools for Welland County

[49] Justin Dewey Fulton, *The Roman Catholic Element in American History* (Cincinnati: Moore, Wilstach, Keys & Overend, 1856), 247-248.

[50] Richard Harcourt, Wikipedia: The Free Encyclopedia, 03/06/2019, https://en.wikipedia.org/wiki/File:Richard_Harcourt.jpg.

and the town of Niagara Falls. From Harcourt's book *The Great Conspiracy Against Our Public Schools*, we have the following:

> This band of foreign priestly conspirators, with no sympathy for the American government or its system of education, are secretly plotting for the destruction of both! They have been watching with untiring vigilance every phase of our system, and they have seen that the public schools were the nurseries of American ideas, of American freedom, of American progress, and that a large number of children born of Roman Catholic parents, who were educated in these schools, were thoroughly Americanized by them. *Therefore, by the advice and co-operation of the pope, they have resolved to take possession of our schools, to Romanize them, or to ruin them.* [51] (Emphasis added)

[51] Richard Harcourt, *The Great Conspiracy Against Our Public Schools*, 1890 (San Francisco: California News Company), 33-34.

[52]

Bernard Fresenborg (1847-?)

Bernard Fresenborg was a Catholic priest when he wrote *Thirty Years in Hell; or, From Darkness to Light*. In his book, he provides firsthand knowledge of the atrocities committed by Catholic clergy, and he also documents his view of the consequences of allowing Catholicism into a country. The excerpts below reflect what he saw as the Catholic Church's attitude toward American public schools. Now his book was written in 1904; the Supreme Court decision was in 1962, and in 1963, the removal of the Bible from public schools was enforced.

> The Catholic world does not hesitate in declaring that our public schools in this country are "Sinks of Iniquity," "Schools of Vice," and "Nurseries of Hell;"

[52] Bernard Fresenborg, *Thirty Years in Hell; or, From Darkness to Light* (St. Louis, Missouri: North-American Book House, 1904), 1.

then why should the followers of Catholicism be permitted to teach in our public schools?[53]

But against this most sacred product of American liberty Rome lifts her unholy hands. Against our schools she hurls her worst anathemas. But it is our purpose in this chapter to let the Roman Catholic Church speak for itself. Its language is plain and needs no interpretation. Listen to Rome's damnable utterances:

1. These public schools are devouring fires and pits of destruction. They ought to go back to the devil, from whence they came. (*The Freeman's Journal*)

2. If your son or daughter is attending a state school, you may be sure that you are violating your duty as Catholic parents and conducting to the everlasting anguish and despair of your child. Take it away. Let it rather never know how to write its name than to become the bound and chained slave of Satan. (*The Shepherd of the Valley*)

3. The common schools of this country are sinks of moral pollution and nurseries of hell. (*Chicago Tablet*)

4. The public or common school system is a swindle on the people, an outrage on justice, a foul

[53] Fresenborg, *Thirty Years in Hell*, 77.

disgrace in matters of morals, and should be abolished forthwith. (*New York Tablet*)[54]

5. We hold education to be a function of the church and not of the state, and in our case we do not and will not accept the state as an educator. (*New York Tablet*)

6. The public school system must be destroyed. It must be done by stopping Bible reading, Psalm singing and eliminating objectionable books. (*Priest Phelan*)[55]

7. Education outside of the control of the Roman Catholic church is a damnable heresy.—*Pius IX.*

There are many more quotes, but I think you get the point. Immediately following that list of curses, Bernard Fresenborg states his opinion of keeping the Bible in American public schools.

> Therefore, we demand that the "book of books" be kept where the rising generation shall come under its moral teaching without party or sectarian comment, so that all may understand the fundamental principles upon which the science of our common law rests, and thus one of the objects of the order is "to maintain the public school system of the United States and to prevent sectarian interference therewith, and upholding the reading of the Holy Bible therein."

---

[54] Ibid., 78.

[55] Ibid., 79.

The argument that the reading of the Bible in the public school should be abolished because it is objectionable to the conscience of some comes only from the Church of Rome, and applies with equal force against the moral code of jurisprudence, because it is objectionable to the conscience of the anarchist, and the conscience of the anarchist is just as sacred and entitled to as much respect, under the law, in this free country of ours as the conscience of anyone else.

We have, just as much right to take the moral code out of our common jurisprudence as to take the Bible out of our public schools, because the moral code of the Bible is the moral code of our common law.[56]

[57]

Paul C. Vitz (August 27, 1935– present)
New York University Professor Emeritus of Psychology

[56] Ibid., 83-84.

[57] http://www.psych.nyu.edu/vitz/.

> In 1985 New York University professor Paul C. Vitz did a study for the U.S. Department of Education. After reviewing scores of books from primary readers to high school history text he found *"It may be easier for a camel to go through the eye of a needle than for a religious figure or for an individual's Christian beliefs to get into the pages of the history books."* For example, one book states that *"Pilgrims are people who make long trips."* Vitz's study clearly demonstrated that an anti-Protestant-Christian agenda exists. He said, *"Those responsible for these books appear to have a deep-seated fear of any form of active contemporary Christianity, especially serious, committed Protestantism."*(*Recovering the Lost Tools of Learning,* Douglas Wilson, 1991, p. 36). Vitz's final assessment: *"When it came to the treatment of history, I can assure you that a bias against Christianity existed."*[58]

It wouldn't be challenging to fill several more pages with additional quotes and references to the involvement of the Catholic Church extending its reach (political arm) to control America. To avoid straying too far off the topic of education, let us look at how the decay of public school has affected a few attributes of our society.

ILLITERACY

America has an illiteracy problem, and here are a few segments from a brief article by Dr. Susan Berry dated October 23, 2017, from the website *Breitbart News*. The title is *"Camille Paglia: Public*

---

[58] Brother Terry, "God and America: Political and Religious Foundations of The United States of America,"9/22/18, http://www.angelfire.com/la2/prophet1/america.html.

Schools Creating Students Who 'Know Nothing,'" and this is what she had to say:

> Outspoken feminist Camille Paglia says the current generation of hyper-sensitive, safety-seeking college students was gradually created by the downward spiral of public education that has left them ignorant of history and geography and focused, instead, on viewing America as an evil nation....
>
> "What has happened is these young people now getting to college have no sense of history of any kind. No sense of history. No world geography. No sense of the violence and the barbarities of history. So they think that the whole world has always been like this, a kind of nice, comfortable world where you can go to the store and get orange juice and milk, and you can turn on the water and the hot water comes out. They have no sense whatever of destruction, of the great civilizations that rose and fell, and so on, and how arrogant people get when they're in a comfortable civilization, etc. So they now are being taught to look around them to see defects in America—which is the freest country in the history of the world—and to feel that somehow America is the source of all evil in the universe, and it's because they've never been exposed to the actual evil of the history of humanity. They know nothing!"
>
> Paglia, a professor at the University of the Arts in Philadelphia, slammed the trend of public schools beginning the teaching of "identity politics," such as that found in "sexual harassment sensitivity training" and "diversity training," all the while true education is absent.
>
> "It's really started at the level of public-school education," she noted. "I've been teaching now for

46 years as a classroom teacher, and I have felt the slow devolution of the quality of public-school education in the classroom."

Sommers described what students indoctrinated in identity politics are learning:

"So young people in a typical Gender Studies class now learn that they inhabit a society with this matrix of oppression and, depending on your identity—you might be advantaged so you have unearned privilege—or you might be burdened because of your race, or maybe you have disability or your gender preference and on and on. But, underneath it all, is this assumption that the United States is a white supremacist, imperialist, capitalist, patriarchal, oppressive society…"

Sommers added that, as early as in junior high school, American students are being indoctrinated in a "very distorted view of the world."[59]

Biblical Illiteracy

The Bible tells us that Jesus is the Word.

> In the beginning was the Word, and the Word was with God, and the Word was God.[60]

[59] Dr. Susan Berry, "Camille Paglia: Public Schools Creating Students Who 'Know Nothing,'" Breitbart, 12/3/2018 https://www.breitbart.com/politics/2017/10/23/camille-paglia-public-schools-creating-students-know-nothing/#disqus_thread.

[60] John 1:1, KJV.

> And the Word was made flesh, and dwelt among us, (and we beheld his glory, the glory as of the only begotten of the Father,) full of grace and truth.[61]

Public school education prohibits the use of the Bible. How has this affected America's Bible illiteracy rate? This rate indicates the condition of America's spiritual armor. Two sources aided my research—the first is *Charisma Magazine*, and the second is *LifeWay Research*. Considering the two articles came to the same conclusion, I will list the points of agreement above and below each other to avoid repeating the same findings.

The title of the article from *Charisma Magazine* is "Dumb and Dumber: How Biblical Illiteracy Is Killing Our Nation." Ed Stetzer, a writer for *Charisma*, starts with the point that America has had many accomplishments to be proud of.

> America can be proud of many things: our innovation, generosity and entrepreneurial spirit are unsurpassed. Yet when it comes to our nation understanding one of the greatest gifts ever given to humanity—the Bible—we're moving from dumb to dumber ... and it's no laughing matter.[62]

> Many people quote bible Scripture in their everyday jargon and are not even aware that its point of origin is the Holy Bible.
>
> "bite the dust" (Psalm 72:9), "land of the living" (Psalm 27:13), "a drop in the bucket" (Isaiah 40:15), "the blind leading the blind" (Matthew 15:14),

---

[61] John 1:14, KJV.

[62] Ed Stetzer, "Dumb and Dumber: How Biblical Illiteracy Is Killing Our Nation," Charisma, 12/3/18, https://www.charismamag.com/life/culture/21076-dumb-and-dumber-how-biblical-illiteracy-is-killing-our-nation?showall=1&start=0.

> "made a scapegoat" (Leviticus 16:22), "go the extra mile" (Matthew 5:41), "leopard can't change its spots" (Jeremiah 13:23), "by the skin of your teeth" (Job 19:20), "fly in the ointment" (Ecclesiastes 10:1), "as old as the hills" (Job 15:7)[63]

Ed Stetzer continues with the sad news that America has become a "post-biblically literate culture." LifeWay Research agrees with this conclusion.

> Study after study in the last quarter-century has revealed that American Christians increasingly don't read their Bibles, don't engage their Bibles, and don't know their Bibles. It's obvious: We are living in a post-biblically literate culture.
>
> Just as critical is the second word of the Bible literacy problem: literacy. Pew Research tells us that 23 percent of us didn't read a single book in the last year. That's three times the number who didn't read a book in 1978. Whether it's the Internet, video games, the TV or increased time spent on entertainment and sports, Americans are spending less time between the pages of any book, not just the Good Book.[64]

---

[63] Ed Stetzer, "Biblical Illiteracy by the Numbers Part 1: The Challenge," Christianity Today, October17,2014, https://www.christianitytoday.com/ed-stetzer/2014/october/biblical-illiteracy-by-numbers.html.

[64] Ed Stetzer, "Dumb and Dumber: How Biblical Illiteracy Is Killing Our Nation," Charisma, 12/3/18, https://www.charismamag.com/life/culture/21076-dumb-and-dumber-how-biblical-illiteracy-is-killing-our-nation?showall=1&start=0.

LIFEWAY

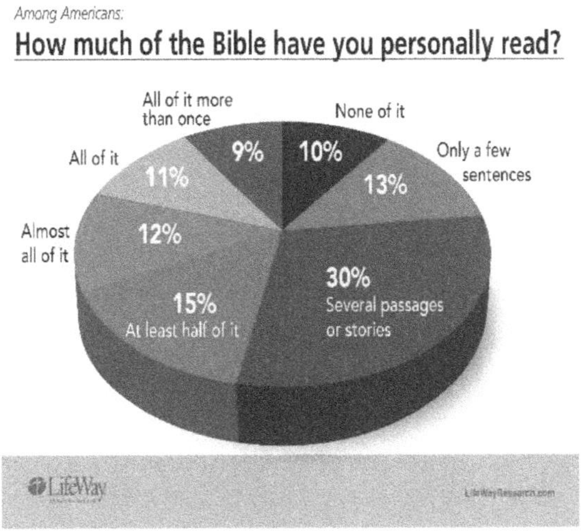

LifeWay's writer Bob Smietana has this to say:

> However, more than half of Americans have read little or none of the Bible.
>
> Less than a quarter of those who have ever read a Bible have a systematic plan for reading the Christian Scriptures each day. And a third of Americans never pick it up on their own, according to a new study from Nashville-based LifeWay Research.
>
> "Most Americans don't know first-hand the overall story of the Bible—because they rarely pick it up," McConnell said. "Even among worship attendees less than half read the Bible daily. The only time most Americans hear from the Bible is when someone else is reading it."[65]

---

[65] Bob Smietana, "LifeWay Research: Americans Are Fond of the Bible, Don't Actually Read It," LifeWay, April 25, 2017,

If this doesn't alarm you, it should. Bible illiteracy has a direct impact on America's moral compass; a deficiency in biblical knowledge transfers to Americans being unprepared for spiritual warfare. Preparedness can only come from taking time to do your biblical studies and verify what is real and what is not—you cannot put such a vital part of your future in the hands of somebody else. How can you identify a lie if you don't know the truth? Stetzer goes on to say:

> This goes beyond simple trivia questions aimed at revealing how few facts we know about our Bibles. American evangelicals increasingly lack a spiritual depth. Our lives betray a lack of Christian character. We don't seem to be very Christlike to a watching world.
>
> The Holy Spirit works though the Scriptures, leading us to maturity in every area. That can't happen if we are not in the Word.[66]

This is important because the Bible instructs that Jesus is the written Word, the Word in the flesh, and that is where you will hear that the Bible is the Living Word because Jesus Christ and His Word are one. The objective here is to be aware that Jesus Christ is the source of our spiritual power to defeat humanity's spiritual enemy. Many people only believe in physical enemies, only what they can see with their eyes and touch with their hands, but there is more.

Not only do we have to contend with our fellow man, but we have unseen enemies in the spiritual realm (a dimension

---

https://lifewayresearch.com/2017/04/25/lifeway-research-americans-are-fond-of-the-bible-dont-actually-read-it/.

[66] Ed Stetzer, "Dumb and Dumber: How Biblical Illiteracy Is Killing Our Nation," Charisma, 12/3/18, https://www.charismamag.com/life/culture/21076-dumb-and-dumber-how-biblical-illiteracy-is-killing-our-nation?showall=1&start=0.

adjacent to our own), the invisible realm, beyond the spectrum our eyes can see. They are hyperdimensional, beyond what we can touch. The Word of God informs us that there is an active spiritual war going on. You may not want to be involved, but you are, whether you like it or not. God's enemy is our enemy. Satan and his demonic hordes are created beings. God is the Creator, and fallen angels and demonic spirits can't contend with God and hope to be victorious. An enemy who is unable to harm his primary target uses the familiar military tactic of attacking secondary targets, targets of value to the primary objective. In this case, the target is humanity because God loves us.

> For God so loved the world, that he gave his only begotten Son, that whosoever believeth in him should not perish, but have everlasting life.[67]

Whether you believe there is a Sovereign God or whether you have no religious orientation (beliefs), you may want to consider that in the spiritual battle, there are only two sides. Those who are with God and those who are not. Some people may believe there is a third side, the neutral position or passive option—the spectator waiting to see how things go before choosing. The difference is that someone wants to either be a willing or unwilling participant in the cosmic battle. God can orchestrate His will, regardless of human choices. By not choosing, you are by default choosing the world system, which is governed by the devil. In Matthew 4:8-9, we find the devil tempting Jesus with the offer of all the kingdoms of the world if He (Jesus) will bow and worship him (the devil).

> Again, the devil taketh him up into an exceeding high mountain, and sheweth him all the kingdoms of the world, and the glory of them; And saith unto

---

[67] John 3:16, KJV.

> him, All these things will I give thee, if thou wilt fall down and worship me.[68]

For that to be a legitimate temptation, the devil would have to currently have legal ownership of the world kingdoms (world system), and he does. Adam forfeited man's dominion by disobeying God and listening to the devil's offer in the Garden. I bring this subject up because man and woman are the targets of Satan. Jesus tells us in the Gospel of John:

> The thief cometh not, but for to steal, and to kill, and to destroy: I am come that they might have life, and that they might have it more abundantly.[69]

If you are a Christian, you have a spiritual bulls-eye painted on you. You made a choice. Choosing to be obedient to God's Word makes you a prime target because being fruitful in any part of your life is damaging to the devil's agenda. Being fruitful gives grounds for a testimony, a witness to the truthfulness and faithfulness of God and His Word. Jesus is the Word, and the Word of God is our weapon against our spiritual enemies.

Simple analysis tells us that if the Word of God is our offensive weapon in spiritual combat and if we don't become knowledgeable of the Bible (the Word of God) to know what power and authority we do have through Jesus, then we are going off to war unprepared. We would be placing ourselves in a position of deadly disadvantage. Trusting in someone else to give you this knowledge in your time of need could be compared to the blind leading the blind.

---

[68] Matthew 4:8-9, KJV.

[69] John 10:10, KJV.

> And he spake a parable unto them, Can the blind lead the blind? shall they not both fall into the ditch?[70]

Wikipedia gives its version of the above verse.

> "The blind leading the blind" is an idiom and a metaphor in the form of a parallel phrase, it is used to describe a situation where a person who knows nothing is getting advice and help from another person who knows almost nothing. It can be traced back to the Upanishads, which were written between 800 BCE and 200 BCE.[71]

The Apostle Paul authored the Epistle to the Ephesians. In Ephesians 6, he provides a breakdown and the purpose of each piece of the armor of God—spiritual armor that believers should wear daily. When should you wear your seatbelt? Always—you never know when you will need it.

> Finally, my brethren, be strong in the Lord, and in the power of his might. Put on the whole armour of God, that ye may be able to stand against the wiles of the devil. For we wrestle not against flesh and blood, but against principalities, against powers, against the rulers of the darkness of this world, against spiritual wickedness in high places. Wherefore take unto you the whole armour of God, that ye may be able to withstand in the evil day, and having done all, to stand. Stand therefore, having your loins girt about with truth, and having on the breastplate

[70] Luke 6:39, KJV.

[71] "The blind leading the blind," Wikipedia, 12/15/2018, https://en.wikipedia.org/wiki/The_blind_leading_the_blind.

> of righteousness; And your feet shod with the preparation of the Gospel of peace; Above all, taking the shield of faith, wherewith ye shall be able to quench all the fiery darts of the wicked. And take the helmet of salvation, and *the sword of the Spirit, which is the word of God*: Praying always with all prayer and supplication in the Spirit, and watching thereunto with all perseverance and supplication for all saints; ... [72] (Emphasis added)

The Word of God is the "sword" in your armor, and a Christian must be experienced with the biblical text, both the Old and New Testament. A mature Christian knows to check his or her spiritual armor daily to identify and repair any weaknesses they might have in their armor.

Biblical illiteracy research and history have provided the following picture. The Bible and prayer have been removed from our public education and replaced with Gnosticism, our Western culture (America) has a high biblical illiteracy rate, and the lack of personal study of Scripture is not as it was in Early America. This being the case, Americans are wide open for the "Great Deception" spoken of in 2 Thessalonians 2:9-12, 1 Timothy 4:1-3, and again in Revelation 13:13-14. If the Lord Jesus and the apostles warn us to be on guard against deception, then obviously, the possibility exists! Jesus warns us,

> And Jesus answered and said unto them, take heed that no man deceive you.[73]

---

[72] Ephesians 6:10-18, KJV.

[73] Matthew 24:4, KJV.

The Apostle Paul warns in Colossians,

> Beware lest any man spoil you through philosophy and vain deceit, *after the tradition of men*, after the rudiments of the world, and not after Christ.[74] (Emphasis added)

A couple of years ago, I was back in college, finally finishing up my bachelor's degree—better late than never. One of the classes I chose was U.S. Military History. Being prior military, I thought that I would enjoy the course and that it would fill in some gaps. The instructor was an active-duty Army captain with high standards, which made it challenging to achieve an "A," but not impossible. The final exam involved writing a lengthy essay. Students were provided a few topics to choose from to write their assignments. I decided to write about whether America was prepared or unprepared for the wars she entered starting from the Spanish American War to Desert Storm. I believed sufficient proof existed to support that America was not prepared for all the wars in that period except for Desert Storm. I enjoyed the research, and the essay was a success.

In my opinion, there is overwhelming proof to claim that, again, America is not ready for war, spiritual war. We have spiritual battles every day, but the persecution and tribulation that Jesus warns us about has not really impacted America as of yet with the cruelty that has been felt by the first-century church, the Christian martyrs of the Catholic Inquisition, and currently being experienced by Christians in the Middle East and other parts of the world. According to the last book of the Bible, Revelation, the spiritual battle has not reached its zenith. Will you be ready?

Just like any soldier who does an inventory of his gear before being deployed to the field, ask yourself, are you ready? You may not believe that there is a spiritual battle to the magnitude

---

[74] Colossians 2:8, KJV.

that the Book of Revelation describes. Yet I urge you to dig deeper and verify for yourself and your loved ones. Unpreparedness in a crisis is a terrible place to be.

The people in New Jersey who suffered through Hurricane Sandy at the end of October 2012 experienced no power in winter, transportation was down, and trucks could not restock stores. They were hungry and cold, and FEMA lacked a plan that would provide help promptly. Most of the affected residents were unprepared—no stocked pantries, no alternate source of heat, and no contingency plan. Before the supermarket chains began popping up, our grandparents and great grandparents were accustomed to maintaining a stocked pantry. Had the victims of Hurricane Sandy kept stocked pantries, they could have made the struggle considerably more tolerable. Preparation makes a difference in a crisis.

> These were more noble than those in Thessalonica, in that they received the word with all readiness of mind, and searched the Scriptures daily, whether those things were so.[75]

> All Scripture is given by inspiration of God, and is profitable for doctrine, for reproof, for correction, for instruction in righteousness: … [76]

UNITED NATIONS, FRIEND OR FOE

Up to this point, I have been focusing on the hidden agenda of the Church of Rome against the education of our young. The United Nations is a secular branch in the tree of deception; this branch, with its global agenda, disguises itself as a seeker of

---

[75] Acts 17:11, KJV.

[76] 2 Timothy 3:16, KJV.

world peace; its goal is the purging of any reference to God in our schools. The process of "learning against learning" is not just something that was tried a couple of hundred years ago and then discarded.

The United Nations has decided that people must conform to a different way of thinking. The United Nations seeks a heteronomous world culture. In this culture, *an ecclesiastical body or a political structure controls the individual citizen's thinking and acting.* In religious history, Roman Catholicism and Islam are working examples of heteronomous systems.

Today, we can see this purging of God from our schools. Christian children are admonished for sharing their views and feelings about God and Jesus Christ. In a three-part article by Berit Kjos titled "Reinventing the World; Conforming People, Schools, Corporations, Governments and Churches to UN standards." The following is from Part I, "The Seamless Communitarian System."

> Schools: A California teacher told seven-year-old Sallie to stop talking with her friends about Jesus in order to "keep [church and state] apart." Her censure makes sense when we remember that the "outcomes" of UNESCO's worldwide Outcome-Based Education (OBE) system include politically correct attitudes. Sallie's loyalty to the Biblical God didn't fit the new standards. Today's systemic transformation includes rewards for schools and teachers whose students demonstrate—on the new student "assessments"—that they have conformed to the beliefs and values of a global citizen. (See Don't Mention Jesus and Zero Tolerance For Non-Compliance) ... We are in the midst of a global transformation, and few of us saw it coming. Silent and unseen half a century ago, this social revolution grew like a stream of water below the surface of our culture for decades. But now,

at the dawn of the new millennium, the benign current has become a malignant torrent flooding the land. Too powerful to be ignored, it challenges us to respond before the old pathways and guideposts have been swept aside in its wake....

Building a Global Framework

... So must the systems that manage the world's natural, social, and human resources. The basic framework for this global network has already been built, and more parts are being added with each month. The resources (including people and facts) that don't fit must be remediated, adapted, or left out.... *Individual thinkers won't fit*. Their quest for vocational success will be blocked by various gatekeepers: teachers, local workforce boards and literacy centers, universities.... These guardians of the new solidarity will *measure and monitor compliance*, shutting doors to economic benefits and social privileges to dissenters who disturb the new consensus....

Shaping the Future

... Those monopolies are fast falling into line. *Teaching and testing the new way of thinking and understanding reality, they quickly sort the adaptable students from the uncompromising students. Those who conform are rewarded with good grades. Others will fail, and their lack of cooperation and understanding will be recorded in their personal, permanent data file for use by future employers.*[77] (Emphasis added)

---

[77] Berit Kjos, "Reinventing the World ~ Part 1: The Seamless Communitarian System," Kjos Ministries, 2001, https://www.crossroad.to/articles2/Reinvent1.htm.

For those of us watching, it may appear that America's education system may not recover or reverse its fall. As individuals, we may not be able to compete with the governmental powers and their puppet masters that are part of America's reconstruction from the inside. But as individuals and as families, we can educate ourselves—it is a matter of desire.

The early Americans educated in the home, and I believe that in the last days, both quality education and factual biblical studies will be done in our homes as well. Consider the time and money you spend on entertainment, which is a distraction put in place on purpose. Is it worth it? Arthur Thompson is the author of the book *To the Victor Go Myths & Monuments*. In Thompson's introductory briefing, he lists the Illuminati's eight goals to change a society.

1. The overthrow of all government
2. The destruction of religion
3. The abolition of private property
4. The death of individualism
5. The deification of sensuality
6. The repudiation of marriage
7. The state control of children
8. The establishment of a world government

This problem brings back a question from chapter one: "Is there an agenda to deliberately hide the truth, keep us ignorant?" This brings us back to the topic of deception. The roots of deception run deep, and its scope is broad. My personal opinions carry no weight with you and your family's beliefs. What is essential for you is the conclusion you draw from the information presented. A determination meant to inform you that a deception of great magnitude exists. Will you trash this presented evidence, will you question it, or will you verify it for yourself?

4

WATCHMAN'S HORN

DECEPTION

As with *propaganda,* the scope and operational arena of *deception* are vast. Its deployment on societies varies in magnitude. The mature and experienced reader has learned that people can have deceitful hearts and minds. This fault is not to be feared but understood.

> Behold, I send you forth as sheep in the midst of wolves: be ye therefore wise as serpents, and harmless as doves.[1]

Deception, accidental or intentional, is taking place around us, but we may not always recognize the indicators. That is the goal now, isn't it, for the recipient to be unaware? As with lies, individuals and nations suffer the effects of deception. It is used to undermine the prosperity and freedoms of a country and destroy the lives of individuals. America started with the potential to be a free nation, and it took the Revolutionary War to hold that freedom. Today, just as in 1776, there still are organizations whose desire is to put all countries under one umbrella; these nations are to be ruled by a centralized government or oligarchy.

---

[1] Matthew 10:16, KJV.

These clandestine organizations are systematic and persistent toward the completion of their goals. A goal this massive in size comes with the understanding that it will take generations to complete.

Foreign powers did not delay in their infiltration of our newly formed United States. The upright in heart saw America as a land of hope and opportunity. The wicked in heart saw it as a land to dominate. The Pilgrims and the Puritans were not the only ones who sailed to the New World. The scheme to subvert the United States' freedoms became possible for Rome after the signing of the Declaration of Independence. Brave men and women of religious faith fled the persecution in Europe with the hope of freedom and safety in the Americas. These men and women are the real *"founders"* of America.

As stated in the previous chapter, it was primarily the Pilgrims and the Puritans who established our educational system and promoted a moral code based on biblical principles. From the beginning of the United States, people of courage gave warning after warning to be vigilant and watchful, for our liberties come at a high price. As soon as we become complacent and offload our responsibility for freedom to others (government), we risk the loss of those liberties. You can only coast one way, and that is downhill. A country that loses its freedom falls back into bondage and persecution. There is a life cycle, a pattern that countries go through. "The cycle of nations" describes the rise and fall of a Republic. Many images on the internet show different versions of this cycle.

Image; Cycle of Nations. [2]

The American Revolutionary War was a war where the enemy, for the most part, was visible. When open warfare on American soil would not bring submission, our enemies were forced to use a different approach. This tactic wasn't new; it had been used in Europe centuries before—bring down the enemy from within, through intrigue, and capture the minds of the young. While we scan the horizon of our borders for danger, we miss what is happening in our backyard. To bring America into submission, our enemy would usurp from within, through our education system, our government, our religion, and our way of life. This form of warfare requires patience because it is slow and progressive. Again, it can take generations to complete.

A gradual dismantling or slow, intentional decay of our nation's foundation would go far less noticed when compared to a direct attack on our borders. It would be like the devil announcing himself to you before asking you to disobey God, but that is not his modus operandi. The devil prefers the art of deception, and he is the master of it. When it comes to the lust for power and the use of fraud, the devil has many earthly apprentices.

---

[2] Commonsensegovernment.com.

Deception is being used to destroy America's right to sovereignty. Our Constitution, our Christian education, and our moral values are all being dismantled slowly, and, done slowly, this process goes unnoticed. The United Nations Charter is superseding our Constitution. Gnosticism has replaced biblical education in our public schools. Our culture is being permitted to promote vice and immorality. Sexual depravity, pornography, abortion, divorce, apathy, excessive alcohol consumption, and drug use have polluted America. Iniquities that are publicly accepted today would cause shock and outrage in 1940s culture.

Dr. Zacharias on a cultural reversal:

> How ironic that sexuality and nudity, which are meant to be private, are now fare for public consumption while spiritual convictions, which are meant to strengthen public polity, are now for private expression only.[3]

One method to convert our culture is to secularize it. A Christian, by default, holds a biblical worldview. Secularization prohibits the freedom of religious expression, especially the Christian faith. Secular powers are privatizing Christianity. Early in chapter one, I explained that we share our worldviews at different levels of exposure due to rejection and ridicule. Our government continually presses for more privatization of America's Christianity. This agenda has confined the body of Christ within church buildings and Christian homes. Jails without guards. Dr. Ravi Zacharias does an excellent job of explaining the effects of secularization and the meaning of privatization. First, Noah Webster defines secular as follows:

---

[3] Zacharias, *Deliver Us From Evil*,108

> Pertaining to the present world, or to things not spiritual or holy; relating to things not immediately or primarily respecting the soul, but the body; worldly. The secular concerns of life respect making provision for the support of life, the preservation of health, the temporal prosperity of men, of states, etc. ...[4]

Paraphrased, God is not allowed. To use Dr. Zacharias' description, in America, Jesus Christ is on house arrest.

> While secularization has cleansed the public arena of religious ideas, privatization insists that though one may choose to believe whatever one wants to it must be kept private. This is the social phenomenon of privatization that magnanimously gives with one hand and militantly takes away with the other --and is then mystified that this benevolence is not appreciated.
>
> Privatization may be defined as the socially required and legally enforced separation of our private lives and our public personas; in effect, privatization mandates that issues of ultimate meaning be relegated to our private spheres.[5]

This allowance for private belief supposedly distinguished democracy from totalitarianism, where one's personal belief is dictated. But in effect the same public outcome results; life's deepest quests and most cherished values are sequestered. Every thinking person knows that to imprison a sacred belief within the private realm is ultimately to fracture, if not to kill, the belief. One could no more sever

---

[4] Webster, *Secular*, http://webstersdictionary1828.com/Dictionary/Secular.

[5] Zacharias, *Deliver Us From Evil*, 105.

> belief from public expression and still live spiritually fulfilled than one could remove the heart from the body and bid the blood flow. The separation kills the life in the body. Such is the impact on privatized spirituality.[6]

This slow process of change reminds me of an analogy that you may have seen in its various forms, "The Frog is Boiling."[7]

The following pages will contain quotes from a variety of authors who differ in profession and entry into history's timeline, but all with the same warning. Their writings provide a different view than is found in public-school history books. The focus will be on the individuals and groups who are responsible for the manipulation, deception, and breakdown of nations—all done to maintain *power* and *control*. The lust for power over humanity extends back to the days of antiquity. Today, we see conflicts for power and control on the nightly news.

The Papacy is one of the oldest political forces left from the ancient world if you consider it is a continuation of the Roman Empire, and it has beachheads in every nation. A vast majority of the historical data printed in this book will expose the activities of both the *papacy* (the *Dynasty of Popes*) and the papacy's private militia, the *Society of Jesus* (the Jesuits). The Church of Rome's hierarchy is, for all practical purposes, a theocracy, a combination of both political and religious power that has universal control as its goal.

A distinction must remain clear—the focus on the Church of Rome is not an attack on the Catholic brothers and sisters who have accepted Jesus Christ as their Savior. When you have an organization as large as the Church of Rome, the laity won't be fully aware of the motives of their hierarchy. The American citizen is not aware of the plans its leaders forge in Washington, DC.

---

[6] Ibid., 106.

[7] https://en.wikipedia.org/wiki/Boiling_frog.

But there must be a separation. This book makes a distinction between Catholic laity (the outer circle) and the Church of Rome's hierarchy (the inner circle). The inner circle, at a minimum, includes the papacy and the Society of Jesus (the Jesuits). It sounds like a conspiracy, right? Within the ranks of priests, nuns, and Jesuits, some have spoken out. And, through personal conviction, they chose to leave.

> And I heard another voice from heaven, saying, *Come out of her, my people, that ye be not partakers of her sins, and that ye receive not of her plagues.*[8] (Emphasis added)

Church memberships fluctuate all the time; people come and go in churches and organizations; this is considered normal human behavior. Some of these individuals are willing to give firsthand, eyewitness accounts of the corruption and inner workings of the Catholic Church. Are the testimonies of these whistle-blowers just more propaganda, or are they like the watchman on the wall, trying to sound the alarm? Whistle-blowers always have a struggle, especially when they are in opposition to organizations of power and influence.

The Vatican has considerable resources at its disposal, and these ex-Catholics who speak out are immediately discredited and labeled as dissenters—some have died under questionable circumstances. Many people within the ranks of the Catholic faith have made significant contributions to society, just as there have been from other cultures worldwide. Historical records still require investigation, and the truth cannot be sugarcoated because it disrupts someone's paradigm. As I have mentioned before, you will have to decide what you consider to be the truth. Investigation, not blind acceptance, is needed here.

---

[8] Revelation 18:4, KJV.

OLD HABITS DIE HARD

The doctrine we choose to adhere to is crucial. You may say, "Great, how do we know who and what to trust as truthful instruction?" The Christian church body already existed outside Catholicism and before Luther's Protestant Reformation. Many of the early Reformers were Catholics themselves. These men didn't always intend to separate from the Church of Rome but desired church reform for the Catholic Church. Being Catholic themselves, they received the indoctrination and *ways* of Catholicism.

Even though they chose to contend with the Catholic Church on reform issues, they committed the same crimes (shedding of innocent blood) as the Church of Rome—maybe not to the degree and longevity of the Church of Rome, but guilty just the same. It would be both foolish and arrogant to claim that one side of the Reformation is entirely evil, and the opposition is completely innocent. We are all sinners in need of salvation.

The late Roderick C. Meredith, the Editor-in-Chief of *Tomorrow's World Magazine,* wrote the Reformation Series titled *"500 Years of The Protestant Reformation."* This series offers an unbiased look at both sides of the Protestant Reformation. In Part 8, *Violent Methods of the Reformers,* we find the following:

> When it came to a showdown, the Protestant reformers were as ready to resort to violence, bloodshed, and persecution as their Roman Catholic adversaries. In any discussion of the methods by which the Reformation triumphed, this fact must be acknowledged.
>
> We have already seen how Luther won the German princes to his cause. How he used them to fight Catholicism and to persecute those who disagreed with him, is another matter. And the same principle may apply to Zwingli and Calvin, and the political

> councils under their sway, and to King Henry VIII and his subservient Parliament and nobility.
>
> Do we remember Luther's raving appeal to the German princes to "smite, strangle, and stab, secretly or publicly" those peasants who had applied the principle of his teachings to their own circumstances? Do we remember that he reversed himself in 1529, and said that Christians were "bound" to resort to arms to defend their Protestant beliefs?
>
> It is also a fact that Luther approved the persecution and martyrdom of the Anabaptists and other sects who rejected his teachings. Commenting on the beheading of Anabaptists in Saxony, he said that "their courage showed that they were possessed by the devil."
>
> After Calvinism was introduced into Scotland, those who professed the Catholic religion were subject to the death penalty, and many paid with their lives for their religious beliefs.

Meredith goes on to write about the martyrdom of Michael Servetus at the hands of John Calvin in Geneva. Under the heading, *The Reason for Protestant Violence and Persecutions,* Meredith explains:

> The answer to the killing of Servetus, then, does not lie in rashness later repented of, nor does it lie in a complete lack of sincerity on Calvin's part. But what is the answer?
>
> The same answer is given, in essence, by many Protestant Historians. It is one that every honest student of the Bible and history must acknowledge.
>
> The answer is that, even long after their separation from Rome and their "conversion" to Protestantism, the early reformers and their followers were

> still literally saturated with the doctrines, the concepts, and the practices of their "mother" church at Rome. "The reformers inherited the doctrine of persecution from their mother church, and practiced it as far as they had the power. They fought intolerance with intolerance. They differed favorably from their opponents in the degree and extent, but not in the principle, of intolerance" (Schaff, Vol. VIII, p. 700).
>
> As we shall see, this frank admission by Schaff reveals why so many of the Protestant doctrines and actions seem so totally inconsistent with their avowed intention of basing everything on "the Bible only."
>
> We have seen that Martin Luther played politics, condoned bigamy, counseled a lie, and encouraged the slaughter of peasants and execution of Anabaptists (which included drowning many of them).
>
> It has been shown that the English revolt began with the lust of Henry VIII, and that he and Queen Elizabeth and their Protestant theologians all had a part in slaughtering hundreds of Catholic, Anabaptist and, later, Puritan dissenters.

A Christian who desires to be obedient to Scripture cannot just accept any doctrine that comes his or her way. Our path is selected, and our life boundaries make the path we walk narrow.

> Because strait is the gate, and narrow is the way, which leadeth unto life, and few there be that find it.[9]

Jesus Christ established His church in the first century with the apostles, and through the Holy Spirit. This event has its

---

[9] Matthew 7:14, KJV.

origin in Acts 2:4, not 300 years later, in the form of a "state church" formed by Emperor Constantine. Who then imposed state church dogma on the existing Christians to unify his empire? Once the Bible became available to the masses, people were able to see for themselves the illegitimacy of the papacy.

During the Dark Ages, inquisitions converted or eliminated individuals and masses of people through torture and death. The victims were those who would not submit to the dogma of the Catholic Church.

Author F. Tupper Saussy says the following about Roman priests controlling sacred writings and excluding the public access to this material:

> The Sibylline and the Aeneid were open only to priests and certain privileged persons. The people learned their sacred content by the trickle-down of priestly retelling. When the Old and New Testaments were adopted as the Empire's official sacred writings, they, too, were given to the exclusive care of the priests. And in accord with *Roman tradition*, the people learned sacred content from discretionary retelling. This had to be, for the sake of the Holy Empire. *For should the people acquire biblical knowledge, they would know that Pontifex "Maximus was not a legitimate Christian entitlement.* Knowing this, they would not bow to his supremacy. The Empire could collapse. And so the monarchial Roman church forcibly suppressed the Bible's intelligent reading. This is why the millennium between Constantine and Gutenberg is known as "the Dark Ages." [10] (Emphasis added)

[10] Saussy, *Rulers of Evil*, 16.

The Oxford Classical Dictionary supports Saussy's statements:

> **The Sibylline Books in Rome**
> ... Two officials in the early Republic had the task of consulting and reporting the advice of the Sibylline Books when dire and unexpected prodigies occurred, or when advice was needed on major matters of state. Their number was later expanded to ten and eventually to fifteen. But the officialdom maintained a tight control over the books. *Only the senate could authorize consultation, no one but the designated officials had access to them,* and their reports went straight to the senate—*which alone decided what and what not to make public.*
>
> ... The Sibylline Books, as employed by the authorities, allowed Romans to reach out to alien wisdom and to reinforce their engagement with the cultures of Greece and the Near East. But the close management of the oracles by an authorized officialdom under the mandate of the *senate limited control to a small circle* and *protected the interests of state.* Augustus reinforced the constricted oversight. He ordered the burning of a host of dubious prophetic oracles, retaining only the Sibylline Books, and was selective even in that retention, setting the remainder apart for safekeeping. The pronouncements that had faded over time were to be copied anew, *but only authorized priests were allowed to do so, lest anyone else might*

> *inspect them. Sibylline pronouncements did not circulate to the public.*[11] (Emphasis added)

Saussy continues:

> By the thirteenth century, these assemblies had grown so vibrant that Pope Gregory IX *declared unauthorized Bible study a heresy*. He further decreed that "it is the duty of *every Catholic to persecute* heretics." To manage the persecution, Gregory established the Pontifical Inquisition.[12] (Emphasis added)

The Roman Catholic Church held the Council of Toulouse (1229), which prohibited the reading of the Bible in vernacular translations, which the Church of Rome considered a vulgar tongue. Author Peter Allix wrote in his book, *Ecclesiastical History of Ancient Churches of the Albigenses*:

> The pastors recommended to the people the having of the books of the New Testament in their mother-tongue, and pressed the reading thereof with so much care and application, that Raymond, Earl of Toulouse, never stirred any whither without taking that holy book with him. This was the certain badge and mark of all these heretics, and that whereby they defended themselves. For which reason, the Council of Toulouse, fearing lest their croisades should not be able to exterminate the Albigenses, as long as they had the Bible in the vulgar tongue, took care to prohibit the having of it in these terms; "We chap. " prohibit the permission of the books of the Old ' "and

---

[11] Gruen, Erich S. "Sibylline Oracles." *Oxford Classical Dictionary*. 22 Dec. 2016; Accessed 31 Oct. 2019. https://oxfordre.com/classics/view/10.1093/acrefore/9780199381135.001.0001/acrefore-9780199381135-e-8134.

[12] Saussy, *Rulers of Evil*, 16.

> New Testament to laymen, except perhaps " they might desire to have the Psalter, or some " Breviary for the divine service, or the Hours of the " blessed Virgin Mary, for devotion; expressly for- " bidding their having the other parts of the Bible " translated into the vulgar tongue." [13]

The Inquisition was during tyrannical times in history. Would you agree? The Dark Ages are considered the past, but the Vatican still favors the use of Inquisitions. The Vatican doesn't have a standing army. The papacy must use the military might of other nations that are tributaries of Rome or have some political agreement. The following chapters will give details to these alliances. Through the instigation of wars and genocides, the Church of Rome eliminates her enemies.

A side effect of research into the unpleasant side of humanity is that it can become discouraging if there isn't hope of victory over the chaos. Gods' Word, the Bible, tells how the story ends—there is light at the end of the tunnel, and that Light is Jesus Christ's return. Friends have asked what benefit does all this research do, and how does it help with *living today* (the present)? I offer this dual answer. You can't identify a lie if you don't know the truth. Second, I find it interesting how some worldviews think deceptions and conspiracies only pertain to the distant past and the prophetic future and not to the here and now. Research of history reveals what is going on now in the present. Granted, you may lose some of your *Pollyanna* worldviews. Is our choice that hard? We can believe the truth once we find it or the programming and indoctrination shoveled to the masses. Every age requires *watchmen*—people (men and women) who are wired to pursue historical research and inform their generation. We can

---

[13] Pierre Allix, *Ecclesiastical History of Ancient churches of the Albigenses* (Oxford, England: Clarendon Press, 1821), 212-213.

choose to learn from history or repeat man's errors because we remain ignorant of them.

> A 19th-century writer. Adolphe Michel, recalled that Voltaire estimated the number of works published over the years, on the Jesuits, to be about six thousand, "What number have we reached a century later?" concluded Adolphe Michel immediately: "No matter. As long as there are Jesuits, books will have to be written against them. There is nothing new left to be said on their account, but new generations of readers come every day ... Will these readers search old books?[14]

COMPLACENCY

The potential for being deceived was significant enough for Jesus Christ and His apostles to warn us to beware of the deceptions and the workings of the spirit of the antichrist. Note, the spirit of the antichrist was already working in the first-century church. The sad thing in today's church is many Christians are asleep at the wheel—*"life is good."* There are causes for spiritual complacency. The false doctrine of *Futurism* is one source of spiritual contentment. This doctrine is covered in greater detail later.

Approximately 25 percent of the Bible is prophetic. Not to diminish the gospel message, but how many churches are warning their flock? Pre-Tribulation rapture teaching has caused Western churches to drop their guard. Jesus Christ said we would experience tribulation and persecution if we followed Him (Matthew 10). False doctrines have lulled Western Christianity into a false sense of security. Western culture has become self-satisfied. America's general population is ignorant of world

---

[14] Edmond Paris, *The Secret History of the Jesuits* (Ontario, California: Chick Publications), 10.

events. This ignorance is partially due to our controlled news outlets. *Ignorance is bliss.*

It will be too late to be informed and be prepared when the problem has reached your doorstep, and if the tribulations that Jesus spoke of delay, then the porch of our children. Parents are responsible for the teaching and life preparation of their children, not only the schools, the church, or the culture around them. From a traditional standpoint, the responsibility to *provide and protect* falls to the man. Men, we cannot shrug off our God-given responsibilities. When a nation's men become weak, that nation is doomed to collapse. The weakness here is more than physical strength. Mental and spiritual strength is needed to hold a culture together. This view is not questioning women's capabilities. I helped for nine years in my church's Divorce Care Ministry. There I witnessed how women had to play both father and mother roles in their homes. Many single moms do fantastic jobs.

Adam was responsible for *protecting the Garden* in Eden. He had the authority to rebuke the serpent, but he didn't. What would the world be like today had Adam done his duty? In the Bible, the church is warned several times by Jesus and the apostles. It takes time to separate the truths from the lies, but I believe it is worth it. Hopefully, the efforts to consolidate and provide a peek behind the curtain will be of help and perhaps motivate you to want to know more. The atrocities and destruction that plague earth will end with the return of Jesus Christ. Until then, Christians have work to do. You may not be called to pastor a church, but you can still share the gospel. Sometimes we are spiritual crossing guards. If you don't know the answers, point that person in need to someone who does.

> Prove all things; hold fast to that which is good.[15]

---

[15] 1 Thessalonians 5:21, KJV.

Not verifying for ourselves means we accept the current paradigm, and some people are perfectly content until change forces its way in! My goal is to share a view that perhaps you are not aware of and prompt you to look deeper for yourself. The references in this book may assist in beginning your investigation. We live in the *Information Age*, where the opportunity to perform research is right at our fingertips and, for most people, within the comfort of their homes. Ignore the mental fillers. The entertainment industry is a multi-billion-dollar industry, and it pushes its views (agenda) on the public (reference the chapter on *propaganda*). Television, sports programs, movies, video games, etc. are pacifiers designed to keep you mentally sedated. This opinion is not a call for a boycott against entertainment but a suggestion for a dose of moderation.

The Roman Empire did the same thing by creating more holidays and colosseums to entertain the masses. America's Early Settlers took full advantage of their freedom to instruct their children. Their daily chores didn't permit all the fruitless distractions we have today. Each American *must distinguish whether they are living in prosperity or a gilded cage*. No nation continues indefinitely. Change will occur, and it can be gradual or catastrophic. Here in America, we see the disastrous results of war taking place overseas while we sit in the presumed safety of our homes. According to recorded history, the American Revolutionary War freed America from England. These same history books once claimed the founding fathers created the United States using Judeo-Christian principles. I find it difficult to fully agree with that view. The architectural design of Washington D.C. is of pagan Greco-Rome, and the buildings and streets are laid out in esoteric design. This construction is far from biblical principles.

While several of the signers of the Declaration of Independence were godly men, it is apparent there were other influential powers at work directly in opposition to God's Word. Where was the public outcry for disapproval?

> Thou shalt have no other gods before me. Thou shalt not make unto thee any graven image, or any likeness of anything that is in heaven above, or that is in the earth beneath, or that is in the water under the earth;[16]

Many of the "Founding Fathers" were members of the secret society of Freemasons. Preliminary research into secret societies reveals Freemasonry was continuously being infiltrated and manipulated by the Jesuits. This research alludes to claims that Freemasonry has roots through the Jesuits to the Rosicrucians and back to the Knights Templar. Freemason Historian Albert G. Mackey rejects the accusations that the Jesuits are the origin of pure Freemasonry. From Albert G. Mackey in the *Encyclopedia of Freemasonry* 1891, he wrote the following about the Jesuits and Freemasonry:

> In the last century the Jesuits were charged with having an intimate connection with Freemasonry, and the invention of the degree of Kadosh was even attributed to those members of the Society who constituted the College of Clermont. This theory of a Jesuitical Masonry seems to have originated with the Illuminati, who were probably governed in its promulgation by a desire to depreciate the character of all other Masonic systems in comparison with their own, where no such priestly interference was permitted.
>
> Yet it cannot be denied that, while the Jesuits have had no part in the construction of pure Freemasonry, there are reasons for believing that they took an interest in the invention of some degrees and systems which were intended to advance their own

[16] Exodus 20:3-4, KJV.

> interests. But wherever they touched the Institution they left the trail of the serpent. They sought to convert its pure philanthropy and toleration into political intrigue and religious bigotry. Hence it is believed that they had something to do with the invention of those degrees, which were intended to aid the exiled house of Stuart in its efforts to regain the English throne, because they believed that would secure the restoration in England of the Roman Catholic religion. Almost a library of books has been written on both sides of this subject in Germany and in France.[17]

Prominent secret society leaders and other historians have written about this clouded link between Freemasonry and the Jesuits. Helena Petrovna Blavatsky was the Russian occultist and philosopher who co-founded the Theosophical Society in 1875. From her book, *Isis Unveiled*, there is the following:

> Count Ramsay, a Jesuit, was the first to start the idea of the Templars being joined to the Knights of Malta. Therefore, we read from his pen the following : " Our forefathers (!!!), the Crusaders, assembled in the Holy Land from all Christendom, wished to unite in a fraternity embracing all nations, that when bound together, heart and soul, for mutual improvement, they might, in the course of time, represent one single intellectual people."...
>
> It is curious to note too that most of the bodies which work these, such as the Ancient and Accepted Scottish Rite, the Rite of Avignon, the Order of the Temple, Fessler's Rite, the Grand Council of the

[17] Albert G. Mackey M.D., *An Encyclopedia of Freemasonry*, (Philadelphia: L.H. Everts and Co., 1891), 382

> Emperors of the East and West Sovereign Prince Mason's, etc., etc., are nearly all the offspring of the sons of Ignatius Loyola. The Baron Hundt, Chevalier Ramsey, Tschoudy, Zinnendorf, and numerous others, who founded the grades in these rites, worked under instructions from the General of the Jesuits.[18]

Author John Daniel states in his book, *The Grand Design Exposed*:

> The truth is, the Jesuits of Rome have perfected Freemasonry to be their most magnificent and effective tool, accomplishing their purposes among Protestants…[19]

From American historian James Parton's book, *The Life of Horace Greeley; Editor of the New York Tribune*, there is this interesting cultural note:

> There are families now, about the country, in which Masonry is a forbidden topic, because its introduction would revive the old quarrel, and turn the peaceful tea-table into a scene of hot interminable contention. There are still old ladies, male and female, about the country, who will tell you with grim gravity that, if you trace up Masonry, through all its Orders, till you come to the grand, tip-top, Head Mason of the world, you will discover that that dread

---

[18] H.P. Blavatsky, Isis Unveiled: *A Master Key to the Mysteries of Ancient and Modern Science and Theology*, (New York: J.W. Bouton, 1878), 384, 390.

[19] John Daniel, *The Grand Design Exposed*, (Middleton, Idaho: CHJ Publishing, 1999), 302.

> individual and the Chief of the Society of Jesuits are one and the same Person![20]

My initial research into Freemasonry is incomplete. However, the question of the Jesuit-Freemason connection being legitimate is overshadowed by how Catholicism was permitted to enter the United States unencumbered after the American Revolutionary War.

The Jesuits manipulate and use any means possible to achieve their goals—*the ends justify the means* for destroying Protestant Christianity. Biblical Christian faith influenced the Pilgrims and Puritans and, therefore, shaped Early America. Early in the United States' history, there were Old World powers not satisfied with America being free.

F. Tupper Saussy's investigation provides a thought-provoking view of the inner workings of the Revolutionary and Civil War. Early American Protestant believers who fled Europe to escape the persecution from the church of England and the Church of Rome established laws to protect America from the papacy and Catholicism. Catholicism was no longer prohibited in predominately Protestant America once the Declaration of Independence was active. The Church of Rome could pollute and disrupt the United States just as it had done with the nations of Europe for centuries. Rome's goal would target our government, our education, and our religion, Protestant Christianity.

> I wanted to know the extent of Jesuit involvement in United States government, presently and historically. What I discovered was a vast Roman Catholic substratum to American history, especially the Revolution that produced the constitutional republic. I found that Jesuits played eminent and under-

[20] James Parton, *The Life of Horace Greeley: Editor of the New York Tribune*, (New York: Mason Brothers, 1855), 102.

> appreciated roles in moving the complacent New Englanders to rebel against their mother country. I discovered facts and motives strongly suggesting that events that made Great Britain divide in 1776 were the outworkings of an ingenious Jesuit strategy. This strategy appears to have been single-handedly designed and supervised by a true founding father few Americans have ever heard of – Lorenzo Ricci (known to British Jesuits as Laurence Richey).[21]
>
> Vatican II affirms Catholic doctrine dating back to 1302, when Pope Boniface VIII asserted that "it is absolutely necessary for the salvation of every human creature to be subject to the Roman Pontiff." This was the inspiration for the papacy to create the United States of America that materialized in 1776, by a process just as secret as the Reagan-Vatican production of Eastern Europe in 1989. What? American government Roman Catholic from the beginning?"[22]

How did the Church of Rome gain so much access to positions of power in America's government? Catholics who were in America before the creation of the United States had limited rights because the concern was, if allowed to be unfettered, they would continue their obligation to obey the Church of Rome and bring all people under the rule of the papacy. The Protestants before the formation of the United States knew this to be the case, and to prevent that from happening in America, Catholics had limited rights. They could not vote or hold positions in government. This all changed with the signing of the Declaration of Independence.

---

[21] Saussy, *Rulers of Evil*, xix.

[22] Ibid., 4.

Before the enactment of the Declaration of Independence, the Catholic population in the Colonies was at its minimum. The Church of Rome had not established a foothold or a beachhead in the North American colonies from which it could politically infiltrate and usurp. That tactical position would change. The Catholics were a minority in a predominantly Protestant America. The Puritans and the Congregationalists of New England distrusted Catholic immigrants because of their "alien allegiance" to the Church of Rome. Protestants, being the majority, imposed limited rights on Catholic immigrants. The website titled The American Revolution offers this information relating to Catholics in British America:

> Before the English settlement of Virginia, a band of Spanish Jesuit priests tried to establish a mission near the Chesapeake Bay in 1570. Indians destroyed it after only a few months. The next Catholics in Virginia were a handful of English, Irish, and Polish Catholic tradesmen who lived and worked in the settlement at Jamestown beginning in 1607. Hindered by proscriptive legislation, however, few Catholics came to the colony.... Catholics fared better in neighboring Pennsylvania, founded by Quaker William Penn in 1681 on a basis of broad religious toleration.... Resentment against the pope and his church reigned in Congregationalist New England throughout the colonial period, and Massachusetts enacted anti-Catholic measures in 1647.... Statistics for Catholics in most of the colonies do not exist due to the lack of resident priests to keep records. In the absence of the oversight and guidance of a Catholic bishop before 1790, the 186 Jesuit priests who worked in British North America between 1634 and the suppression of their order in 1773 struggled to fulfill their missions.... When the new states began

> crafting constitutions in 1776, with Virginia, Pennsylvania, and Maryland pondering proposals for religious toleration, many Catholics stepped forward in service to their nation. John Barry helped found the United States Navy. Stephen Moylan became Washington's muster master-general. Daniel Carroll joined Congress from Maryland, and Thomas FitzSimons represented Pennsylvania.... By the end of the Revolution, Catholics in the United States numbered about 25,000 out of a general population of 4,000,000.[23]

The Protestant Reformation was dividing Europe. And as was shared earlier in this chapter, religious persecution was committed on both sides of the Reformation. Neither party, Protestant nor Catholic, could claim to be completely innocent. The New England Puritans were extremely harsh in their intolerance of those outside of their faith. England was no longer a safe place for Catholics. Englishman George Calvert chose the colonies for religious refuge. George Calvert obtained a land grant from King Charles I, which is the state of Maryland today. George's son Cecelius Calvert would be the Calvert to complete his father's dream.

> Cecilius Calvert, the second Baron Baltimore, established Maryland as a place of refuge for Catholics, when two ships, the Ark and the Dove, arrived with his brother and some three hundred colonists in early 1634.[24]

Catholic immigrants found Maryland to be a safe haven. Protestant America's distrust of the Catholic Church was

---

[23] "Catholics in British America," The American Revolution, November 2, 2019, http://www.ouramericanrevolution.org/index.cfm/page/view/p0155.

[24] Ibid.

justified. Europe was in chaos due to the Catholic Church's interference in the political affairs of Europe's sovereigns, but their persecution of the Catholic laity was not justified.

The Toleration Act of 1649 helped provide religious freedom in the Americas for non-Protestants. The wording of the Toleration Act closely resembled the text of Roman church dogma used to accuse those who opposed the papacy. The punishments for violating the Toleration Act were similar to that of the Inquisition.

The Maryland Toleration Act of 1649

> Forasmuch as in a well governed and Christian Common Wealth matters concerning Religion and the honor of God ought in the first place to bee taken, into serious consideration and endeavoured to bee settled, Be it, therefore, ordered and enacted by the Right Honourable Cecilius Lord Baron of Baltimore absolute Lord and Proprietary of this Province with the advise and consent of this Generall Assembly:
>
> That whatsoever person or persons within this Province and the Islands thereunto belonging shall from henceforth blaspheme God, that is Curse him, or deny our Saviour Jesus Christ to bee the sonne of God, or shall deny the holy Trinity the father sonne and holy Ghost, or the Godhead of any of the said Three persons of the Trinity or the Unity of the Godhead, or shall use or utter any reproachfull Speeches, words or language concerning the said Holy Trinity, or any of the said three persons thereof, *shalbe punished with death and confiscation or forfeiture of all his or her lands and goods to the Lord Proprietary and his heires.*
>
> And bee it also Enacted by the Authority and with the advise and assent aforesaid, *That whatsoever person or persons shall from henceforth use or utter any reproachfull words or Speeches concerning the blessed*

> *Virgin Mary the Mother of our Saviour or the holy Apostles or Evangelists* or any of them shall in such case for the first offence forfeit to the said Lord Proprietary and his heirs Lords and Proprietaries of this Province the summe of five pound Sterling or the value thereof to be Levyed on the goods and chattells of every such person soe offending, but in case such Offender or Offenders, shall not then have goods and chattells sufficient for the satisfyeing of such forfeiture, or that the same bee not otherwise speedily satisfyed that then such Offender or Offenders shalbe *publiquely whipt* and *bee imprisoned during the pleasure of the Lord Proprietary* or the Lieutenant or cheife Governor of this Province for the time being. And that every such Offender or Offenders for every second offence shall forfeit tenne pound sterling or the value thereof to bee levyed as aforesaid, or in case such offender or Offenders shall not then have goods and chattells within this Province sufficient for that purpose then to *bee publiquely and severely whipt and imprisoned as before is expressed.* And that every person or persons before mentioned offending herein the *third time,* shall for such third Offence *forfeit all his lands and Goods and bee for ever banished and expelled out of this Province....* [25] (Emphasis added)

King George II granted the Charter of 1732, which prohibited religious freedom for Roman Catholics:

> The charter contained contradictions. The colonists were entitled to all the rights of Englishmen, yet

[25] "The Maryland Toleration Act 1649," American History; From the Revolution to Reconstruction and Beyond, http://www.let.rug.nl/usa/documents/1600-1650/the-maryland-toleration-act-1649.php.

> there was no provision for the essential right of local government. *Religious liberty was guaranteed, except for Roman Catholicism and Judaism.* A group of Jews landed in Georgia without explicit permission in 1733 but were allowed to remain.[26]

The Catholic population numbers vary, but the concern of the Vatican having politically and religious influence in the Colonies was a concern for the predominately Protestant America. History had already shown what the destructive results were of having the papacy and its Jesuit militia influence allowed in a country. Protestant America already had religious freedom; the American Revolution provided freedom from British rule. The Declaration of Independence offered religious freedom for religions other than the Protestant faith and opened the door for the Church of Rome to infiltrate America. F. Tupper Saussy makes the following comments about the American Revolution in his book *Rulers of Evil*:

> BEFORE THE American Revolution, Roman Catholics were barred from voting or holding public office throughout the British colonies. They were a persecuted minority everywhere but in the proprietary domain of William Penn (Pennsylvania and Delaware). Some of their most energetic persecutors, in fact, were the very Huguenots whom the Catholics had chased out of France in the wake of Louis XIV's revocation of the Edict of Nantes.
>
> The basis of Roman Catholic persecution was political. Catholics owed allegiance to Pontifex Maximus, the Bishop of Rome. The Bishop of Rome was a foreign ruler who, as a matter of public policy,

[26] Cashin, Edward J. "Trustee Georgia, 1732-1752." New Georgia Encyclopedia. 02 September 2015. Web. 01 November 2019.

regarded the British king and his *Protestant church as heretics to be destroyed*. From the American colonists' standpoint, to allow Catholics to vote or hold office was tantamount to surrendering their colonies to a foreign conqueror. A crucial part of *maintaining personal liberty in Protestant colonial America* was keeping *Roman Catholics out of government*. But then came the Revolution. The colonial citizenry fought for and won their independence from Great Britain. They established a Constitution that amounted to... surrendering their country to a foreign conqueror. *Consider the legalities. Before the Constitution was ratified, American Catholics had few civil rights; after ratification, they had them all....* the Constitution welcomed *agents* of Pontifex Maximus, the *world's chief enemy of Protestantism*, into the ranks of government.

Of the 2,500,000 enumerated inhabitants in 1787 America, the Roman Catholic population consisted of no more than 16,000 in Maryland, 7,000 in Pennsylvania, 1,500 in New York, and 200 in Virginia.[27] (Emphasis added)

Once the Constitution was in place, a steady influx of European immigrant s transformed Roman Catholicism from America' s smallest to largest religious denomination. By 1850, the *higher powers at Rome* could view the United States as a viable *tributary*, if not another *papal state*.[28] (Emphasis added)

---

[27] Estimation in 1784 of then Father Superior of the American Mission, John Carroll, a Jesuit priest and brother of Daniel Carroll, upon whose land, "Rome," the U.S. Capitol building was erected.

[28] Saussy, *Rulers of Evil*, 85-86.

The Catholic Church considers the Protestant church to be heretics. What is a heretic?

Noah Webster's 1828 definition

HER'ETIC, *noun*

1. A person under any religion, but particularly the Christian, who holds and teaches opinions repugnant to the established faith, or that which is made the standard of orthodoxy. In strictness, among Christians, a person who holds and avows religious opinions contrary to the doctrines of Scripture, the only rule of faith and practice.
2. Anyone who maintains erroneous opinions.[29]

Merriam-Webster

1. religion: a person who differs in opinion from established religious dogma (see DOGMA SENSE 2) *especially*: a baptized member of the Roman Catholic Church who refuses to acknowledge or accept a revealed truth. The church regards them as heretics.
2. one who differs in opinion from an accepted belief or doctrine: NONCONFORMIST.[30]

Noah Webster

[29] Webster, *Heretic,* http://webstersdictionary1828.com/Dictionary/Heretic.

[30] Merriam-Webster, Online Dictionary, *Heretic,* https://www.merriam-webster.com/dictionary/heretic.

> DOGMA, *noun* [Gr., to think; Latin] A settled opinion; a principle, maxim or tenet; a doctrinal notion, particularly in matters of faith and philosophy; as the dogmas of the church; the dogmas of Plato.
> Compliment my dogma and I will compliment yours.[31]

Merriam-Webster

> Definition of *dogma*
> 1a: something held as an established opinion
> *especially*: a definite authoritative tenet
> b: a code of such tenets, pedagogical dogma
> c: a point of view or tenet put forth as authoritative without adequate grounds,
> 2: a doctrine or body of doctrines concerning faith or morals formally stated and authoritatively proclaimed by a church[32]

> … In the mouth of two or three witnesses shall every word be established.[33]

Based on historical records and a myriad of testimonies, the Church of Rome was behind many of history's most heinous crimes to be committed against humanity. Anyone who opposed Rome's dogma was subject to this *intolerance,* this hatred. One person's opinion is insufficient to bring accusations to the masses, but a history of witnesses and historical accounts that span centuries is proof for such a claim.

---

[31] Webster, Dogma, http://webstersdictionary1828.com/Dictionary/Dogma.

[32] Merriam-Webster, Online Dictionary, *Dogma,* https://www.merriam-webster.com/dictionary/dogma.

[33] 2 Corinthians 13:1, KJV.

In the following pages, I will bring voices from the past within the range of those living in the present. These individuals from different walks of life and different periods of time give their warning, their testimony of how Catholicism has done great harm to the body of Christ. The next two chapters detail these accusations. You, the reader, will be the juror to determine whether a solid case exists for false doctrine and deception. These records offer a firm criticism against the Church of Rome. Is a Christian only to be defensive in this battle between good and evil? When dealing with workers of evil, we are to expose them.

> And have no fellowship with the unfruitful works of darkness, but rather reprove them.[34]

In what manner are we directed to bring the reproach against a brother or sister in Christ?

> Moreover if thy brother shall trespass against thee, go and tell him his fault between thee and him alone: if he shall hear thee, thou hast gained thy brother. But if he will not hear thee, then take with thee one or two more, that in the mouth of two or three witnesses every word may be established. And if he shall neglect to hear them, tell it unto the church: but if he neglect to hear the church, let him be unto thee as an heathen man and a publican.[35]

Paraphrasing the biblical text, if a brother or sister in Christ begins to backslide, develop a sinful lifestyle, that person's fellow Christian brothers or sisters are to, in a loving way, bring it to their attention privately and then, if needed, to the church

[34] Ephesians 5:11, KJV.

[35] Matthew 18:15-17, KJV.

elders. The desired end is to restore that individual's walk with God. Consider the following verse from Galatians:

> Brethren, if a man is overtaken in any trespass, you who are spiritual restore such a one in a spirit of gentleness, considering yourself lest you also be tempted.[36]

The Bible does not direct us to have an *inquisition,* to torture the fallen Christian or unbeliever into accepting church doctrine. Nor are we led to burn a "heretic" alive. Jesus Christ already paid the ultimate price for our salvation at Calvary, where He made the *way* of reconciliation with God. We must make every attempt to rescue that wayward person.

The Church of Rome had accused millions of believing brothers and sisters in Christ of heresy. Heresy as defined by Catholic dogma, not God's Word. Even if a brother or sister in Christ was in error according to Scripture, there is no command in the New Testament to imprison these fallen ones and torture them to death. Great is God's mercy and grace.

> The Lord is not slack concerning his promise, as some men count slackness; but is longsuffering to usward, not willing that any should perish, but that all should come to repentance.[37]

> For I have no pleasure in the death of him that dieth, saith the Lord GOD: wherefore turn yourselves, and live ye.[38]

---

[36] Galatians 6:1, KJV.

[37] 2 Peter 3:9, KJV.

[38] Ezekiel 18:32, KJV.

Launching a deceptive plan could require years of preparation. The *Superior General* is the leader of the Jesuits and is known as the black pope. The Jesuits are skilled, patient, and relentless for a one-world government.

Americans were not the only ones to sound the alarm about the Jesuits. The website Worlds Last Chance produced an article titled "Catholic Confidential; Deplorable Jesuit Secrets Revealed!"[39] At this time, the video with the same name is currently available on YouTube and includes several quotes from prominent historical figures. Some of which I will share with you. These are the watchmen from time past, sounding the alarm to make us aware of the dangers. These warnings, these historical records, are accessible in the public domain for anyone willing to search.

Before reviewing the history of the Jesuits, it would be helpful to have insight into the mindset, the indoctrination, of a Jesuit. The following oath explains the workings of the Jesuits from the sixteenth century to the middle of the twentieth century. From "The Jesuit Extreme Oath of Induction as recorded in the Journals of the 62nd U.S. Congress, 3rd Session, House Calendar No. 397, House Bill 1523, Contested election case of Eugene C. Bonniwell, against Thos. S. Butler, Feb. 15, 1913, pp. 3215-3216," we have the following:

The Jesuit's Extreme Oath of Induction

> I ______, now in the presence of Almighty God, the Blessed Virgin Mary, the Blessed Michael the Archangel, the Blessed St. John the Baptist, the Holy Apostles, Peter and Paul, and all the Saints, sacred hosts of Heaven, and to you, my ghostly Father, the Superior General of the Society of Jesus, founded by

[39] https://www.worldslastchance.com/end-time-prophecy/catholic-confidential—deplorable-jesuit-secrets-revealed.html.

St. Ignatius Loyola, in the Pontification of Paul the Third, and continued to the present, do by the womb of the virgin, the matrix of God, and the rod of Jesus Christ, declare and swear that his holiness, the Pope, is Christ's Vice-regent, and is the true and only head of the Catholic or Universal Church throughout the earth; and that by the virtue of the keys of binding and loosing, given to his Holiness by my Savior, Jesus Christ, he hath power to depose heretical kings, princes, states, commonwealths and governments, all being illegal without his sacred confirmation, and that they may be safely destroyed.

I do further declare, that I will help and assist and advise all or any of his Holiness' agents in any place wherever I shall be, and do my utmost to extirpate the heretical Protestant or Liberal doctrines and to destroy all their pretended powers, legal or otherwise.

I do further promise and declare, that notwithstanding I am dispensed with to assume any religion heretical, for the propagating of the Mother Church's interest, to keep secret and private all her agents' counsels, from time to time as they may instruct me, and not to divulge directly or indirectly, by word, writing, or circumstances whatever; but to execute all that shall be proposed given in charge or discovered unto me, by you, my ghostly father. ...

I do further promise and declare, that I will have no opinion or will of my own, or any mental reservation whatever, even as a corpse or cadaver but unhesitatingly obey each and every command that I may receive from my superiors in the Militia of the Pope and Jesus Christ.

That I will go to any part of the world, whatsoever, without murmuring and will be submissive in all things whatsoever communicated to me.... I do further promise and declare, that I will, when opportunity presents, make and wage relentless war, secretly or openly, against all heretics, Protestants and Liberals, as I am directed to do to extirpate and exterminate them from the face of the whole earth, and that I will spare neither sex, age nor condition, and that I will hang, waste, boil, flay, strangle and bury alive these infamous heretics; rip up the stomachs and wombs of their women and crush their infants heads against the wall, in order to annihilate forever their execrable race.

That when the same cannot be done openly, I will secretly use the poison cup, the strangulation cord, the steel of the poniard, or the leaden bullet, regardless of the honor, rank, dignity or authority of the person or persons whatsoever may be their condition in life, either public or private, as I at any time may be directed so to do by any agent of the Pope or superior of the Brotherhood of the Holy Faith of the Society of Jesus.[40]

QUOTATIONS FROM HISTORY:

Ignatius of Loyola (1491–1556), the founder of the Society of Jesus, and First Superior General (black pope)

Nor will it contribute a little to our advantage, if, with caution and secrecy, we foment and heighten the animosities that arise among princes and great men, even to such a degree that they may weaken

[40] The Jesuit Extreme Oath of Induction, https://archive.org/details/JesuitExtremeOathOfInduction_201302

each other. But if there appear any likelihood of reconciliation, then as soon as possible let us endeavor to be the mediators, lest others prevent us."[41]

"Finally,—Let all with such artfulness gain the ascendant over princes, noblemen, and the magistrates of every place, that they may be ready at our beck, even to sacrifice their nearest relations and most intimate friends, when we say it is for our interest and advantage.[42]

Paolo Sarpi (1552–1623), a Venetian patriot, scientist, scholar, and church reformer

They are a public plague, and the plague of the world ... From the Jesuit colleges there never is sent a pupil obedient to his father, devoted to his country, loyal to his prince.[43]

Every species of vice finds its patronage in them. There is no perjury, nor sacrilege, nor parricide, nor incest, nor rapine, nor fraud, nor treason which cannot be masked as meritorious beneath the mantle of their dispensation.[44]

---

[41] W.C. Brownlee, *Secret Instructions of the Jesuits* (New York: American and Foreign Christian Union, 1857), 141.

[42] Mary Frances Cusak, *The black pope: A History of the Jesuits* (London: Marshall, Russell & Co. Ltd., 1896), 86.

[43] Ibid., 356.

[44] John Alfred Kensit, *The Jesuits: Their History and Crimes* (London: Protestant Truth Society, 1918), 30.

Priest Antoine Arnauld (1612–1694)

> Do you wish to excite troubles, to provoke revolution, to produce the total ruin of your country? Call in the Jesuits ... and build magnificent colleges for these hot-headed religionists; suffer those audacious priests, in their dictatorial and dogmatic tone, to decide on affairs of State.[45]

Michelangelo Tamburini (1648–1730), the 14th Superior General of the Society of Jesus

> See, sir, from this chamber I govern not only to Paris, but to China, not only to China, but to all the world, without any one to know how I do it.[46]

John Adams (1735–1826), the Second President of the United States of America

> In 1816, John Adams wrote to Thomas Jefferson (third President of the United States), regarding the restoration of the Society of Jesus: "My history of the Jesuits is not eloquently written, but it is supported by unquestionable authorities, is very particular and very horrible. Their restoration is indeed a step toward darkness, cruelty, perfidy, despotism, death ... I do not like the appearance of the Jesuits. If ever there was a body of men who merited eternal

---

[45] Hector Macpherson, *The Jesuits in History* (Springfield, Missouri: Ozark Book Publishers, 1997; originally published in Edinburgh, 1914), 32.

[46] Jacopo Leone, *The Jesuit Conspiracy: The Secret Plan of the Order* (London: Chapman and Hall, 1848), 134.

damnation on earth and in hell, it is this Society of Loyola's."[47]

Shall we not have regular swarms of them here, in as many disguises as only a king of the gypsies can assume, dressed as painters, publishers, writers and schoolmasters? If ever there was a body of men who merited eternal damnation on earth and in hell it is this Society of Loyola's ... we are compelled by our system ... to offer them asylum.[48]

Adam Weishaupt (1748–1830), a Jesuit, German philosopher and believed to be the founder of the Order of Illuminati

The degree of power to which the representatives of the Society of Jesus had been able to attain in Bavaria was all but absolute. Members of the order were the confessors and preceptors of the electors; hence they had a direct influence upon the policies of government. The censorship of religion had fallen into their eager hands, to the extent that some of the parishes even were compelled to recognize their authority and power. *To exterminate all Protestant influence* and to render the Catholic establishment complete, *they had taken possession of the instruments of public education*. It was by Jesuits that the majority of the Bavarian colleges were founded, and by them they were

[47] J.E.C. Shepherd, *The Babington Plot* (Toronto, Canada: Wittenburg Publications, 1987), 18.; quoting a letter dated May 5, 1816.

[48] George Riemer, *The New Jesuits* (Boston, Massachusetts: Little, Brown & Co., 1971), xiv.

> controlled. *By them also the secondary schools of the country were conducted.*[49] (Emphasis added)

Marquis de LaFayette (1757–1834), French General and Statesman

> It is my opinion that if the liberties of this country—the United States of America—are destroyed, it will be by the subtlety of the Roman Catholic Jesuit priests, for they are the most crafty, dangerous enemies to civil and religious liberty. They have instigated MOST of the wars of Europe.[50]

Napoleon Bonaparte (1769–1821), crowned emperor of France in 1804

> The Jesuits are a military organization, not a religious order. Their chief is a general of an army, not the mere father abbot of a monastery. And the aim of this organization is: POWER. Power in its most despotic exercise. Absolute power, universal power, power to control the world by the volition of a single man. Jesuitism is the most absolute of despotisms: and at the same time the greatest and most enormous of abuses … The general of the Jesuits insists on being master, sovereign, over the sovereign. Wherever the Jesuits are admitted they will be masters, cost what it may. Their society is by nature dictatorial, and therefore it is the irreconcilable enemy of all

---

[49] https://redice.tv/news/jesuit-pope-agenda-meet-the-templars-knights-of-malta-and-blackwater-xe-exterminators.

[50] James L. Chapman, *Americanism versus Romanism: or the cis-Atlantic battle between Sam and the pope* (Nashville, Tennessee: 1856), 127.

constituted authority. Every act, every crime, however atrocious, is a meritorious work, if committed for the interest of the Society of the Jesuits, or by the order of the general.[51]

Friedrich von Hardenberg (1772–1801), a German philosopher

Never before in the course of the world's history had such a Society [i.e., the Jesuit Order] appeared. The old Roman Senate itself did not lay schemes for world domination with greater certainty of success.[52]

Samuel Morse ((1791–1872), American inventor of the telegraph, the creator of Morse Code

They are Jesuits. This society of men, after exerting their tyranny for upwards of two hundred years, at length became so formidable to the world, threatening the entire subversion of all social order, that even the pope, whose devoted subjects they are, and must be, by the vow of their society, was compelled to dissolve them. They had not been suppressed, however, for fifty years, before the waning influence of Popery and Despotism required their useful labors, to resist the light of Democratic liberty, and the pope (Pius VII), simultaneously with the formation of the Holy Alliance, revived the order of the Jesuits in all their 'ower. From their vow of 'unqualified submission to

[51] Charles Chiniquy, *Fifty Years in the Church of Rome* (Grand Rapids, Michigan: Baker Book House, 1968; originally published in 1885) 487, 488; quoting Memorial of the Captivity of Napoleon at St. Helena, by General Montholon, Vol. II, 62, 174.

[52] Theodor Griesinger, *The Jesuits: Their Complete History* (London: W. H. Allen & Co., 1903; originally published in 1873), 654.

the Sovereign Pontiff," they have been appropriately called the pope's Body Guard. *"And do Americans need to be told what Jesuits are? ... they are a secret society, a sort of Masonic order, with superadded features of revolting odiousness, and a thousand times more dangerous.* They are not merely priests, or of one religious creed; they are merchants, and lawyers, and editors, and men of any profession, having no outward badge, (in this country) by which to be recognized; they are about in all your society. "They can assume any character, that of angels of light, or ministers of darkness to accomplish their one great end, the service upon which they are sent, whatever that service may be. They are all educated men, prepared and sworn to start at any moment, and in any direction, and for any service, commanded by the general of their order, bound to no family, community, or country, by the ordinary ties which bind men; and sold for life to the cause of the Roman Pontiff."[53] "And who are these agents? They are for the most part, Jesuits, an ecclesiastical order proverbial through the world for cunning, duplicity, and total want of moral principle; an order so skilled in all the arts of deception that even in Catholic countries, in Italy itself, it became intolerable, and the people required its suppression.[54] (Emphasis added)

[53] J. Wayne Laurens, *The Crisis: Or, the Enemies of America Unmasked* (Philadelphia, Pennsylvania: G. D. Miller, 1855), 265-267.

[54] Samuel Morse, *Foreign Conspiracy Against the Liberties of the United States* (Boston, Massachusetts: Crocker & Brewster, 1835), Vol. I, 55.

Orestes Augustus Brownson (1803–1876), a New England activist, intellectual and labor organizer, preacher and noted Catholic convert and writer

> Undoubtedly it is the intention of the pope to possess this country [America]. In this intention he is aided by the Jesuits, and all the Catholic prelates and priests. If the Catholic church becomes predominant here, Protestants will all be exterminated.[55]

Abraham Lincoln (1809–1865), the 16th President of the United States

> This war [American Civil War, 1860–1865] would never have been possible without the sinister influence of the Jesuits. We owe it to Popery that we now see our land reddened with the blood of her noblest sons. Though there were great differences of opinion between the South and North, on the question of slavery, neither Jeff Davis nor any one of the leading men of the Confederacy would have dared to attack the North, had they not relied on the promise of the Jesuits, that, under the mask of Democracy, the money and the arms of the Roman Catholics, even the arms of France, were at their disposal if they would attack us.[56]

> The Protestants of both the North and South would surely unite to exterminate the priests and the Jesuits, if they could learn how the priests, the nuns, and

---

[55] Charles Chiniquy, *Fifty Years in the Church of Rome* (Chicago: Adam Craig, 1891), 678, See also, *The Papal Conspiracy Exposed*, by Edward Beecher (Boston: Stearns and Company, 1855), 26.

[56] Chiniquy, *Fifty Years in the Church of Rome*, 699.

the monks, which daily land on our shores, under the pretext of preaching their religion ... are nothing else but the emissaries of the pope, of Napoleon III, and the other despots of Europe, to undermine our institutions, alienate the hearts of our people from our constitution, and our laws, destroy our schools, and prepare a reign of anarchy here as they have done in Ireland, in Mexico, in Spain, and wherever there are any people who want to be free.[57]

'I am so glad to meet you again,' he said: 'you see that your friends, the Jesuits have not yet killed me. But they would have surely done it when I passed through their most devoted city, Baltimore, had I not defeated their plans, by passing incognito a few hours before they expected me ...' 'New projects of assassination are detected almost every day, accompanied with such savage circumstances, that they bring to my memory the massacre of St. Bartholomew and the Gunpowder Plot. We feel, at their investigation, that they come from the same masters in the art of murder, the Jesuits ...' 'So many plots have already been made against my life, that it is a real miracle that they have all failed, when we consider that the great majority of them were in the hands of skillful Roman Catholic murderers, evidently trained by the Jesuits.'[58]

---

[57] Ibid.

[58] Chiniquy, *Fifty Years in the Church of Rome*, 691-692, 703, and 709.

> I know that Jesuits never forget nor forsake. But man must not care how and where he dies, provided he dies at the post of honour and duty.[59]

Charles Chiniquy (1809–1899), a Canadian ex-Catholic priest

> From that time, the Catholic priests, with the most admirable ability and success, have gathered their Irish legions into the great cities of the United States, and the American people must be very blind indeed, if they do not see that if they do nothing to prevent it, the day is very near when the Jesuits will rule their country, from the magnificent White House at Washington, to the humblest civil and military department of this vast Republic.[60]

Luigi Desanctis (1808–1869), a parish priest in Rome who left the Roman Catholic Church because he had contentions with the moral and doctrinal corruption of the Roman Church, became a Protestant pastor.

> All these things cause the Father-General [of the Jesuits] to be feared by the pope and sovereigns ... A sovereign who is not their [the Jesuits] friend will sooner or later experience their vengeance.[61]

> At what then do the Jesuits aim? According to them, they only seek the greater glory of God; but if you examine the facts you will find that they aim at

---

[59] Ibid., 664.

[60] Chiniquy, *Fifty Years in the Church of Rome*, 670.

[61] Luigi Desanctis, *Popery, Puseyism and Jesuitism* (London: D. Catt, 1905; Maria Betts, translated from the original, *Roma Papale*, 1865), 136.

> universal dominion alone. They have rendered themselves indispensable to the pope, who, without them, could not exist, because Catholicism is identified with them. They have rendered themselves indispensable to governors and hold revolutions in their hands; and in this way, either under one name or another, it is they who rule the world."[62]
>
> He who thinks he knows the Jesuits by having read all the books that were written in the past century [the Eighteenth Century] to unmask them, would be grossly deceived. The Jesuitism of that day was an open war against the gospel and society; the Jesuitism of the present is a slow but contagious and deadly disease, which secretly insinuates itself; it is a poison taken under the name of medicine.[63]

Richard W. Thompson (1809–1900), Secretary of the Navy, United States of America

> [The Jesuits] are the deadly enemies of civil and religious liberty. "[The Jesuit General] occupies the place of God, and must be obeyed, howsoever the peace and welfare of the multitude may be imperiled, or the nations be convulsed from center to circumference. The society of Jesuits must obtain the mastery, even if general anarchy shall prevail, or all the world besides be covered with the fragments of a universal wreck!"[64]

---

[62] Ibid., 139.

[63] Ibid., 138.

[64] R. W. Thompson, *The Footprints of the Jesuits* (New York: Hunt & Eaton, 1894) 59.

> The sovereigns of the 'Holy Alliance' had massed large armies, and soon entered into a pledge to devote them to the suppression of all uprisings of the people in favor of free government; and he [Pius VII] desired to devote the Jesuits, supported by his pontifical power, to the accomplishment of that end. He knew how faithfully they would apply themselves to that work, and hence he counseled them, in his decree of restoration, to strictly observe the 'useful advices and salutary counsels' whereby Loyola had made absolution the cornerstone of the society.[65]

Brigadier General Thomas M. Harris (1817–1906), Union General during the Civil War and a physician

> The organization of the Roman Catholic hierarchy is a complete military despotism, of which the pope is the ostensible head ... The black pope is the head of the order of the Jesuits, and is called a General. He not only has command of his own order, but directs and controls the general policy of the Roman Catholic church. He is the power behind the throne, and is the real potential head of the hierarchy ... There is no independence of thought, or of action, in its subordinate parts. Implicit and unquestioning obedience to the orders of superiors in authority, is the sworn duty of the priesthood of every grade .... "It would seem that the Jesuits had had it in mind, from the beginning of the war [the American Civil War of 1861-1865], to find an occasion for the taking off [i.e., the

[65] Ibid., 251.

> assassination] of Mr. [Abraham] Lincoln. The favorite policy of the Jesuits [is] that of assassination.[66]

Francis Parkman (1823–1893), American Historian best known for "The Oregon Trail"

> The Jesuits, then as now, were the most forcible exponents of ultramontane principles. The church to rule the world; the pope to rule the church; the Jesuits to rule the pope: such was and is the simple programme of the Order of Jesus, and to it they have held fast, except on a few rare occasions of misunderstanding with the Viceregent of Christ.[67]

Ellen G. White (1827-1915), an American Christian pioneer who formed the Seventh-day Adventist church

> ... Jesuitism inspired its followers with fanaticism ... There was no crime too great for them to commit, no deception too base for them to practice, no disguise too difficult for them to assume ... It was a fundamental principle of the order that the end justifies the means. By this code, lying, theft, perjury, assassination, were not only pardonable but commendable, when they served the interests of the church. Under various disguises the Jesuits worked their way into

---

[66] General Thomas M. Harris, "*Rome's Responsibility for the Assassination of Abraham Lincoln,*" 1897. See http://www.antichristconspiracy.com/HTML%20Pages/Rome's%20Responsibility%20for%20the%20Assassina tion%20of%20Lincoln.htm.

[67] Frances Parkman, *France and England in North America* (New York: The Viking Press, 1983; originally published in 1865), Vol. I, p. 1172. 1173.

offices of state, climbing up to be the counselors of kings, and shaping the policy of nations.[68]

Margaret F. Cusack (1829–1899), converted nun of Kenmare

The great idea of the Jesuit has always been a universal spiritual [and Temporal] monarchy, in which … the Jesuit should reign supreme. England has always been the place desired for the base of operations necessary for this end. Hence the blood, the tears shed, and the schemes undertaken in this country by the Jesuit. He has by no means ended his efforts for the subjugation of the world to Rome through England."[69] "When the Jesuit is expelled from one place he is not slow to find another. France may reject him, not without cause, but England opens her arms to him. Catholic Italy may deprive him of the glories of his once famous home in the Gesu, but America opens her doors to him. He is the wandering Jew of the Romish church; he is followed by the execrations of those by whom he was once beloved, until they discovered his iniquities.[70]

Charles Haddon Spurgeon (1834–1892), a famous British Baptist preacher and was known as the "Prince of Preachers"

Our ancient enemies have small belief in our common sense if they imagine that we shall ever be able to trust them, after having so often beheld the depths

[68] Ellen G. White, *The Great Controversy* (Deland, Florida: Laymen for Religious Liberty, 1990; originally published in 1888), 234, 235.

[69] Cusak, *The black pope*, 285.

[70] Ibid., 286-287.

> of Jesuitical cunning and duplicity. The sooner we let certain Archbishops and Cardinals know that we are aware of their designs, and will in nothing cooperate with them the better for us and our country. Of course, we shall be howled at as bigots, but we can afford to smile at that cry, when it comes from the church which invented the Inquisition, 'No peace with Rome' is the motto of reason as well as of religion.[71]

G. B. Nicolini, Italian ex-Catholic who authored History of the Jesuits *in 1854*

> ... take the Jesuit for what he ought or appears to be, and you commit the greatest of blunders. Draw the character after what the Jesuit seems to be in London, you will not recognize your portrait in the Jesuit of Rome. The Jesuit is the man of circumstances. Despotic in Spain, constitutional in England, republican in Paraguay, bigot in Rome, idolater in India, he shall assume and act out in his own person, with admirable flexibility, all those different features by which men are usually to be distinguished from each other. He will accompany the gay women of the world to the theatre, and will share in the excesses of the debauchee. With solemn countenance, he will take his place by the side of the religious man at church, and he will revel in the tavern with the glutton and the sot. He dresses in all the garbs, speaks all languages, knows all customs, is present everywhere though nowhere recognized –and all this, it should seem (O

---

[71]Charles Haddon Spurgeon, *Geese in Their Hoods: Selected Writings on Roman Catholicism* (Publisher unknown, 1873).

monstrous blasphemy!), for the greater glory of God – ad majorem Dei gloriam.[72]

The members of the Society are divided into four classes—the Professed, Coadjutors, Scholars, and Novices. There is also a secret fifth class, known only to the General and a few faithful Jesuits, which, perhaps more than any other, contributes to the dreaded and mysterious power of the order. It is composed of laymen of all ranks, from the minister to the humble shoe-boy … These are affiliated to the Society, but not bound by any vows … they are persons who will make themselves useful … they act as the spies of the order … and serve, often unwittingly, as the tools and accomplices in dark and mysterious crimes. [The Jesuit] Father Francis Pellico … candidly confesses that "the many illustrious friends of the Society remain occult, and obliged to be silent."[73]

There is no record in history of an association whose organization has stood for three hundred years unchanged and unaltered by all the assaults of men and time, and which has exercised such an immense influence over the destinies of mankind … 'The ends justify the means,' is his favorite maxim; and as his only end, as we have shewn, is the order, at its bidding the Jesuit is ready to commit any crime whatsoever.[74]

---

[72] G.B. Nicolini of Rome, *History of the Jesuits: Their Origin, Progress, Doctrines and Designs* (London: Henry G. Bohn, 1854), 42.

[73] Nicolini, op. cit., 45-46.

[74] Ibid., 495-496.

> The immense wealth of the Jesuits has been bequeathed to them by wills made at the last hour![75]

Adolf Hitler (1889–1945), German politician and the leader of the Nazi Party

> I have learnt most of all from the Jesuit Order ... So far, there has been nothing more imposing on earth than the hierarchical organization of the Catholic Church. A good part of that organization I have transported direct to my own party ... The Catholic Church must be held up as an example ... I will tell you a secret. I am founding an Order ... In Himmler I see our Ignatius de Loyola![76]

Walther Friedrich Schellenberg (1910–1952, German SS-Brigadeführer and leader in foreign intelligence

> The SS had been organized by Himmler according to the principles of the Jesuit Order. The rules of service and spiritual exercises prescribed by Ignatius de Loyola constituted a model which Himmler strove carefully to copy. Absolute obedience was the supreme rule; every order had to be executed without comment.[77]

---

[75] Ibid., 42.

[76] Edmond Paris, A. Robson, tr., *The Vatican Against Europe* (London: P. R. MacMillan, Ltd., 1961), 252, 256.

[77] Ibid., 253.

Avro Manhattan (1914–1990), a man of many talents. He was a writer, philosopher and was considered a polymath. May best be known for his criticisms of the Roman Catholic Church.

> The Jesuits are one of the largest stockholders in the American steel company, Republic and National. They are also among the most important owners of the four greatest aircraft manufacturing companies in the U.S., Boeing, Lockheed, Douglas and Curtis-Wright.[78]

> No political event or circumstance can be evaluated without the knowledge of the Vatican's part in it. And no significant world situation exists in which the Vatican does not play an important explicit or implicit role.[79]

Alberto Rivera (1935–1997), an Ex-Jesuit, anti-Catholic activists

> The higher I went in the Jesuit Order, the more corruption I saw within the institution. I was invited to attend a secret black mass by high-ranking Jesuits [including Superior General Pedro Arrupe] in a monastery in the northern part of Spain. When I knelt to kiss the ring of a high official, I saw a symbol on that ring that made my blood run cold. It was a Masonic symbol [the compass and the square]! A thing I hated and I had been told to fight against it …

---

78 Avro Manhattan, *The Vatican Billions* (Chino, California: Chick Publications, 1983), 184.

79 Edmond Paris, *The Vatican Against Europe* (Springfield, Missouri: Ozark Book Publishers, 1993), 308.

> I found out the Jesuit General was also a Mason and a member of the Communist Party in Spain.[80]

Edmond Paris (1894–1970), author of The Secret History of the Jesuits

> The public is practically unaware of the overwhelming responsibility carried by the Vatican and its Jesuits in the starting of the two world wars – a situation which may be explained in part by the gigantic finances at the disposition of the Vatican and its Jesuits, giving them power in so many spheres, especially since the last conflict."[81] "The Jesuits ... are a secret society – a sort of Masonic order – with superadded features of revolting odiousness, and a thousand times more dangerous."[82] "The Fuhrer had come to power, thanks to the votes of the Catholic Zentrum [Center Party overseen by Jesuit Ludwig Kaas], only five years before [1933], but most of the objectives cynically revealed in Mein Kampf were already realized; this book ... was written by the Jesuit [controlled] Father [Bernhardt] Stempfle and signed by Hitler. For ... it was the Society of Jesus which perfected the famous Pan-German programme as laid out in this book, and the Fuhrer endorsed it.[83]

---

[80] Jack Chick, *Alberto* (Chino, California: Chick Publications, 1979), Part 1, 27-28.

[81] As quoted on http://www.chick.com/catalog/books/0191.asp.

[82] As quotes on http://bibletruth.org/free.com/articles/QuotesOnJesus.pdf.

[83] Edmond Paris, *The Secret History of the Jesuits* (Chino, California: Chick Publications, 1975; originally published in 1965), 138.

Michael Bunker, American writer known for "Surviving Off-Grid."

> There is a conspiracy against Christendom.... But who are Satan's agents in this conspiracy? The "agents" are the Jesuits. Even though the Jesuits exude vast influence and control in the areas of theology, education, recorded history and current media, I am still perplexed that virtually no literature exists exposing the Jesuit's influence on mainline Protestantism.... In this work, the author uncovers forgotten history regarding the cooperative salvation theology of the Jesuits. . . From Cain to Charles [G.] Finney, this book proves that modern Protestantism has abandoned the Doctrines of Grace and embraced the [Satanic] doctrines of cooperative salvation.[84]

In the next chapter, we will review a historical timeline that acknowledges the concerns of the above witnesses as legitimate. These are documented accounts of the manipulation and interference by the Church of Rome into the politics, national laws, and education of foreign nations that resulted in the death of millions of innocent men, women, and children through the centuries.

[84] Michael Bunker, *Swarms of Locusts: The Jesuit Attack on the Faith* (New York: Writers Club Press, 2002), 13-14.

5

Blood-Stained Hands Part 1

In chapter four, I introduced you to the warnings and testimonies from prominent figures in history. These historical figures made their indictments against the Church of Rome's hierarchy (the papacy, the *white pope*) and the Society of Jesus, the papacy's private militia. The *Superior General* (the *black pope*) is the head of the Jesuit Order. The warnings are specific—do not allow Catholicism into your country. Catholicism is pseudo-Christianity.

The Vatican, the papacy, is a theocracy that has established political beachheads in foreign countries behind the guise of religion. The Society of Jesus, the Order of the Jesuits, is the papacy's infiltrators aimed at gaining positions of influence and power within the targeted nation. From that point, the papacy can pursue its agenda by influencing the governing authorities of an infiltrated country.

The watchmen have sounded the alarm to warn us of this hidden order, which has continuously manipulated the rulers of Europe and other nations through the centuries. This resulted in bloodshed from the Inquisitions, later masked in wars, toppled regimes, assassinations, revolutions, and the indoctrination of innocent children's minds. Author Edmond Paris shared the following from his book *The Secret History of the Jesuits*.

> And something even better: the Jesuit must see in his superior not a fallible man, but Christ Himself. J. Huber, Professor of Catholic theology in Munich and author of one of the most important works on the Jesuits, wrote: "Here is a proven fact: the 'Constitutions' repeat five hundred times that one must see Christ in the person of the General."[1]
>
> It is the same today: the 33,000 official members of the Society operate *all over the world in the capacity of her personnel,* officers of a truly secret army containing in its ranks heads of political parties, high ranking officials, generals, magistrates, physicians, faculty professors, etc., all of them striving to bring about, in their own sphere, "I 'Opus Dei," God's work, in reality the plans of the papacy.[2] (Emphasis added)

The watchmen have made their indictment, but is there a written record of these atrocities, or are these claims just biased opinions or unjustified intolerance? The focus of this book is to identify, when possible, the origin of doctrines; one method of identification is to shine the spotlight on false beliefs that are spread by counterfeit Christianity. Not only does the Bible warn the Christian not to fall prey to the Great Deception of end times, but the Bible is also the tool by which we are to filter questionable doctrines.

---

[1] J. Huber, "Les Jesuites": 71, 73. in *The Secret History of the Jesuits,* ed. Edmond Paris (Ontario, California: Chick Publications, 1983), 37.

[2] Paris, *The Secret History of the Jesuits,* 41.

> All Scripture is given by inspiration of God, and is profitable for doctrine, for reproof, for correction, for instruction in righteousness:[3]

These next two chapters are constructed to show a continuous timeline of atrocities directly connected to the Roman Catholic Church or indirectly through Rome's proxy secular arms. The goal is to draw congruent accounts recorded in history together to show a consistent timeline of the Catholic Church's interference in the politics of foreign nations, which ended in the death of millions of innocent people over the centuries. Most of the referenced text will provide details, including names of key figures, dates, locations, and titles of the Catholic Church representatives and their accomplices, which aided in the completion of these crimes. Through the study of historical events, we can determine what type of "spiritual root" is feeding the Church of Rome's hierarchy. The spirit of this world is in opposition to God and His Holy Spirit.

While all of humanity is in a fallen state and has the propensity to sin and even commit vicious crimes, the common man or woman is not claiming to be the "Infallible Vicar of Christ." The *fruit* identifies the *root*. With the source identified—and the associated acts (fruits), whether they be righteous or evil—those actions can then be compared to the "spiritual fruits" described in the Bible. This comparison will answer the question of which spirit is guiding the Church of Rome's hierarchy—is it the Spirit of God, or is it the spirit of the antichrist, which is behind the world's system. Is the Church of Rome's objective about saving souls or about controlling them? Is it about maintaining *power?* Is the *Dynasty of the Popes* about being vicars for Christ or about being Roman emperors?

---

[3] 2 Timothy 3:16, KJV.

Dr. Alberto Rivera, ex-Jesuit, provides the introduction to Edmond Paris's book, *The Secret History of the Jesuits,* and Dr. Rivera states the following:

> The Bible puts the power of a local church into the hands of a Godly pastor. But the cunning Jesuits successfully managed over the years to remove that power into the hands of denomination headquarters, and have now pushed almost all of the Protestant denominations into the arms of the Vatican. This is exactly what Ignatius de Loyola set out to accomplish: a universal church and the end of Protestantism.[4]

The subject of the universal church is covered more in-depth in the *Ecumenical Trap* chapters.

Was the *Dynasty of the Popes* throughout the historical timeline of atrocities fully aware of what was taking place within their sphere of influence? As the proposed highest infallible church representative on earth with vast resources, did they make any attempt to stop the bloodshed? Did the Vatican condone this loss of life or instigate it? The Church of Rome has the world's oldest and best intelligence network. Is the Vatican ignorant of the carnage that was or is taking place within its sphere of influence and power to change? Dr. Alberto Rivera continues with the following statement:

> Having at his disposition at all times, and from every quarter, the regular reports from the bishops ... could he ignore what the German military heads could never pretend to: the tragedy of the concentration camps—the civilians condemned to deportation—the cold-blooded massacres of those who

[4] Dr. Alberto Rivera, "Introduction" in *The Secret History of the Jesuits,* ed. Edmond Paris (Ontario, California: Chick Publications, 1983), 8.

> 'stood in the way'—the terror of the gas chambers where, for administrative reasons, millions of Jews were exterminated? And if he knew about it why didn't he, as trustee and first chorister of the Gospel, come out dressed in white, arms extended in the shape of the cross, to denounce a crime without precedent, to shout" No!?...[5]

The Roman Catholic Church dealt cruelly with those who would not submit to its dogma. Authors Dave Hunt, Peter De Rosa, and historian Will Durant concur:

> Every citizen in the empire was required to be a Roman Catholic. Failure to give wholehearted allegiance to the pope was considered treason against the state punishable by death. Here was the basis for slaughtering millions. As Islam would be a few centuries later, a paganized Christianity was imposed upon the entire populace of Europe under the threat of torture and death.[6]

> Thus Roman Catholicism became "the most persecuting faith the world has ever seen ... [commanding] the throne to Innocent III murdered far more Christians in one afternoon ... than any Roman emperor did in his entire reign."[7]

> Compared with the persecution of heresy in Europe from 1227 to 1492, the persecution of Christians by Romans in the first three centuries after Christ was a mild and humane procedure.

---

[5] Ibid.

[6] Hunt, *A Woman Rides the Beast*, 243.

[7] De Rosa, *Vicars of Christ*, jacket.

> Making every allowance required by an historian and permitted to a Christian, we must rank the Inquisition, along with the wars and persecutions of our time, as among the darkest blots on the record of mankind, revealing a ferocity unknown in any beast.[8]

ROME DEMANDS ABSOLUTE AUTHORITY

The goal of the Jesuit Order is for the masses to submit in absolutism to the prerogatives of the pope. The Jesuit's desire is *ultramontanism*. Catholicism keeps its church laity from knowing a complete sense of biblical salvation, redemption from their sins, from their fallen state. The pope and his clergy to whom he delegates are the dispensers of grace, the mediators a Catholic must go to for confession and forgiveness of sins.

For the Catholic, there appears to be a catch in the form of superstitious belief. The Catholic Priest forgives the Catholic layperson of their sin, but there is still an unjustified penalty assigned to that sin. Catholic dogma dictates the forgiven sinner also must receive punishment for the forgiven sins. This punishment requires an act of penitence by the layperson, and the Roman Catholic Church doctrine decides what form of remorse fits as punishment for a particular iniquity. If a Catholic should die before completing their earthly penitence, they are considered in-debt, and a balance is due.

Purgatory is an unscriptural holding area between heaven and earth. The Catholic enters purgatory to complete any unfinished temporal punishment and cleansing of remaining sins before entering heaven. However, the pope and his clergy not only are the dispensers of grace (error 1), but they also can grant or

---

[8] Will Durant, *The Story of Civilization* (New York: Simon and Shuster, 1950), vol. IV, 784.

sell indulgences to the Catholic member (error 2). These indulgences are pretty much a *"get of jail free card"* for those who are behind in their penitence.

Rome uses the granting of indulgences as fiat money for bribery. Salvation is complete through Jesus Christ's sacrificial death on the cross; this is where He paid with His blood the wages of our sins. If humanity could atone for their sins, then Jesus being the sacrificial Lamb of God was for nothing. God's plan of redemption is complete. For example, while humanity views sins with different levels of tolerance and punishment, God does not. He is not biased in His judgments.

> For there is no respect of persons with God.[9]

> For the wages of sin is death (eternal separation from God); but the gift (salvation) of God is eternal life through Jesus Christ our Lord.[10]

There is a price for sin, and the price for the remission and cleansing of sin is the shedding of blood. While some readers may not understand or agree with this type of judgment, my purpose is to inform. It was recognized by Old Testament Law:

> And almost all things are by the law purged with blood; and without shedding of blood is no remission.[11]

The Old Testament Law required almost a continuous act of shedding of blood, animal sacrifices for the wiping away of sins. The New Testament reveals God's New Covenant. Jesus Christ

---

[9] Romans 2:11, KJV.

[10] Romans 6:23, KJV.

[11] Hebrews 9:22, KJV.

offered Himself as the perfect and holy sacrifice for humanity's sins. Jesus shed His blood for all. Note Jesus' words in Matthew:

> For this is my blood of the new testament, which is shed for many for the remission of sins.[12]

Why do I bring this up in with such focus? To expose the error of confession to a human (priest) for the forgiveness of sins.

> For there is one God, and one mediator between God and men, the man Christ Jesus;[13]

From Edmond Paris and Will Durant, we have the following:

> The Jesuits wanted to impose this monarchial absolutism on the Roman church and they maintained it in civil society as they had to look upon the sovereigns as temporal representatives of the Holy Father, true head of Christianity; as long as those monarchs were entirely docile to their common lord, the Jesuits were their most faithful supporters. On the other hand, if these princes rebelled, they found in the Jesuits their worst enemies.[14]

> The pope *offered "a plenary indulgence* to the king and nobles of France for aid in suppressing the Catharist heresy. To Philip Augustus, in return for such aid, the pope offered the lands of all who should fail to

[12] Matthew 26:28, KJV.

[13] 1 Timothy 2:5, KJV.

[14] Paris, *The Secret History of the Jesuits*, 35.

> join in a crusade against the Albigensians."[15] (Emphasis added)
>
> Comte Le Maistre, in his letters written in 1815 to justify the Spanish Inquisition, states that it existed "by virtue of the bull of the sovereign pontiff" and that the Grand Inquisitor "is always either an archbishop or bishop."[16]
>
> If the authorities refused to execute the condemned, they would themselves be brought before the Tribunal and consigned to the flames.[17]
>
> Of the eighty popes in a line from the thirteenth century on, not one of them disapproved of the theology and apparatus of the Inquisition. On the contrary, one after another added his own cruel touches to the workings of this deadly machine.[18]

If you have wondered how the Church of Rome accumulated so much wealth and property, rest assured it wasn't from tithes, offerings, and the selling of indulgences alone. The Church of Rome obtained much of its wealth by theft, stealing from the victims of the Inquisitions. The executed victims of the Inquisition had all they owned confiscated by the Church of Rome; the victim's family were left with nothing and became homeless. During the Inquisitions, the dead were dug up to face trial. Upon conviction, which was guaranteed, the Church of

---

[15] Durant, *The Story of Civilization*, 774.

[16] Le Maistre, op. cit., p.39, in R. W. Thompson, *The Papacy and the Civil Power* (New York: Harper and Brothers Publishers, 1876), 83.

[17] Hunt, *A Woman Rides the Beast*, 244-245.

[18] De Rosa, *Vicars of Christ*, 175.

Rome then confiscated the property from the heirs of the deceased. This charade was known as the "corpse trials."

As you can see above, the popes offered lands that were not legally theirs to give, and those lands would be illegally confiscated and used however the papacy saw fit. Author Dave Hunt has this to add about the wealth of Rome being ill-gotten gain:

> Most of Rome's wealth has been acquired through the *sale of salvation*. Untold billions of dollars have been paid to her by those who thought they were purchasing heaven on the installment plan for themselves or loved ones. The practice continues to this day—blatantly where Catholicism is in control, less obviously here in the United States. No greater deception or abomination could be perpetrated.
>
> In addition to such perversions of the gospel which have led hundreds of millions astray, there are the further abominations of corrupt banking practices, laundering of drug money, trading in counterfeit securities, and dealings with the Mafia (fully documented in police and court records), which the Vatican and her representatives around the world have long employed. Nino Lo Bello, former *Business Week* correspondent in Rome and Rome bureau chief for *New York Journal of Commerce*, writes that the Vatican is so closely allied with the Mafia in Italy that[19] many people ... believe that Sicily ... is nothing more than a Vatican holding."[20]

[19] Ibid., 76.

[20] Nino Lo Bello, The Vatican Empire (Trident Press, 1968), 167, in A Woman Rides the Beast, ed. Dave Hunt, 76.

THE PILGRIM CHURCH

This historical timeline is about providing a witness, evidence in written form, to the unchanging personality of the Vatican through its Catholicism, atrocities, and interference in the political affairs of foreign nations. Take notice of the actions and doctrine that motivate the Jesuits, which serve the papacy. Italy is where the Jesuits came into being.

The Protestant Reformation was birthed out of Catholicism in Germany. As time progressed from Emperor Constantine's formation of his state church, which evolved into today's Catholicism, through the Protestant Reformation, there has been neglect to mention the Pilgrim church. The Pilgrim church was not birthed out of Catholicism as Protestantism was but struggled through centuries of persecution to hold onto the teachings of the apostles. This church identified the papacy with the antichrist centuries before Martin Luther.

The people groups that made up this Pilgrim church were spread out over Europe and had many names: Waldenses, Poor Men of Lyons, Bogomils, Albigensians, and Anabaptists. As we will see, they were hunted and persecuted everywhere they went by the Church of Rome. The deeper one looks into the history and pulls out of time the atrocities of the Church of Rome, the more difficult it becomes to consider it a church at all, for it resembles the Old Roman Empire more than it does a church. There were different elements of the Pilgrim church and accusations made about what kind of people they were. In E. H. Broadbent's book, *The Pilgrim Church,* we find this informative description:

> In Languedoc and Provence in the South of France, there was a civilization in advance of that in other countries. The pretensions of the Roman church to rule had been generally opposed and set aside there. The congregations of believers who met apart from

the Catholic church were numerous and increasing. They are often called Albigenses, a name taken from Albi, a district where there were many of them, but this name was never used by them, nor of them until a later period. They had intimate connections with the brethren—whether called Waldenses, Poor Men of Lyons, Bogomils, or otherwise—in the surrounding countries, where churches spread among the various peoples. Pope Innocent III required of the Count of Toulouse, Raymond VI, who ruled in Provence, and of the other rulers and prelates in the South of France, that the heretics should be banished. This would have meant the ruin of the country. Raymond temporised, but was soon involved in a hopeless quarrel with the pope, who in 1209 proclaimed a crusade against him and his people. Indulgences, such as had been given to the Crusaders who went at great risk to themselves to rescue the Holy Places in Palestine from the Mohammedan Saracens, were now offered to all who would take part in the easier work of destroying the most fruitful provinces of France. This, and the prospect of booty and licence of every kind attracted hundreds of thousands of men. Under the presidence of high clerical dignitaries and led by Simon de Montfort, a military leader of great ability and a man of boundless ambition and ruthless cruelty, the most beautiful and cultivated part of Europe at that time was ravaged, became for twenty years the scene of unspeakable wickedness and cruelty and was reduced to desolation.[21]

---

[21] E. H. Broadbent, *The Pilgrim church* (London: Pickering and Inglis LTD., 1931), 88.

Dave Hunt had this to say about Broadbent's excerpt and then follows by pointing to Historian Will Durant:

> These simple believers were burned at the stake or slain with the sword (and most of their records were destroyed) when their towns and villages were razed by papal armies.... Though some of the worst tales are told about the Cathari, one can only agree with their beliefs as described by Durant:[22]

> They denied that the church (Church of Rome) was the church of Christ; St. Peter had never come to Rome, had never founded the papacy; *the popes were successors to the emperors,* not to the apostles. Christ had no place to lay His head, but the pope lived in a palace; Christ was propertyless and penniless, but Christian prelates were rich; surely, said the Cathari, these lordly archbishops and bishops, these worldly priests, these fat monks, were the Pharisees of old returned to life! The Roman church, they were sure, was the Whore of Babylon, the clergy were a Synagogue of Satan, the pope was Antichrist. They denounced the preachers of crusades as murderers. Many of them laughed at indulgences and relics.[23] (Emphasis added)

Throughout the list of recorded events in the following pages, a continuous pattern emerges for all to see. Under the authority of the Vatican, where the popes are the head, orders are given to kill and eliminate all those who oppose Rome's doctrines. History also records the murder of innocent Catholic laity, either as collateral damage or in retaliation by a group or groups

---

[22] Hunt, *A Woman Rides the Beast,* 255.

[23] Durant, *Story of Civilization,* 772.

who oppose Rome. Any killing of innocents is unjustified. This pattern of intolerance by the Church of Rome is still in place today; the Vatican has not changed its dogmas or repented of its crimes. It would mean that the papacy would have to admit that the *Dynasty of the Popes* is not infallible.

> Though no exact figures are available, the slaughter of these Christians by the popes probably ran into the millions during the thousand years before the Reformation.[24]

> (Pope) Innocent was satisfied with nothing less than complete and entire submission to his will. And, true to the teachings of the False Decretals, he *inaugurated measures of force and oppression to compel obedience to the doctrines of the church*. He issued a bull to his legate, Dominic, commanding him to put all the inhabitants of the city of Beziers, in France, to the sword; and, in obedience to it, *sixty thousand Vaudois were buried beneath its ashes*, none being saved but young girls and boys, who were abandoned to the brutality of the soldiers.[25]

Sixty thousand souls in one day wiped out. This is where the Vatican sent seasoned mercenaries who served in the Crusades to liberate Jerusalem from the Muslims to rural southern France, technically a foreign nation in relationship to the Vatican. If any other foreign land committed such a crime, it would be considered an act of war, because it is war. But who dares to oppose Rome? While reading this portion of my research, I recalled my college class on military history. During World War I, the *Battle of the Somme* was recorded as the bloodiest day in British military

---

[24] Hunt, *A Woman Rides the Beast*, 256.

[25] R.W. Thompson, *The Papacy and the Civil Power*, 418.

history. The mixture of French and British troops that were killed or lost was close to 60,000. That was horrific in itself. The victims in Beziers France were not trained soldiers; they were defenseless against trained mercenaries.

Peter De Rosa, author of the book *Vicars of Christ: The Darkside of the Papacy*, writes how Pope Innocent III gloated over the blood of thousands of men, women, and children as the crowning glory of his papacy. And here we have an account where the Catholics of France opposed what the Church of Rome, a foreign political power, was doing in their country. The Catholics in Southern France chose to help and stand by their fellow citizens, which resulted in the forfeiting of their own lives along with the rest.

Peter De Rosa writes:

> The only dissenters were the heretics. The second part of this book will deal with the crowning glory of Innocent's reign, namely, the crushing of the Albigensians in the south of France. Hundreds of thousands of them were put to death, by fire and sword, at his bidding. Being the sole depository of truth, Innocent felt free to eradicate heresy by every means at his disposal. It was he who gave a fresh impetus to the Inquisition and injected a special kind of intolerance into Catholicism that was to last for centuries.[26]

Broadbent writes in reference to Pope Innocent III's crowning achievement:

> When the town of Beziers was summoned to surrender, the Catholic inhabitants joined with the Dissenters in refusing, though warned that if the place were taken no soul should be left alive. The town was

[26] De Rosa, *Vicars of Christ*, 73.

> captured, and of the tens of thousands who had taken refuge there none were spared.[27]

Rome considered the Waldenses an enemy of the church. The bounty hunters who captured and put to death the Waldenses also destroyed any record of their core beliefs. However, it is possible to use the comments from the Waldenses' enemies to gleam what they believed. Author John Paul Perrin writes in his book, *History of the Waldenses; Anterior to the Reformation:*

> King Louis XII having received information from the enemies of the Waldenses, dwelling in Provence, of several heinous crimes which they fathered upon them, sent to the place Monsieur Adam Fumee, Master of Requests, and a certain Sorbonnist Doctor, called Parui, who was his confessor, to inquire into the matter. They visited all their parishes and temples, and neither found there any images, or sign of the ornaments belonging to the mass, or ceremonies of the Romish church. Much less could they discover any of those crimes with which they were charged. But rather, that they kept the Sabbath duly; caused their children to be baptized according to the primitive church; taught them the articles of the Christian faith, and the commandments of God. The king, having heard the report of the said commissioners, said, with an oath, that they were better men than himself or his people.[28]

---

[27] E. H. Broadbent, *The Pilgrim Church,* 102.

[28] J. Paul Perrin, *History of the Waldenses: Anterior to the Reformation* (Philadelphia: Griffith and Simon, 1846), 36.

16TH AND 17TH CENTURY EUROPE

The Waldenses in Italy did not escape persecution. Wherever the Church of Rome desired to establish its hold, the blood of the innocent would flow.

Italy

> Italy had been hardly touched by the Reformation. Nevertheless, the Waldenses, who had survived since the middle ages in spite of persecutions and established themselves in the north and south of the peninsula, joined the Calvinist church in 1532. On a report from the *Jesuit Possevino,* Emmanuel Philibert of Savoy launched another bloody persecution against his "heretic" subjects in 1561. The same thing happened in Calabria, at Casal di San Sisto and Guardia Fiscale.[29] (Emphasis added, Father Possevino is a name you will see again.)
>
> The Jesuits were implicated in these massacres; they were busy converting the victims ... [30]
>
> As for *Father Possevino*: " ... he followed the Catholic army as their chaplain, and recommended the extermination by fire of the heretic pastors as necessary and holy act."[31] (Emphasis added)

---

[29] Paris, *The Secret History of the Jesuits*, 44.

[30] J. Huber, *Les Jesuites*, 165, in *The Secret History of the Jesuits*, ed. Paris, 44.

[31] H. Boehmer, professor at the University of Bonn, "Les Jesuites" (Armand Colin, Paris 1910, pp.89) in *The Secret History of the Jesuits*, ed. Edmond Paris (Ontario, California: Chick Publications, 1983), 44.

Spain and Portugal were strongholds for the Jesuits. Where the Jesuits were inconsistent in their tenure in France, England, and Russia, they were able to maintain agreements with Spain and Portugal. And as history notes, Spain was to follow her *mother church* and have her Inquisition.

Portugal

Portugal was a choice country for the Order.

> Already under John III (1521-1559), it was the most powerful religious community in the kingdom.[32]

Its influence grew even more after the revolution of 1640, which put the Braganza on the throne.

> "Under the first king of the house of Braganza, Father Fernandez was a member of the government and, under the minority of Alphonse VI, the counselor most heeded by the regent Queen Louise. Father de Ville was successful in overthrowing Alphonse VI 1667, and Father Emmanuel Fernandez was made a deputy to the 'Cortes' in 1667 by the new King Peter II ... In fact, we can see the results by the decadent state into which this unfortunate land fell. All the energy and perspicacity of the Marques of Pombal, in the middle of the 18th century, were needed to tear Portugal out of the Order's deadly grip.[33]

---

[32] Ibid., 45.

[33] Paris, *The Secret History of the Jesuits*, 45.

Spain

> During the 17th century, they (the Jesuits) are all powerful in Spain, among the high classes and at Court. Even Father Neidhart, former German cavalry officer, fully governed the kingdom as Counselor of State, prime minister and Grand Inquisitor ... In Spain as in Portugal, the kingdom's ruin coincided with the rise of the Order ... [34]

Spain spills her share of innocent blood. In the book of Revelation, we find attributes of wickedness that characterize the *woman who rides the beast*—she is drunk with the blood of the saints. The verse reads as follows:

> And I saw the woman drunken with the blood of the saints, and with the blood of the martyrs of Jesus: and when I saw her, I wondered with great admiration.[35]

Bible students familiar with church history could relate the above verse to the *Dark Ages* and the *Roman Catholic Inquisition*. While conquering Spain, the French army under the command of Napoleon Bonaparte was witness to the Spanish Inquisition at the hands of the Dominican Order. Where the killings in Southern France were at the hands of the pope's ex-crusaders and mercenaries, the Spanish Inquisition was at the hands of Dominican Friars, a branch of Catholic Church clergy. The Dominican Order is a mendicant Catholic religious order, which was established by Spanish priest Dominic of Caleruega in the year 1216. By definition, a religious order that is considered "mendicant," lives on

---

[34]H. Boehmer, professor at the University of Bonn, "Les Jesuites" (Armand Colin, Paris 1910, pp.85-88) in *The Secret History of the Jesuits*, ed. Edmond Paris (Ontario, California: Chick Publications, 1983), 46.

[35] Revelation 17:6, KJV.

the alms they received and are busy with *apostolic activities*. The Dominican's actions were horrific enough to turn the stomachs of hardened, seasoned French troops in Napoleon's army.

From author R.W. Thompson's book, *The Papacy and the Civil Power,* and Catholic Historian Peter De Rosa's book, *Vicars of Christ: The Darkside of the Papacy,* we are given the following accounts of the Spanish Inquisition:

> One thinks immediately of the Inquisitions (Roman, Medieval, and Spanish) which for centuries held Europe in their terrible grip. In his *History of the Inquisition,* Canon Llorente, who was Secretary to the Inquisition in Madrid from 1790-92 and had access to the archives of all the tribunals, estimated that in Spain alone the number of condemned exceeded 3 million, with about 300,000 burned at the stake.[36]

Peter De Rosa gives the following account of Napoleon and the Spanish Inquisition.

> When Napoleon conquered Spain in 1808, a Polish officer in his army, Colonel Lemanouski, reported that the Dominicans [in charge of the Inquisition] blockaded themselves in their monastery in Madrid. When Lamanouski's troops forced and entry, the inquisitors denied the existence of any torture chambers. The soldiers searched the monastery and discovered them under the floors. The chambers were full of prisoners, all naked, many insane. The French troops, used to cruelty and blood, could not stomach the sight. They emptied the torture-

[36] R. W. Thompson, *The Papacy and the Civil Power* (New York: Harper & Brothers Publishers, 1876), 82.

> chambers, laid gunpowder to the monastery and blew the place up.[37]

These acts of butchery, torture, murder, and lust for blood were done by men who believed they acted in the name of a holy God. To have a desire to commit such evil and think it to be a righteous act shows the power of indoctrination. It is something that is programmed in. When comparing the wickedness and cruelty of the Dominican friars during the Spanish Inquisition to the works of Christ's apostles in the book of Acts, the question arises, what can cause the minds of those friars to believe that torturing another human being is a righteous act? Two possible reasons immediately come to mind—first, the indoctrination of the soul with false teaching and, second, the influence of the spirit of the antichrist working in the hearts of these deceived individuals, not to exclude demonic possession.

To wring out confessions from these poor creatures, the Roman Catholic Church devised ingenious tortures so excruciating and barbarous that one is sickened by their recital. Church Historian Bishop William Shaw Kerr writes:

> The most ghastly abominations of all was the system of torture. The accounts of its cold-blooded operations make one shudder at the capacity of human beings for cruelty. And it was decreed and regulated by the popes who claim to represent Christ on earth....
>
> Careful notes were taken not only of all that was confessed by the victim, but of his shrieks, cries, lamentations, broken interjections and appeals for mercy. The most moving things in the literature of the Inquisition are not the accounts of their

---

[37] Peter De Rosa, *Vicars of Christ: The Darkside of the Papacy* (New York: Crown Publishers, 1988), 172.

> sufferings left by the victims but the sober memoranda kept by the officers of the tribunals. We are distressed and horrified just because there is no intention to shock us.[38]
>
> Rome has not changed at heart no matter what sweet words she speaks when it serves her purpose.[39]

Edgar Quinet (1803–1875), a French historian, poet, and political philosopher, had the following to say about the Jesuits. According to the Encyclopedia Britannica,[40] Quinet had sympathy for all religions, but his radical views separated him from the Church of Rome.

> Wherever a dynasty dies, I can see, rising up and standing behind her, a kind of bad genie, one of those dark figures that are the confessors, gently and paternally luring her towards death … [41]

The Jesuits found repeatable success in the strategy of entering a country and immediately focusing on winning the minds and favor of the ruling classes. If you can control the head, then you can control the tail. The Vatican found it necessary to guide the political activities of foreign nations. Without this control, the papacy would lose the use of those nations' armed forces. By proxy, the popes used these external military forces to continue

---

[38] Bishop William Shaw Kerr, op. cit., 239-240, in *A Woman Rides the Beast*, ed. Dave Hunt (Eugene, Oregon, 1994), 80.

[39] Hunt, *A Woman Rides the Beast*, 81.

[40] "Edgar Quinet," Encyclopedia Britannica, 02/25/2019, https://www.britannica.com/biography/Edgar-Quinet.

[41] Michelet et Quinet: "Des Jesuites," (Hachette, Pauline, Paris 1845, pp.259), in *The Secret History of the Jesuits*, ed. Edmond Paris (Ontario, California: Chick Publications, 1983), 47.

their Inquisitions. The Vatican's Inquisitions would now come under new names to murder on a massive scale, names such as war and genocide. These strategies used by Rome will be seen repeatedly.

> The fighting spirit developed more and more as time went on as, beside foreign missions, the activities of Loyola's sons started to concentrate on the souls of men, especially amongst ruling classes. Politics are their main field of action, as all the efforts of these "directors" concentrates on one aim: *the submission of the world to the papacy, and to attain this the "heads" must be conquered first*. And to realize this ideal? Two very important weapons: *to be the confessors of the mighty and those in high places and the education of their children.* In that way, the present will be safe while the future is prepared.[42]

The Protestant tide was growing in Europe, and this was a significant threat and concern for the Vatican. The Holy Roman Empire was losing territory in its backyard, which made up a large part of its power base. The Protestant Reformation was born in Germany, which created a struggle to regain lost territory, which also meant revenue from tributary taxes and the selling of indulgences. Central Europe is vital to Rome. This point will keep Europe almost in a continuous state of war for centuries. The catalyst of instigation for this lack of peace in Europe will be the Church of Rome.

We know from history it was the Houses of Wittelsbach and the Habsburg that helped the Jesuit Order hold back the Protestant tide from dividing Europe into two separate religious camps. The Protestants are a thorn in the Vatican's side, and this doesn't take into account the Vatican's burden from the Eastern

---

[42] Paris, *The Secret History of the Jesuits*, 33-34.

Orthodox church, which has as its head the Russians Czars. The Bolshevik Revolution and World War II will change the status of the Eastern Orthodox church's impact on Rome.

To maintain favor in the ruling courts, the Jesuits were the confessors for the ruling class. This inside information significantly increased the success of preserving support in the courts. For the Jesuits, the ends always justify the means. Control of the ruling class was at least a two-fold strategy, for the Jesuits were also the tutors and instructors of the ruling classes' youth. Where the monarchal parents resisted accepting the pope's agenda, the Jesuits would succeed with the minds of the would-be heirs to the thrones of Europe. They would sway the very souls that were next in line to rule. Once the minds of the heirs were secure, the future was stable, and the parents were now expendable.

The House of Wittelsbach ruled in Bavaria from the 1100s to 1918. In 1214, Otto II, through marriage, gained the Palatinate of the Rhine. When the Duke of Bavaria, in 1294, became Holy Roman Emperor Louis IV, he secured through the Treaty of Pavia the Wittelsbach lands for his nephew. There were other popes from this family, and this connection allowed Rome to control Bavaria and part of the Rhine for centuries.

The House of Habsburg,[43] or traditional spelling Hapsburg, was a powerful and distinguished ruling family in Europe. Several popes were drawn from this house and several emperors and kingdoms: the Kingdom of Bohemia, the Kingdom of England, the Kingdom of Germany, the Kingdom of Hungary, the Kingdom of Croatia, the Kingdom of Illyria, the Second Mexican Empire, the Kingdom of Ireland and the Kingdom of Portugal, and the Kingdom of Spain.

Like the House of Wittelsbach, its power and influence came to an end with World War I. Note how these houses assisted the Church of Rome in maintaining control as Tributaries to the

---

[43] "House of Hapsburg," Wikipedia: The Free Encyclopedia, 03/15/2019, https://en.wikipedia.org/wiki/House_of_Habsburg.

Vatican. The following excerpts are from Edmond Paris's book *Secret History of the Jesuits*:

Germany

> It was not southern Europe, but central Europe: France, Holland, Germany, Poland, which were the site for the historical struggle between Catholicism and Protestantism, So these countries were the main fields of battle for the Society of Jesus.[44]
>
> In Bavaria, the young Duke Albert V, son of a zealous Catholic and educated at Ingolstadt, the old Catholic city, called on the Jesuits to combat effectively the heresy: "On the 7th of July 1556, 8 Fathers and 12 Jesuit teachers entered Ingolstadt.... the Roman Catholic conceptions directed the politics of princes and the behavior of the high classes.... Loyola's emissaries won the country's heart and mind from the start ... [45]
>
> One can judge the state of mind of the Fathers introduced to this stronghold of faith by reading the following: "The Jesuit Mayrhofer of Ingolstadt taught in his "Preacher's mirror:" "We will not be judged if we demand the killing of Protestants, any more than

[44] H. Boehmer, professor at the University of Bonn, "Les Jesuites" (Armand Colin, Paris 1910, pp. p.89, 104, 112, 114) in *The Secret History of the Jesuits*, ed. Edmond Paris (Ontario, California: Chick Publications, 1983), 47.

[45] Ibid.

we would by asking for the death of thieves, murderers, counterfeiters and revolutionaries."[46]

From 1563 on, he (Albert V) pitilessly expelled all recalcitrant, and had no mercy for the Anabaptists who had to suffer drownings, fire, prison and chains, all of which were praised by Jesuit Agricola ... In spite of all this, a whole generation of men had to disappear before the persecution was crowned a complete success.[47]

In 1617, the archduke Ferdinand was crowned king of Bohemia by the emperor. "Influenced by his Jesuit confessor Viller, Ferdinand started at once to combat Protestantism in his new kingdom. This signaled the start of that bloody war of religion which, for the next thirty years, kept Europe in suspense.[48]

When the Thirty Years War came to an end, and peace was concluded assuring German Protestants the same political rights enjoyed by the Catholics, the Jesuits did their uttermost to continue the fighting; it was in vain.[49]

The deep misery which followed the war of religion, the powerless politics, the intellectual decadence, the moral corruption, a frightful decrease in the population and

---

[46] Rene Fulop-Miller: "Les Jesuites et le secret de leur puissance" (Plon, Paris, 1933, p.98,102) *in The Secret History of the Jesuits*, ed. Edmond Paris (Ontario, California: Chick Publications, 1983), 48.

[47] Paris, *The Secret History of the Jesuits*,.49.

[48] Ibid., 50.

[49] Rene Fulop-Miller, op. cit., II, pp. 104-105, in *The Secret History of the Jesuits*, ed. Edmond Paris (Ontario, California: Chick Publications, 1983), 51.

impoverishment of the whole of Germany: these were the results of the Order's actions.[50] (Emphasis added, results of allowing the Jesuit Order in a country)

Switzerland

America had its 13 states at the time of the American Revolution. The Republic of Switzerland had its 13 cantons at the time of the Reformation. Before the Reformation, we can see that the Swiss defended their independence through several historical battles with foreign powers. The House of Habsburgs from Austria in 1315, King Louis XI of France in 1444, and Duke Charles the Bold of Burgundy 1476–1477.[51] There were many others. The Swiss were not immune or isolated enough from the conflict of Reformation and Counter-Reformation. At the time of the Reformation, Switzerland was a Confederation with independent cantons. Whether the townships were large or small, each carried equal voting power. This power permitted some of the less populace cantons to reject Protestantism. As in the rest of Europe, the Roman Catholic Church in Switzerland had its corruption and needed reform.

---

[50] J. Huber, *Les Jesuites* (Sandoz et Fischbacher, Paris 1875, pp. 183-186), in *The Secret History of the Jesuits*, ed. Edmond Paris (Ontario, California: Chick Publications, 1983), 52.

[51] Philip Schaff, "*History of the Christian Church, Volume VIII: Modern Christianity. The Swiss Reformation,*" Christian Classic Ethereal Library, 2002-11-27, http://www.ccel.org/ccel./schaff/hcc8.html, 7.

[52]

Swiss Historian Philip Schaff lived from January 1, 1819, to October 20, 1893. Educated in Germany, Schaff was a Protestant theologian and ecclesiastical historian. From his works, we have the following about the condition of the Catholic Church in Switzerland:

> The church (Roman Catholic) in Switzerland was corrupt and as much in need of reform as in Germany. The inhabitants of the old cantons around the Lake of Lucerne were, and are to this day, among the most honest and pious Catholics; but the clergy were ignorant, superstitious, and immoral, and set a bad example to the laity. The convents were in a state of decay, and could not furnish a single champion able to cope with the Reformers in learning and moral influence. Celibacy made concubinage a common and pardonable offence. The bishop of Constance (Hugo

[52] "Schaff," Wikipedia: The Free Encyclopedia, 03/18/2019, https://upload.wikimedia.org/wikipedia/commons/6/6b/Schaff_P.jpg.

> von Hohenlandenberg) *absolved guilty priests on the payment of a fine of four guilders for every child born to them, and is said to have derived from this source seventy-five hundred guilders in a single year* (1522). In a pastoral letter, shortly before the Reformation, he complained of the immorality of many priests who openly kept concubines or bad women in their houses, who refuse to dismiss them, or bring them back secretly, who gamble, sit with laymen in taverns, drink to excess, and utter blasphemies.[53] (Emphasis added)

The 16th-century Reformation spawned several Evangelical denominations. Zwingli and Calvin in Switzerland went further than German reformers. While both the German and Swiss reformers agreed to be in opposition with the Church of Rome, the Swiss reformers were very strict about the sovereign glory of God and held to strict scriptural interpretation of the first and second commandments. Wherever the Protestant Evangelicals were saving souls, the Jesuits would be sure to plan their counterattacks; these confrontations seemed to always end in bloodshed. There were innocent lives lost in both camps, both Catholic and Protestant. From, *The Secret History of the Jesuits*, Paris writes:

> It was only during the 17th century that the Jesuits established themselves successfully in Switzerland, after having been called, then banished, by a few cities of the Confederation, during the second half of the 16th century.[54]
>
> Charles Borromee wrote to his confessor that the Company of Jesus (the Jesuits), governed by heads

---

[53] Schaff, *History of the Christian Church, Volume VIII*, 8.

[54] Paris, *The Secret History of the Jesuits*, 53.

> more political than religious, is becoming too powerful to preserve the necessary moderation and submission ... She rules over kings and princes, and governs temporal and spiritual affairs; the pious institution has lost the spirit which animated her originally; we shall be compelled to abolish it.[55]

> At the same time in France, the famous legal expert Etienne Pasquiet wrote: "Introduce this Order in our midst and, at the same time, you will introduce dissension, chaos and confusion."[56]

Philip Schaff's note on Cardinal Charles Borromeo:

> The provincial governors were often oppressive, sold the subordinate offices to partisans, and enriched themselves at the expense of the inhabitants. The Protestants were distracted by internal feuds. The Roman Counter-Reformation was begun with great zeal and energy in Upper Italy and Switzerland by the saintly Cardinal Charles Borromeo, archbishop of Milan. Jesuits and Capuchins stirred up the hatred of the ignorant and superstitious people against the Protestant heretics. In the Grisons themselves the Roman Catholic party under the lead of the family of Planta, and the Protestants, headed by the family of Salis, strove for the mastery.[57]

---

[55] J. Huber op. cit., p. 131, in *The Secret History of the Jesuits,* ed. Edmond Paris (Ontario, California: Chick Publications, 1983), 53.

[56] Cite by H. Fulop-Miller: "Les Jesuites et le secret de leur puissance" (Plon, Paris, 1933, p.57), in *The Secret History of the Jesuits,* ed. Edmond Paris (Ontario, California: Chick Publications, 1983), 53.

[57] Schaff, *History of the Christian Church, Volume VIII,* 95.

> Any plan forged in Rome, or by other foreign powers, against Protestantism in Switzerland was assured of the Jesuits full support ... In 1620, they were successful in making the Catholic population of the Veltlin rise against the Protestants and they slaughtered six hundred. *The pope gave indulgences to all those who took part in that horrible deed.*[58] (Emphasis added)

> Today, article 51 of the Swiss constitution forbids the Society of Jesus to hold any cultural or educative activity on the territory of the Confederation, and efforts made to abolish this rule have always been defeated.[59]

The Swiss operate under democratic principles today, and like France, they had learned from the destruction and chaos caused by the opening of their doors to the Jesuits.

Poland

If you recall, Jesuit Possevino is responsible for launching the "bloody persecution" in his home country of Italy just 20 years earlier in 1561. And as you will see, he has no trouble involving himself in intrigue and deceit if it will accomplish what is best for Rome. Even acting as the mediator between Poland and Russia, his motives had nothing to do with the success of either country, only that of Rome. For the Jesuit, the underlying motto is "*the ends justify the means.*" French author H. Boehmer, who is considered a moderate historian, writes:

---

[58] Paris, *Secret History of the Jesuits*, 54.

[59] Ibid., 55.

> Of all the States, Poland, who had millions of orthodox Christians in her midst, should have had religious tolerance as one of the most essential principles of her interior politics. The Jesuits did not allow that. They did worse: they put Poland's exterior politics at the service of Catholic interests in a fatal manner.[60]

> In 1581, Father Possevino the pontifical legate in Moscow, has done his best to bring together the Czar Ivan the Terrible and the Roman church. Full of glad hopes, Possevino made himself, in 1584, the mediator of the peace of Kirewora Gora between Russia and Poland, a peace which saved Ivan from inextricable difficulties.[61]

Ivan got what he wanted, peace, and afterward, he had no further use for the Jesuits. Possevino leaves Russia empty-handed. A couple of years later, at the time of Ivan's assassination, Grischka Ostrepjew, a Russian monk of no rank, claims to be Dimitri the son of Ivan the Terrible. Possevino quickly seizes the opportunity. The false Dimitri colludes to submit Moscow to Rome if he sits as Czar on the throne. The Jesuit Possevino wastes no time and introduces Ostrepjew to the Palatine of Sandomir, who gives his daughter in marriage.

Speaking for the false Dimitri to King Sigismond III of Poland, an agreement is made to move against the Czar Boris Godounov. Possevino's reward for his successful dethroning of Czar Godounov is Dimitri renouncing the religion of his fathers at Crascovie. The Jesuits begin their establishment in Moscow.[62]

---

[60] H. Boehmer, op. cit., p. 135, in *The Secret History of the Jesuits*, ed. Edmond Paris (Ontario, California: Chick Publications, 1983), 56.

[61] Paris, *Secret History of the Jesuits*, 57.

[62] Ibid.

The law of sowing and reaping—or in a secular view, cause and effect—can be applied to the deceit of Father Possevino. He helped Dimitri obtain the Russian throne, where he denounced the faith of his forefathers. The Czars, like the popes, were the head of their church; the Orthodox church did not stand with this false Czar. Edmond Paris writes:

> But it was these favors from the Catholics which unleashed the hatred of the Russian Orthodox church against Dimitri. On the 27th of May 1606, he was massacred with several hundred Polish followers. Until then, one could hardly speak of a Russian national sentiment; but now, this feeling was very strong and took immediately the form of a fanatical hatred for the Roman church and Poland.[63]

Sweden

The Scandinavian countries were stout in their Lutheranism. Mr. Pierre Dominque writes:

> Lutheranism submerged everything else and, when the Jesuits made their counter-attack, they did not find what was found in Germany: a Catholic party in the minority, but still strong.[64]

There was an attempt to gain a foothold in 1574 by Father Nicolai and other Jesuits. But the conditions and circumstances were rejected by the Roman Curia, and the Jesuits had to leave.

---

[63] Ibid., 59.

[64] Pierre Dominique: "*La politique des Jesuites*" Grasset, Paris 1955, p. 76, in *The Secret History of the Jesuits*, ed. Edmond Paris (Ontario, California: Chick Publications, 1983), 59.

> Fifty years later, the Order won another great victory in Sweden. Queen Christine, daughter of Gustave-Adolphe, the last of the Wasas, was converted under the teaching of two Jesuit professors, who managed to reach Stockholm pretending to be travelling Italian noblemen. But, in order to change her religion without conflicts, she had to abdicate on the 24th of June 1654.[65]

England

> When Elizabeth came to the throne in 1558, Ireland was still entirely Catholic and England 50 per cent so . . .[66]

The Jesuits built seminaries with the goal of training the English. There was an agreement between Philip II of Spain and the Roman Curia to overthrow Queen Elizabeth 1 and replace her with Catholic Mary Stuart. Rome instigated an Irish uprising, and it failed. The Jesuits had a large Catholic Assembly in Southwark.[67] The Jesuits continued their schemes in England and attempted a plot at Edinburgh in favor of King James of Scotland, but this also failed, and the result was the execution of Mary Stuart in 1587. Spain was a problem for a while with their Naval Armada. The Jesuits continued to train English priests, and they continued their propaganda secretly under the direction of Father Garnett.

---

[65] H. Boehmer, op. cit., pp. 137-139, in *The Secret History of the Jesuits*, ed. Edmond Paris (Ontario, California: Chick Publications, 1983), 60.

[66] Ibid.

[67] Paris, *The Secret History of the Jesuits*, 60.

> After the Gunpowder Plot against James I, successor of Elizabeth, this Father Garnett was condemned for complicity and hanged, like Father Campion.[68]

The Jesuits were relentless in their attempts to gain a foothold in England, through the use of their *craft* with Charles I, Charles II, and a treaty with Louis XIV. During the reign of Charles I, which at that time was in Cromwell's Commonwealth, there were Jesuits who paid with their lives for their intrigues. Charles II, who enjoyed being king and wasn't interested in what plans the Jesuits had, "... hanged five Fathers for high treason at Tyburn ..." [69]

> All these combinations were the main cause for the 1688 revolution. The Jesuits had to go against a stream to powerful. Then, England had twenty Protestants for each Catholic.
>
> The king was overthrown; all the members of the Company put in prison or banished. For some time, the Jesuits recommenced their work of secret agents, but it was nothing more than a futile agitation. They had lost the cause.[70]

France

The history of relationships between Rome and France goes back centuries. To document all the accounts would generate books. The Vatican and her loyal watchdogs, the Jesuits, would interfere with the sovereigns of France on hundreds of occasions. Before the 16th century, where we find the Reformation and the Society

---

[68] Ibid., 61.

[69] Ibid., 61.

[70] Pierre Dominique, op. cit., pp. 101-102, in *The Secret History of the Jesuits*, ed. Edmond Paris (Ontario, California: Chick Publications, 1983), 62.

of Jesus in contention, there were several examples of how the popes will demand that one sovereign country attack another sovereign nation to do the will of Rome. At the end of the 12th century and the beginning of the 13th century, we have such an example.

Many of us are familiar with the stories of Robinhood, which has its setting during the temporal reign of Prince John of England. Prince John (John Lackland) became king in the year 1199 when Richard the Lionheart died. John, living up to his character portrayed in the stories told later, conflicted with Pope Innocent III. The pope would threaten him with a letter of interdict and excommunication, and the now King John would tax the Catholic clergy in order to support his war with France. King John went so far as to confiscate church property.

Pope Innocent III decides to depose John and directs King Philip II of France to prepare himself to expel King John. The story ends with King John submitting to the papacy. The Vatican does not have a standing army of its own. So to exercise its secular arm, it must either employ the use of a foreign nation's troops or buy the service of mercenaries with the incentive of receiving indulgences. The Church of Rome will use tolerances as bribery repeatedly throughout the centuries. Note that before the 19th century, the French have done the bidding of Rome with the high cost to the health of France.

The 16th-century ushers the Jesuits into France. It was in 1551 that the Jesuit Order began to plant roots in France again, and the French suffered greatly due to the counsel of the Jesuits. France would purge itself of this religious cancer only to fall into relapse from the craft of Jesuit persuasion. The Jesuits would manipulate their way back in, only to set France up for more devastation.

> The Faculty of Theology, whose mission is to safeguard the principles of religion in France, decreed on the 1st of December 1554, that 'this society appears to

> be *extremely dangerous regarding the faith, she is an enemy of the church's peace,* fatal to the monastic state and seems to have been born to bring ruin rather than edification.'[71] (Emphasis added)
>
> The famous Lainez, the man at the Council of Trent, distinguished himself in polemics, especially at the Colloquy of Poissy, in an unhappy attempt to conciliate the two doctrines (1561).[72]
>
> Thanks to the Queen-Mother Catherine of Medici, the Order opened its first Parisian establishment, the College of Clermont, which was in competition with the University.[73]

As previously discussed, it was the Medici family through *Cosimo d'Medici* who helped increase the level of Gnosticism into Catholicism. Wikipedia had this to say about Catherine of Medici:

> Some historians have excused Catherine from blame for the worst decisions of the crown, though evidence for her ruthlessness can be found in her letters. In practice, her authority was always limited by the effects of the civil wars. Her policies, therefore, may be seen as desperate measures to keep the Valois monarchy on the throne at all costs, and her patronage of the arts as an attempt to glorify a monarchy whose prestige was in steep decline. Without

---

[71] Gaston Baily: "Les Jesuits" (Chamberry, Imprimerie Nouvelle, 1902, p.69, in *The Secret History of the Jesuits*, ed. Edmond Paris (Ontario, California: Chick Publications, 1983), p.63.

[72] Paris, *The Secret History of the Jesuits*, 64.

[73] Ibid.

> Catherine, it is unlikely that her sons would have remained in power. The years during which they reigned have been called "the age of Catherine de' Medici." According to Mark Strage, one of her biographers, Catherine was the most powerful woman in sixteenth-century Europe.[74]

The 16th century started to see a change in Europe; Protestantism began to replace Rome's pseudo-Christianity. Rome's preferred answer to these heretics was the Inquisition, assassination of rulers, and interdicts against states that resisted the pope. The Massacre of St. Bartholomew made countries wary of accepting Catholicism's missionaries. By church law, Catholics are citizens of the Vatican first before they are citizens of their host country that they currently call home.

The pope decrees the killing of heretics, then Catholics in foreign lands do the will of the papacy, a distant political power. Dedicated Catholics can be viewed as patriots to an external power by the laws of Catholicism. We will see this struggle again in Europe during World War II, with the persecution of non-Catholics, mainly the Jews. Racism is not intrinsic; it is taught or bred into the minds of people. The Vatican condemns intolerance today in the ecumenical movement, but throughout history, the Church of Rome has shown no tolerance whatsoever for any people group who wish to practice their religion peacefully.

> There is no need to ask if the Jesuits "consented" to the Saint Bartholomew Massacre (1572). Did they "prepare" it? Who knows?... The Company's politics, subtle and supple in their proceedings, have very clear aims; it is the popes' politics: "destroy heresy." Everything must be subordinated to this

---

[74] "Catherine de' Medici," Wikipedia: The Free Encyclopedia, 03/09/2019, https://en.wikipedia.org/wiki/Catherine_de%27_Medici.

> major aim. "Catherine of Medici worked towards this aim and the Company could count on the Guises.[75]

Peter De Rosa explains how the Vatican a monarchy believes it should rule everywhere, and individual freedom is not permitted. America is the land of the free, and these freedoms, the same privileges that non-Catholics tried to exercise in the 16th century Europe was "alien to the pontiff's notion of Christian faith."[76] De Rosa gives the following examples of the Church of Rome's response to religious freedom:

> In 1520, Leo X condemned Luther for daring to say that burning heretics is against the will of God. Gregory XIII commemorated with joy the Massacre of St Bartholomew on the night of 24 August 1572 when thousands of Huguenot Protestants died. Clement VIII attacked the Edict of Nantes in 1598 because it gave equality of citizenship to all, regardless of their religion. The Edict was revoked in 1685 to the church's delight: within three years, fifty thousand Protestant families left France, scattered further abroad, said Voltaire, than even the Jews. Innocent X had meanwhile condemned the Peace of Westphalia for daring to grant toleration to all citizens, regardless of their religion or lack of it. In every instance and over centuries, the Catholic church proudly proclaimed its dogma of religious intolerance.[77]

---

[75] Pierre Dominique, op. cit., pp. 84, in *The Secret History of the Jesuits*, ed. Edmond Paris (Ontario, California: Chick Publications, 1983), 64.

[76] De Rosa, *Vicars of Christ*, 145.

[77] Ibid.

Three years later, it was the League, after the assassination of the duke de Guise, nicknamed "the king of Paris" and the appeal to His Most Christian Majesty to fight the Protestants.

The shrewd Henry III did his best to avoid war of religion.... *"The Jesuits, powerful in Paris, protested that the king of France had surrendered to heresy ... So Henry III was assassinated.* As the heir was a Protestant, the murder seemed at first glance to have been for other than political reasons; but is it not possible that those who planned it and persuaded the Jacobin Clement to carry it out were hoping for an uprising of Catholic France against the Huguenot heir?...

In 1592, a certain Barriere who tried to assassinate Henry IV confessed that *Father Varade, rector of the Jesuits in Paris had persuaded him to do it.*

In 1594, another attempt was made by Jean Chatel, former pupil of the Jesuits who had heard his confession just before carrying it out. [78] (Emphasis added)

The Father was hanged at Greve while the king confirmed an edict of Parliament banishing the sons of Loyola from the kingdom, as "corrupters of youth, disturber of public peace and enemies of the State and crown of France ... "

The edict was not carried out fully and, in 1603, it was revoked by the king against the advice of Parliament.

... The fact is, Henry IV chose as his confessor and tutor for the Dauphin one of the most distinguished members of the *Company, Father Cotton.*

---

[78] Paris, *The Secret History of the Jesuits*,.64-65.

> On the 16th of May 1610, on the eve of his campaign against Austria, he was murdered by Ravaillac who confessed having been inspired by the writings of *Fathers Mariana and Suarez*. These two sanctioned the murders of heretic "tyrants" or those insufficiently *devoted to the papacy's interests.*[79]
>
> Fortunately, Aquaviva was still there. Once again, this great general schemed well; he condemned most severely the legitimacy of tyrannicide. *The Company always had authors who, in the silence of their studies, exposed the doctrine in all its rectitude; she also possessed great politicians who, when necessary, would put the right masks on it.*[80] (Emphasis added)

France and Spain are two European countries in which the Jesuits were able to establish lengthy entrenchments of power. Rarely was the blood of a Jesuit spilled; the French didn't seem to see that when it came to Rome taking a loss due to defeat, the French paid with their blood. The pope was safe back in the Vatican. Father Cotton maintained control of the situation, and the Jesuits came out with a victory. "Her wealth, adherents and establishments increased."[81] Henry IV, like his father Henry III, was assassinated. Louis the XIII reigned for 33 years and died of multiple illnesses. Then Louis XIV takes the throne, and the Jesuits experience some very successful intrigues.

> The accession of Louis XIV marked the start of the most prosperous time for the Order....In spite of it, the secure place they held at Court assured them victory, ... It goes without saying that they had only

---

[79] Ibid., 66.

[80] Pierre Dominique, op. cit., p.95, in *The Secret History of the Jesuits*, ed. Edmond Paris (Ontario, California: Chick Publications, 1983), 66-67.

[81] Paris, *Secret History of the Jesuits*, 67.

> unwillingly accepted the religious peace assured through the Edict of Nantes, and had continued a secret war against the French Protestants....As Louis XIV was getting older, he turned more and more to bigotry under the influence of Madame de Maintenon and Father La Chaise, his confessor.... Finally, on the 17th of October 1685, he signed the "Revocation of the Edict of Nantes." Making those of his subjects who refused to embrace the Catholic religion outlaws.[82]

The *Edict of Nantes* was signed and put in place by Henry IV in 1598 to grant Calvinist Protestants of France, which were known as the Huguenots, substantial rights in France. History shows that when a government signs an agreement to give human beings liberties that were already bestowed upon them by God, it is not long before the prejudice returns when new rulership comes to power.

The story of Joseph in the book of Genesis parallels the broken promises of the Edict of Nantes. Joseph was promoted to prime minister by Pharaoh. A future Pharaoh forgets the promises made to the Israelites and enslaves the Hebrew people. History proves time and again that signing a document doesn't guarantee to change the heart of man. The prophet Jeremiah makes this remark about the human condition:

> *The heart is deceitful above all things, and desperately wicked: who can know it?*[83]

> According to Marshal Vauban, France lost in that way 400,000 inhabitants and 60 million francs. Manufactures, merchants, ship owners, skillful artisans

[82] Ibid., 67-68.

[83] Jeremiah 17:9, KJV.

went to other countries and brought them the benefit of their abilities.[84]

India, Japan, and China

India

> The conversion of "pagans" had been the first objective of the Society of Jesus' founder ... Their theocratic ideal: to bring the world under the Holy See's authority, required that they should go into all the regions of the globe, *in the conquest of souls.*
>
> Francis Xavier, one of Ignatius' first companions who, like him, was canonized by the church, was a great promoter of Asia's evangelization. In 1542, he disembarked at Goa and found there a bishop, a cathedral and convent of Franciscans who, together with some Portuguese priests, had already tried to spread around them the religion of Christ.[85]

In 1549 Francis Xavier left for Japan.

> His successor in India, Robert de Nobile, applied in that country the same methods the Jesuits used in Europe ... He adopted the clothes, habits and way of living of the Brahmins, mixed their rites with Christian ones, all with the approval of Pope Gregory XV, Thanks to this ambiguity, he "converted" so he claimed, 250,000 Hindus. But, "about a century after his death, when the intransigent pope Benedict XIV forbade the observance of these Hindu rites,

[84] Paris, *Secret History of the Jesuits*, 68.

[85] Ibid., 71.

> everything collapsed and the 250,000 pseudo-Catholics disappeared.[86]

Japan and China

To summarize the mission to Japan and China quickly, the Jesuits were not able to successfully manipulate the culture as they did in Europe.

The Americas

There is no country that Rome has not tried to dominate. The Aztec and Inca Empires had established societies. To the outside world, they appeared as simple people, even barbaric. They had their gods and their way of life. Their education level varied among the tribes. How could the South American nations compete with the power and wealth of Rome? Our school history lessons tell us how in 1519, Herman Cortez and his conquistadors conquered the Aztec empire. They were slaughtered by the thousands, and what the sword and cannonballs didn't kill, the disease carried by these white invaders did. It wasn't evangelism; it was imperialism. Here is an example of how Catholicism seeks to control souls rather than save them. The Conquistadors didn't free the South American Indians; they enslaved them.

> The missionaries of the Society of Jesus found the New World much more favorable to their proselytism than Asia. There, they found no old and learned civilizations, no religious solidly established, nor any philosophical traditions, but only poor and

---

[86] "Les Jesuites," in "Le Crapouillot," Nr. 24, 1954, p.42, in *The Secret History of the Jesuits*, ed. Edmond Paris (Ontario, California: Chick Publications, 1983), 72.

barbarian tribes, unarmed spiritually as well as temporally before the white conquerors.

Only Mexico and Peru, with memory of Aztec and Inca gods still fresh in their minds, resisted this imported religion for quite a long time. Also, the Dominicans and Franciscans had already established themselves solidly.

In Canada, the Hurons, peaceful and docile, accepted easily their catechism, but their enemies, the Iroquois, attacked the stations created around Fort Sainte Marie and massacred the inhabitants. The Hurons were practically exterminated within ten years and in 1649, the Jesuits had to leave with about three hundred survivors....

But Paraguay was the land for the great "experience" of Jesuitical colonization; the country spread then from the Atlantic to the Andes ...

These good savages were duly catechized and trained to live a sedentary life under a discipline as gentle as it was strong: "as an iron hand in a velvet glove.[87]

The Jesuits watch over them like fathers; and, like fathers also, they punish the smallest mistakes ... The whip, fasting, prison, pillory on the public square, public penance in the church, these are the chastisements they use ... [88]

Dave Hunt makes note that Latin America had not forgotten the crimes of the Catholic Church when Pope John Paul II made his visit to Latin America.

---

[87] Paris, *The Secret History of the Jesuits*, 78-79.

[88] Ibid., 80.

> Nor have the descendants of Aztecs, Incas, and Mayas forgotten that Roman Catholic priests, backed by the secular sword, gave their ancestors the choice of conversion (which often meant slavery) or death. They made such and outcry when John Paul II in a recent visit to Latin America proposed elevation Junipero Serra (a major eighteenth-century enforcer of Catholicism among the Indians) to sainthood that the pope was forced to hold the ceremony in secret.[89]

Edmond Paris continues:

> Let us consider how it affected the intellectual and moral advancement of the beneficiaries of that system, these "poor innocents" as they were called by the Marques de Loreto: "The missions' high culture is nothing more than an artificial product from a hothouse, carrying in itself a seed of death. Because, in spite of all this breaking in and training the Guarani remained deep down what he was a lazy savage, narrow-minded, sensual, greedy and sordid.[90]
>
> The Guarani's moral life enriched itself very little under the Father's discipline. He became a devout and superstitious Catholic who sees miracles everywhere and seems to enjoy flagellating himself until blood appears; he learned to obey and was attached to the good Fathers, who cared so well for him, with a filial gratitude which, even though not very deep, was nevertheless very tenacious. This not very brilliant

[89] Hunt, *A Woman Rides the Beast*, 71.

[90] Paris, *The Secret History of the Jesuits*, 80-81.

> result proves that there was some important defect in the educative methods of the Fathers.[91]

What was that defect?

> The fact that they never tried to develop, in their "red" children, the inventive faculties, the need for activity, the feeling of responsibility; they themselves invented games and recreations for their Christians, they thought for them instead of encouraging them to think for themselves; they merely submitted those who were under their care to a mechanical "breaking in" instead of actually educating them.[92]

> How could it be otherwise when they themselves had gone through a "breaking in" that lasted for fourteen years? Were they going to teach the Guaranis and their white pupils to "think for themselves," when they were absolutely forbidden to do so?"
>
> The education of Paraguay's natives was done on the same principles the Fathers used to apply, now apply and will apply on everyone everywhere; their aim, deplored by Mr. Boehmer, but which is ideal to the eyes of those fanatics: the renouncement of all personal judgment, all initiative, a blind submission to the superiors.[93]

Returning to ex-Catholic priest Bernard Fresenborg, whom we heard from back in chapter three. From his book *Thirty Years*

---

[91] Ibid., 81-82.

[92] H. Boehmer, op. cit., pp. 204-205, in *The Secret History of the Jesuits*, ed. Edmond Paris (Ontario, California: Chick Publications, 1983), 82.

[93] Paris, *The Secret History of the Jesuits*, 82-83.

in Hell; or, From Darkness to Light, he had this to say about the effects of Rome on a nation's education. When it comes to the dogmas of Catholicism, we see that a ceiling, a cap must be placed on what degree or permission to think or to discern for yourself is permitted. This cap was necessary to maintain control.

> Education in its literal meaning, means an infusion of intelligence that lifts up the minds of man, and it is generally so accepted by the world at large, but education, as far as Catholicism goes, means only a rehearsal of abominations, which have been practiced upon the followers of this creed for centuries in the past and does not in the least bear upon the principles of true education.[94]
>
> Now, do you expect an institution which teaches such doctrines to elevate a nation above their own' doctrine? If you do, you are expecting something unreasonable, and if the inhabitants of Cuba, Porto Rico and the Philippine Islands are not to be elevated above such abominations can the future hold anything for them but misery?[95]

France Late 19th Century

> Having been made president of the Republic on the 10th of December 1848, Louis Napoleon Bonaparte gathers several ministers around himself, one of which is M. de Falloux. Who is this M. de Falloux? A tool of the Jesuits ... On the 4th of January 1849, he

---

[94] Fresenborg, *Thirty Years in Hell,* 40.

[95] Ibid., 48-49.

> institutes a commission whose job is to 'prepare a big legislative reform of primary and secondary education' ... A law on teaching is being prepared which would "make amends" to the Jesuits. In the past, the State and the University had been protected against the Jesuits invasions; we were wrong and unjust; we demanded that the government applied its laws against these *agents from a foreign government* and we ask their forgiveness for it.... *"Put in their hands the teaching of the young generations."*[96] (Emphasis added)

Indoctrinating the youth of a nation to seize control of that nation is a recurring strategy; America is experiencing this very same strategy. This fact is such a crucial point that it can't be overstated. What determines the course of a nation's future is the education of the next generation, its youth! The Jesuits were well aware of this principle and made effective use of it. Each time the Jesuits planned to enter a country, they used their practice of "mission adaptation" and focused on building relationships with the ruling classes to have access to the courts.

Part two of the connection with the ruling classes is the education of their children for indoctrination, the next generation scheduled to lead. As was mentioned in chapter three on *Education,* before the signing of the Declaration of Independence, Catholics in America had limited rights. Early Americans restricted the political rights of Catholics as an act of National Defense. Catholics are citizens of the Vatican, a foreign power. All Catholics may not take their citizenship and obligation to the Vatican seriously. Catholics who hold a position of political power in the United States and swear to obey Roman church law, devoted to the will of the popes, can't fulfill their oath to both nations. These individuals may be compromised with a conflict of interest.

---

[96] Paris, *The Secret History of the* Jesuits, 109-110.

F. Tupper Saussy brings this point up in his book *Rulers of Evil*. The following two comments by Saussy should shed some additional light on the subject. First, shortly after the *American Revolution,* we have this insight from Saussy:

> Eight years after the sacrifice, Congress met in the Capitol for the first time. Washington gave the appearance of a Roman Catholic settlement. The most imposing houses in the city belonged to Daniel Carroll and his brother-in-law, secularized Jesuit priest Notley Young. The city's mayor was Carroll's nephew, Robert Brent, who was also purveying stone for most of the federal buildings. Over on the west side of town stood Georgetown College, established by Bishop John Carroll in 1789. *Georgetown quickly became the foremost incubator of federal policy, foreign and domestic. It is still administered by the Society of Jesus.*[97] (Emphasis added)

His second comment on the subject:

> America's understanding has been systematically bent to the will of the church Militant, while the intellectual means for sensing the capture have been disconnected. Most of the content of modern media, whether television, radio, print, film, stage, or web, is state-of-the-art Jesuit *ratio studiorum* (Latin for method of study). The Jesuit college is no longer just a chartered institution; it has become our entire social environment - the movies, the mall, the school, the home, the mind. Human experience has become a Spiritual Exercise managed by charismatic spiritual directors who know how to manipulate a

---

[97] Saussy, *Rulers of Evil,* 231-232.

> democracy's emotions. Logic, perspective, national memory, and self-discipline are purged to the point that "unbridled emotional responses," as economist Thomas Sowell put it, "are all we have left."[98] (Bold emphasis added)

Returning to the timeline in France:

> This in fact is the aim of the law of the 15th of March 1850. This law appoints a superior council for Public Instruction in which the clergy dominates. (first art.); it makes the clergy masters of the schools, (art. 44); it gives religious associations the right to create free schools, without having to explain about the non-authorized congregations (Jesuits), (art. 17,2); it said that the *letters of obedience* would be their diplomas, (art. 49); M. Barthelemy Saint-Hilaire tries in vain to demonstrate that the aim of the authors of that project is to give the monopoly to the clergy, and that this law would be fatal to the University ... [99] (Emphasis added)
>
> Victor Hugo exclaims, also vainly: "This law is a monopoly in the hands of those who try to make teaching come out of the sacristy and the government out of the confessional."[100]

The law gets passed, and it is a great victory for the Jesuits. The methods of logical and rational opposition have not

---

[98] Ibid., 74.

[99] Paris, *Secret History of the Jesuits*, 110.

[100] Adolphe Michel, *Les Jesuites* (Sandoz et Fischbacher, Paris 1845, p. 66ff., in *The Secret History of the* Jesuits, ed. Edmond Paris (Ontario, California: Chick Publications, 1983), 110.

changed. Listen to what French publicist and historian Count Montalembert had to say in response to the objections of passing the law:

> We will be swallowed up if we don't stop immediately the current trend of rationalism and demagogy; what's more, it can be stopped only with the help of the church (Protestant).[101]

> Louis-Napoleon, President of the Republic, had favored the Jesuits in every way. Now emperor, he refused nothing to his accomplices and allies. The clergy poured out its blessings and "Te Deum" profusely on the massacres and proscriptions of the 2nd of December. The one responsible for this abominable ambush was looked upon as a providential savior: "The archbishop of Paris, Monsignor Sibour, who saw the massacres on the boulevard, exclaims: "The man who was prepared by God has come; the finger of God was never more visible than in the events which produced these great results.[102]

Crimean War, 200,000 Casualties for All Involved, 1853–56

There is a familiar aphorism from philosophy professor George Santayana, which you may have heard. "*Those who do not learn history are doomed to repeat it.*" According to a Google search, there is an original version of the phrase, and it goes like this, "*Those who cannot remember the past are condemned to repeat it.*" Many of us are caught in a paradox. We cannot recall a past we are

[101] Paris, *The Secret History of the Jesuits*, 110.

[102] Ibid., 111.

destined to repeat because our memories contain no such events to forget.

France is doomed to repeat her error of not remembering what happens when she allows the Jesuits and the influence of Rome to dictate what justifies going to war. Here we have the *Crimean War*, which has as its catalyst the simple argument between the monks of the Eastern Orthodox church and the Latin monks of the Roman Catholic Church. Both churches were claiming the right to protect the holy places in Palestine. Who is to supervise the churches in Bethlehem? The Orthodox church is supported by the Russian Czar, and the Catholic Church has its Emperor, who poses as a Vicar of Christ.

Here we see the repeat of Rome using the blood of foreign troops to advance the interests of the Vatican. This error in memory will cost France 100,000 dead. Also, the wars will weaken France as she approaches the doorstep of World War I. While France is becoming weaker, her neighbor to the East, Prussia, is becoming stronger. In the Epistle of James, he asks the question, "Why do we war?"

> From whence come wars and fightings among you? come they not hence, even of your lusts that war in your members? Ye lust, and have not: ye kill, and desire to have, and cannot obtain: ye fight and war, yet ye have not, because ye ask not. Ye ask, and receive not, because ye ask amiss, that ye may consume it upon your lusts.[103]

From the *Secret History of the Jesuits*, Paris writes:

> ... The Crimean war was regarded as a compliment to the Roman expedition ... It was praised by the

---

[103] James 4:1-3, KJV.

whole clergy, full of admiration for the religious fervor of the troops besieging Sebastopol....[104]

What was this expedition which aroused the enthusiasm of the clergy? M. Paul Leon, member of the Institute, explains: "A quarrel between monks revives the question of the East: it was born out of rivalries between the Latin and Orthodox churches regarding the protection of the Holy places (in Palestine). Who would watch over Bethlehem's churches, hold the keys, direct the work?... But behind the Latin monks is France's Catholic party, provided with ancient privileges and supporter of the new regime; ... [105]

The Czar invokes the protection of the Orthodox church which he has to assure and, to make it effective, asks that his fleet should use the Dardanelles passage; England, which is backed by France, refuses and the war breaks out.[106]

France and England can reach the Czar only through the Black Sea and the Turkish alliance ... From now on, the war of Russia becomes the Crimean war and is entirely centered on the siege of Sebastopol, a costly episode without issue. Bloody battles, deadly

---

[104] Abbe J. Brugerette: "Le Pretre francais et la societe contempraine" (Lethielleux, Paris 1933, I, pp. 168,180), in *The Secret History of the Jesuits*, ed. Edmond Paris (Ontario, California: Chick Publications, 1983), 112.

[105] Paul Leon, of the Institute, "La gurre pour la Paix," (Ed. Fayard, Paris 1950, pp. 321-323, in *The Secret History of the Jesuits*, ed. Edmond Paris (Ontario, California: Chick Publications, 1983), 112-113.

[106] Paris, *The Secret History of the Jesuits*, 113.

> epidemics and inhuman sufferings cost France one hundred thousand dead.[107]

> The Crimean war, between France and Russia, is not a political war, but a holy war; it is not a State fighting another State, people fighting other people, but singularly a war of religion, a Crusade … [108]

Mexico

The Mexican objective is straightforward. The Reformation/Counter-Reformation battle is alive and well. Where would Mexico be today if Protestantism had been allowed to spread into Mexico? Would the United States be experiencing the current issue of illegal immigration and the building of the wall to protect the United States' southern border? Many Protestant countries are free and have free markets, educational opportunities for all levels of society, a high standard of living, etc. This is speculation, but the probability of the Mexican and United States relationship may have turned out like the Canadian and United States relationship, more stable with prosperity on both sides.

> To transform a lay-republic into an empire and offer it to Maximilien, archduke of Austria. Austria is the papacy's number one pillar. The aim is also to erect a barrier which would contain the influence of the

---

[107] Paul Leon, of the Institute, "La gurre pour la Paix," (Ed. Fayard, Paris 1950, pp. 321-323), in *The Secret History of the Jesuits*, ed. Edmond Paris (Ontario, California: Chick Publications, 1983), 113.

[108] Quoted by Monsignor Journet: "Exigences chretiennes en politique" (Ed. L.V.F. Paris 1945, p.274), in *The Secret History of the Jesuits*, ed. Edmond Paris (Ontario, California: Chick Publications, 1983), p.113.

> Protestant United States of the States of South America, strongholds of the Roman church.[109]
>
> M. Albert Bayet wrote with sagacity: "The war's aim is to establish a Catholic empire in Mexico and curtail the peoples' right to self rule; as during the Syrian campaign and the two Chinese campaigns, it tends especially to serve catholic interests.[110]
>
> We know how, in 1867, after the French army had reembarked, Maximilien, the unfortunate champion of the Holy See, was made a prisoner when Queretaro surrendered and was shot dead, ...
>
> Nevertheless, the time was getting nearer when France was to pay, once again, much more dearly for the *political support the Vatican* assured the imperial throne. While the French army was spilling its blood in the four corners of the world, and getting weaker while *defending interests which were not hers*, Prussia, under the heavy hand of the future "iron chancellor," was busy expanding its military might in order to unite the German states in a single block.[111] (Emphasis added)

THE DECLINE OF THE FRENCH EMPIRE

France begins to desire to enter the Modern Age. But as we will see in the coming two World Wars, France was not in a position

---

[109] Paris, *The Secret History of the Jesuits*, 114.

[110] Albert Bayet: "Histoire de France" (Ed. Du Sagattaire, Paris 1938, p.282), in *The Secret History of the Jesuits*, ed. Edmond Paris (Ontario, California: Chick Publications, 1983), 114.

[111] Paris, *The Secret History of the Jesuits*, 114.

to defend her sovereign aspirations. To the Jesuits and the papacy, France is a pawn in their chess game; they are nothing but a means to an end. They can be discarded as soon as a suitable substitute is available.

> The artillery is out of date. Our cannons are still loaded through the muzzle," wrote Rothan, French minister at Frankfurt who can see disaster coming....
>
> The war instigators (Jesuits) are not concerned....
>
> France declared war; this "war of 1870, which history proved to be the work of the Jesuits." As M. Gaston Bally wrote.[112]

> The consequences were: the collapse of the Empire and the counter-coup for the papal throne which followed ... The imperial edifice and the papal edifice, crowned by the Jesuits, fell in the same mud, in spite of the Immaculate Conception and papal infallibility; but alas, it was over the ashes of France.[113]

> In 1864, Pius IX published the encyclical letter "Quanta Cura," accomplished by the "Syllabus" which anathematized the best political principles of the contemporary societies. "Anathema on all that is dear to modern France! Modern France wants the independence power. Modern France wants the liberty of conscience and liberty of worship; the 'Syllabus' teaches that the Roman church has the right to use force and reinstate the Inquisition.[114]

---

[112] Ibid., 115.

[113] Gaston Bally, op. cit., pp. 100,101, in *The Secret History of the Jesuits*, ed. Edmond Paris (Ontario, California: Chick Publications, 1983), 115.

[114] Paris, *The Secret History of the Jesuits*, 117-118.

These are the doctrines taught by the Jesuits in their colleges. They are at the front of the army of counter-revolution ... *Their mission consists of bringing up the youth put in their care with hatred for the principles on which French society rests*, principles laid down by former generations at a great cost....[115] (Emphasis added. We see this in the United States today.)

... Through the 'Syllabus' of 1864 which they themselves drew up, Pius IX declared war on all free thought and sanctioned, a few years later, the dogma of infallibility which is a real historical anachronism and of which modern science could not care less.[116]

No need to say that the Jesuits, all-powerful in Rome, as much because of their spirit as of their organization, were going to engage the papacy in international politics more and more, as M. Louis Roguelin wrote: "Since she lost her temporal power, the Church of Rome took advantage of every opportunity to regain all the ground she was constrained to abandon, through recrudescence of diplomatic activities; *as her cleverly concealed scheme is to divide in order to reign, she tried to turn every conflict in her favor*.[117] (Emphasis added)

---

[115] Adolphe Michel: op. cit., p. 77ff, in *The Secret History of the Jesuits*, ed. Edmond Paris (Ontario, California: Chick Publications, 1983), 118.

[116] Louis Roguelin: "L'Eglise cretienne primitive et le catholicisme' (Paris, Maurice Boivent, 1927, pp. 79-81), in *The Secret History of the Jesuits*, ed. Edmond Paris (Ontario, California: Chick Publications, 1983), p.121.

[117] Paris, The Secret History of the Jesuits, 122.

Dreyfus Affair

The Republic side of France grew tired of the Roman yoke. The Jesuits prefer a monarchy that they can manipulate and control. The country begins to experience a rift, and the Catholic regions were located in the West and the South. Those favorable to the church supported the Royal Family of Chambord. There was an attempt in 1873 to restore a monarchy, and the clergy spread their propaganda and claimed that anyone desiring to vote for the *"free-thinkers" is guilty of sin.*

The Catholic Church breeds in or indoctrinates superstitions from generation to generation. Maintaining control is supreme for the papal monarchy, or it will collapse without its absolutism to Rome. Both sides of the power struggle committed coercive events and boycotts. The people grew tired of "Jesuitic ultramontanism." The country was divided. It was a simple distinction. Those with a high level of religious faith voted for the Catholic candidate and the opposing side that desired a Republic form of government voted for the anticlerical deputies and senators. In 1889, there was another attempt to reestablish the throne with General Boulanger, a dictatorial candidate, but it failed. In 1890, the rulership of France was no longer a monarchy but a general staff of elected officials. The Jesuits did not just halt their intrigues. France experienced a rift of its masses. On one side, you had those of religious faith, and on the other, those that wish for less interference in their lives from the clergy of a foreign power. Here was an opportunity to divide and conquer while the chaos was still fresh. The Dreyfus Affair caused a second rift, which would separate the people from their nations' military. The Lord Jesus made the following statement about a kingdom that is divided against itself:

> And Jesus knew their thoughts, and said unto them, Every kingdom divided against itself is brought to

> desolation; and every city or house divided against itself shall not stand:[118]

The Dreyfus conspiracy is described by Catholic historian, Adrien Dansette as follows:

> ... On the 22nd of December 1894, the Captain of artillery Alfred Dreyfus is proved guilty of treason, condemned to deportation for life imprisonment and cashiering. Three months earlier, our intelligence Service had discovered, at the German Embassy. A list of several documents to do with national defense; it established a resemblance between the writing of Captain Dreyfus and the one on that list. Immediately, the general-staff cried out: "it's him, it's the Jew."[119]

There is much more available to read on the injustice forced on Captain Dreyfus, who was innocent and was eventually freed and vindicated, but not before serving part of his sentence on the infamous "Devil's Island" and not before completing another rift in France. France was already weakened from serving as Rome's proxy military, the changes in government, and having the emotional divide of the people from their patriotism for their nation's military, all this on the doorstep of World War I. Wikipedia provides this brief description about the Dreyfus Affair:

> The Dreyfus Affair (French: *l'affaire Dreyfus,* pronounced [la.fɛʁ dʁɛ.fys]) was a political scandal that divided the Third French Republic from 1894 until its resolution in 1906. The affair is often seen as a modern and universal symbol of injustice, and it

---

118 Matthew 12:25, KJV.

119 Paris, *The Secret History of the Jesuits,* 138.

> remains one of the most notable examples of a complex miscarriage of justice and antisemitism. The major role played by the press and public opinion proved influential in the lasting social conflict.[120]

The persecution of the Jews in World War II traces its roots in centuries of antisemitism being cultivated in Europe, only to bloom into the unholy flower of the Holocaust. In the following article printed in the Church of Rome's "Civilta Cattolica," we can clearly decipher that the Jews are the scapegoat for the disharmony in Europe.

> Let us see now what was published in Rome itself by the "Civilta Cattolica," the Jesuits official publication, under the title "Il caso Dreyfus:[121]
>
> The Jews' emancipation has been the result of the so-called principles of 1789, whose yoke weighs heavily on all French people ... The Jews hold the Republic in their hands, which is more Hebraic than French ... The Jew has been created by God to be used as a spy wherever some treason is being prepared ... It is not only France, but also in Germany, Austria and Italy that the Jews must be excluded from the nation. Then, with the great harmony of former times re-

---

[120] "Dreyfus affair," Wikipedia: The Free Encyclopedia, 01/12/19, https://en.wikipedia.org/wiki/Dreyfus_affair.

[121] Paris, *The Secret History of the Jesuits*, 149.

> established, nations will find again their lost happiness.[122]

This may seem absurd to today's reader, but it was another successful deployment of propaganda to promote antisemitism into the minds that adhere to Catholicism. This was done decades before Hitler's rise to power, and it only fueled the flame for the Holocaust. If you go to the website for the *La Civilta Cattolica*[123], you will find the phrase; "Reflecting the Mind of The Vatican Since 1850."

Edmond Paris writes:

> After reading all this, written and published in the "Civilta Cattolica," it would be superfluous to dwell even deeper on the Order's culpability and we can only agree with what Joseph Reinach wrote then: "You see, it is the Jesuits who contrived this dark affair. And, for them, Dreyfus is only a pretext. What they want, and they admit it, is to strangle the laity and a redirected French Revolution … abolish foreign gods, the dogmas of 1789.[124]
>
> As we can see, Father Baily, Founder of "La Croix," had what it takes to make a saint: persecute the innocent, curse those who defend him, give them up to be murdered, uphold with all one's strength lying and iniquity, stir up discord and hatred: these are, to the eyes of the Roman church, solid titles for glory,

---

122 The "Civilta Cattolica" of the 5th February 1898, in *The Secret History of the Jesuits*, ed. Edmond Paris (Ontario, California: Chick Publications, 1983), 149.

123 https://laciviltacattolica.com/english-edition/.

124 Paris, *The Secret History of the Jesuits*, 150.

and we can understand her wish to bestow the halo on the author of these pious deeds.[125]

Abbe Brugerette says: "Today, when we consider those calls for the Inquisition to be brought back, for the persecution of the Jews, for the murder of Dreyfus' defenders, it is like listening to the delirious imaginations of wild and grotesque fanatics. Nevertheless, these are presented to us by the "La Croix" as great, comforting and cheering spectacle.[126]

Eminent historian Pierre Gaxotte stated the following:

The Dreyfus Affair was the decisive turning point ... judged by officers, it involved the military institution ... The Affair grew, became a political conflict, divided families, cut France into two. It had the effects of a war of religion ... It created hatred against the officers' corps ... It started anti-militarism.[127]

Justice had nevertheless triumphed in the end and the Abbe Fremont, who did not fear mentioning the sinister crusade led by Innocent III against the Albigenses when referring to the Affair, seemed to be a true prophet when he said:[128]

---

[125] Paris, *The Secret History of the Jesuits*, 152-153.

[126] Abbe Burgerette: "Le Pretre francals et la societe contemporaine" (Lethielleux, Paris 1933, II, pp. 450, in *The Secret History of the Jesuits*, ed. Edmond Paris (Ontario, California: Chick Publications, 1983), 152.

[127] Pierre Gaxotte, de l' Academie Francaise, "Historie de Francais" (Flammarion, Paris 1951, tome II, pp. 515-517, in *The Secret History of the Jesuits*, ed. Edmond Paris (Ontario, California: Chick Publications, 1983), 153.

[128] Ibid., 155.

> The Catholics are winning and they think they will overthrow the Republic because of the hatred for the Jews. But they will, I am afraid, only overthrow themselves.[129]

Above, we can see the preparations for World War I forming and the imbalance of France's military strength in comparison to Prussia. Austria was the first victim; the Hapsburg Monarchy had been a faithful stronghold within the Germanic lands. The Vatican would have to find a secular arm with the ability to stop the German expansion. The French Empire of Napoleon III was not prepared. Win or lose, the Vatican does not spill its own blood for its conquests but requires tributary payment in blood from those nations who are foolish enough to submit to the papacy.

> So during the 20th century, we see the Vatican actively engaged in the interior and exterior politics of countries, and even govern them thanks to Catholic parties. What's more, we will see it support "providential" men such as Mussolini and Hitler who, because of its help, will unleash the worst kind of catastrophes.[130]

In the 20th century, we find printed in the Catholic News Paper *La Croix*:

> In this text, published by "La Croix" on the 9th of August 1955, we can read: "The church does not want auxiliaries of another type than those of this *Company*

---

[129] Agnes Siegfried: "L'Abbe Fremont" (F. Alcan, Paris 1932, II, p. 163), in *The Secret History of the Jesuits*, ed. Edmond Paris (Ontario, California: Chick Publications, 1983), 155.

[130] Ibid., 123.

> *... may the sons of Loyola strive to follow the footprints of former ones ...* [131] (Emphasis added)

The Church of Rome's dogma has not changed; instead of change, *we found missionary adaptation*! In the next chapter, we will continue with Part 2 of the historical timeline in the 20th century.

[131] Ibid.

6

Blood-Stained Hands Part 2

1900–1914 Doorstep of World War I (WWI)

In the 20th century, we find France still plagued with the intrigues of the Jesuits and the plans of the Vatican. Europe is still in turmoil and desires to be free from the foreign chains of Rome. After all, it is the Industrial Age; what happened in the Middle Ages is history, right? France pushes for separation from Rome; this will build contention between France and the papacy. The papacy will hold a grudge against France and remind them that the popes don't like to lose.

> Waldek-Rousseau, president of the Council, declared in a speech pronounced at Toulouse on the 28th of October 1900: "Dispersed, but not suppressed, the religious Orders formed themselves again, bigger in numbers and more militant; they cover the territory with the network of a political organization whose links are innumerable and tightly knit, as we have seen through a recent trial."
>
> At last 1901, a law is passed, ruling that no Congregation can be formed without an authorization, and that those who do not ask for it within legal time

> will be automatically dissolved.... The law of 1904 abolished the teaching Orders.... After that, the friction between the French government and the Holy See will be constant.[1]
>
> We know that we will shock many people when we declare that we will necessarily be involved in politics. But anyone wanting to judge fairly can see that the *Sovereign Pontiff, invested by God with a supreme authority,* doesn't have the right to separate politics from the domain of faith and morals.[2] (Emphasis added)

The above-quoted statements bring to mind a sad truth which may justly apply to the *Dynasty of the Popes*. The popes believe they are the infallible substitute for God here on earth. Many popes have claimed to be God; this was also a common characteristic of pagan Rome's emperors. Are the popes exhibiting sinful pride and arrogance? Let the words of the popes speak for themselves:

1. Pope Innocent III (1198-1216) wrote: "We may according to the fullness of our power, dispose of the law and dispense above the law. Those whom the pope of Rome doth separate, it is not a man that separates them but God. For the pope holdeth place on earth, not simply of a man but of the true God." (1 Book of Gregory 9 Decret. c. 3)

---

[1] Paris, *The Secret History of the Jesuits*, 156.

[2] Agnes Siegfried: "L' Abbe Fremont" (F. Alcan. Paris 1932, II, 342.) in *The Secret History of the Jesuits*, ed. Edmond Paris (Ontario, California: Chick Publications, 1983), 157.

2. The Lateran Council addressing Pope Julius II in an oration delivered by Marcellus said: "Take care that we lose not that salvation, that life and breath which thou hast given us, for thou art our shepherd, thou art our physician, thou art our governor, thou art our husbandman, thou art finally another God on earth." (Council Edition. Colm. Agrip. 1618)

3. Pope Nicholas said of himself: "I am in all and above all, so that God Himself and I, the vicar of God, hath both one consistory, and I am able to do almost all that God can do... wherefore, if those things that I do be said not to be done of man, but of God, what do you make of me but God? Again, if prelates of the church be called of Constantine for gods, I then being above all prelates, seem by this reason to be above all gods. Wherefore, no marvel, if it be in my power to dispense with all things, yea with the precepts of Christ." (Decret. par. Distinct 96 ch. 7 edit. Lugo 1661)

4. The RC New York Catechism states: "The pope takes the place of Jesus Christ on earth... by divine right the pope has supreme and full power in faith, in morals over each and every pastor and his flock. He is the true vicar, the head of the entire church, the father and teacher of all Christians. He is the infallible ruler, the founder of dogmas, the author of and the judge of councils; the universal ruler of truth, the arbiter of the world, the supreme judge of heaven and earth, the judge of all, being judged by no one, God himself on earth."

5. The title "Lord God the pope" appeared in the Canon Law of Rome. "To believe that our Lord God the pope has not the power to decree as he is decreed, is to be deemed heretical." (The Gloss extravagances of Pope John XXII Cum. Inter, tit XIV Ad Callem Sexti Decretalium, Paris, 1685)

   Father A. Pereira acknowledged: "It is quite certain that Popes have never disapproved or rejected this title "Lord God the pope" for the passage in the gloss referred to appears in the edition of the Canon Law published in Rome by Gregory XIII."

6. Pope Nicholas I declared that "the appellation of God had been confirmed by Constantine on the pope, who being God, cannot be judged by man." (Labb IX Dist.: 96 Can 7 Satis Evidentur Decret Gratian Primer Para)

7. Speaking [in] the name of the pope (a rhetorical device) Cardinal Manning said: "I acknowledge no civil superior, I am the subject of no prince, and I claim more than this, I claim to be the supreme judge on earth and director of the consciences of men, I am the last supreme judge of what is right and wrong." (Sermon in the Pro Cathedral, Kensington, Tablet Oct 9, 1864)[3]

The popes are exalting themselves just as Lucifer did before his fall. Refer to Isaiah 14:13-14, *the five I wills*.

---

[3] "Have Popes Really Claimed to be God?" July 3, 2019, http://www.geoffhorton.com/PapalClaims.html.

1. I will ascend into heaven.
2. I will exalt my throne above the stars of God.
3. I will sit also upon the mount of the congregation.
4. I will ascend above the heights of the clouds.
5. *I will be like the Most High.*

The popes claim to be the Vicar of Christ, acting as His Ambassador to the world. Noah Webster's definition of *ambassador* refers to the word "embassador."

> EMBAS'SADOR, noun;
> 1. A minister of the highest rank employed by one prince or state, at the court of another, *to manage the public concerns of his own prince* or state, and *representing the power and dignity of his sovereign*. Embassadors are ordinary, when they reside permanently at a foreign court; or extraordinary, when they are sent on a special occasion. They are also called ministers. Envoys are ministers employed on special occasions, and are of less dignity.[4] (Emphasis added)

Up to this point in the historical timeline, we have reviewed the capabilities of Rome's Vicars of Christ. These Vicars have stained their hands with the death and blood of millions of innocent people through the centuries. The papacy believes it is just in the sight of God, but the Bible refutes that point. We are warned by God's t*hird commandment* not to take the Lord's name in vain. Don't claim His name in emptiness or falsehood.

---

[4] "Embassador," *Webster's Dictionary* 1828-Online Edition, 03/21/2019, http://webstersdictionary1828.com/Dictionary/Embassador.

> Thou shalt not take the name of the LORD thy God in vain; for the LORD will not hold him guiltless that taketh his name in vain.[5]

With this false belief of authority, supposedly from God, the papacy, along with the Jesuit Order, has committed some of the most heinous atrocities against humanity. It appears that they have committed every sin known to man through the centuries. Jesus Christ made it very clear about those who take His name in vain.

> Wherefore *by their fruits* ye shall know them. Not every one that saith unto me, Lord, Lord, shall enter into the kingdom of heaven; but he that doeth the will of my Father which is in heaven. Many will say to me in that day, Lord, Lord, have we not prophesied in thy name? And in thy name have cast out devils? And in thy name done many wonderful works? And then will I profess unto them, I never knew you: depart from me, *ye that work iniquity.* [6] (Emphasis added)

Let's continue with the timeline.

> So Pius X, as soon as he had acceded to Saint-Peter's throne, publicly declared that, for him, the pope's authority must be felt in every domain, and that political clericalism is not only a right but a duty. He also chose for his secretary of State a Spanish prelate, Monsignor Merry del Val who was thirty-eight years

---

[5] Exodus 20:7.

[6] Matthew 7:20-23, KJV.

> old and, like him, *passionately pro-German and anti-French.*[7] (Emphasis added)
>
> Other conflicts arose concerning French bishops, considered in Rome to be too Republican. At last, tired of the constant difficulties arising from the Vatican's infringements of the terms of the Concordat, the French government put an end, on the 29th of July 1904, to "relations which were made void by the Holy See."[8]

From Edward Bernays' book *Propaganda*:

> ... Formerly the rulers were the leaders. They laid out the course of history, by the simple process of doing what they wanted. And if nowadays the successors of the rulers, those whose position or ability gives them power, can no longer do what they want without the approval of the masses, they find in propaganda a tool which is increasingly powerful in gaining that approval. Therefore, propaganda is here to stay.[9]

The above quote is inserted here to set the premise for the transition into the 20th century. Below is a quote by General Wernz (*black pope*) demanding obedience to his authority. *Old World* rulers did as they pleased if it was within their power to do so. These rulers were acting on illegitimate power. Wernz's quotation brings up the distinction between power and authority again. Below we see the *black pope,* Father Wernz, claiming authority over a foreign nation, France.

---

[7] Paris, *The Secret History of the Jesuits*, 157.

[8]" Ibid., 159.

[9] Bernays, *Propaganda,* 27.

Any political entity with enough power can unjustly impose its authority over others. It's known as tyranny. We have seen this exercised time and time again consistently, by the Church of Rome through the centuries, only to result in the death of thousands of innocent people. Without the craft of the Jesuits to manipulate foreign nations into doing the bidding of Rome, the Vatican would not have the power it exercises. Catholicism uses superstition and religious dogma to bind the Catholic mind.

Rome is standing on the doorstep of the 20th century, and its old paradigms are now antiquated. The Vatican can no longer bludgeon and do as she pleases. The opinion of the masses will matter. Rome has not changed, but the world's circumstances have. The Vatican must take a more subtle approach. The Vatican is one of the eldest powers left by the *Old World*. In those days, the papacy could issue a Bull, and thousands of "heretics" would be slaughtered. The genocides still take place, but the connection to Rome is better concealed.

As said before, Rome has not changed its dogmas or repented of its Inquisitions. These approaches are still the first choice for Rome. However, the global backlash would expose the Vatican for what it is. Rome will have to use smoke and mirrors to appease public opinion, while behind the scenes, it is business as usual. Now the quote from the black pope.

> Besides, it was at that time that Father Wernz, general of this Order, wrote: "The State is under the church's jurisdiction, *so secular authority* is indeed *under the subjection of ecclesiastical authority* and has to obey."[10] (Emphasis added)

---

[10] Pierre Dominique: "La politique des Jesuites" Grasset, Paris 1955, p.241, in *The Secret History of the Jesuits*, ed. Edmond Paris (Ontario, California: Chick Publications, 1983), 160.

That is the doctrine of these intransigent champions of theocracy, counselors as well as those who execute their commands, who made themselves indispensable at the Vatican, so much so that, today, it would be absolutely impossible to distinguish even the smallest difference between "the black pope" and "the white pope": they are one and the same, And, when we refer to the politics of the Vatican, we simply mean the Jesuits politics.[11]

While the Jesuits had effectually worked, through the "Dreyfus Affair," at dividing the French people and weakening the prestige of our army, in Germany, they were doing the exact opposite. Bismark who, himself, had launched in the past the "Kulturkampf" against the Catholic church, was being loaded with her favors. This is what we are told by the Catholic writer, Joseph Rovan, who also explains it:[12]

Bismark will be the first Protestant to receive the "Order of Christ" with jewels, one of the highest honors of the church. The German government allows newspapers devoted to it to publish the fact that the chancellor would be ready effectually to uphold the pope's pretentions of a partial restoration of his temporal authority.[13]

---

[11] Paris, *The Secret History of the Jesuits,* 160.

[12] Ibid., 161.

[13] Joseph Rovan: "Le catholicisme politique en Allemagne" Paris 1956, pp. 121, 150ff, in *The Secret History of the Jesuits,* ed. Edmond Paris (Ontario, California: Chick Publications, 1983), 161.

> His (Bismark) secretary of State wrote to the nuncio of Munich: "In view of the approaching revision of the religious legislation which, as we have reasons to believe, will be carried out in a conciliatory manner, the Holy-Father wishes that the Centre promote, in every possible way, the projects of the military."[14]

WORLD WAR I

Vatican Secretary of State, Merry del Val:

> "During the audience I had that day with His Holiness, the Holy-Father, who started the conversation by mentioning our energetic steps taken in Belgrade, he made some characteristic remarks: "It would certainly have been better," said his Holiness, "if Austria-Hungary had punished the Serbians for all the wrongs they had done.[15]
>
> However, the affair dragged on in 1913. But on the 28th of June 1914, the archduke Francois-Ferdinand was murdered at Sarajevo. The Serbian government had nothing to do with this crime committed by a Macedonian student, but it was the perfect excuse for the emperor Francois-Joseph to start hostilities.[16]

Unlike the term for the Presidency of the United States, which may extend from four to eight years, an elected pope's

---

[14] Jean Bruhat, "Le Vatican contre les peoples" (Paralleles, 21st December 1950), in *The Secret History of the Jesuits*, ed. Edmond Paris (Ontario, California: Chick Publications, 1983), 162.

[15] "Document" P.A. XI/291, in *The Secret History of the Jesuits*, ed. Edmond Paris (Ontario, California: Chick Publications, 1983), 165.

[16] Paris, *The Secret History of the Jesuits*, 164-165.

papacy may last decades. As with France, when the Vatican wants revenge and time extends beyond a pope's tenure, he merely passes this desire on to the next elected pope, as a runner passes the baton in a track meet. Rome weaves her revenge into the next available political intrigue. Above and below, we have quotes giving clarity that Pope Pius X strongly expressed his desire to inflict punishment on the Serbian nation. For the papacy, this desire will come to fruition in the second World War, through the most horrifying means.

The opinion of the Curia, Secretary of State:

> It would have been impossible to detect any spirit of indulgence and conciliation in the words of His Eminence. It is true that he described the note to Serbia as very harsh, but he nevertheless approved of it entirely and, at the same time and indirectly, *expressed the wish that the Monarchy would finish the job*. Indeed, added the cardinal, it was a pity that Serbia had not been humiliated much earlier, as it could have been done. Then, without such great risks attached. *This declaration echoes the wishes of the pope who, over the past few years, often expressed regret that Austria-Hungary had neglected 'chastising' her dangerous neighbor on the Danube.*[17] (Emphasis added)
>
> So the Holy See was fully conscious of the "great risks" represented by a conflict between Austria and Serbia, but, *nevertheless, did all in its power to encourage it. The Holy-Father and his Jesuit counselors were not concerned about the sufferings of "Christian nations." It was not the first time that these nations were used for the*

---

[17] "Veroffentlichungen der (Commission fur Neuere Gescuichte Osterreichs," 26 Wien-Leipzig 1930, pp. 893-894, in *The Secret History of the Jesuits*, ed. Edmond Paris (Ontario, California: Chick Publications, 1983), 166.

> *benefit of Roman politics. The opportunity wished for had come at last to use the Germanic secular arm against Orthodox Russia, "godless" France which needed a "thorough bleeding," and, as a bonus, against "heretic" England. Everything seemed to promise a "lively and happy" war.*[18]

Being a theocracy, the Vatican wields its influence in two spheres, one that is political and the other religious. Both are a means of control. Had Pope Pius X indeed been infallible and genuinely the Vicar of Christ, would it have been rational for him to obey the Holy Bible and implement the instructions about revenge given by the Apostle Paul in the Book of Romans when dealing with Serbs?

> Recompense to no man evil for evil. Provide things honest in the sight of all men. If it be possible, as much as lieth in you, live peaceably with all men. Dearly beloved, avenge not yourselves, but rather give place unto wrath: for it is written, Vengeance is mine; I will repay, saith the Lord.[19]

The papacy has repeatedly offered its hand of grace to individuals and nations who submit to Rome's wishes. Is that grace? History's annuals give a perspective of Catholicism's hierarchy using the godless tactics that other world tyrants have used.

> If this was satire, it could not be put in a better way. A few years before 1914. M. Yves Guyot, a true prophet, said:[20] "If war breaks out, listen, you men who think that the Roman church is the symbol of

---

[18] Paris, *The Secret History of the Jesuits*, 167.

[19] Romans 12:17-19, KJV.

[20] Paris, *The Secret History of the Jesuits*, 168.

order and peace, and do not search for blame outside the Vatican: it will be the sly instigator, as in the war of 1870."[21]

INTRODUCTION TO WORLD WAR II (WWII)

What does the word Inquisition trigger in your past education? Do you think of your school days history classes? Were you taught that the Roman Catholic and Spanish Inquisitions were during the Middle Ages, the Dark Ages? A time long ago, when men were barbaric, where the Roman Catholic Church and its religious tributaries tortured and killed millions in the name of God? Those who would not submit to Catholicism's dogma suffered the most extreme cruelty and torture. If hell were a place on earth, the Inquisitors of the Roman Catholic Church would be its keepers.

In this section, we will be reviewing the debate, which implies there was a connection between the papacy, Hitler's Nazi regime, Mussolini, and Ante Pavelic's terrorist group, the "Ustashe." Did the Church of Rome (Vatican hierarchy) perpetuate the Holocaust with its approval and its participation by its clergy?

There was a hatred for the Jews in Catholic Europe, but what was the origin of this hatred? This hatred warranted the Nazis to murder millions of Jewish men, women, and children. As in previous chapters, I have introduced historical accounts for you. Do these accounts answer the following questions? Was the Vatican fully aware of the Holocaust atrocities that were happening within the papacy's sphere of influence? Did the Church of Rome with her political power and wealth look the other way when she could have intervened?

---

[21] Yves Guyot: "Bilan polituque de I'Eglise," p.139, in *The Secret History of the Jesuits*, ed. Edmond Paris (Ontario, California: Chick Publications, 1983), 168.

Without a doubt, the Inquisitions are not the will of a holy God. And to clarify, I am speaking of the God of the Bible, where Jesus came to offer salvation, not the slaughter and torture of millions of innocent people. The Jesuits and papacy failed to regain control over European nations through World War I, the *Great War*. Rome was unable to punish the Serbian people as Pope Pius X had wished. The papacy saw the Eastern Orthodox church as a thorn in its side. The Bolshevik Revolution provided Rome's desired persecution for the Eastern Orthodox church. The protector of the Orthodox church was the Russian Czars. The Russian Imperial Romanov Family of Czar Nicholas II was murdered during the revolution, thereby removing the Eastern Orthodox church's primary protector.

[22]

The Inquisition didn't end. The Vatican would use the Jesuit's craft, and Rome's political power and wealth, to make pacts with the secular forces of foreign countries to do Rome's bidding. Where the papacy's failed in WWI to punish the Serbian people, the Church of Rome will succeed in WWII through Ante Pavelic. Ante Pavelic ferociously persecuted the Serbian people. Where

[22] https://en.wikipedia.org/wiki/Execution_of_the_Romanov_family#/media/File:Russian_Imperial_Family_1913.jpg.

the Hapsburgs of the Austria-Hungary Empire failed, the Vatican would raise another Austrian to complete the assignment, Adolf Hitler.

Previous pages reviewed the portion of the timeline that covered centuries before WWI and WWII. During that time, the massacres (Inquisition) of the innocent continued. The period from WWI and WWII falls into a period known as the *Second Industrial Revolution*—a time many of us would consider the *Modern Age*. The Church of Rome was establishing the Jews to take the fall for Europe's problems long before the World Wars. Racism is not intrinsic in Catholic Europe. We can look back to the beginning of the second millennium after Jesus's first Advent. From Dave Hunt's book, *A Woman Rides the Beast,* we have:

> Pope Urban II (1088-99), inspirer of the first Crusade, decreed that all heretics were to be tortured and killed. That became a dogma of the church. Acclaimed as the 'angelic doctor,' even St. Thomas Aquinas taught that non-Catholics, or heretics, could, after a second warning, be legitimately killed. His exact words are: "*they have merited to be excluded from the earth by death.*"[23]
>
> The popes themselves were the authority behind the Inquisitions. They wielded the power of life and death even over emperors. Had any pope opposed the Inquisition, he could have stopped it during his papacy at least. Where do we read that the popes thundered anathemas against the secular authorities who imposed so many and such gruesome deaths upon their victims? Never! Civil magistrates would

---

[23] St. Thomas Aquinas, *Summa Theologica* (Louis Guerin, Barri-Ducis, 1857), vol. 4, p.90, *in A Woman Rides the Beast*, ed. Dave Hunt (Eugene, Oregon: Harvest House Publishers, 1994), 246-247.

> have desisted from these loathsome murders in order to save their own souls, but papal orders to stop the Inquisitions never came.[24]

> In 1096 Pope Urban II inspired the first crusade to retake Jerusalem from the Muslims. With the cross on their shields and armor, the Crusaders massacred Jews across Europe on their way to the Holy Land. Almost their first act upon taking Jerusalem "for Holy Mother church" was to herd all of the Jews into the synagogue and set it ablaze. These facts of history cannot be swept under the carpet of ecumenical togetherness as though they never happened.[25]

The pope's Crusaders killed Jews on their way to liberate Jerusalem. If the Crusaders executed the Jews with the Muslims, who were the Crusaders rescuing in Jerusalem?

The Spanish Inquisition was no different; the Jews suffered greatly. In 1492, the Catholic Monarchs Ferdinand and Isabel of Castile and Aragon declared an edict to expel all Jews who would not convert to Catholicism. Centuries later, visitors to the City of Girona, Spain were able to receive a tourist's pamphlet that told a portion of the Spanish Inquisition that related to the expelling of the Jews:

> ... issued the edict expelling the Jews from Spanish territory ... [they had] no other choice but renunciation of religious belief or compulsory expatriation. Those who chose to convert to Christianity in order to avoid expulsion faced the full fury of the Inquisition, which had already begun to prosecute heretics

---

[24] Hunt, *A Woman Rides the Beast*, 247.

[25] Ibid., 82.

> in Girona in 1490 ... Some Jewish families were virtually wiped out at the hands of the Inquisitors.[26]

Rome was promoting, through action and indoctrination, a hatred for Jews to the Catholic laity. Not every Catholic agreed with Rome's racism; many Jews were saved during the Holocaust by loving Catholics. Note the centuries of *doctrine*, propaganda, and hatred by the Vatican's Catholicism toward the Jews. The Bible speaks of the church as the body of Christ and Jerusalem as the Holy City. Both descriptions are singular. The Vatican, with its Catholicism, tries to claim these titles, on the premise that the Jews forfeit this right because they killed Jesus Christ. Jesus gave His life willingly! God's plan was beyond man's understanding. Jesus gave His life of His own obedient choice to fulfill His Father's will for the completion of a *New Covenant* to reconcile humanity back to God—the whole world, including the Jews.

> Therefore doth my Father love me, because I lay down my life, that I might take it again. *No man taketh it from me, but I lay it down of myself.* I have power to lay it down, and I have power to take it again. This commandment have I received of my Father.[27] (Emphasis added)

We can reference God's Word, where the Apostle Paul writes in the Book of Romans that Israel, the Jewish nation is to be saved.

> For I would not, brethren, that ye should be ignorant of this mystery, lest ye should be wise in your own conceits; that blindness in part is happened to Israel,

---

[26] Hunt, *A Woman Rides the Beast*, 271.

[27] John 10:17-18, KJV.

> until the fulness of the Gentiles be come in. And so all Israel shall be saved: as it is written, There shall come out of Sion the Deliverer, and shall turn away ungodliness from Jacob: For this is my covenant unto them, when I shall take away their sins. As concerning the gospel, they are enemies for your sakes: but as touching the election, they are beloved for the fathers' sakes. For the gifts and calling of God are without repentance.[28]

God has not forgotten His promises to the Jewish nation. Revelation 7 and 14 explain how God will use 12,000 Jewish men from each tribe of Israel to fulfill prophecy. These 144,000 witnesses will preach the everlasting gospel. If the Jews are still part of God's plan, then ask yourself who or what spiritual being is behind the motivation of killing the Jews? And who are the devil's human pawns?

WWII comes along, and Hitler's Nazi regime systematically murder the Jews. When you read the letters and autobiographies of the Nazi SS leaders Hitler, Himmler, and Rudolf Hoess (Commandant of Auschwitz), these men believed they were in the right. If you want to remove any doubt that evil is real, read the de*tails of the Holocaust and the butchering of the Serbian people during WWII. Men possessing an evil spirit could only do these horrific acts.* This same spirit operated in the minds of the men who tortured and killed during the Inquisitions. The following pages list written accounts of the Nazi Party, the Catholic Church, and puppet regimes that took part in the Holocaust. These account for the death of millions by the time the war was over.

---

[28] Romans 11:25-29, KJV.

PREPARATION FOR WWII

> In 1919, the sons of Loyola reaped the bitter fruits of their criminal politics. *France had not succumbed to the "thorough bleeding."* The apostolic empire of the Hapsburgs, which they had *encouraged to "punish the Serbians,"* had disintegrated, liberating the Orthodox Slavs from the yoke of Rome. Russia, instead of coming back to the Roman fold, had become Marxist, anti-clerical and officially atheistic. As for invincible Germany, it floundered in the chaos. But the proud nature of the Company would never consider confessing a sin. When Benedict XV died in 1922, it was ready to start again on a new basis. Is it not all-powerful in Rome?[29] (Emphasis added)

The mission of the Jesuits had failed, but this was only a temporary setback. The Jesuits would again weave a new plan where the ends justify the means. France and the Serbian people were still in the crosshairs of Rome.

The subsequent paragraphs contain excerpts from the authors, professors, and historians. The passages are offered to go beyond a suggestion for those that may still doubt the involvement of the Roman Catholic Church in the political affairs of foreign nations. These writings will aid in recreating the imagery of the struggle for the Catholic Church in Germany during the rise of the Nazi Party. Documents also refute the papacy's claimed neutrality. In the past, the Vatican would threaten Catholic kings or political leaders with excommunication to bring them back under papacy control. But Hitler and Mussolini received no such threat or public admonishment. Why?

Large portions of the German people were confused by the division in their church leadership. The Church of Rome is far

---

[29] Paris, *The Secret History of the Jesuits*, 174.

from innocent of being the catalyst for Hitler and Mussolini's rise to power and their associated massacres of thousands of innocent men, women, and children. From French Historian Adolphe Michel, we have the following:

> Of all the factors which have played a part in the international life of a century full of confusion and upheavals, one of the most decisive—nevertheless best recognized—resides in the ambition of the Roman church. Her secular desire to extend her influence towards the East made her the "spiritual" ally of Pan-Germanism and its accomplice in the attempt to gain supreme power which twice 1914 and 1939, brought death and ruin to the peoples of Europe.
>
> The public is practically unaware of the overwhelming responsibility carried by the Vatican and its Jesuits in the start of the two world wars, a situation which may be explained in part by the gigantic finances at the disposition of the Vatican and its Jesuits, giving them power in so many spheres, especially since the last conflict. In fact, the part they took in those tragic events has hardly been mentioned until now, except by apologists eager to disguise it.[30]

The *Mercure de France*—a French gazette and literary magazine—Catholic writer Joseph Royan, author Edmond Paris, and the Catholic newspaper *La Croix* offer insight into the connection between the papacy and Hitler before WWII. There are times when the real agenda of political leaders are not fully known until they are enabled—having the necessary resources at their

[30] See Edmond Paris: Le Vatican contre L'Europe (Fischbacher, Paris) (also P.T.S. London) and L. Duca "L' Or du Vatican" (Laffront, Paris), in *The Secret History of the Jesuits*, ed. Edmond Paris (Ontario, California: Chick Publications, 1983), 12.

disposal. It is at that point a political leader can bring their hidden plans to fruition.

> On the first of May 1938, the "Mercure de France" reminded us of what was said four years earlier: "The Mercure de France of the 15th of January 1934 said—and nobody contradicted it—that it was Pius XII who 'made' Hitler. He came to power, not so much through legal means, but because the pope influenced the Centrum (German Catholic party) ... Does the Vatican think it made a political error in opening the way to power to Hitler? It doesn't seem so..."[31]

> Mr. Joseph Rovan, Catholic writer, comments on the diplomatic agreement between the Vatican and the Nazi Reich on the 8th of July 1933: "The Concordat brought to the national socialist government, considered nearly everywhere to be made up of usurpers, if not brigands, the seal of an agreement with the oldest international power (the Vatican). In a way, it was the equivalent of a diploma of international honorability.[32]

> Many Catholic authors couldn't hide their surprise—and grief—when writing about the inhuman indifference shown by Pius XII in the face of the worst kind of atrocities committed by those in his favor.[33]

---

[31] Paris, *The Secret History of the Jesuits*, 13.

[32]" Le catholicisme politique en Allemagne, Paris 1956, p. 231, Ed. Du Seuil, in *The Secret History of the Jesuits*, ed. Edmond Paris (Ontario, California: Chick Publications, 1983), 13.

[33] Paris, *The Secret History of the Jesuits*, 16.

Listen to what Mr. Alfred Grosser, professor at the Institute of political studies of Paris University, says: "The very concise book of Guenter Lewy: "The Catholic church and Nazi Germany" (New York, McGraw Hill-1964) says that all the documents agree to show the Catholic church cooperating with the Hitler regime ... In 1933, when the Concordat forced the bishops to swear an oath of allegiance to the Nazi government, the concentration camps were already open ... the reading of quotations compiled by Guenter Lewy proves this overwhelmingly. We find in them some crushing evidence from personalities such as Cardinal Faulhaber and the Jesuit Gustav Gundlach."[34]

The thurifers of the Vatican must bow their heads in shame when an Italian member of parliament cries out: *"The pope's hands are dripping with blood."* (Speech by Laura Diaz, member of parliament for Livourne, delivered at Ortona on the 15th of April 1946)[35], or when the students of Cardiff University College choose as the theme for a conference: "Should the pope be brought to trial as a war criminal?"[36] (Emphasis added)

---

[34] Saul Friedlander: "Pie XII et le IIIe Reich" (Ed. Du Seuil, Paris 1964) in *The Secret History of the Jesuits*, ed. Edmond Paris (Ontario, California: Chick Publications, 1983), 18.

[35] Paris, *The Secret History of the Jesuits*, 18.

[36] "La Croix." 2nd April 1946.

GERMANY BEFORE WWII

The German Catholic faith began to flourish again; it experienced a resurgence of its strength in Germany. When compared to the days of Protestant rule under Chancellor Otto von Bismarck, who was Lutheran, the Nazi Party increased in political power, and the Catholic leadership in Germany became divided. Some saw the Nazi incompatibility with church doctrine, while others leaned toward their nationalism and desired to see Germany return to power. There were conflicting decisions against Catholics becoming a member of the Nazi Socialist Party due to its non-compatibility with Catholicism. Any Catholic choosing to become members were prohibited from receiving the sacraments. Professor Guenter Lewy writes:

> Some Catholics were surprised and confused, for only a few weeks earlier they had been told to vote against Hitler and *for* the Catholic-led Center and Bavarian People's parties. [37]

> Catholic intellectual life flourished and men like Max Scheler and Romano Guardini and Catholic publications such as the Allgemeine Rundschau, Hochland and Stimmen der Zeit enjoyed high prestige among non-Catholics too. The Catholic daily press was strong. Moreover, German Catholics were able to strengthen their political influence, for the Catholic Center party, founded in 1870 as a counterforce to widespread anti-Catholic sentiments in Bismarck's Germany, now assumed a key role.[38]

---

[37] Guenter Lewy, *The Catholic Church and Nazi Germany*, rev. ed. (Da Capo Press, 2000) 4, Original print 1964.

[38] Ibid., 5.

Jesus Christ offers salvation, beyond the restraints of man, but here we see Catholic dogma being used as a means of control, a way to direct the Catholic masses. It is used to prohibit a Catholic's freedom of choice. This dogma doesn't have the same superstitious power today as it once held, but for the indoctrinated Catholic, this bridle still exists in varying degrees.

Many German Catholics were dissatisfied with their country's political and economic problems. There was also the displeasure with the outcome of the Treaty of Versailles. The Catholic laity did not make doctrinal decisions; the rank of Bishop and above make doctrinal decisions. The laity's responsibility was to follow the decisions of the church hierarchy, which was erratic at times. This indecision put the church laity in a moral struggle.

Here the primary focus in on the Roman Catholic Church's hierarchy, not the church laity. The hierarchy makes the decisions that control and dictate Catholicism's doctrine to the laypeople. The divided Catholic leadership only added to the turmoil. The fluctuation of what was considered acceptable to church doctrine, and what was not, began to create a division within the German Catholic Church clergy, which then disseminated down to the laymen. For many Germans, it became a struggle to obey the church blindly or follow their conscience.

Where was the freedom for the individual Catholics to follow their hearts or to be led by the Holy Spirit? The Catholic was forced to choose between *natural law* or obedience to church superiors. Natural law is the inherent knowledge that tells one that the extermination of a race of people (Jews) or the slaughter of thousands (Serbs) in the name of religion or ideology is wrong. Church doctrine dictated how they should vote.

Here is an example where the Catholic is expected to be a loyal citizen of the Vatican first before a loyal citizen of their host nation. History records the German bishops being of differing views on what to do and how to respond to the growing strength of the Nazi Party. From the beginning, it was the Catholic vote that established the Nazi Party. From Edmond Paris, we have the following accounts of the rise of Fascism with Mussolini and Hitler's climb to power during the reign of Pope Pius XI:

> In the defeat they just suffered, the sons of Loyola can see a glimmer of some hope. The Russian revolution, by eliminating the Czar, protector of the Orthodox church, had it not decapitated the great rival and helped the penetration of the Roman church?[39]

> On the 16th of November 1922, Parliament elected Mussolini by 306 votes to 116. In the meeting, one saw the Catholic group of don Sturzo, supposedly Christian-Democrat, voting unanimously for the first fascist government.[40]

> The pope, in February 1929, at the time of the treaty of Lateran, calls Mussolini "the man whom Providence allowed us to meet." Rome does not condemn what is commonly called the "Ethiopian aggression" and, in 1940, the Vatican is still Mussolini's sincere friend.[41]

> Ten years later, the same maneuver brought about a similar result in Germany. The Catholic "Zentrum" of Monsignor Kass assured, by its massive vote, the dictatorship of Nazism.[42]

---

[39] Paris, *The Secret History of the Jesuits*, 175.

[40] Pietro Nenni "Six and de guerre civile en Italie" (Librarie Valois, Paris 1930, p.146), in *The Secret History of the Jesuits*, ed. Edmond Paris (Ontario, California: Chick Publications, 1983), 177.

[41] Paris, *The Secret History of the Jesuits*, 176.

[42] Ibid., 177.

The Lateran Treaty, by which Mussolini showed his gratitude to the papacy, gave the Holy See, apart from the payment of one thousand 750 million liras (i.e., £20,000,000) the temporal sovereignty over the territory of Vatican City. Monsignor Cristiani, prelate of His Holiness, explains the significance of this event: *"It is certain that the Constitution of the Vatican City was a matter of prime importance in order to establish the papacy as a political power."*[43] (Emphasis added)

Hitler receives his impetus from Mussolini; the ideal of the Nazis is the same as in Italy ... Since Mussolini is at the head, all the sympathies are for Berlin... In 1923, his Fascism merges with National-Socialism; he becomes friends with Hitler to whom he supplies arms and money.[44]

From amongst these agitators, the choice of Germany's "regenerators "will fall upon Hitler, who is destined to triumph over the "democratic mistakes" under the Holy Father's standard. Of course, he is Catholic, like his principal collaborators.[45]

The Nazi regime is like a return to the government of southern Germany. The names and origins of its chiefs demonstrate it: Hitler is specifically Austrian,

---

[43]" Monsignor Cristiani: "Le Vatican politique," Imprimatur 15th of June 1956 (Ed. Du Centurion, Paris 1957, p.136), in *The Secret History of the Jesuits*, ed. Edmond Paris (Ontario, California: Chick Publications, 1983), 179.

[44]" Antonio Aniante: "Mussolini" (Grasset, Paris 1932, p.123ff), in *The Secret History of the Jesuits*, ed. Edmond Paris (Ontario, California: Chick Publications, 1983), 180.

[45] Paris, *The Secret History of the Jesuits*, 181-182.

Goering is Bavarian, Goebbels is Rhenish, and so on.[46]

In 1924, the Holy See signs a Concordat with Bavaria. In 1927, we read in "Cologne's Gazette": "Pius XI is certainly the most German pope who ever sat on the throne of Saint-Peter.[47]

Mercure de France, French Gazette writes:

The "Mercure de France" gave an excellent study in 1934: "In the beginning of 1932, German Catholics did not consider they had lost the cause but, in the spring, their chiefs seemed somewhat irresolute: they had been told that 'the pope was personally in favor of Hitler.'"[48]

That Pius XI was sympathetic to Hitler should not surprise us ... For him, Europe could settle down again only through Germany's hegemony ... The Vatican had thought of changing the centre of gravity of the Reich, through the Anschluss, for a long time, and the Company of Jesus was openly working towards that aim (Ledochowski's plan), especially in Austria. We know how Pius XI depended on Austria to make what he called his politics triumph. What had to be prevented was the hegemony of Protestant Prussia and, as the Reich was the one to dominate

[46] Gonzague de Reynold: "D'ou vient l'Allemagne" (Plon, Paris 1939, p.185.), in *The Secret History of the Jesuits*, ed. Edmond Paris (Ontario, California: Chick Publications, 1983), 182.

[47] Paris, *The Secret History of the Jesuits*, 182.

[48] Ibid., 182-183.

> Europe … a Reich had to be rebuilt where the Catholics would be masters … [49]

> In March 1933 "…Von Papen leaves for Rome. This man, whose past is so wicked, becomes a pious pilgrim with the mission to conclude a Concordat (for the whole of Germany) with the pope. He too will have to emulate Mussolini's overtures towards the Vatican." [50]

Again, early on, things looked promising for Germany. In the beginning, Hitler had the pope's acceptance. His political power appeared to be on the side of Catholics. This premise caused an increase in the strength of the German Catholic faith. However, doubts were also beginning to develop about whether the Nazi Party's rhetoric and promises toward the church could be trusted. Some clergy put their nationalism above their religion. This dilemma is an excellent example of how Christianity and the world system of politics cannot be yoked together.

Hitler executed many Catholic laities, priests, and bishops who took a stand in opposition to him. Grober of Freiburg had a priest, Max Josef Metzger, who was a pacifist and generated a manifesto for a new government after Germany lost the war. Metzger intended the Swedish Archbishop Eidem to receive his declaration. Metzger's error was his choice of couriers; his courier was an informant for the Gestapo. The Gestapo arrested Metzger for treason in June of 1943. Guenter Lewy documents the following:

---

[49] Ibid., 183.

[50] "Mercure de France;" "Pius XI and Hitler" (15th of January 1934), in *The Secret History of the Jesuits*, ed. Edmond Paris (Ontario, California: Chick Publications, 1983), 182-183.

> Appeals for clemency having failed, Metzger was put to death on April 17, 1944, one of seventy-four German Catholic priests executed or murdered by the Nazis.[51]

Hitler allowed the Catholic churches of Germany to operate as long as they didn't interfere with his plans. This strategy undermined the papacy's control, but Hitler, being a Catholic, only duplicated the Vatican's diplomacy. This same diplomacy was used by the Vatican when dealing with monarchs, regimes, and tributary states through the centuries.

The political systems of this world fall under the influence of Satan, who has the current rule over the World's operating system. The Church of Rome is guilty of some of the worst atrocities that can be committed against humanity. These acts of cruelty span centuries and point to the spirit of the antichrist, not the Holy Spirit, as the influencing force in the minds of these men.

It was the Catholic vote that put Hitler in power. Once the German people realized their error, the cost of putting the evil genie back in its bottle was too high. The Vatican wasn't in full agreement with Hitler, and never publicly denounced this member of the Catholic Church or publicly announced that the church laity should reject the Nazi regime. Had the Vatican made a strategic error, or is this the use of the Hegelian dialectic? The Vatican's desire to find an opposing force against Communism helped bring Mussolini's fascism and Hitler's Nazi regime to power. Unlike the monarchs of the past, the Vatican was unable to control these two tyrants; her only option was to reduce collateral damage to church interest. Author Dave Hunt writes:

> On March 13, 1933, at a conference of Bavarian bishops, Cardinal Faulhaber, just back from Rome,

[51] Lewy, *The Catholic Church and Nazi Germany, xxiii.*

reported that "the Holy Father, Pius XI, had publicly praised the Chancellor Adolf Hitler for the stand which he had taken against Communism....[R]eports were circulation again that the Vatican was anxious for the friendly co-operation of German Catholics with the Hitler government...."[52]

On March 23, Hitler announced that "the government of the Reich, [which] regards Christianity [Catholicism] as the unshakable foundation of the morals and the moral code of the nation, attach[es] the greatest value to friendly relations with the Holy See and [is] endeavoring to develop them." Five days later the German bishops publicly withdrew their previous opposition to the Nazi Party.[53] The strategy that Hitler had earlier outlined to Rauschning was working:

[52] Hunt, *A Woman Rides the Beast*, 274.

[53] Guenter Lewy, *The Catholic Church and Nazi Germany* (McGraw-Hill, 1964), in A Woman Rides the Beast, Dave Hunt.

[54]

Hermann Rauschning was an ex-Nazi and is considered a conservative revolutionary. He had briefly joined the Nazi Party, and in 1934, he renounced it. Rauschning left Germany in 1936 and eventually emigrated to the United States. He spoke out against the Nazi Party and wrote several books. In *Voice of Destruction,* Rauschning writes of Hitler's contempt for the Catholic clergy. If the clergy would not submit to Hitler's agenda, then he was willing to expose their secrets and hypocrisy to the world through the cinema. Rauschning quotes Hitler as follows:

> We should trap the priests by their notorious greed and self-indulgence. We shall thus be able to settle everything with them in perfect peace and harmony. I shall give them a few years' reprieve. Why should

[54] https://en.wikipedia.org/wiki/Hermann_Rauschning#/media/File:Hermann_Rauschning.jpg.

we quarrel? They will swallow anything in order to keep their material advantages.[55]

Persecution of the Jews

From Peter De Rosa's, *Vicars of Christ:*

> In 1936, Bishop Berning of Osnabruch had talked with the Fuehrer for over an hour. Hitler assured his lordship there was no fundamental difference between National Socialism and the Catholic church. Had not the church, he argued, looked on Jews as parasites and shut them in ghettos?
>
> "I am only doing," he boasted, "what the church has done for fifteen hundred years, only more effectively." Being a Catholic himself, he told Berning, he "admired and wanted to promote Christianity."[56]

Guenter Lewy writes:

> In 1939, Archbishop Grober declared that—The embarrassing fact that Jesus had been a Jew was handled in a similar manner. In a pastoral letter of 1939 Archbishop Grober conceded that Jesus Christ could not be made into an Aryan, but the Son of God had been fundamentally different from the Jews of his time—so much so that they hated him and demanded his crucifixion, and "*their murderous hatred had continued in later centuries.*" Jesus had been a Jew, admitted Bishop Hilfrich of Limburg in his pastoral letter for Lent 1939, but "the Christian religion has

---

[55] Hermann Rauschning, *The Voice of Destruction* (New York, G.P. Putman's Sons, 1940), 53.

[56] De Rosa, *Vicars of Christ*, 5.

> not grown out of the nature of this people, that is, is not influenced by their racial characteristics. Rather it has had to make its way against this people." The Jewish people the Bishop added, were guilty of the murder of God and had been *under a curse* since the day of the crucifixion....[57] (Emphasis added)

Archbishop Grober's pastoral letter is a sad example of the hypocrisy of the Catholic Church. Catholicism has hunted and persecuted and murdered non-Catholic religions for centuries. The Church of Rome's hierarchy, now in the 20th century, has not changed its intolerance of other religions. When the Vatican does bend its view, it is in the form of *missionary adaptation* to complete the papacy's agenda. We will see more missionary adaptation in the following chapter on the *ecumenical movement*.

From von Papen's memoirs as cited in Paris's, *Secret History of the Jesuits*:

> This fervor is easily explained when we read the following from von Papen: "The general terms of the Concordat were more favorable than all other similar agreements signed by the Vatican." and, "the Chancellor Hitler asked me to assure the papal secretary of State (Cardinal Pacelli) that he would immediately muzzle the anticlerical clan."[58]

Dave Hunt points out Hitler's spiritual convictions:

> That Hitler was a Catholic in good standing made his promises of peaceful partnership with the church believable. He had been raised in a traditional Catholic

[57] Lewy, *The Catholic Church and Nazi Germany*, 277.

[58] Franz von Papen: "Memoires" (Flammarion, Paris 1953, pp. 207, in *The Secret History of the Jesuits*, ed. Edmond Paris (Ontario, California: Chick Publications, 1983), 184.

> family, had regularly attended Mass, had served as an altar boy, had hoped at one time to become a priest, and had attended school as a boy in a Benedictine monastery at Lambach. The abbot was heavily involved in the occult and Eastern mysticism, and it was at this monastery that Hitler first encountered the Hindu swastika which he later adopted.[59]
>
> For Hitler, however, the Holocaust was a highly spiritual undertaking. In line with his conviction that he was doing God's will in exterminating the Jews, Hitler ordered that the Final Solution be executed "as humanely as possible." In spite of his persecution of the church whenever he perceived that it stood in his way, Hitler insisted to the very end, "I am now as before a Catholic and will always remain so." He was convinced that the plan he had conceived as a good Catholic would complete the massacre of "those Christ killers" which the Catholic church had begun during the Middle Ages but had executed so poorly.[60]

Edmond Paris continues as if right on cue:

> This was not an empty promise. Already during that year (1933), apart from the massacre of Jews and assassinations perpetrated by the Nazis, there were 45 concentration camps in Germany, with 40,000 prisoners of various political opinions, but mostly liberals. *Franz von Papen, the pope's secret chamberlain,* defined perfectly the deep meaning of the *pact between the Vatican and Hitler* by this phrase worth

---

[59] Hunt, *A Woman Rides the Beast,* 275.

[60] Ibid., 280.

> engraving: "Nazism is a Christian reaction against the spirit of 1789."
>
> In 1937, Pius XI, under the pressure of world opinion, "condemned" the racial theories as incompatible with Catholic doctrine and principles, in what his apologists amusingly call the "terrible" encyclical letter *"Mit brennender Sorge."* Nazi racism is condemned, but not Hitler, its promoter: *"Distinguio."* And the Vatican takes care not to denounce the "advantageous" Concordat concluded, four years earlier, with the Nazi Reich.[61] (Emphasis added)

The Roman Catholic representatives in Germany were aware of the extermination of the Jews. Dave Hunt points out how so many that could have interceded on behalf of the Jews remained silent.

> Cardinal Bertram, head of the East German church province, and Archbishop Grober, head of the Upper Rhenish province, along with other bishops, expressed concern for the dismissals of Catholic civil servants by the new government. At the same time, however, the *bishops rejected reports* of brutality in the new concentration camps. Grober even became a "promoting member" of the SS and kept up his financial contributions to the bitter end.[62] (Emphasis added)

Edmond Paris concurs:

> ... The Sovereign Pontiff had not condemned Mussolini's politics and had left the Italian clergy fully

---

[61] Paris, *The Secret History of the Jesuits*, 184.

[62] Hunt, *A Woman Rides the Beast*, 282.

> free to co-operate with the Fascist government ... The ecclesiastics, from the priests of humble parishes to the cardinals, spoke in favor of the war ... "One of the most striking examples came from the Cardinal-Archbishop of Milan, Alfredo Ildefonso Schuster (Jesuit), who went as far as *calling the campaign "a Catholic crusade."* "Italy," clarified Pius XI, "thinks this war is justified because of a pressing need for expansion ... [63] (Emphasis added)

> Pius XII was known for his outspoken warnings to the faithful against the "abuse of human rights," yet he was silent about the Holocaust. He never spoke a public word against Hitler's systematic extermination of the Jews, *because to do so would have condemned his own church for its similar deeds.* This silence, historians agree, encouraged Hitler and added to the unspeakable genocide.[64] (Emphasis added)

The topic of Pius XII speaking out against the Nazi's extermination of the Jews seems to be one of scholarly debate! According to *Wikipedia* and *Encyclopedia Britannica,*

> The Catholic Church had been offering condemnations of Nazi racism since the earliest days of the Nazi movement. The 1942 Christmas address is significant for the light it throws on the ongoing scholarly debate around the war time policies of Pius XII in response to what would later be termed The Holocaust (the systematic murder of Europe's Jews by the Nazis). Pius' cautious approach has been a subject of controversy. According to the Encyclopedia

[63] Paris, *The Secret History of the Jesuits* 185.

[64] Hunt, *A Woman Rides the Beast*, 284.

> Britannica, his "strongest statement against genocide was regarded as inadequate by the Allies, though in Germany he was regarded as an Allied sympathizer who had violated his own policy of neutrality."[2] According to concentration camp prisoner, Father Jean Bernard of Luxembourg, treatment of clergy imprisoned in the Priest Barracks of Dachau Concentration Camp worsened when Pope Pius or the German bishops were critical of Hitler or the Nazis. [65]
>
> At the pope's command, Pacelli helped draft the anti-Nazi encyclical *Mit brennender Sorge* ("With Deep Anxiety"), written partly in response to the Nürnberg Laws and addressed to the German church on March 14, 1937. In it the papacy condemns racial theories and the mistreatment of people because of their race or nationality *but does not refer to Hitler or the Nazis by name*. The pope, aware of Pacelli's strong desire to prevent a break in relations between the Vatican and Berlin, commissioned the American Jesuit John La Farge to prepare an encyclical demonstrating the incompatibility of Catholicism and racism and excluded Pacelli from participating.[66] (Emphasis added)

The German Catholic clergy initiated several attempts to generate official church documents opposing the Nazi Party. Each attempt ended with failure. As the clergy's paper or initiative approached the finish line, the process derailed into the ditch

---

[65] "Pope Pius XII's 1942 Christmas address," Wikipedia: The Free Encyclopedia, 03/08/2019, https://en.wikipedia.org/wiki/Pope_Pius_XII%27s_1942_Christmas_address#cite_note-2.

[66] "Pius XII," Encyclopedia Britannica, 03/08/2019, https://www.britannica.com/biography/Pius-XII.

of indecision. The sacrifice was considered too high. The concern was that it would tear Catholic Germany apart, especially once Hitler had committed Germany to war. Guenter Lewy had this to say from his book, *The Catholic Church and Nazi Germany*:

> ... Bishop Preysing of Berlin headed a faction calling for a line of more vigorous opposition,
>
> ... fall of 1941. Preysing and four other bishops had composed the draft of a joint pastoral letter that they wanted to be read by all members of the episcopate. The letter was bold and outspokenly critical of the regime.[67]

> The draft pastoral letter was approved by about two-thirds of the episcopate; however, Cardinal Bertram objected to the project, and the proposed joint public protest therefore never took place.
>
> ... The courageous joint pastoral letter of 1941, which Preysing helped draft, quite deliberately omitted the Jewish issue.
>
> ... Preysing was not sure that he would have the backing of a majority of his priests and laity.[68]

Here we see one example of the division in the German Catholic Church. Cardinal Bertram was pro-Hitler to the end. Hitler died on April 30, 1945. His death was announced publicly on May 2, 1945. Bertram, being pro Hitler, gives his instructions to the parish priests of Breslau. The parish priests are to hold a service in memory of Hitler and the German soldiers who died for the German Homeland.[69] Bertram chose nationalism over

---

[67] Guenter Lewy, *The Catholic Church and Nazi Germany*, rev. ed. (De Capo Press, 2000), xx.

[68] Ibid., xxi.

[69] Ibid.

church doctrine. Lewy gives this reasoning for Bertram's instructions:

> But the very fact that this order was issued indicates that Bertram adhered to his line of compromise and conciliation not simply as a result of tactical considerations, but because he continued to see and respect Hitler as the legitimate Catholic head of state.[70]

Preysing's document was never accepted, even after corresponding with Pope Pius XII. The pope did respond. Most of the actions were just internal communications. These communications did not result in any public opposition to Hitler.

> The documents released by the Vatican confirm that from 1942 on the pope had reliable information about the systematic slaughter of the Jews of Europe. In letters addressed to Pius in early 1943, Archbishop Preysing mentioned a "new wave of deportations of Jews" and inquired whether the pope "could not do something in this matter [such as] issue an appeal on behalf of the unfortunates."
>
> Pius XII replied on April 30, 1943, that he had alluded to the fate of these unfortunates in his Christmas message of 1942 and that much money was being expended on behalf of non-Aryan refugees.
>
> Both Preysing and Pius XII, it thus appears, encouraged each other to issue public protests against the massacre of the Jews, yet each found compelling reasons not to do so.[71]

---

[70] Ibid., xxii.

[71] Lewy, *The Catholic Church and Nazi Germany*, xxiii.

From author Avro Manhattan's book, *The Vatican in World Politics*, he states:

> The very day Pius XII commenced his pontificate, Mussolini expelled Italy's 69,000 Jews and the pope said nothing. A few weeks later Italy invaded Albania. The pope protested, but "not because a country had been wantonly attacked, but because the aggression had been carried out on a Good Friday."[72]

The Fascist aggression against Albania, on Good Friday in 1939:

> "...From the political point of view, the annexation of the country by a Catholic power was bound to improve the position of the church and please the Vatican.[73]

Spain

Spain was to experience the same undermining as Italy and Germany. The rebellion in Spain was supported with money, arms, and ammunition by the Italian fascist party. The Vatican played its part by threatening the established government. Spain's rulers no longer fit into the papacy's plans. The pope excommunicated them, and through Archbishop Goma—the new Primate of Spain—the papacy proclaimed civil war. The Vatican acknowledged Franco's government on August 3, 1937, almost two years before Spain's civil war ended. The Vatican repeats this pattern,

[72] Avro Manhattan, *The Vatican in World Politics* (New York: Gaer and Associates, 1949), 126.

[73] Camille Cianfarra: "La Guerre et le Vatican" (Le Portulan, Paris 1946, pp.46-48, in *The Secret History of the Jesuits*, ed. Edmond Paris (Ontario, California: Chick Publications, 1983), 185.

and if it is not the instigator of the conflict, it seeks the position of a mediator to reap the spoils from the chaos—like a vulture who patiently waits for the predator to abandon its prey. Paris gives this historical account:

> So this "protected hunting-ground" was soon provided with a dictator similar to those who had been already successful in Italy and Germany. The adventure of General Franco only started in mid-July 1936 but, on the 21st of March 1934, the "Pact of Rome" had been sealed, between Mussolini and the chiefs of Spain's reactionary parties, one of whom was M. Goicoechea, chief of the "Renovacion Espanola.[74]

> The pope excommunicated the heads of the Spanish Republic and declared spiritual war between the Holy See and Madrid. Then he produced the encyclical letter 'Dilectissimi Nobis' ... Archbishop Goma, new primate of Spain, proclaimed the civil war.[75]

Belgium

A good example of *propaganda's effective use* to sway the minds of the masses is in Belgium, before the German invasion. The Jesuits guided the *Catholic Action* and the propaganda machine *Christus Rex*. The traitor Leon Degrelle headed Christus Rex. This trio was responsible for the successful manipulation of the Belgian people. Monsignor Picard and the Jesuits promoted a politicly fascist gospel of spiritual renewal to Belgium. Mussolini's fascism influenced the tactics of the Catholic Action. Historically, the *Catholic*

---

[74] Paris, *The Secret History of the Jesuits*, 186.

[75] Andre Ribard: "1960 et le secret du Vatican" (Libr. Robin, Paris 1954, p.45), in *The Secret History of the Jesuits*, ed. Edmond Paris (Ontario, California: Chick Publications, 1983), 186.

Action did its best to change societies that fell under anti-clerical regimes. The Catholic Action, like the Jesuits, were dedicated to the prerogatives of the pope. Belgium fell prey to the same strategy used in Germany, Italy, and Spain—the call for a new regime. Replace the head, and the tail will still follow.

Belgium's Catholic clergy betrayed its people by serving as a fifth-column, the group that would undermine the Belgium people from within. The Catholic laity in Belgium, as in Germany, was seeking guidance from their religious leaders. Below, you will see that documents from the past will witness the Catholic Church leading Belgium to capitulate to the German invasion and to discard its alliance with England and France. Edmond Paris writes:

> The ground had to be prepared for the approaching invasion of the Fuhrer's armies. So under the pretense of "spiritual renewal," the Hitlerite Fascist gospel was diligently preached there by Monsignor Picard, Jesuit, Father Arendt, Jesuit, Father Foucart, Jesuit, etc.[76]

> After 1928, the group of Leon Degrelle regularly collaborated with Monsignor Picard ... Monsignor Picard enlisted the help of Leon Degrelle for a particularly important mission: to manage a new publishing house at the Catholic Action centre. This publishing house was given a name which soon became famous: it was 'Rex' ... [77]

> The calls for new regime multiplied ... Founded on similar principles, the 'rexist' team started an *active propaganda program* in the country, their meetings

[76] Paris, *The Secret History of the Jesuits*, 187.

[77] Ibid.

soon attracted a few hundred, then thousands of listeners.[78] (Emphasis added)

Being only a pale shadow of these two (Mussolini & Hitler), Leon Degrelle, chief of "Christus Rex," was the beneficiary of the same support (the papacy)—but for a very different purpose, as his job was to open his country to the invader.[79]

Other Catholics as well, in the Autumn of 1940, looked towards the great tower of Saint-Rombaut ... Many entered the episcopal palace to ask the advice of Monsignor Van Roey or his entourage, concerning the morality, usefulness or necessity of collaboration ... [80]

More than one thousand Catholic Burgomasters, all the general secretaries, even though carefully chosen, adapted themselves immediately to the new Order ... All those good people imprisoned or insulted in 1944 must have wondered, in 1940: What does Malines think? But who would believe that neither Malines, their bishops, nor their priests had been able to put their minds at rest?[81]

Eight out of ten Belgian collaborationists were Catholics ... During those decisive weeks, because of the

---

[78] Jacques Saint-Germain, "La Bataille de Rex" (Les oeuvres francaises, Paris 1937, pp.67,69), in *The Secret History of the Jesuits*, ed. Edmond Paris (Ontario, California: Chick Publications, 1983), 187.

[79] Paris, *The Secret History of the Jesuits*, 188.

[80] Ibid., 191-192.

[81] Ibid., 192.

choice which had to be made, Malines and various bishoprics never issued written or verbal negative advice, to myself or to all those other collaborationists. "Even though not very pleasant, this, is the plain or naked truth. The attitude of the high Catholic clergy abroad could only strengthen the conviction of the faithful that collaboration was perfectly compatible with the faith … [82]

All these efforts were aiming at nothing less than Belgium's break-up, as we are reminded by another Catholic writer, M. Gaston Gaillard: "The Flemish-speaking Catholics and the autonomist Catholics of Alsace justified their attitude by their tacit support always given to Germanic propaganda by the Holy See. When they referred to the memorable letter sent by Pius XI to his secretary of State, Cardinal Gaspari, on the 26th of June 1923, they were easily convinced that their politics had the approval of Rome, and, of course, Rome did nothing to persuade them otherwise.[83]

We smile when we read the following from R. P. Fessard (Jesuit): "In 1916 and 1917, we waited for the American reinforcements with so much impatience. In 1939, we sadly realized that, even after war had been declared, Hitler was looked upon favorably by a large part of American opinion; even, and especially by Catholics. In 1941 and 1942, we wondered

---

[82] Ibid.

[83] Ibid., 193-194.

again if the United States would or would not intervene.[84]

For, and this is an historical fact, the "Christian Front," a Catholic movement opposed to the United States intervention, was directed by *the Jesuit Father Coughlin, a notorious pro-Hitlerite*. This pious organization lacked nothing and received, from Berlin, a plentiful supply of propaganda material prepared by Goebbels' office.[85] (Emphasis added)

Through its publication 'Social Justice" and *radio broadcasts, the Jesuit Father Coughlin, apostle of the swastika, reached a vast public*. He also looked after secret "commando cells" in the main urban centers, led according to the sons of Loyola's methods and trained by Nazi agents.[86]

The Fuhrer had come to power, thanks to the votes of the Catholic Zentrum, only five years before, but most of the objectives cynically revealed in 'Mein Kampf were already realized; this book, an insolent challenge to the western democracies, was *written by the Jesuit Father Staempfle and signed by Hitler. For –as so many ignore the fact—it was the Society of Jesus which perfected the famous Pan-German program as laid out in*

---

[84] R. P. Fessard S.J.: Libre meditation sur un message de Pie XII," (Plon, Paris 1957, p.202, in *The Secret History of the Jesuits*, ed. Edmond Paris (Ontario, California: Chick Publications, 1983), 194.

[85] Paris, *The Secret History of the Jesuits*, 195.

[86] Edmond Paris: "The Vatican against Europe" (P.T.S., London 1959, p.141).

> *this book, and the Fuhrer endorsed it.*[87] (Emphasis added)

In Germany and Belgium, we see the Catholic Church directing the decisions of its laity to either support the Nazi Party or capitulate to its invasion. The Catholic leadership, all the way up the chain of command, could have strongly influenced the minds of Catholic German soldiers. Consistently, the Vatican was more concerned with her interests and self-preservation over the needs of the people. It has never been about saving souls as it has been about controlling them.

A significant portion of Europe's population was faithful members of the Catholic Church, both civilian and military. There was an opportunity for the Vatican to use its influential powers for the good of these nations. The debate is what would have saved more lives—the Vatican to firmly denounce Fascism and Nazi agendas or surrendering to the Fascist and Nazi regime with their stubborn wills? This latter choice would allow the papacy to reap what it could in the aftermath. Mussolini, Hitler, and Franco were only doing what the Church of Rome has done for centuries, showing intolerance to the degree of murder to all who oppose their will. For the papacy to reverse its support would be to admit that it is not infallible and fail with its scheme to regain control over Europe.

Austria

As Hitler was moving across Europe, the Catholic Church was clearing the way politically for the German invasion. This brings up the instructions given by Ignatius Loyola, the founder of the Society of Jesus (the Jesuits) to his followers centuries ago. A Jesuit, whenever possible, should be the mediator in political affairs. The papacy consistently dictated its interests throughout

---

[87] Paris, *The Secret History of the Jesuits*, 196.

the war, even though the Vatican publicly announced its neutrality, it was working like the devil behind the scenes—pun intended.

Note the following excerpts that document the Catholic Church's involvement in Austria, Poland, and Czechoslovakia. They leave the reader with a repetitive story. Compare the following events with the strategies used in Germany and Belgium. From the book by W.C. Brownlee, *Secret Instructions of the Jesuits*, we have Ignatius Loyola's instructions:

> Nor will it contribute a little to our advantage, if, with caution and secrecy, we foment and heighten the animosities that arise among princes and great men, even to such a degree that they may weaken each other. But if there appear any likelihood of reconciliation, then as soon as possible let us endeavor to be the mediators, lest others prevent us.[88]

Edmond Paris provides detailed accounts of the Vatican's involvement:

> In the early days of May (1936), von Papen entered into secret negotiations with Dr. Schussnigg (Austrian Chancellor) working on his weak point and showed him how advantageous a reconciliation with Hitler would be as far as the Vatican's interests were concerned; the argument may seem odd, but Schussnigg was very devout, and von Papen the pope's chamberlain.[89]

---

[88] W.C. Brownlee, *Secret Instructions of the Jesuits*, 141.

[89] G.E.R. Gedye, "Suicide de l' Autriche" (Union latine d' editions, Paris 1940, p.188), in *The Secret History of the Jesuits*, ed. Edmond Paris (Ontario, California: Chick Publications, 1983), 197.

Not surprisingly, it was the secret chamberlain who led the whole affair which ended, on the 11th of March 1938, with the resignation of the pious Schussnigg (pupil of the Jesuits), in favor of Seyss-Inquart, chief of the Austrian Nazis. The following day, the German troops entered Austria and the puppet government of Seyss-Inquart proclaimed the union of the country to the Reich. This event was welcomed by an enthusiastic declaration of Vienna's archbishop: Cardinal Innitzer (Jesuit).[90]

Cardinal Innitzer, highest representative of the Roman church in Austria, also wrote in his declaration: "I invite the chiefs of Youth organization to prepare their union to the organization of the German Reich."[91]

So not only did the cardinal-archbishop of Vienna, followed by his episcopate, throw in his lot with Hitler most enthusiastically, *but he handed over also the "Christian" youth to be trained according to Nazi methods*; these methods had been "officially condemned" in the "terrible" encyclical letter: "Mit brennender Sorge![92] (Emphasis added)

Then the "Mercure de France" justifiably observed: "These bishops have not taken a decision which involves the church as a whole on their own accord;

---

[90] Paris, *The Secret History of the Jesuits*, 198.

[91] Ernest Pezet, former vice-president of the Commission for Foreign Affairs, "L, Autriche et la paix" (Ed. Self, Paris 1945, p.149), in *The Secret History of the Jesuits*, ed. Edmond Paris (Ontario, California: Chick Publications, 1983), 198.

[92] Paris, *The Secret History of the Jesuits*, 198-199.

the Holy See gave them directives which they merely followed.[93]

This obvious. But what other "directives" could be expected from this Holy See which brought to power Mussolini, Hitler, Franco and, in Belgium, created the "Christus-Rex" of Leon Degrelle?[94] (Emphasis added)

Poland

In fact, it (the Holy See) did not frown at the brutal regrouping of Catholics in Central Europe, according to the plan of the Jesuits general, Halke von Ledechowski.

The Vatican's licensed thurifers keep on reminding their readers that Pius XII "protested" against the aggression in the encyclical letter "Summi Pontifcatus." In reality, this ludicrous document, like all other such documents, which numbers no less than 45 pages, contains only one phrase at the end, concerning Poland crushed by Hitler. And this short allusion is an advice to the Polish people to pray much to the Virgin Mary![95]

To those who would be surprised at such behavior towards a Catholic country, we will quote a famous precedent: after the first division of Poland in 1772, a catastrophe in which the Jesuits intrigues played a

[93] Austria and Hitler ("Mercure de France," 1st May 1938, p.720), in *The Secret History of the Jesuits*, ed. Edmond Paris (Ontario, California: Chick Publications, 1983), p.199.

[94] Paris, *The Secret History of the Jesuits*, 199.

[95] Ibid., 199-200.

> large part, Pope Clement XIV, when writing to the Empress of Austria, Marie-Therese, expressed his satisfaction as follows:
>
> "The invasion and division of Poland were not done for political reasons only; it was in the interests of religion, and necessary to the spiritual profit of the church, that the Court of Vienna should extend its domination over Poland as much as possible."[96]

Czechoslovakia

> In Czechoslovakia, the Vatican did even better: it provided Hitler with one of its own prelates, a secret chamberlain, to be made into the head of this satellite state of the Reich.[97]

Note: The Vatican turned a deaf ear to calls for help. M. Francois Charles Roux tells us:

> In the middle of August, I had tried to persuade the pope that he speaks in favor of peace—a just peace, of course... My first attempts were unsuccessful.
>
> All my attempts," adds the former French ambassador, "received the same answer from Pius XI: "It would be useless, unnecessary, inopportune." I could not understand his obstinacy in keeping silent.[98]

---

[96] Ibid., 200-201.

[97] Ibid., 201.

[98] Francios Charles-Roux: "Huit and au Vatican" (Flammarion, Paris 1947, pp. 127-128), in *The Secret History of the Jesuits*, ed. Edmond Paris (Ontario, California: Chick Publications, 1983), 201.

As anticipated, on the 15th of March 1939, Hitler annexed the rest of Bohemia and Moravia, and put the Republic of Slovakia, which he created with a stroke of his pen, "under his protection." At the head, he placed *Monsignor Tiso (Jesuit), "who dreamed of combining Catholicism and Nazism.*[99] (Emphasis added)

Catholicism and Nazism," Proclaimed Monsignor Tiso, "have much in common; they work hand in hand at reforming the world.[100]

In June 1940, Radio Vatican announced: "*The declaration of Monsignor Tiso, chief of the Slovakian state,* stating his intention to build up Slovakia according to a Christian plan, has the *full approval of the Holy See.*"[101]

Tiso's regime, in Slovakia, was especially afflicting for the Protestant church of that country, which comprised one fifth of the population. Monsignor Tiso tried to reduce the Protestant influence to its minimum, and even eliminate it ... *Influential members of the Protestant church were sent to concentration camps.*[102] (Emphasis added)

---

[99] Paris, *The Secret History of the Jesuits*, 202.

[100] Henriette Feuillet: "France Nouvelle," 25th of June 1949., in *The Secret History of the Jesuits*, ed. Edmond Paris (Ontario, California: Chick Publications, 1983), 202-203.

[101] Henriette Feuillet: "France Nouvelle," 25th of June 1949, in *The Secret History of the Jesuits*, ed. Edmond Paris (Ontario, California: Chick Publications, 1983), 203.

[102] "Reforme," 17th of August 1947., in *The Secret History of the Jesuits*, ed. Edmond Paris (Ontario, California: Chick Publications, 1983), 203.

Note: The credible witness Lord Russell wrote the following of Liverpool, who was also a judicial counselor during the trials for the war criminals:

> These could count themselves fortunate, as we consider this declaration from the Jesuits general Wernz, a Prussian (1906-1915): "The church can condemn heretics to death as any rights they have is because of our forbearance." Let us see now what kind of apostolic gentleness was used by the gauleiter prelate Tiso towards the Jews: "in 1941, the first contingent of Jews from Slovakia and upper-Silesia arrive at Auschwitz; from the start, those who were not able to work are sent to the gas chamber, in a room of the building containing the crematory furnaces.[103]
>
> Another high dignitary of the Roman church, in a neighboring country, could have appropriated this declaration of Monsignor Tiso to himself. For, if the foundations of the Slovakian "City of God" were hatred and persecution, according to the steadfast tradition of the church, *what can be said of the eminently Catholic state of Croatia, offspring of the collaboration between the killer Pavelitch and Monsignor Stepinac, and with the assistance of the pontifical legate Marcone.*[104] (Emphasis added)

After researching this next section, I understood the hatred the Serbian people have held onto through the decades that followed WWII. The Holocaust of the Jews is in public school

---

[103] Lord Russell of Liverpool, "Sous le signe de la criox games," (L' Ami du livre, Geneva 1955, p.217)., in *The Secret History of the Jesuits*, ed. Edmond Paris (Ontario, California: Chick Publications, 1983), 203.

[104] Paris, *The Secret History of the Jesuits*, 204.

textbooks, and we can all agree that it is wicked and horrible to exterminate any race of people systematically. While conducting research for this book, I sadly found what level of barbarism man can fall too. The whitewashing of the historical facts waters down the truth. This dilution hides who the actual war criminals are from the public.

Many of us have been shielded from the terrors of war, and understandably so. Depending on the age of the child, it is necessary at times to protect their minds from truths beyond their emotional comprehension. At what age should we expose them or ourselves to the realities of the world? It is not about having a doomsday worldview; it is about knowing the truth. We all have a basic understanding of war, but our public school history books and mainstream media give a censored look of warfare. Controlling powers don't want to disturb the herd too much unless it achieves the desired manipulation. To show the depth of evil would be too much for the average armchair viewer, sitting in their presumed safety. You and I need to know there is a big difference between the reality of war and what the media dishes out. Evil goes beyond the death of war.

During WWII, Serbia suffered a horrific slaughter of its people. These atrocities were butchery, not just death from war. In this case, it is essential not to lose the details in translation, so I will give you the text as I found it. Several excerpts will be listed again as a testimony to which individuals and groups were directly or indirectly in contact with the Vatican, thereby connecting the crimes to Rome.

ATROCITIES OF THE "OUSTACHIS

> What these "Assassins in the Name of God," as they were so rightly nicknamed by M. Herve Lauriere, did over four years defies all imagination, and the annals of the Roman church, even though so rich in such material, cannot produce the equivalent in

Europe.... Do we need to add that the crony of the blood-thirsty Ante Pavelitch was Monsignor Stepinac, another Jesuit?[105]

The Croatian terrorist organization of the "Oustachis." Led by Pavelitch, had come to the notice of the French people through the assassination, in Marseille, of King Alexander the First of Yugoslavia and our Foreign-Affairs' minister, Louis Barthou, in 1934.[106]

The chief of terrorists, hired by Mussolini, "worked" for the Italian expansion on the Adriatic coast. When, in 1941, Hitler and Mussolini invaded and divided Yugoslavia, this supposed Croatian patriot was put, by them, at the head of the satellite they created under the name of "Independent State of Croatia." ... *May 18th, 1941 Pius XII gave a private audience to Pavelitch and his 'friends', one of whom was Monsignor Salis-Sewis, vicar-general to Monsignor Stepinac.*[107] (Emphasis added)

So the Holy See did not fear shaking hands with a certified murderer, sentenced to death by default for the murder of King Alexander the First and Louis Barthou, a chief of terrorists having the most horrible crimes on his conscience. *In fact on the 18th of May 1941, when Pius XII gladly welcomed Pavelitch and his gang of killers, the massacre of Orthodox Croats was at its*

---

[105] Ibid.

[106] Ibid., 204-205.

[107] Ibid., 205.

height, concurrently with forced conversions to Catholicism.[108] (Emphasis added for connection)

The "Osservatore Romano" informs us that, on the 22nd of July 1941, the pope received on hundred members of the Croatian Security Police, led by the chief of Zagreb's police, Eugen Kvaternik-Dido. This group of Croatian S.S., the pick of the executioners and torturers operation in the concentration camps, were presented to the Holy-Father by one who perpetrated crimes so monstrous that his own mother committed suicide in despair.[109]

Mile Budak, minister for Worship, exclaimed in August 1941, at Karlovac: "The Oustachi movement is based on religion, All out work rests on our loyalty to religion and the Catholic church.[110]

Besides, on the 22nd of July, at Gospic, the same minister for Worship had perfectly defined this work: "We will kill some Serbians, deport others, and the rest will be compelled to embrace the Roman Catholic religion."[111]

---

[108] Cf. Herve Lauriere: "Assassins in the Name of God," (Ed. Dufour, Paris 1951, p.40ff)., in *The Secret History of the Jesuits*, ed. Edmond Paris (Ontario, California: Chick Publications, 1983), p. 205.

[109] Edmond Paris, *The Secret History of the Jesuits*, 207.

[110] Cf. Herve Lauriere: "Assassins in the Name of God," (Ed. Dufour, Paris 1951, p.97)., in *The Secret History of the Jesuits*, ed. Edmond Paris (Ontario, California: Chick Publications, 1983), 208.

[111] "L 'Ordere de Paris," 8th February 1947., in *The Secret History of the Jesuits*, ed. Edmond Paris (Ontario, California: Chick Publications, 1983), 208.

This German Jesuit, well-known before Hitler's advent made it known in 1928 in a book whose foreword was written by Monsignor Pacelli (*soon to be Pius the XII*), then apostolic nuncio in Berlin. Muckermann expressed himself as follows: "The pope appeals in favor of the Catholic Action's new crusade. He is the guide who carries the standard of Christ's Kingdom ... The Catholic Action means the gathering of world Catholicism. It must live its heroic age ... The new epoch can be acquired for Christ only through the price of blood.[112]

To this bloody list of honors, we must enter the names of the Abbe Bozidar Bralo, the priest Dragutin Kamber, the Jesuit Lackovic and the Abbe Yvan Salitch, secretaries to Monsignor Stepinac, the priest Nicolas Bilogrivic, etc ... and numberless Franciscans; one of the worst of these was Brother Miroslav Filipovitch, main organizer of those massacres, chief of and executioner at the concentration camp of Jasenovac, the most hideous of these earthly hells.[113]

When Pavelitch and his 4,000 "Oustachis"—which included archbishop Sarie, a Jesuit, bishop Garic and 400 clerics—left the scene of their exploits to go first to Austria then on to Italy, they left behind part of their "treasures": films, photographs, recorded speeches of Ante Pavelitch, chests full of jewels, gold coins, gold and platinum from teeth, bracelets,

---

[112] Cf. Herve Lauriere: "Assassins in the Name of God," (Ed. Dufour, Paris 1951, p.82,84-84., in *The Secret History of the Jesuits*, ed. Edmond Paris (Ontario, California: Chick Publications, 1983), 209.

[113] Edmond Paris, The *Secret History of the Jesuits* (Ontario, California: Chick Publications, 1983), 209.

> wedding rings and pieces of dentures made of gold and platinum. This spoil taken from the poor wretches who had been murdered were hidden at the Archiepiscopal palace where they were eventually found.[114]
>
> *As for the fugitives, they took advantage of the "Pontifical Commission for Assistance," created expressly to save war criminals.* This charitable institution hid them in convents, mainly in Austria and Italy, *and provided the chiefs with false passports which enabled them to go to "friendly" countries, where they would be able to enjoy the fruits of their robberies in peace.*[115] (Emphasis added)

The Catholic Church's use of convents and monasteries to help criminals escape justice is an old practice. Bernard Fresenborg recounts such activities in his book. The following is from Chapter VIII titled; *Monasteries Are Often the Abode of Criminals, and Nunneries the Slaughter Pens of Virtue*. The following remarks relate directly to WWII:

> These asylums are used by Catholicism to shuffle criminals of their following into, in defiance of law and justice, as these asylums are notorious among those who are on the inside workings of this creed, as to places where Catholic criminals can be concealed without fear of having the civil law bring them to justice, as these places are a retreat for Catholic criminals who are pursued by the minister of justice, and where, so long as they remain, they cannot be arrested; but in order to elevate these "asylums" to the plane of religion, they, are called by different

---

[114] Ibid., 210-211.

[115] Ibid., 211.

> names which are misnomers, and are only raised to the level of religious institutions to cover up the infamy of their actual missions, as *Catholicism has learned that as long as she can throw around and about herself a religious glamor, that she is permitted to go ahead and violate the laws of man without molestation.*[116] (Emphasis added)

Continuing with the Timeline:

> The archbishop of Zagreb was then made a member of the holy cohort in his lifetime by Pius XII who hastened to confer on him the title of "Cardinal" in recognition of "his apostolate which displays the purest brightness.... We are acquainted with the symbolic meaning of the Cardinals' Purple: the one who dons it must be ready to confess his Faith "usque ad sanguinis effusionem": to the point of shedding blood....[117]

In our world, there is a lust for power and wealth, both inside and outside religious organizations. Within Catholicism's hierarchy, clergy are promoted to higher positions of power and influence, not due to their benevolent deeds but due to their malevolent acts in the service of the popes. This advancement is nothing more than a payment for services rendered. Again, note the identifying Bible verse:

> And the woman was arrayed in *purple and scarlet colour*, and decked with gold and precious stones and pearls, having a golden cup in her hand full of

---

[116] Bernard Fresenborg, *Thirty Years in Hell; or, From Darkness to Light* (Saint Louis, Missouri: North American Book House, 1904), 56.

[117] Paris, *The Secret History of the Jesuits*, 212.

abominations and filthiness of her fornication:[118] (Emphasis added)

If that is the case, the right to cardinalship of Monsignor Stepinac cannot be contested. In the diocese of Gornji Karlovac, part of his archbishopric, of 460,000 Orthodox people who lived there, 50,000 were able to hide in the mountains, 50,000 were sent to Serbia, 40,000 were converted to Catholicism through the regime of terror and 280,000 were massacred.[119]

The truth is that the veil thrown over these infamies in an attempt to hide them is transparent and not wide enough. To cover Stepinac, others have to be uncovered: Bishops Saric, Garic, Simrak, the priests Bilogrivic, Kamber Bralo and their associates—the Franciscans and Jesuits have to be uncovered, and finally the Holy See.[120]

On the 10th of February 1960, the infamous archbishop of Zagreb, Alois Stepinac, died at his native village of Karlovice, where he had been made to reside. This death gave the Vatican an opportunity to organize one of its spectacular manifestations for which it excels. [121]

---

[118] Revelation 17:4, KJV.

[119] Cf. Jean Hussard: "Vu en Yougoslavie" (Lausanne 1947, p.216)., in *The Secret History of the Jesuits*, ed. Edmond Paris (Ontario, California: Chick Publications, 1983), 212.

[120] Paris, *The Secret History of the Jesuits*, 216.

[121] Ibid., 218.

> ... So the Holy See surpassed itself to give this apotheosis all the pomp possible. The "Osservatore Romano" and all the Catholic press dedicated many columns to the rapturous praise of the "martyr," his "spiritual testament." And the speeches of His Holiness John XXIII proclaiming "his respect and supernatural affection..."[122]

FRUIT INSPECTORS

This section may have a humorous title, but it is a serious matter when the fruit is spiritual. We have reviewed only the tip of the iceberg when it comes to the Vatican's historical record of intrigue and corruption with the regimes of Europe. It isn't necessary to list every atrocity that can be attached to the Catholic Church to show consistency in the timeline. The Church of Rome at different levels of her clerical hierarchy—from the simple monks to the popes—are guilty of the intentional manipulating doctrine to control the minds of the Catholic laity, the indoctrination of the young, the inquisitions, the massacres, the assassinations of kings, the torture of the innocent, etc.

It is regrettable for the Catholic Church to have a list of atrocities against humanity that spans centuries. The Church of Rome committed these acts behind the guise of service to a holy God when the real motivation was simply the lust for power and control over foreign nations. Based on the historical accounts of the Catholic Church, it would appear the watchmen and martyrs from the past are right that the spirit behind Catholicism's hierarchy is not the Holy Spirit, but the spirit of the antichrist—using a counterfeit Christianity to deceive the masses. It's the same spirit the apostles warned us of, and the same spirit both the

---

[122] Ibid.

Pilgrim church and the Protestant Reformers claimed to be the motivating force behind the *Dynasty of the Popes*.

Here God's Word is the deciding judge, as it can evaluate the fruit produced by the Vatican and the Society of Jesuits' actions through the centuries. The type of fruit produced identifies the tree and its root system, be it good or evil. What are the Roman Catholic Church hierarchies spiritually rooted to? Using the biblical analogy of being grafted in the vine, we can choose what we spiritually graft to—be it the Holy Spirit or the spirit behind the "prince of the power of the air."

What are the fruits of the flesh? Compare the historical timeline to the Scripture listed below. Today's drive to control individual thinking and to be politically correct has produced the phrase *"don't judge me."* But, in fact, we are told to judge, to evaluate, to identify who can be trusted and who cannot.

> For all the law is fulfilled in one word, even in this; Thou shalt love thy neighbour as thyself. *But if ye bite and devour one another*, take heed that ye be not consumed one of another. beware lest you be consumed by one another. This I say then, Walk in the Spirit, and ye shall not fulfil the lust of the flesh. *For the flesh lusteth against the Spirit, and the Spirit against the flesh: and these are contrary the one to the other: so that ye cannot do the things that ye would.*[123] (Emphasis added)

> But if ye be led of the Spirit, ye are not under the law. Now the works of the flesh are manifest, which are these; Adultery, fornication, uncleanness, lasciviousness, *Idolatry, witchcraft, hatred, variance, emulations, wrath, strife, seditions, heresies, Envyings, murders, drunkenness, revellings,* and such like: of the which I tell you before, as I have also told you in time past,

[123] Galatians 5:14-17, KJV.

> that they which do such things shall not inherit the kingdom of God.[124] (Emphasis added)

Jesus gave the analogy of the "True Vine" to show that if you are not in Him, then you cannot produce the fruit of the Holy Spirit.

> I am the true vine, and my Father is the husbandman. Every branch in me that beareth not fruit he taketh away: and every branch that beareth fruit, he purgeth it, that it may bring forth more fruit. Now ye are clean through the word which I have spoken unto you. Abide in me, and I in you. As the branch cannot bear fruit of itself, except it abide in the vine; no more can ye, except ye abide in me. [125]

> I am the vine, ye are the branches: He that abideth in me, and I in him, the same bringeth forth much fruit: for *without me ye can do nothing*. If a man abide not in me, he is cast forth as a branch, and is withered; and men gather them, and cast them into the fire, and they are burned.[126] (Emphasis added)

Through the Holy Spirit, believers are motivated to produce good fruit, and these fruits are as follows.

> But the fruit of the Spirit is love, joy, peace, longsuffering, gentleness, goodness, faith, Meekness, temperance: against such there is no law. And they that

---

[124] Galatians 5:18-21, KJV.

[125] John 15:1-4, KJV.

[126] John 15:5-6, KJV.

> are Christ's have crucified the flesh with the affections and lusts.[127]

The Word of God warns the world to be wary of counterfeit Christianity and false teachers of the Word—churches that work and respond to the way the world works and responds. Compare these churches to the fruits of the Holy Spirit and the commandments Jesus told us to follow.

The World

> This then is the message which we have heard of him, and declare unto you, that God is light, and in him is no darkness at all. If we say that we have fellowship with him, and *walk in darkness*, we lie, and do not the truth … [128]

> Love not the world, neither the things that are in the world. If any man love the world, the love of the Father is not in him. For all that is in the world, the lust of the flesh, and the lust of the eyes, and the pride of life, is not of the Father, but is of the world.[129]

Counterfeits

> For such are *false apostles, deceitful workers*, transforming themselves into the apostles of Christ. And no marvel; *for Satan himself is transformed into an angel of light*. Therefore it is no great thing if his ministers also be transformed as the ministers of

[127] Galatians 5:22-24, KJV.

[128] 1 John 1:5-6, KJV.

[129] 1 John 2:15-16, KJV.

> righteousness; whose end shall be according to their works.[130] (Emphasis added)

These last two chapters provided just a portion of what the past reveals about the Catholic Church's mission. These historical documents validate that past warnings of deceit are real. The false doctrine of Catholicism will continue until the last days. Do not be deceived is the caution given by Jesus Christ and the New Testament apostles. Judge the doctrine by what it produces—the semantics and clever rhetoric are just a veil to hide the real agenda.

There is speculation of what event or world power could unite the world's religions under one banner—many of these world religions conflict doctrinally. A cosmic deception has been suggested, such as an alien visitation, be it real or fabricated. You may or may not know that the Vatican takes this possibility very seriously, again, always looking for the opportunity to be a mediator of power. For the world's religions to come under one banner, they would have to find common ground or surrender their doctrinal beliefs. The next two chapters will discuss the topic of a universal church and how the Catholic Church is spearheading the ecumenical movement.

---

[130] 2 Corinthians 11:13-15, KJV.

7

Ecumenical Trap Part 1

In the last 50-plus years, the ecumenical movement has received considerable attention and push for world acceptance. In this chapter, we'll explore the question of what is the ecumenical movement, the motivation behind it, and the goal to centralize religious control back to Rome—the "mother church." We'll also

- Consider statements made by the popes.
- Review warnings and oppositions to the ecumenical movement.
- Consider biblical text relating to the origin of the other world religion's gods.
- Review the propaganda that promotes all religions as talking to the same God.

Definition

If you have not heard of the "ecumenical movement," you may be familiar with the term *universal church*. Here are a couple of quick definitions, first from Wikipedia and second from the Encyclopedia Britannica.

> Ecumenism is any interdenominational initiative aimed at greater cooperation among Christian churches. Ecumenism is the idea of a Christian unity in the literal meaning: *that there should be a single church*. Ecumenism is separate and distinct from nondenominational Christianity, which seeks no common organizing principle.[1]

Above, we can see a move to increase control of the masses. Power and authority become centralized. Exercising this power and influence is then available to a limited number of individuals who are sold out on the hierarchy's mission statement.

> Ecumenism, the movement or tendency toward worldwide Christian unity or cooperation. The term, of recent origin, emphasizes what is viewed as the universality of the Christian churches.[2]

The movement has been symbolized by "coexist" signs, rhetoric, and bumper stickers. The chief decision for the fundamental Christian is whether to support or reject this movement.

Catholicism and Protestantism are utterly opposed. The first question you must ask is whether any changes exist in either the Protestant or Catholic Church doctrines which indicate the possibility of reconciliation. You must be able to identify these changes before centuries of opposition can be considered resolved. The Roman Empire, before the creation of Rome's state church, persecuted the first-century church of the apostles.

The Christian church was established on the day of Pentecost, as written in Acts 2. Satan made a strategic move by giving

---

[1] "Ecumenism," Wikipedia: The Free Encyclopedia, 2/21/19, en.wikipedia.org/wiki/Ecumenism.

[2] "Ecumenism," Encyclopedia Britannica, 02/21/19, https://www.britannica.com/topic/ecumenism.

Emperor Constantine the vision to create a state church. Before the Emperor's dream, Rome slaughtered the Christians in its coliseums. After Constantine's dream, Christianity became the Empire's new religion. The relief the Christians experienced from persecution was short-lived. Their suffering would continue, but now by the newly formed state Church of Rome. Christians suffered torment for refusing to accept the state-mandated dogma. This state-mandated doctrine was a blend of Christianity and Mithraism. Catholicism has its roots in the Roman Empire's new state religion, which Emperor Constantine formed to unify his Empire.

In this chapter, it will be necessary to return to the Protestant Reformation of 1517, considering it is the main focus of the ecumenical documents. Has the Catholic Church changed its doctrinal beliefs since the Council of Trent or the Councils of Vatican I and Vatican II? Or have the Protestant church "leaders" of today blindly accepted the dogma of Rome based on clever semantics? The Vatican Councils were to strengthen the Church of Rome as the primary church (mother church).

With the ramp-up of the ecumenical movement, there have been several pompously displayed ceremonies full of hoopla over the signing of documents expressing "unity" between the Catholic Church, several world religions, and liberal denominations of the Protestant church.

1. Vatican II Vatican Council, Second. Second Vatican Council, popularly called Vatican II, 1962–65, the 21st ecumenical council (see council, ecumenical) of the Roman Catholic Church, convened by Pope John XXIII and continued under Paul VI.

2. *Evangelicals and Catholics Together: The Christian Mission in the Third Millennium*, published in 1994.

3. *Joint Declaration on the Doctrine of Justification;* by the Lutheran World Federation and the Catholic Church 1999.

4. The World Methodist Council adopted the Declaration on 18 July 2006.

5. *Manhattan Declaration: A Call of Christian Conscience;* drafted on October 20, 2009, released on November 20, 2009.

6. Pope Francis calls for all religions to unite, March 21, 2013.

7. World Alliance of Religions for Peace Summit Seoul, South Korea, 18th September 2014. All the world religions are agreeing to a pantheistic god they have been preaching on the United Nations. They have come together; who is missing from the signing ceremony? The hard-core Protestants, Evangelicals, and Lutherans not present.

8. John 17 Movement. That prayer of Jesus in the 17th Chapter of the Gospel according to John is the reason Roman Catholics and a variety of Protestant Christians met together on May 23rd, 2015 in Phoenix, Arizona. The movement is linked to Rome and has the pope's blessing.[3]

9. Vatican correspondent January 26, 2015, Rome. At the end of a week devoted to the press for Christian unity, Pope Francis said on Sunday

---

[3] Vatican, "Letter from Vatican," http://v2.garykinnaman.com/wp-content/uploads/2014/03/letterfromvatican.jpg.

that the way ahead is for various denominations to reject "proselytism and competition" among themselves.

10. The World Communion of Reformed churches (representing the "80 million members of Congregational, Presbyterian, Reformed, United, Uniting, and Waldensian churches"), adopted the Declaration in 2017.

Many Protestant church leaders have greeted the ecumenical movement with open arms. These leaders failed to recognize the devil's deception. God's Word predicted this fraud in the first century. The Apostle Paul writes:

> Now the Spirit speaketh expressly, that in the latter times some shall depart from the faith, giving heed to seducing spirits, and doctrines of devils;[4]

> For if he that cometh preacheth *another Jesus*, whom we have not preached, or if ye receive *another spirit*, which ye have not received, or *another gospel*, which ye have not accepted, *ye might well bear with him*.[5] (Emphasis added)

PURPOSE

In the 20th century, we can look at the *ecumenical movement* from World War I with the World Council of Churches (WCC).

> The WCC originated out of the ecumenical movement, which, after World War I, resulted in two

[4] 1 Timothy 4:1, KJV.

[5] 2 Corinthians 11:4, KJV.

> organizations. The Life and Work Movement concentrated on the practical activities of the churches, and the Faith and Order Movement focused on the beliefs and organization of the churches and the problems involved in their possible reunion. Before long, the two movements began to work toward establishing a single organization. In 1937 the Faith and Order Conference at Edinburgh and the Life and Work Conference at Oxford accepted the plan to create one council. A conference of church leaders met in 1938 in Utrecht, Neth., to prepare a constitution; but World War II intervened, and the first assembly of the WCC could not be held until 1948. In 1961 the International Missionary Council united with the WCC.
>
> The WCC's members include most Protestant and Eastern Orthodox bodies but not the Roman Catholic Church. The Southern Baptists of the United States are among Protestant nonmembers. The controlling body of the WCC is the assembly, which meets at intervals of approximately six years at various locations throughout the world. The assembly appoints a large central committee that in turn chooses from its membership an executive committee of 26 members, which, along with specialized committees and 6 copresidents, carries on the work between assemblies. The headquarters of the council, in Geneva, has a large staff under a general secretary.[6]

The World Council of Churches provides the following description of what they claim to represent:

---

[6] "World Council of Churches," Encyclopedia Britannica, 02/21/19 https://www.britannica.com/topic/World-Council-of-churches.

> The World Council of Churches is a fellowship of churches which confess the Lord Jesus Christ as God and Saviour according to the Scriptures, and therefore seek to fulfill together their common calling to the glory of the one God, Father, Son and Holy Spirit.
>
> It is a community of churches on the way to visible unity in one faith and one eucharistic fellowship, expressed in worship and in common life in Christ. It seeks to advance towards this unity, as Jesus prayed for his followers, "so that the world may believe." (John 17:21)[7]

To avoid pretense in uniting the world's religions under a single banner, all parties involved need a common motivating goal. All parties would agree on world peace and ending world hunger. Many of the objectives are political, social, and non-religious. Combating against world hunger, against abortion, and human rights violations, etc. are legitimate crusades. There is no rational argument to be made against the combing of international efforts to solve problems that exist on a global scale. International teamwork and alliances have been formed by nations in the past to resolve international issues; an example was the Berlin Airlift in 1948.

It may be interesting to note that many of the countries coming together are the same countries creating problems. The restructuring of the world through the chaos (Hegelian dialectic)! How many poor third world countries do we see causing destruction on an international scale? World powers and governments want to keep and gain more power and control over their populations. These entities have global agendas. We must look behind the cover story and propaganda given by political powers to determine their actual end game.

---

[7] "What is the World Council of Churches," World Council of Churches, 02/21/19, https://www.oikoumene.org/en/about-us.

There is a difference between combining church doctrines and combining efforts to use resources to solve major social issues efficiently. Any group can participate in international aid without surrendering or being forced to abandon their religious beliefs and doctrines. Cooperation rather than war is for the good of the world, a no-brainer, right?

Two of the world's religions move to the front of the line when it comes to shedding the blood of millions through holy wars, jihads, and crusades—Catholicism and Islam. The premise, *for the good of the people and world peace,* has been used throughout history as a cover story and definitely by *wolves in sheep's clothing.* The Catholic Church is leading the ecumenical movement, and the papacy, as you may expect, is the head. The Church of Rome's historical record dates back over a thousand years and consists of deceit, toppled regimes, assassinations, and the death of millions. Once you remove your ignorance of the Church of Rome's history and the Vatican hierarchy's true nature, it's not hard to believe deceit is the motivator behind the ecumenical movement.

Rome has attempted to combine world religions before! This unification was done in the fourth century by Emperor Constantine when he created the "state" church religion, which has evolved into today's Catholicism. The Christians that remained from the church of the apostles were forced to comply. Is the ecumenical movement a means for Rome to centralize its power, ultimately for the purpose of maintaining dominance?

The Gospel Herald, a Catholic website, shares an article about Pope Francis, who has called for unity among evangelicals, Catholics, and Christians from other denominations. The pope emphasizes that "we are one in Christ" and *warns that division between the groups is the work of the devil.* According to biblical Scripture, there is only one body of Christ, the true Christian church. Many religions claim to be a part of that body, and Catholicism is one of them. The body of Christ is not a religion but the worldwide amalgamation of individuals who have faith in

Jesus Christ as Lord and Savior, accompanied by their obedience to God's Word. The Church of Rome proves itself illegitimate for such a claim by the evidence of her crimes and spiritual fruit.

About Pope Francis's remarks—is standing on your faith "the work of the devil"? It sounds like the *heretic* labeling has returned. Could this be considered the beginning of targeting religious denominations as spoken of in the book of Revelation? God commands a Christian to be separate from the *spirit* behind the world system. On the website *Bible Reasons,* under the topic *"Being Set Apart,"* the author, Fritz Chery, writes the following and supports his view with biblical Scriptures at the end.

> When it comes to being set apart for God, know that it cannot be done by our own efforts. You must be saved. You must repent of your sins and trust in Christ alone for salvation. God desires perfection. Jesus died on the cross and became that perfection on our behalf. He satisfied the wrath of God. We must have a change of mind about who Jesus is and what was done for us. This will lead to a change of lifestyle. The sanctification process is when God works in His children's life to make them more like Christ until the end. Christians are a new creation through Christ, our old life is gone. We can't go back to when we used to live in sexual sin, drunkenness, wild parties, and anything that goes against the Bible. We don't live for man, we live to do God's will.[8]

In the article "Pope Francis Calls for Unity Between Evangelicals, Catholics: 'Division Is the Work of devil,'" Pope Francis states the following about not conforming to the ecumenical movement:

---

[8] Fritz Chery, "Being Set Apart," Bible Reasons, 01/45/19, https://biblereasons.com/being-set-apart/.

> Pope Francis has called for unity among evangelicals, Catholics, and Christians from other denominations, emphasizing that "we are one in Christ" and warning that division between the groups is the work of the devil. "Division is the work of the Father of Lies,": the 'Father of Discord,' who does everything possible to keep us divided," Francis said in a video message to a gathering sponsored by the John 17 Movement, according to Catholic Herald.[9]

Be wary of those saying peace, peace.

> For when they shall say, Peace and safety; then sudden destruction cometh upon them, as travail upon a woman with child; and they shall not escape.[10]

Warnings from the Past

Today, for many people, it is difficult to remain informed about world events. And it is even more challenging to find the time to study history. We study history not to repeat the errors of those who have come before us. Some authors have taken the time to complete much-needed research and make studies available to the public. This research will assist in reviewing the track record and history of political and religious doctrines of a nation, groups, or individuals. Of course, it is prudent to validate which source is trustworthy and which is false; this is not a quick task. Don't let the validation process (time) discourage you from

---

[9] Leah Marieann Klett," Pop Francis Calls for Unity Between Evangelicals, Catholics: 'Division Is the Work of devil,' The Gospel Herald, 01/18/19, http://www.gospelherald.com/articles/55719/20150526/pope-francis-calls-for-unity-between-evangelicals-catholics-division-the-work-of-devil.htm.

[10] 1 Thessalonians 5:3, KJV.

doing your due diligence. Nothing is free; if something has value, it will cost you.

The Vatican is a nation within the country of Italy, per the Lateran Treaty of 1929. It has its flag, ambassadors to foreign countries, and a position in the United Nations; it is not only a power of religious power but a political one. The Vatican does not have separation of church and state; it is a theocracy.

For those of you who study biblical prophecy, is it a stretch to make the connection between the ecumenical movement and the prophesied formation of a one-world religion? This religion is to be ruled by the final antichrist. The ecumenical movement is not something new. Global agendas take time, and Rome has been working progressively behind the scenes to accomplish the goal of a one-world church, a restoration of the so-called "mother church."

> And all that dwell upon the earth shall worship him, whose names are not written in the book of life of the Lamb slain from the foundation of the world.[11]

> Who opposeth and exalteth himself above all that is called God, or that is worshipped; so that he as God sitteth in the temple of God, shewing himself that he is God.[12]

Many churches, as well as individuals, claim the name of Jesus Christ but do not adhere to the biblical Scriptures. Consider this admonishment from the Lord Jesus:

> Many will say to me in that day, Lord, Lord, have we not prophesied in thy name? And in thy name have cast out devils? And in thy name done many

[11] Revelation 13:8, KJV.

[12] 2 Thessalonians 2:4, KJV.

> wonderful works? And then will I profess unto them, *I never knew you*: depart from me, *ye that work iniquity*.[13] (Emphasis added)

> This people draweth nigh unto me with their mouth, and honoureth me with their lips; but their heart is far from me. But in vain they do worship me, *teaching for doctrines the commandments of men*.[14] (Emphasis added)

> *And why call ye me, Lord, Lord, and do not the things which I say?*[15] (Emphasis added)

As with any prophetic event, time will tell whether the ecumenical movement is another step in a sequence of events that will lead to the apostate church. Do you view the topic of the *Great Deception* as something that is coming and has not arrived on the world stage? This Deception has been gradually building, conditioning, and manipulating the hearts and minds of the masses.

> The only people in the world, it seems, who believe in the conspiracy theory of history are those of us who have studied it. While Franklin D. Roosevelt might have exaggerated when he said, "Nothing happens in politics by accident; if it happens, it was planned that way." Carroll Quigley—Bill Clinton's favorite professor at Georgetown University—boldly admitted in his *Tragedy & Hope* (1966) that (a) the multitudes were already under the control of a

---

[13] Matthew 7:22-23, KJV.

[14] Matthew 15:8-9, KJV.

[15] Luke 6:46, KJV.

> small but powerful group bent on world domination and (b) Quigley himself was a part of that group.[16]

According to a debunked website, the following quote by J. Edgar Hoover is about communism:[17]

> Yet the individual is handicapped by coming face to face with a conspiracy so monstrous he cannot believe it exists. The American mind simply has not come to a realization of the evil which has been introduced into our midst. It rejects even the assumption that human creatures could espouse a philosophy which must ultimately destroy all that is good and decent. The Elks Magazine (August 1956).[18]

Hoover's quote is for the reader who has difficulty believing clandestine conspiracies have existed for centuries. The goal of these hidden organizations is power over the masses. When you have all the money that you will ever need, another item the devil promotes is the lust for power, the desire to control. If you don't think this is possible, consider who controls the food industry, transportation, and technology, the ability to have clean water, the monetary system, etc. We live in a world that is ruled by a minority of power and wealth. It is not something we want to hear much less believe on a grand scale.

God is sovereign; it is not possible to stop the coming prophetic events. *The warnings of the coming Great Deception are not*

---

[16] Saussy, *Rulers of Evil,* ix.

[17] Mick West, "Debunked: "A conspiracy so monstrous he cannot believe it exists" (Hoover)," Metabunk.org, 01/18/2019, https://www.metabunk.org/debunked-a-conspiracy-so-monstrous-he-cannot-believe-it-exists-hoover.t330/.

[18] Ibid.

about creating fear but about being aware that the Great Deception threatens spiritual destinies. Many readers need more persuasion, more proof that there are organizations with wicked intentions. The evidence offered here comes in the form of organizational background and history. Organizations like the Church of Rome and the United Nations speak peace, but in their hearts, they seek control over the free world. Satan wants the destruction of humankind. An article published from *Under the Radar Media*, "Bill Clinton's mentor Carroll Quigley Reveals Fraud of the 'Two-Party System,'" shows that conspiracies are no longer in the shadows but out in the open.

> The argument of two parties should represent opposed ideas and policies, one perhaps, of the Right and the other of the Left, *is a foolish idea acceptable only to doctrinate and academic thinkers*. Instead, *the two parties should be almost identical*, so that the American people can "throw the rascals out" at any election *without leading to any profound or extensive shifts in policy*. The policies that are vital and necessary for America are no longer subjects of significant disagreement, but are disputable only in details of procedure, priority, or method.[19] (Emphasis added)

From Saussy's book, *Rulers of Evil*:

> What the Seal of the United States of America represents, to anyone who takes it seriously, is a *Ministry of Sin*. A speech by Jesuit political scientist Michael Novak, published in the January 28, 1989 issue of America, the weekly magazine of American Jesuits,

---

[19] "Bill Clintons Mentor Carroll Quigley Reveals Fraud of the Two-Party System," Under the Radar Media, 1/18/2019, https://undertheradarmedia.wordpress.com/2012/07/19/bill-clintons-mentor-carroll-quigley-reveals-fraud-of-the-two-party-system/.

> sums it up eloquently enough: The framers wanted to build a "novus ordo" that would secure "liberty and justice for all ..." The underlying principle of this new order is the fact of human sin. To build a republic designed for sinners, then, is the indispensable task... There is no use building a social system for saints. There are too few of them. And those there are are impossible to live with!... Any effective social system must therefore be designed for the only moral majority there is: sinners.[20] (Emphasis added)

A puzzle of a thousand pieces does not become a recognizable picture until the appropriate number of the pieces are in their correct placement. We can view end-time prophecy in the same way. It can be challenging to distinguish which prophecies are rising toward fulfillment and which can be considered history. Scholars and theologians debate over unfulfilled prophetic events. I will not be foolish and claim to have a full understanding of prophecy. However, this does not exclude us from heeding the warnings of deception made by Jesus Christ and the apostles. We are not to be ignorant of the devil's tactics.

When putting a puzzle together, you have the puzzle box cover to provide a coherent image of all the pieces in assembled form. God also provides a picture of end-time events in the Bible, specifically the Book of Daniel and the Book of Revelation. The apostles asked Jesus in Matthew 24:3, "What shall be the sign of thy coming, and of the end of the world?" There are harbingers to these coming events to prevent us from falling victim to the deceptions.

> And he shall send his angels with a great sound of a trumpet, and they shall gather together his elect from the four winds, from one end of heaven to the other.

---

[20] Saussy, *Rulers of Evil*, 224.

> Now learn a parable of the fig tree; When his branch is yet tender, and putteth forth leaves, ye know that summer is nigh: So likewise ye, when ye shall see all these things, know that it is near, even at the doors.[21]

Prophetic events are appointed times in history, never early and never late. What would be a rational understanding of a deception of great magnitude? Are we to believe that yesterday didn't contain any deception building, and then suddenly tomorrow, the Great Deception spoken of in the Bible is successfully poured out on the masses? Deception of a global magnitude is a process that requires preconstruction, conditioning the minds of the masses, and setting up the victim or prey for believing the lie. It is my hope the research in this book will create questions that you can't ignore. Is the problem that the masses have been spiritually duped or lulled into a passive state of mind? Jesus Christ and the apostles give their warnings. Believers are to beware of the devil's trickery. As in the 1st century, the deeds of the antichrist are at work today. The Apostle Paul states:

> Now the Spirit speaketh expressly, that in the *latter times* some shall depart from the faith, giving *heed* to *seducing spirits,* and *doctrines of devils*; Speaking lies in hypocrisy; having their conscience seared with a hot iron; *Forbidding to marry,* and commanding to *abstain from meats,* which God hath created to be received with thanksgiving of them which believe and know the truth.[22] (Emphasis added)

The above verse describes the priesthood. Can we assign this verse to the Catholic Church's priests, or is it too vague to

---

[21] Matthew 24:31-33, KJV.

[22] 1 Timothy 4:1-3, KJV.

identify the Catholic Church? Noah Webster defines the word "heed" in the following way:

> HEED, verb transitive, To mind; to regard with care; to take notice of; to attend to; to observe.[23]

Seducing spirits, seduce is defined as follows:

> To draw aside or entice from the path of rectitude and duty in any manner, by flattery, promises, bribes or otherwise; to tempt and lead to iniquity; to corrupt; to deprave.[24]

"Doctrine" has already been defined; it relates to teaching and can be true or false. The verse describes the doctrine as being of devils, which means wickedly based. Forbidding to marry is one of the requirements of the Catholic Church's priests and other religions.

> In most types of Buddhism, monks and nuns must remain celibate.... Certain schools of Hinduism require celibacy to advance toward liberation; but depending on the school, this is either a short-term period in life or a permanent decision. Some Brahmans can marry, others can't.... Jainism encourages celibacy of monks, but not of laymen.[25]

Today's news documents tragic stories about Catholic priests and their victims. The Catholic Church could have

---

[23] Webster, *Heed*, http://webstersdictionary1828.com/Dictionary/Heed.

[24] Webster, *Seduce*, http://webstersdictionary1828.com/Dictionary/Seduce.

[25] Hank Owings, "What religions in the world require chastity or celibacy by their religious leaders/priests?" Quora, July 5, 2012, https://www.quora.com/What-religions-in-the-world-require-chastity-or-celibacy-by-their-religious-leaders-priests.

avoided countless sexual crimes committed inside and outside the church. Celibacy is an individual choice, so priests being unmarried and celibate is not supported in the Bible. By making it mandatory, the Church of Rome put a burden on the priesthood. The woman who rides the beast in Revelation 17 is also described as the "mother of harlots and abominations." From Dave Hunt's book, *A Woman Rides the Beast*, we have the following excerpt that relates to the doctrine of forbidding marriage in the priesthood:

> The great apostle Paul was a celibate and recommended that life to others who wanted to devote themselves fully to serving Christ. He did not, however, make it a condition for church leadership as the Catholic church had done, thereby imposing an unnatural burden upon all clergy that very few could bear. On the contrary, he wrote that a bishop should be "the husband of one wife" (1 Timothy 3:2) and set the same requirement for elders (Titus 1:5,6).[26]
>
> Not only has celibacy made sinners of the clergy who engage in fornication, but it makes harlots out of those with whom they secretly cohabit. Rome is indeed "the mother of harlots"! Her identification as such is unmistakable. No other city, church, or institution in the history of the world is her rival in this particular evil.[27]

Ex-Priest Bernard Fresenborg had this to say in his book *Thirty Years in Hell; or From Darkness to Light*:

> Now, the Good Lord was either right or wrong when He made this declaration, and who is there that

---

[26] Hunt, *A Woman Rides the Beast*, 77.

[27] Ibid., 78.

> would declare that the Lord was mistaken in His injunction? Not one! Therefore, we must acknowledge that either the Lord our God made a declaration that was nonsensical and unreasonable, or else the Roman Priestcraft is living a life which is diagonally contrary to the commands and demands of God Almighty, for when the Roman church declares that her Priests shall not wed, they at once set up a rule for their teachers which is in violation, to not only the laws of God, but the laws of man, as the silent whisperings of man's nature demands a helpmeet. [28]

From ex-priest Charles Chiniquy's chapter titled, "The Vow of Celibacy," he writes:

> WERE I to write all the ingenious tricks, pious lies, shameful stories called miracles, and sacrilegious perversions of the Word of God made use of by superiors of seminaries and nunneries to entice their poor victims into the trap of perpetual celibacy, I should have to write ten large volumes, instead of a short chapter. Sometimes the trials and obligations of married life are so exaggerated that they may frighten the strongest heart. At other times the joys, peace and privileges of celibacy are depicted with such brilliant colors that they fill the coldest mind with enthusiasm.
>
> The pope takes his victim to the top of a high mountain, and there shows him all the honors, praise, wealth, peace and joys of this world, united to the most glorious throne of heaven, and then tells him: *"I will give you all those things if you fall at my feet,*

[28] Fresenborg, *Thirty Years in Hell*, 60.

> *promise me an absolute submission, and swear never to marry in order to serve me better."*[29] (Emphasis added)

During the Festival of Easter (Ishtar), Catholics practice what is called Lent, and during the forty days of Lent, they are at times to abstain from eating meats (fasting). One such practice is not eating the flesh of animals, as directed by Canon Law 1251.

> Canon 1251: Abstinence from eating meat or another food according to the prescriptions of the conference of bishops is to be observed on Fridays throughout the year unless they are solemnities; abstinence and fast are to be observed on Ash Wednesday and on the Friday of the Passion and Death of Our Lord Jesus Christ.[30]

On the website *Got Questions,* the question was asked, "Is ecumenism biblical? Below is the writer's reply. Once you move past some definitions of ecumenism, you come to the writer's answers.

> First of all, are those we are joining with truly Christians in the biblical sense of the word? Many people and organizations reference the name of Jesus Christ and even state He is Lord and Savior yet clearly reject what the Bible says about Him. Obvious examples of this are Mormons and Jehovah's Witnesses, who call themselves followers of Jesus Christ and claim to be "Christian" yet deny what the Bible declares concerning Christ's nature and work. A not-so-obvious example is liberal Christianity. Liberal

---

[29] Charles Chiniquy, *50 Years in the Church of Rome* (Chicago: Adam Craig, 1891), 129.

[30] Colin B. Donovan, STL, "Fasting and Abstinence," Catholic Online, 02/27/2019, https://www.catholic.org/lent/abfast.php.

Christianity is found in almost every denomination, and, although it may seem Christian, it usually rejects several essential truths. Liberals often deny or diminish the inspiration and authority of the Bible (2 Timothy 3:16), the exclusive nature of salvation in Christ (John 14:6; 1 Timothy 2:5), and the total dependence upon God's grace, apart from human works, for salvation (Romans 3:24, 28; Galatians 2:16; Ephesians 2:8–9)....

There is a major emphasis in our day on ecumenical unity among evangelicals and Roman Catholics. Those who promote such unity state that both groups are Christian and both are God-honoring systems of faith. But there are substantial differences between the two groups. *Biblical Christianity and Roman Catholicism are two different religions that practice and believe different things about how one is saved, the authority of the Bible, the priesthood of believers, the nature of man, the work of Christ on the cross, etc.* The list of irreconcilable differences between what the Bible says and what the Roman Catholic Church says make any joint mission between the two impossible. Those who deny this are not being true to what they say they believe, no matter which side they are on. Any Catholic who is serious about his faith will reject what a serious evangelical Christian believes, and vice-versa....

Regarding ecumenical ventures, we need to ask whether or not these goals are being pursued. Often, sharing the gospel becomes an afterthought, if it is even thought of at all. In place of the gospel, ecumenism tends to focus on political and social messages. Rather than seek to transform hearts, ecumenical endeavors often seek to transform environments—political, social, or financial.

> *The ultimate goal of our actions should be the salvation of lost sinners (Ephesians 2:1–3).*[31] (Emphasis added)

A Christian with "fundamental disciplines" who desires to adhere to the Scriptures literally will be persecuted for his or her stand.[32] It happened to the early Christian church when Constantine the Great of Rome decided to take Christianity as the "state" religion. Jesus said that if you follow Him, you will have tribulation.

> These things I have spoken unto you, that in me ye might have peace. In the world ye shall have tribulation: but be of good cheer; I have overcome the world.[33]

The Reformation

Some view the ecumenical movement with caution, as something to be wary of! By reviewing the Protestant Reformation and the Catholic Church's *Counter-Reformation,* we can see the puzzle of the Great Deception taking form. Some of the puzzle pieces were put in their respective places centuries ago, for example, "*learning against learning.*" Recall the chapter on *propaganda.*

For the most part, today's Christians have been lulled into complacency, a false sense of security. You may say that is a harsh statement. It is not said with ill intention but with care for my fellow brothers and sisters in Christ. It is to make you inquire. The knowledge of the Protestant Reformation and the Catholic Church's *Counter-Reformation* has either been forgotten or

---

[31] "Is ecumenism biblical?" Got Questions, November 11, 2018, https://www.gotquestions.org/ecumenism-ecumenical.html.

[32] Ephesians 6:10-13.

[33] John 16:33, KJV.

intentionally left out of the teaching in today's Western churches. To forget something, you would have to have known of its existence prior. Take notice of how often, if at all, the curriculum in church Bible study classes provides instruction on the details of the Protestant Reformation of 1517 and what the Catholic Church has done in response.

The Pilgrim church existed long before Martin Luther came on the world stage. What is missing in the teaching of church history is the moves and counter-moves made between the Protestant church and the Catholic Church. Knowledge of this history would have changed today's movement for a universal Christian church from one of blind acceptance to one of caution and warning. The doctrine of *pre-tribulation rapture* and the *ecumenical movement* are widely accepted.

It is time to sound the alarm and give forewarning; every generation needs *watchmen*. Have we forgotten all the blood of the martyrs—those individuals who refused to deny Christ as Savior and stood against the Church of Rome's tyranny? The Reformation was more than just a complaint against the selling of indulgences, which led Martin Luther to the investigation of how Rome viewed forgiveness and justification; it was light breaking through the darkness.

> The sixteenth century presents the spectacle of a stormy sunrise after a dismal night. Europe awoke from the long sleep of superstition. Nations shook off their chains. The dead arose. The witnesses to truth who had been silenced and slain stood up once more and renewed their testimony. The martyred confessors reappeared in the Reformers. There was a cleansing in the spiritual sanctuary. Civil and religious liberty were inaugurated. The discovery of printing and revival of learning accelerated the movement. There was progress everywhere. Columbus struck across the ocean and opened a new

> hemisphere to view. Rome was shaken on her seven hills, and lost one-half of her dominions. Protestant nations were created. The modern world was called into existence.[34]

The *Dark Ages* had been imposed on Europe for close to a thousand years by Rome. Without the light of God's Word being made available to the masses, they truthfully were in the dark. As a Bible-believing Christian, try to imagine yourself not having your current knowledge of God—not having the hope, the relationship, the scriptural discernment, and understanding He gives you. What a sense of emptiness that would be—having your knowledge limited to oppression, fear, and superstitious dogma.

The Church of Rome forced this reality on the masses. The popes suppressed any opposition, and if you were accused of, or even suspected of, being a "heretic," then you were the guest of honor at the next bonfire. Compare that to the liberty and freedom you now have. Currently, in many countries, people are still able to open a Bible and read it for themselves without the threat of persecution, but that is changing. The Holy Spirit gives discernment of the Scriptures to believers.

> But the natural man receiveth not the things of the Spirit of God: for they are foolishness unto him: neither can he know them, because they are spiritually discerned.[35]

Human discernment, at its basic level, offers enough understanding to know that the world we live in is no accident—there is intelligent design.

---

[34] H. Grattan Guinness, *Romanism and the Reformation* (Toronto: S.R. Briggs, 1887), 223.

[35] 1 Corinthians 2:14, KJV.

> For the invisible things of him from the creation of the world are clearly seen, being understood by the things that are made, even his eternal power and Godhead; so that they are without excuse:[36]

Before Johannes Gutenberg's printing press, the common man had limited-to-no access to God's written Word. The general population was ignorant of what the Bible honestly had to say about salvation—faith in the atoning sacrifice of Jesus Christ at Calvary, redemption through the blood of Jesus, the simplicity of the gospel message. Martin Luther read the prophecies in the Book of Daniel and the Book of Revelation.[37] Further study of these prophetic books identified the spirit of the antichrist working through Catholicism and the *Dynasty of Popes*.[38] Gutenberg's printing press aided the masses; they were able to read or hear the Word of God for themselves.

> So then faith cometh by hearing, and hearing by the word of God.[39]

Scripture makes it clear the papacy has no biblical authority over the *body of Christ*, the Christian church. Note this verse where Jesus, not man, is the head of the Christian Church.

> And he is the head of the body, the church: who is the beginning, the firstborn from the dead; that in all things he might have the preeminence.[40]

---

[36] Romans 1:20, KJV.

[37] Humanity is saved by grace; this was the revelation that Martin Luther received from Ephesians 2:8-9.

[38] Matt 24:5, Revelation 6:2, 17:1-6.

[39] Romans 10:17, KJV.

[40] Colossians 1:18, KJV.

The papacy has considerable political and religious power but does not have God-given authority to exercise those powers over the masses. To restate the difference between *power* and *authority,* I repeat, anyone with enough power can force others into submission; history is full of tyrants. Righteous authority is *justly given* and authorizes the right to wield the hand of power.

The Dark Ages were over; the Reformation brought the light of the gospel, and Scripture was available once again to the masses. The papacy was losing control. Hundreds of thousands of people across Europe turned away from Rome and to the truth of the Scriptures. This exodus resulted in both a loss of control and loss of financial revenues for the Catholic Church. The selling of indulgences to the masses of tributary nations was the primary source of funding for the construction of St. Peter's Cathedral. The Church of Rome had to do something. The Catholic Church tried to stop the common man and woman from reading God's Word for themselves by burning Bibles and burning Reformers (heretics). This action only reinforced the revelation that the popes were indeed a form of the final Antichrist and that Catholicism was the *woman riding the beast* in Revelation 17.

> In the reaction which followed, all the powers of hell seemed to be let loose upon the adherents of the Reformation. War followed war; tortures, burnings, and massacres were multiplied. Yet the Reformation stood undefeated and unconquerable. God's word upheld it, and the energies of His almighty spirit. It was the work of Christ as truly as the founding of the church eighteen centuries ago; and the revelation of the future which He gave from heaven that prophetic book with which the Scripture closes was one

> of the mightiest instruments employed in its accomplishment[41]

The Catholic Church had to devise a different approach to suppress and destroy Protestantism. I have noted three specific actions the Church of Rome implemented in their *Counter-Reformation,* requiring further study. The *Council of Trent,* the *Society of Jesus,* and the doctrine of *Futurism.*

> The council of Trent (1545-1563) was a turning point in the history of Catholicism when dogma and disciplinary reforms were passed.
>
> In Trent, the council discontinuously met over 18 years *Concile de Trente.*
>
> A reform of the church and of the clergy was called for by humanists and some members of the clergy for years, because churches were getting empty, behaviours of the regular and secular clergy were criticised, priests often were ignorant. The 5th council of Latran ended in 1517 but had come to nothing.
>
> The development of the Reformation urged Charles V to call for another council meeting. Pope Paul III sent the first notice in 1536, but the council finally met in Trent, on Empire ground, in 1545.
>
> The council of Trent, through five popes' reigns, held 25 sessions over 18 years, with long interruptions. Around 1550, during the second session, Charles V asked a Lutheran Protestant delegation to attend, but no dialogue ensued.
>
> The council enabled the church to define its dogma and discipline:

---

[41] H. Grattan Guinness, F.R.G.S., *Romanism and the Reformation* (Toronto: S.R. Briggs, 1887), 251.

- faith has two origins—i.e., the Bible and the *tradition,*
- man's salvation rests on God, *but also on the believer's participation,*
- seven sacraments still exist,
- *Christ's presence in the bread and the wine* of the communion is real and substantial,
- the canon of the Scriptures, namely the list of the books in the Bible considered as God given, is determined,
- *indulgences are kept,* but not to be marketed,
- rules concerning ecclesiastic discipline are established,
- *inquisition is maintained,*
- the *purgatory* is asserted and prayers for the deceased still required,
- the *legitimacy of saints' worship* is asserted.[42] (Emphasis added)

At times, the Church of Rome appears to be easing up on its unwillingness to change church dogma. Without this appeasement, the ecumenical movement would not succeed. This illusion is where the ends justify the means, and the Church of Rome is using her technique of missionary adaptation. In F. Tupper Saussy's book *Rulers of Evil,* he explains it this way:

> This is explained as "the adjustment of the mission subject to the cultural requirements of the mission object" so that the papacy's needs will be brought "as much as possible in accord with existing socially shared patterns of thought, evaluation, and action,

[42] "The Catholic Reformation or Counter-Reformation in 16th century," Musee, 01/18/2019, https://www.museeprotestant.org/en/notice/the-catholic-reformation-or-counter-reformation/.

> so as to avoid unnecessary and serious disorganization.[43]

The late Dave Hunt co-authored *The Seduction of Christianity; Spiritual Discernment in the Last Days*, and authored the well-documented book *A Woman Rides the Beast*. In *A Woman Rides the Beast*, Hunt gives a detailed study of the relationship between the Catholic Church and Revelation 17. Here are some of his excerpts about the Catholic Church's willingness to change dogma.

> To understand Roman Catholicism one must ignore the public posturing and public-relations-motivated profile offered by the Catholic church. The face that Rome shows to the world varies from country to country depending upon the control it has and what it can effect. Instead, we must look to Catholicism's official doctrines, which never change.
>
> Vatican II is thought by most Catholics and non-Catholics to have liberalized Catholicism. In fact, it reaffirmed the canons and decrees of previous key councils: "This sacred council accepts loyally the venerable faith of our ancestors ... and it proposes again the decrees of the Second Council of Nicea, of the Council of Florence, and the Council of Trent." The Council of Trent denounced the Reformation and dammed evangelicals' beliefs with more than 100 anathemas. All these condemnations of the Gospel of God's grace are endorsed and reaffirmed by Vatican II.[44]
>
> To escape that destructive enslavement, the Reformers urged submission to God's pure Word as the

---

[43] Saussy, *Rulers of Evil*, 13.

[44] Hunt, *A Woman Rides the Beast*, 89.

> ultimate authority rather than to the church or the pope. The basic issue that sparked the Reformation (and which remains the basic issue today) was whether to continue in blind submission to Rome's dogmas, even though they contradicted the Bible, or to submit to God's Word alone as the final authority.[45]
>
> The Reformers made that choice in favor of Scripture and their central cry became *Sola Scriptura*! That liberating truth was rejected at the Council of Trent by bishops who were unwilling to surrender control of the people under them. It was even considered to be harmful for the people to possess the Bible in their own tongue because they might take it literally, which Rome argues even today must not be done. From her viewpoint only a specially trained elite can understand the Bible:
>
> ...Trent's view that the authority for the Catholic is the church, not the Bible, remains in force today. Only Scripture scholars trained at the Pontifical Biblical Institute in Rome with "a degree in theology [and]mastery of six or seven languages (including Hebrew, Aramaic, and Greek ...)" are capable of understanding the Bible. Having earned "a Licentiate in Sacred Scripture ... the Catholic church's license to teach Scripture." They alone can teach the Bible. No layman is qualified. Vatican II insists: ... [46]

The root of the word Protestantism is *"protest,"* just as the word Christian became a way of identifying people who believed and followed the "Way" of Jesus Christ. People who were

---

[45] Ibid., 329, 330.

[46] Ibid., 330.

in agreement with Martin Luther rejected and protested the Edict of Worms by Emperor Charles V of Habsburg and became known as Protestants. The Edict of Worms forced or bound Habsburgs' Empire of 300 princely states and free territories to Roman Catholicism. The motivation for Luther's Reformation wasn't totally for religious reasons. The papacy was putting a financial strain on the German princes. Roderick C. Meredith, Editor in Chief of *Tomorrow's World Magazine,* wrote a study on the *500 Years of The Protestant Reformation*. In it, he provides details to Martin Luther's connection with the German princes.

John Mosheim describes this abuse of power:

> Among these artifices, what were called indulgences—that is, liberty to buy off the punishments of their sins by contributing money to pious uses—held a distinguished place. And to these, recourse was had as often as the papal treasury became exhausted, to the immense injury of the public interests. Under some plausible, but for the most part false pretext, the ignorant and timorous people were beguiled with the prospect of great advantage by the hawkers of indulgences, who were in general base and profligate characters.
>
> These scandals provided a very adequate reason in the eyes of many German princes, for instance, to throw off the papal yoke—whether by "reform" or revolt—in order to free themselves from papal taxation and interference, and to seize the wealth of the churches and monasteries. Luther's later attack on the papal financial policy and taxation instantly made him a champion of the German middle class and, indirectly, of all his countrymen, who had long

> harbored feelings of resentment toward the crafty and easy-living Italians.[47]

Above, we can see how the *Edict of Worms* forced the German princes to pay tribute to Rome. How can the Vatican justify the demand for tributary taxes? John the Baptist, Jesus Christ, and the apostles never *forced* anyone to convert or to pay tribute to the New Testament church. God permits each of us to exercise our ability to choose.

Protestant Reformers and the Church of Rome were in a standoff. This stalemate was similar to WWI Trench Warfare. Here we have two opposing sides digging in for the long haul, and neither one was willing to give up conquered ground. The Lutheran faith consisted of the Augsburg Confession.[48] The stalemate continued until Pope Paul III called for both sides to meet in a small Italian cathedral in the city of Trent. Here we see the Jesuit's *craft* played its strategic part. The Council of Trent was not for ecumenical reasons.

> Then the Jesuits moved in. Diego Lainez, Alfonso Salmeron, two of the original companions, and Claude LeJay, all three in their early thirties, distinguished themselves at Trent early on by spurning the grand style of the other delegates. They set up housekeeping in a "narrow, smoke-blackened baker's oven" and wore clothing so heavily patched and greasy that other priests were embarrassed to associate with them. They carried with them intricate

---

[47] Roderick C. Meredith, "The Truth Behind the Protestant Reformation, Part 2, Setting the Stage for Revolution," Tomorrow's World, March-April 2017, https://www.tomorrowsworld.org/magazines/2017/may-june/setting-the-stage-for-revolution.

[48] Glen L. Thompson, "The Unaltered Augsburg Confession: A.D. 1530," St. Paul's Lutheran church and School, 01/20/2019, https://www.stpls.com/uploads/4/4/8/0/44802893/augsburg-confession.pdf.

> advisories from Ignatius himself, written from the delegates' point of view, as for example: ... When the matter that is being debated seems so manifestly just and right that I can no longer keep silent, then I should speak my mind with the greatest composure and conclude what I have said with the words 'subject of course to the judgment of a wiser head than mine.' If the leaders of the opposing party should try to befriend me, I must cultivate these men, who have influence over the heretics and lukewarm Catholics, and try to win them away from their errors with holy wisdom and love....[49]

The Council of Trent denied every petition the Reformers brought to the table. The Roman Catholic Church had no intention of amending its dogma. The council hurled over a hundred anathemas and damnations at the Protestant Reformers. The Council of Trent is where the *white pope* is said to begin taking orders from the *black pope*. One generation later, the guidelines (*Directorium Inquisitorum, 1584*) for what became known as the Roman Catholic Inquisition were published under the Jesuit supervision and the command of the Cardinals Inquisitors General. Is the Church of Rome a Christian church or a continuation of the Roman Empire under the guise of a church? This Empire has its Emperors, the popes, who, like previous Roman emperors, claimed to be infallible and to be God on earth. There is the private army of the papacy, the military order of the Jesuits.

The Jesuits had one mission at the Council of Trent—to destroy Protestantism and return the people to the "mother church." The Inquisition, with its use of torture and burning Christians at the stake, was only one method in their arsenal. Twisting the interpretation of Scriptures would also have to be used, "learning against learning." Misinterpretation of

[49] Saussy, *Rulers of Evil*, 56.

Scriptures was the only way to separate the pope's actions from that of the antichrist.

The *Dynasty of the Popes* is a working example, a shadow of the final Antichrist. The same individual prophesized in the Book of Daniel and the Book of Revelation. It was believed long before the Protestant Reformation that the spirit of the antichrist was working through the papacy. The Reformation and the invention of the printing press helped propagate this view. Dr. David Jeremiah, author and Senior Pastor of Shadow Mountain Community Church in San Diego, California, has published several books. Dr. Jeremiah's book *"The Handwriting on the Wall"* is a study on the Book of Daniel. The following comparison is about the papacy and the spirit of the antichrist:

> Before the Protestant Reformation, the most accepted idea was that the Antichrist was the Catholic pope. Saint Bernard in the twelfth century called Pope Anacletus the Antichrist. In the thirteenth century, Frederick II, ruler of the Holy Roman Empire, accused Pope Gregory IX of being the Antichrist. It wasn't the Protestants doing the name calling, it was the Catholics who had fallen out of favor with the papal regime that was in power at the time.
>
> Not only disgruntled Catholics, but also some of the most responsible Protestant scholars and theologians were convinced that the Antichrist was living in Rome disguised as the pope. The list is impressive: Martin Luther, leader of the Protestant Reformation; Philip Melanchthon, German reformer; John Calvin, French reformer in Geneva; Huldreich Zwingli, Swiss reformer; William Tyndale, English reformer and Bible translator. All of these illustrious men and

> more pointed their finger at the pope as the guilty one.[50]

Francisco Ribera was a Jesuit priest who, like all Jesuits, took the *Jesuit Blood Oath,* dedicating himself to the interests of the papacy. With his education in theology, he developed a prophetic conclusion that was different from what the victims of Rome were voicing based on the Scriptures. Ribera changed the interpretation of Scripture; rather than the spirit of the antichrist working progressively toward the *last days,* Ribera's revision changed the translation to mean that one evil man will arrive on the world stage just before the Lords' return.

Ribera shifted the connection of the antichrist with Catholicism and the *Dynasty of the Popes* to a future world leader, who will arrive on the scene when the Jews rebuild their temple. Ribera published his commentary in 1590 and passed his *baton of deception* to another professor of theology, Jesuit scholar Cardinal Robert Bellarmine (1542–1621). Bellarmine published his works on the Reformation, *Polemic Lectures Concerning the Disputed Points of Christian Belief Against the Heretics of This Time*. Bellarmine agrees with Ribera, which is no surprise; the Jesuits work together as a unified army. The *Futurist* school of thought became accepted by Catholics, and these works are known as *Jesuit Futurism.*

> Futurism (Christianity) is the proposal that the Book of Revelation does not bear the application to the Middle Ages or the papacy, rather the "future" (more particularly to a period immediately prior to the Second Coming). The Dictionary of Premillennial Theology (1997) states that Ribera was an Augustinian amillennialist, whose form of futurism proposed

[50] David Jeremiah, with C.C. Carlson, *The Handwriting on the Wall: Secrets from the Prophecies of Daniel* (Dallas: Word Publishing, 1992), 147.

that only the introductory chapters of "Revelation referred to ancient Rome, and the remainder referred to a literal three and half years at the end of time. His interpretation was then followed by Robert Bellarmine and the Spanish Dominican Thomas Malvenda.[51]

In truth, the Counter-Reformation wasn't really much of a "reformation" of Catholicism, at least not from a theological perspective. It was truly a "counter to the Reformation"; that is, it was primarily concerned with refuting and silencing Protestant disagreements. Much of the Counter-Reformation was driven by politics. In Spain, for example, kings and queens were more than happy to apply Catholic resources toward stamping out dissenters—*in their case, mostly Protestants. Deportation, excommunication, and execution were common tools used in the Counter-Reformation.*

However, on the most critical issues, the Council of Trent, like the rest of the Counter-Reformation, was mostly a doubling-down on entrenched Catholic theology. This council, and the other Counter-Reformers, doggedly defended transubstantiation, upheld the necessity of sacraments for salvation, rejected sola fide, and claimed outright that Catholic tradition was as equally authoritative as the Bible. In addition, the council members determined that the Latin Vulgate was the one and only acceptable Bible for church use. And they insisted that, since politics

---

[51] "Francisco Ribera," Wikipedia: The Free Encyclopedia, 1/21/2019, https://en.wikipedia.org/wiki/Francisco_Ribera#Futurism.

> was instituted by God, all political leaders were subject to papal authority.[52] (Emphasis added)

By falsely projecting the devil's plans to a forward time, this teaching creates a pause in the prophetic timeline where there isn't one. Also, Futurism fabricates the premise of thought for those who have accepted the indoctrination. Is it rational to think the devil is going take a break, back off on his agenda when his time is limited? This break, midstream in history's regular timeline, builds a false sense of security. Whether we are the generation to experience the Apocalypse or not, this teaching is deceitful. With a quick look at history, we can easily see that the wickedness and the evil in the world have not taken a sideline. Scripture records Gods' prophetic judgment against Satan; we can look at the first and last books of the Bible, Genesis and Revelation, for these prophecies.

> And I will put enmity between thee and the woman, and between thy seed and her seed; it *shall bruise thy head,* and thou shalt bruise his heel.[53] (Emphasis added)

> And the great dragon was *cast out, that old serpent, called the devil, and Satan,* which *deceiveth the whole world*: he was cast out into the earth, and his angels were cast out with him.[54] (Emphasis added)

> Therefore rejoice, ye heavens, and ye that dwell in them. *Woe* to the *inhabiters of the earth*_and of the sea! for the *devil is come down unto you,* having *great wrath,*

---

52 "Counter Reformation," Got Questions, 01/21/2019, https://www.gotquestions.org/Counter-Reformation.html.

53 Genesis 3:15, KJV.

54 Revelation 12:9, KJV.

> because he knoweth that *he hath but a short time.*[55] (Emphasis added)

> And the devil that deceived them was *cast into the lake of fire* and brimstone, where the beast and the false prophet are, and shall be tormented day and night for ever and ever.[56] (Emphasis added)

The Apostle Peter believed the devil was presently active in his desire for human destruction. Note Peter's warning:

> Be sober, *be vigilant;* because your *adversary* the devil, as a roaring lion, walketh about, seeking whom *he may devour:*[57] (Emphasis added)

Vigilance means we are to remain watchful, stay alert, be attentive to avoid danger, and provide safety. Peter gives that warning because Satan is active 24 hours a day, seven days a week, and is not on holiday. Adam forfeited the title deed to creation through his disobedience, and Jesus Christ's sacrifice and atoning work at Calvary redeemed what Adam lost. Both the Apostles John and Paul make it clear in Scripture that the spirit of the antichrist was already working in the first-century church. Before listing a few verses to show that the spirit of the antichrist was already at work in the early church, let's consider the definition of the noun "anti." Noah Webster defines "anti" as: "A preposition signifying against, *opposite,* contrary, or *in place of;* …"[58] (Emphasis added)

---

[55] Revelation 12:12, KJV.

[56] Revelation 20:10, KJV.

[57] 1 Peter 5:8, KJV.

[58] "Anti," *Webster's Dictionary,* 01/21/2019, http://webstersdictionary1828.com/Dictionary/Anti.

> For *false Christs* and false prophets shall rise, and shall shew signs and wonders, to seduce, if it were possible, even the elect.[59] (Emphasis added)

> Little children, it is the last time: and as ye have heard that antichrist shall come, even now are there *many antichrists*; whereby we know that it is the last time.[60] (Emphasis added)

> Beloved, *believe not every spirit, but try the spirits whether they are of God*: because many false prophets are gone out into the world. Hereby know ye the Spirit of God: Every spirit that confesseth that Jesus Christ is come in the flesh is of God: And every spirit that confesseth not that Jesus Christ is come in the flesh is not of God: and this is that spirit of antichrist, whereof ye have heard that it should come; and *even now already is it in the world*.[61] (Emphasis added)

Author Steve Wohlberg wrote a book titled *The Left Behind Deception*; he also produced a short article that relates, titled "Left Behind by the Jesuits." Under the heading *Defining the Issue*, we find the following:

> Before we go much farther, let's define some terms. Historicism is the belief that biblical prophecies about the little horn, the man of sin, the Antichrist, the Beast, and the Babylonian Harlot of Revelation 17, all apply to the developing history of Christianity and to the ongoing struggle between Jesus Christ and Satan within the Christian church, culminating

[59] Mark 13:22, KJV.

[60] 1 John 2:18, KJV.

[61] 1 John 4:1-3, KJV.

> at the end of time. Historicism sees these prophecies as having a direct application to Papal Rome as a system whose doctrines are actually a denial of the New Testament message of free salvation by grace through simple faith in Jesus Christ, apart from works. Historicism was the primary prophetic viewpoint of the Protestant Reformers. In direct opposition to Historicism, and rising up as a razor-sharp counterattack on Protestantism, was that of the Jesuits with their viewpoint of Futurism, which basically says, "The Antichrist prophecies have nothing to do with the history of Papal Rome, rather, they apply to only one sinister man who comes at the end."
>
> *Thus Jesuit Futurism sweeps 1,500 years of prophetic history under the proverbial rug by inserting its infamous GAP.* This theory teaches that when Rome fell, prophecy stopped, only to continue again right around the time of the rapture, thus the "gap" was created. The ten horns, the little horn, the Beast, and the Antichrist have nothing to do with Christians until this "last-day Antichrist" should appear. According to this viewpoint, there were no prophecies being fulfilled during the Dark Ages![62] (Emphasis added)

Before continuing to the next topic, let's reconsider the prophecies of the Book of Daniel and the writing of the Apostle Paul in 2 Thessalonians without the Jesuit's false doctrine of *Futurism*. Then, the belief held by the early church fathers and the Pilgrim church is valid. The spirit of the antichrist has been working throughout church history. This view is in agreement with the biblical text. This same spirit is historically seen working through the Papacy.

---

[62] Steve Wohlberg, "Left Behind by the Jesuits," Assembly of Yahweh, 01/22/2019 http://assemblyoftrueisrael.com/Documents/Leftbehind.htm.

For the false doctrine of Futurism to be believable, the Jesuits would twist the true meaning of prophecies in the Book of Daniel, Book of Revelation, and the Apostle Paul's remarks in 2 Thessalonians 2. This twisting is done to misdirect the identification of the antichrists away from the papacy. "Anti" means in place of, so do the popes claim to occupy the place of God the Father and Jesus Christ on earth? Read the Apostle Paul's comments on the man of sin:

> Let no man deceive you by any means: for that day shall not come, except there come a *falling away first,* and that *man of sin be revealed, the son of perdition;* Who *opposeth* and *exalteth himself above all that is called God,* or that is worshipped; so that *he as God sitteth in the temple of God, shewing himself that he is God....* For the *mystery of iniquity doth already work*: only he who now letteth (hold fast-restrain) will let, until he be taken out of the way. [63] (Emphasis added)

The Apostle Paul's remarks in 2 Thessalonians and the prophecy from Daniel about the rise of the "little horn" are speaking of the workings of the antichrist here on earth. This reign is through the bishops of Rome, the dynasty of the popes, beginning in A.D. 538.

The Apostle Paul spoke of a restrainer that held back the arrival of the antichrist, the man of sin. Many prophecy teachers say that the restrainer is the Holy Spirit. And when the Lord raptures the church, the Holy Spirit will leave with the church—thereby allowing the antichrist to enter the world stage. A historical view held by early church fathers is the power and strength of the Roman Empire is the restrainer spoken of by the Apostle Paul. When that power falls away, it will allow the popes to establish their kingdom. The Apostle Paul could share this truth in

---

[63] 2 Thessalonians 2:3,4,7 KJV.

private with the early church. However, he couldn't write it in his epistles because it would only increase the persecution of the Christian church, which was already under Roman oppression.

The popular view of Nebuchadnezzar's dream in Daniel 2 shows the fourth kingdom to be Rome represented as the *legs of iron* and not being conquered but disbanding into ten kingdoms represented by the statues' ten toes made of iron and clay. The ten kingdoms were the Alamanni (Germans), Anglo Saxons (English), Burgundian (Swiss), Franks (French), Heruli (extinct A.D. 493), Lombards (Italian), Ostrogoths (extinct A.D. 538), Suevi (Portuguese), Vandals (extinct A.D. 534), and the Visigoths (Spanish). These ten kingdoms were in Europe. The statue of Daniel 2 has two legs of iron representing the East and West capitals of the Roman Empire. However, the "little horn," which represents the antichrist, rises from within the 10 horns, the 10 kingdoms which are the Western half of the Empire, Europe. Let's consider the prophecies. The Bible uses the word "beast" to represent a kingdom, and a "horn" can mean a king or a kingdom.

> After this I saw in the night visions, and behold a *fourth beast*, dreadful and terrible, and strong exceedingly; and it had great iron teeth: it devoured and brake in pieces, and stamped the residue with the feet of it: and it was diverse from all the beasts that were before it; and it had *ten horns*.[64] (Emphasis added)

> I considered the horns, and, behold, there came up among them another *little horn*, before whom there were *three of the first horns plucked up by the roots*: and,

[64] Daniel 7:7, KJV.

> behold, in this horn were eyes like the *eyes of man*, and a *mouth speaking great things*.[65] (Emphasis added)

This little horn uproots three of the 10 kingdoms: the Heruli, Ostrogoths, and the Vandals. By uprooting, there was no chance for continued existence or future return. Emperor Justinian issued a decree in A.D. 533 that the bishop of Rome is the chief bishop over all the churches and the *corrector of heretics*. Emperor Justinian focused more on his religious desires and less on being a soldier, his desire to build the kingdom of God on earth. Here we have the falling away of the emperors of Rome's power. The power of the empire shifted to the papacy in A.D. 538 Vigilius ascended to the papal office in A.D. 538 under the military protection of General Belisarius.

> Vigilius' statement to Justinian is a very strong rebuttal of theological enthusiasm of the emperor by a pope. Justinian in fact left already the Chiefs of Staff position at the military in 538 since he was more involved in the synods and seminaries than in the army barracks. This is the diffusion of the Roman Empire and the final fall of the Roman Empire. When politics took up theology, power of that entity shifted to the most trained in theology, the papacy, although he was not going to receive this honored space for some time.[66]

Henry Grattan Guinness was a Protestant Christian preacher and author. He evangelized during the Evangelical

---

[65] Daniel 7:8, KJV.

[66] "538 A.D. and the Transition from Pagan Roman Empire to Holy Roman Empire: Justinian's Metamorphosis from Chief of Staffs to Theologian," International Journal of Humanities and Social Sciences, January 1, 2017, http://www.ijhssnet.com/view.php?u=https://www.ijhssnet.com/journals/Vol_7_No_1_January_2017/7.pdf.

awakening of the 1859 Ulster Revival and had this to say in his book *Romanism and the Reformation:*

> Paul distinctly tells us that he knew, and that the Thessalonians knew, what that hindrance was, and that it was then in existence. The early church, through the writings of the Fathers, tells us what it knew upon the subject, and with remarkable unanimity affirms that this "let," or hindrance, *was the Roman empire* as *governed by the Caesars*; that *while the Caesars held imperial power, it was impossible for the predicted antichrist to arise,* and that on the *fall of the Caesars* he would arise. Here we have a point on which Paul affirms the existence of knowledge in the Christian church. The early church knew, he says, what this hindrance was. The early church tells us what it did know upon the subject, and no one in these days can be in a position to contradict its testimony as to what Paul had, by word of mouth only, told the Thessalonians. It is a point on which ancient tradition alone can have any authority. Modern speculation is positively impertinent on such a subject.[67] (Emphasis added)

From Tertullian, an early church father, A.D. 200:

> And now ye know what *detaineth,* that he might be revealed in his time. For the mystery of iniquity doth already work; only he who now *hinders* must hinder, until he be taken out of the way." What obstacle is there but the *Roman state,* the *falling away of which,* by

[67] H. Grattan Guinness, *Romanism and the Reformation* (Toronto: S.R. Briggs, 1887), 194.

> being scattered *into ten kingdoms, shall introduce Antichrist upon (its own ruins)*? [68] (Emphasis added)

Rev. Edward Elliot lived from 1793-1875. He was an English clergyman—a scholar who graduated from Trinity College, Cambridge. Rev. Elliott believed in the historicist view of biblical eschatology—that the Book of Revelation covered history's timeline from the Apostle John until the Second Advent of Jesus Christ.

> With which view well accorded what was added in his prophecy by St. Paul. For he spoke of the seed of the apostacy, which was to bring forth antichrist, as already sown: but that there was a certain hindrance first to be removed out of the way,—a hindrance well under stood in the church to mean the Roman Empire as at that time constituted,—ere room could be made for the antichrist's development. And when then might the first of these changes occur, and imperial heathen Rome fall to make way for him? [69]

Historically the Papacy has mirrored the traits of Daniel 7's *little horn*. Both the prophet Daniel and the Apostle Paul tell how the antichrist will sit in place of God and speak great blasphemies. The Pharisees accused Jesus Christ of these same blasphemies. The difference is that Jesus Christ is the Son of God and not guilty of the sin of blasphemy. The Bible provides examples of what is considered blasphemy.

---

[68] Tertullian, *Ante-Nicene Fathers Vol. 3*, trans. Peter Holmes (Buffalo, New York: Christian Literature Publishing Co., 1885), 1049.

[69] Edward B. Elliott, *Commentary on the Apocalypse* (London: Seeley, Burnside and Seeley, 1847), 68-69.

> I and my Father are one.[70]

> The Jews answered him, saying, For a good work we stone thee not; *but for blasphemy*; and because that thou, *being a man, makest thyself God*.[71] (Emphasis added)

> And when he saw their faith, he said unto him, *Man, thy sins are forgiven thee*.[72] (Emphasis added)

> And the scribes and the Pharisees began to reason, saying, Who is this which speaketh *blasphemies? Who can forgive sins, but God alone?*[73] (Emphasis added)

Here we will let the words from the Church of Rome speak for themselves. From the *Catholic Encyclopedia Vol. 12,* under the heading of *The Pope's Universal Coercive Jurisdiction*:

> ... It is theirs to judge offenses against the laws, to impose and to remit penalties. This judicial authority will even include the power to pardon sin.[74]

From Michael Muller's 1872 book, *The Catholic Priest*:

> Seek where you will, through heaven and earth, and you will find one created being who can forgive the sinner, who can free him from the chains of hell. That

---

[70] John 10:30, KJV.

[71] John 10:33, KJV.

[72] Luke 5:20, KJV.

[73] Luke 5:21, KJV.

[74] Charles G. Herbermann, "The Catholic Encyclopedia," Vol. 12: Philip II-Reuss, November 12, 2019, p.659, http://www.ccel.org/ccel/herbermann/cathen12.html.

> extraordinary being is the priest, the Roman Catholic priest.[75]

St. Alphonsus De Liguori writes in *Dignity of the Priest*, 1889:

> And God himself is obliged to abide by the judgment of his priests, and either not to pardon or to pardon, according as they refuse or give absolution, provided the penitent is capable of it. "Such is," says St. Maximus of Turin, "this judiciary power ascribed to Peter that its decision carries with it the decision of God." The sentence of the priest precedes, and God subscribes to it,[76]

Rev. L. Giustiniani, D.D., writes about Pope Leo the XII in his book, *Papal Rome As It Is*:

> Given in Rome from our Palace, the first of February 1817, the XIV. jurisdiction of the most holy Pontiff and Father in Christ, and Lord our God, the Pope Leo XII. through the Divine Providence, the IV year of his reign...[77]

From Pope Leo XIIIs, Encyclical Letter Praeclara Gratulationis Publicae, June 20, 1894:

---

[75] Michael Muller, *The Catholic Priest* (Baltimore: Kreuzer Brothers, 1872), 78-79.

[76] St. Alphonsus De Liguori, *Dignity of the Priest*; or Selva (New York: Benziger Brothers, 1889), 27.

[77] Rev. L. Giustiniani, D.D., *Papal Rome As It Is* (Baltimore: Publication Rooms No.7, 1843),181.

> But since We hold upon this earth the place of God Almighty... [78]

From Catholic Professor Alfred Baudrillart's lectures at the Catholic Institute of Paris in early 1904, we have the following:

> Nevertheless when confronted by heresy she does not content herself with persuasion; arguments of an intellectual and moral order appear to her insufficient and she has recourse to force, to corporal punishment, to torture. She creates tribunals like those of the Inquisition, she calls the laws of State to her aid, if necessary she encourages a crusade, or a religious war and all her " horror of blood " practically culminates into urging the secular power to shed it, which proceeding is almost more odious for it is less frank than shedding it herself.[79]

The Apostle Paul stated clearly in 1 Timothy who mediates on the behalf of man:

> For there is one God, and one mediator between God and men, the man Christ Jesus...[80]

Mark of the Beast

The devil is the master counterfeiter. The Old Testament prophets, by God's power, performed signs and wonders; so too will

[78] Catholic church, *The Great Encyclical Letters of Pope Leo XIII* (New York: Benziger Brothers, 1903), 304.

[79] Alfred Baudrillart, The Catholic church; The Renaissance and Protestantism (London: Kegan Paul, Trench, Trubner & Company. LTD., 1907), 182-183.

[80] 1st Timothy 2:5, KJV.

the false prophet by the Dragon's power show signs and wonders to deceive the masses. Jesus Christ tells the following to His apostles who asked about what signs to look for in the end days:

> For there shall arise false Christs, and false prophets, and shall shew great signs and wonders; insomuch that, if it were possible, they shall deceive the very elect.[81]

The Old Testament identifies a sign or mark of obedience to God as keeping His commandments. The Antichrist will have his opposing "mark." *Obedience,* who will you obey, who will you worship even if it means sacrificing your life? God established the Sabbath day in Genesis.

> And on the seventh day God ended his work which he had made; and he rested on the seventh day from all his work which he had made. And God blessed the seventh day, and sanctified it: because that in it he had rested from all his work which God created and made.[82]

God sanctified the Sabbath day in Genesis, making it His holy day. This event is before the Mosaic Law, and the giving of the Ten Commandments at Mount Sinai. The sanctity of the Sabbath continued by its' placement in the Decalogue given to Moses; there, God tells the Israelites to remember His Sabbath. The stone tablets containing the Ten Commandments are inside the Ark of the Covenant. The Decalogue is different from the *Book of the Law* containing the ceremonial laws the Jewish priests followed. That book of the law sat beside the Ark.

---

[81] Matthew 24:24, KJV.

[82] Genesis 2:2-3, KJV.

> Take this book of the law, and put it in the side of the ark of the covenant of the LORD your God, that it may be there for a witness against thee.[83]

Jesus Christ, as our High Priest, sacrificed Himself at Calvary, thereby fulfilling all the ceremonial requirements for atonement. The sacrificial system of the Jews was a shadow of what Jesus' completed at Calvary. The Lord made the earthly sacrificial system obsolete. God made this known by tearing the veil that covered the Holy of Holies (Mark 15:38), where the Ark rested. New Testament followers of Jesus Christ are not under the *book of the law,* the *Mosaic Law*. Redemption through Jesus removed the condemnation from the book of law (Galatians 3:10), which was placed next to the Ark (Deuteronomy 31:26). The Ten Commandments, the *Moral Law* written on stone tablets, are inside the Ark. The Apostle Paul states in Romans 8:1.

> There is therefore now no condemnation to them which are in Christ Jesus, who walk not after the flesh, but after the Spirit.[84]

This liberty does not abolish the Ten Commandments. History records that the Pilgrim church, also known as the Primitive church, worshiped on the seventh day as well. Dr. Tho. Morer, Rector of the United Parishes of SS Ann and Agnes, Church of England wrote in 1701:

> We must yield therefore that the Primitive Christians had a great veneration for the Sabbath, and spent the Day in Devotion and Sermons. And 'tis not to be doubted but they derived this Practice from the

[83] Deuteronomy 31:26, KJV.

[84] Romans 8:1, KJV.

> Apostles themselves, as appears by several Scriptures to that purpose; ...[85]

The Apostle Paul taught and shared the Gospel message on the Sabbath. From Acts, there are the following verses:

> But when they departed from Perga, they came to Antioch in Pisidia, and went into the synagogue on the sabbath day, and sat down.[86]

> And when the Jews were gone out of the synagogue, the Gentiles besought that these words might be preached to them the next sabbath.[87]

> And Paul, as his manner was, went in unto them, and three sabbath days reasoned with them out of the scriptures...[88]

> And he reasoned in the synagogue every sabbath, and persuaded the Jews and the Greeks.[89]

From English clergyman John Ley, pastor of Great Budworth in Cheshire, he wrote the following in 1641, referencing the dishonoring of the Sabbath:

> To these Testimonies (most what of the adverse party assenting to that which will inferre their

---

[85] Dr. Tho. Morer, *A Discourse in Six Dialogues on the Name, Notion an Observation of the Lords's Day,* (London: Golden Ball in St. Paul's Church-yard, 1701), 189.

[86] Acts 13:14, KJV.

[87] Acts 13:42, KJV.

[88] Acts 17:2, KJV.

[89] Acts 18:4, KJV.

> conviction for application of the name Sabbath) I will annexe other evidences, both for the Apostles time, and for some succeeding ages of the Church.
>
> First, for the time of the Apostles, their practice for religious and solemne Assemblies on the Jewes Sabbath is plaine, in the relation of their acts by St. Luke, whereof they that doubt may reade their owne resolution, and receive satisfaction in Acts.13.ver. 14,42, 44. Acts.16.23. and chap.27.ver.2. besides other places.
>
> Secondly, from the Apostles time untill the councell of Laodicea, which was about the yeare 364, the holy observation of the Jewes Sabbath continued, as may be proved out of many Authors; yea (notwithstanding the Decree of that Councell against it.) about the yeare 380. Greg. Nyssen passionately complained of the violation of the old Sabbath (as an holy brother to the new Lords day) questioning the profaners of it thus : (as the Bishop of Ely brings him in) With what face (saith he) dost thou looke upon the Lords day, who hast dishonoured the Sabbath:...[90]

Protestant America, like the Church of Rome, observes Sunday as the day of worship. Is this a crucial error? Emperor Constantine changed the day of rest to honor Mithra, the god of the Sun; Protestants claim that Sunday honors the day of the Lord's resurrection. Mithraism was prominent in the Roman Empire. Author and Professor Samuel Dill at Queens College, Belfast wrote in 1905:

[90] John Ley, *Sunday a Sabbath,* (London: R. Young, 1641), 163.

> Of all the oriental religions which attracted the devotion of the West in the last three centuries of the Empire, that of Mithra was the most powerful.[91]

I am not suggesting a mass migration to the Seventh Day Adventist Church, but there are no Bible scriptures that instruct the body of Christ to change their day of worship from the seventh day to the first day of the week. I am suggesting that to accept this view, you must accept what is implied by tradition. Jesus Christ admonished the Pharisees for practicing the traditions of man in place of God's commandments.

> For laying aside the commandment of God, ye hold the tradition of men, as the washing of pots and cups: and many other such like things ye do.[92]

From the Book of Isaiah, we find God declaring the Sabbath His holy day.

> If thou turn away thy foot from the Sabbath, from doing thy pleasure on my holy day; and call the Sabbath a delight, the holy of the LORD, honourable; and shalt honour him, not doing thine own ways, nor finding thine own pleasure, nor speaking thine own words:[93]

Is it foolish to think that God maintained His holy day in the Old Testament and will in His coming kingdom, but accepts worship from man on a pagan worship day during the New Testament period? Note another verse by the Prophet Isaiah:

---

[91] Samuel Dill, M.A., *Roman Society from Nero to Marcus Aurelius,* (London: Macmillan and Co., 1905), 585.

[92] Mark 7:8, KJV.

[93] Isaiah 58:13, KJV.

> For as the new heavens and the new earth, which I will make, shall remain before me, saith the LORD, so shall your seed and your name remain. And it shall come to pass, that from one new moon to another, and from one sabbath to another, shall all flesh come to worship before me, saith the LORD.[94]

When looking at the fourth commandment, we can see what qualifies as a royal seal. Even today, we recognize a seal as a symbol of authenticity and ownership. What are the minimum requirements for a royal seal? Well, there is the name, e.g., George; there is the title or authority, e.g., King of England; then there is the jurisdiction of the authority, e.g., all of England and its' territories. Exodus 20 records the Ten Commandments. Looking specifically at the 4th commandment in Exodus 20:8-11:

> Remember the sabbath day, to keep it holy. Six days shalt thou labour, and do all thy work: But the seventh day is the Sabbath of the LORD thy God: in it thou shalt not do any work, thou, nor thy son, nor thy daughter, thy manservant, nor thy maidservant, nor thy cattle, nor thy stranger that is within thy gates: For in six days the LORD made heaven and earth, the sea, and all that in them is, and rested the seventh day: wherefore the LORD blessed the sabbath day, and hallowed it.[95]

Here the name on the seal is *the Lord*. The title of authority is *God the Creator*. And His jurisdiction is *"heaven and earth, the sea, and all that in them is."* There is much speculation about what the "mark of the beast" in Revelation 13 might be. The beast's mark

---

[94] Isaiah 66:22-23, KJV.

[95] Exodus 20:8-11, KJV.

has to do with worship. Those who refuse the mark will be economically banned. Note the following verse from Revelation 13, which is followed by the Catholic Church's ruling at the Council of Tours A.D. 1163:

> And he causeth all, both small and great, rich and poor, free and bond, to receive a mark in their right hand, or in their foreheads: And that no man might buy or sell, save he that had the mark, or the name of the Beast, or the number of his name.[96]

> 4. Is directed against the Albigenses, and forbids all intercourse with them; forbids even to give them a retreat or protection, or to buy and sell with them.[97]

God is not capricious. The doctrine to keep God's commandments are found both in the Old and New Testament. Exodus 31 states the following:

> Speak thou also unto the children of Israel, saying, Verily my sabbaths ye shall keep: for it is a *sign* between me and you throughout your generations; that ye may know that I am the LORD that doth sanctify you.... Wherefore the children of Israel shall keep the Sabbath, to observe the Sabbath throughout their generations, for a *perpetual covenant*.... It is a *sign* between me and the children of Israel for ever: for in six days the LORD made heaven and earth, and on

---

[96] Revelation 13:16-17, KJV.

[97] Rev. Edward H. Landon. M.A., A Manual of Councils of the Holy Catholic Church, (Edinburgh: John Grant, 1909), 177.

> the seventh day he rested, and was refreshed.[98] (Emphasis added)

Above we see God establishing a covenant. Consider what God says about His spoken word.

> My covenant will I not break, nor alter the thing that is gone out of my lips.[99]

> So shall my word be that goeth forth out of my mouth: it shall not return unto me void, but it shall accomplish that which I please, and it shall prosper in the thing whereto I sent it.[100]

Strong's Concordance for "sign," H226, tells us this is a sign, a distinguishing mark. The Lord spoke through His prophets. In Ezekiel 20, the emphasis is placed on keeping the Sabbath as being a sign.

> Moreover also I gave them my sabbaths, to be a sign between me and them, that they might know that I am the LORD that sanctify them.[101]

> And hallow my sabbaths; and they shall be a sign between me and you, that ye may know that I am the LORD your God.[102]

The Israelites don't own the sabbaths. The verse reads, "my sabbaths," expressing the ownership belonging to God. In the

---

[98] Exodus 31:13,16,17, KJV.

[99] Psalm 89:34, KJV

[100] Isaiah 55:11, KJV.

[101] Ezekiel 20:12, KJV.

[102] Ezekiel 20:20, KJV.

Deuteronomy 11:13-18, we find God establishing a conditional promise to the Israelites, an if-then, promise. God tells the Israelites that if they obey His commandments, they will be blessed, and He warns them not to be deceived by serving other gods. Disobedience will incur God's wrath. In verse 18, there are the following instructions.

> Therefore shall ye lay up these my words in your heart and in your soul, and bind them for a *sign* upon your *hand,* that they may be as *frontlets between your eyes.*[103] (Emphasis added.)

God's instructions for the *hand* and the *forehead* (frontlets) is where Satan derives his counterfeit mark that opposes God. God's sign, or mark, is to represent a believer's willingness to obey His commandments. This harmony is expressed through both action (hand) and thought (forehead). Jesus kept and taught that we should keep the commandments.

> If ye keep my commandments, ye shall abide in my love; even as I have kept my Father's commandments, and abide in his love.[104]

Some Bible teachers refer to a few New Testament passages to justify Sunday worship, but no New Testament scripture instructs making a change. Satan has his sign or mark. The beasts in Daniel's prophecies represent kingdoms. The mark of the beast identifies adherence to that kingdom.

The Book of Daniel tells of the rise and fall of great kingdoms. The satanic spirit governing these kingdoms migrates from one kingdom to the next, always ready to oppose God.

---

[103] Deuteronomy 11:18, KJV.

[104] John 15:10, KJV.

The Church of Rome persecuted Christians for over a thousand years. The popes have spoken blasphemies against God. Revelation 13:16-17 states the beast will cause all to receive a mark in their right hand or their foreheads. And without this mark, you will not be able to buy or sell. The mark indicates allegiance to the name or number of the beast, a system, an earthly kingdom that takes the worship that rightfully belongs to God. Note Revelation 12:17, which is before the new heaven and the new earth.

> And the dragon was wroth with the woman, and went to make war with the remnant of her seed, which keep the commandments of God, and have the testimony of Jesus Christ.[105]

Today there's a fascination with the *mark of the beast* being a technological device, visible or implanted. The mark identifies your allegiance. Author Christian Edwardson wrote *Facts of Faith* in 1942. Edwardson explains how a religious system marks you without a tech device. Edwardson's view focuses on the Church of Rome. In 1942, Catholicism continues its Counter Reformation to oppose Biblical Christianity. Today, with the rise of Islam, there is another example of an antichrist mark on the head and hand. It is the Shahada, the Creed worn by Islamic terrorists' groups. The ecumenical movement wishes to include Islam into its fold as well.

> This mark must belong to religion, for it has to do with "worship" (Revelation 13:12), and it must have originated with the Papacy, for it is "his mark" (Revelation 15:2), and yet it must be something both Catholics and Protestants agree upon, for "all" will receive it (Revelation 13:12, 16). It is something in which not

---

[105] Revelation 12:17, KJV.

> only the people but also "the earth" on which they dwell, can show obedience. (Revelation 13:12) There is but one thing that answers to all these specifications; namely, Sunday keeping. Sunday is a religious institution that originated with the Catholic Church, and yet Protestants agree to keep it, and we shall now show how the earth can have a part in receiving the mark.
>
> Some will ask how a day can be a mark in a person's forehead or hand. But we read in Exodus 13:3, 4, 9 that a day can be "for a sign unto thee upon thine hand, and for a memorial between thine eyes." But some one will ask how this "mark" can be received by some only "in their right hand," while others receive it "in their foreheads." (Revelation 13:16) That is easy to see. Many people tell us: "We know that the seventh day is the right Sabbath, but we have to work on that day or lose our jobs." Such people have no Sunday-Sabbath in their mind, or forehead, because they do not believe in it; but their "hand" obeys it, and so they receive it in their hand. There are others who see the seventh day is the true Sabbath in the New Testament, but they love their old friends and their old ways more than the unpopular truth, and wish they did not have to obey it.[106]

Currently, it is not mandatory to worship on Sunday. The prophetic day of having to choose which mark we will submit to is coming. This type of edict has been imposed in the past by Rome. And has been requested again! Emperor Constantine's signed an edict in A.D. 321 to make Sunday, the day of the Sun,

---

[106] Christian Edwardson, *Fact of Faith,* (Southern Publishing Association, 1942), 190-191.

a day of rest. Pope John Paul II requested in his apostolic letter "On Keeping the Lord's Day Holy," in 1998 to have civil legislation support the observance of Sunday. That is a request for *civil enforcement*. In September of 2007, Pope Benedict XVI, while celebrating mass in Vienna, appealed for a renewed respect for Sunday. The Catholic Church acknowledges that Sunday worship is her doing. The following is from the Catholic Church.

From "The Catholic World," March 1894:

> The church took the pagan philosophy and made it the buckler of faith against the heathen. She took the pagan, Roman Pantheon, temple of all the gods, and made it sacred to all the martyrs; so it stands to this day. She took the pagan Sunday and made it the Christian Sunday. She took the pagan Easter and made it the feast we celebrate during this season. Sunday and Easter day are, if we consider their derivation, much the same. In truth, all Sundays are Sundays only because they are a weekly, partial recurrence of Easter day. The pagan Sunday was, in a manner, an unconscious preparation for Easter day. The Sun was a foremost god with heathen-dom. Balder the beautiful, the White God, the old Scandinavians called him. The Sun has worshippers at this hour in Persia and other lands.... There is, in truth, something royal, kingly about the Sun, making it a fit emblem of Jesus, the Sun of Justice. Hence the church in these countries would seem to have said, to 'Keep that old pagan name [Sunday]. It shall remain consecrated, sanctified.' And thus the pagan

> Sunday, dedicated to Balder, became the Christian Sunday, sacred to Jesus.[107]

Jesuit Adrien Nampon's book *Catholic Doctrine as Defined by the Council of Trent*:

> "Tradition, not Scripture, Lessing says, "is the rock on which the church of Jesus Christ is built."[108]

From the "American Sentinel 1893," Father Enright writes the following:

> The Bible says, "Remember that thou keep holy the Sabbath day." The Catholic Church says: " No! By my divine power I abolish the Sabbath day, and command you to keep holy the first day of the week." And, lo! The entire civilized world bows down in reverent obedience to the command of the holy Catholic Church.[109]

From the Council of Laodicea in A.D. 364, Canon 29:

> Christians shall not Judaize (keep Sabbath) and be idle on Saturday (Sabbath original) but shall work on that day; but the Lord's day they shall especially honor.

---

[107] William Gildea, D. D., *The Catholic World*, Vol. 58, (New York: The Office of the Catholic World, 1894), 809.

[108] Rev. Adrien Nampon, SJ., *Catholic Doctrine as Defined by the Council of Trent*, (Philadelphia: Peter F. Cunningham and Son, 1869), 157.

[109] T. Enright, CSS. R., *American Sentinel*, Vol. 8, Number 22, (New York: Pacific Press Publishing Company, 1893), 173.

If you are a Christian who is doing their best to obey God's Word, it will not matter where on history's timeline you were born; you are in opposition to the culture around you. Why? Since the fall of man, the devil has ruled the kingdoms of the world. Having the seal of God, His distinguishing mark, will bring *persecution,* but it will also be a *shield.* This mark indicates we believe God's Word, and we back it up by our actions. Note the prophecy I have used before in Revelation 9, where the locust-like creatures come out of the abyss and attack humans, only those without the seal of God in their foreheads.

> And he opened the bottomless pit; …And there came out of the smoke locusts upon the earth: and unto them was given power, as the scorpions of the earth have power. And it was commanded them that they should not hurt the grass of the earth, neither any green thing, neither any tree; but only those men which have not the seal of God in their foreheads….[110]

Much more can be said on this subject. However, I have briefly covered this topic due to its' grave importance.

Today, there are several views, doctrines on the rapture of the church. Do I believe there is going to be a rapture? Yes! The question is when. Should our goal be to count on a particular view of the rapture or to be spiritually prepared for the persecution which is prophesied to come? Depending on whom you speak with, some hold to the belief in a pre-tribulation, mid-tribulation and post-tribulation rapture.

---

110 Revelation 9:2-5, KJV.

In 1 Thessalonians 4:13-18, the Apostle Paul alluded to the rapture of the church to give the Thessalonians spiritual comfort for dealing with their loved ones who had died. Some Thessalonians believed the rapture of the church was so close they stopped working. In 2 Thessalonians, Paul tells the church not to focus on the actual day the Lord returns but to continue doing that which is good. Paul admonishes believers who are not about God's work but are being lazy, waiting on the Lord.

THE COMFORT OF THE RAPTURE

> But I would not have you to be ignorant, brethren, concerning them which are asleep, that ye sorrow not, even as others which have no hope. For if we believe that Jesus died and rose again, even so them also which sleep in Jesus will God bring with him. For this we say unto you by the word of the Lord, that we which are alive and remain unto the coming of the Lord shall not prevent them which are asleep. For the Lord himself shall descend from heaven with a shout, with the voice of the archangel, and with the trump of God: and the dead in Christ shall rise first: Then we which are alive and remain shall be caught up together with them in the clouds, to meet the Lord in the air: and so shall we ever be with the Lord. Wherefore comfort one another with these words.[111]

> For even when we were with you, this we commanded you, that if any would not work, neither should he eat. For we hear that there are some which walk among you disorderly, working not at all, but are busybodies. Now them that are such we

[111] 1 Thessalonians 4:13-18, KJV.

> command and exhort by our Lord Jesus Christ, that with quietness they work, and eat their own bread. But ye, brethren, be not weary in well doing. [112]

The focus is to shed light on the origin of the pre-tribulation rapture doctrine, to unveil what is a deception. It does not appear to be what the early church was taught or believed. Regarding the rapture (to be caught up) of the church, the body of Christ, the commonly referenced verses are those from the Apostle Paul's letters to the Thessalonians, who shared this knowledge to offer comfort.

> For if we believe that Jesus died and rose again, even so them also which sleep in Jesus will God bring with him.[113]

> For this we say unto you by the word of the Lord, that we which are alive and remain unto the coming of the Lord shall not prevent them which are asleep.[114]

> For the Lord himself shall descend from heaven with a shout, with the voice of the archangel, and with the trump of God: and the dead in Christ shall rise first:[115]

---

[112] 2 Thessalonians 3:10-13, KJV.

[113] 1 Thessalonians 4:14, KJV.

[114] 1 Thessalonians 4:15, KJV.

[115] 1 Thessalonians 4:16, KJV.

> Then we which are alive and remain shall be caught up together with them in the clouds, to meet the Lord in the air: and so shall we ever be with the Lord.[116]
>
> Wherefore comfort one another with these words.[117]

Pre-tribulation rapture doctrine is where the Christian church is removed from Earth before the Great Tribulation begins. To add food for thought, let's take a closer look. Verse 4:15 above states those who are alive when Jesus returns are not raptured before those that are dead. Verses 16 and 17 say the dead in Christ shall rise (be resurrected) first, and then those of us who are alive shall be caught up to be with the Lord. Here, I am merely offering the question of what the biblical text says. My current understanding is the rapture of Christians who are alive cannot happen until the dead are resurrected first. Consider the following scriptural verses from the Book of Revelation.

> And I saw thrones, and they sat upon them, and judgment was given unto them: and I saw the souls of them that were beheaded for the witness of Jesus, and for the word of God, and which had not worshipped the beast, neither his image, neither had received his mark upon their foreheads, or in their hands; and they lived and reigned with Christ a thousand years.[118]

Here we have the witnesses who were killed during the tribulations mentioned in the Book of Revelation. For their faith until death, they shall reign with Christ in the Millennial Kingdom.

---

[116] 1 Thessalonians 4:17, KJV.

[117] 1 Thessalonians 4:18, KJV.

[118] Revelation 20:4, KJV.

> But the rest of the dead lived not again until the thousand years were finished. *This is the first resurrection.*[119]

Revelation 20:5 states it is the first resurrection of the dead. If that is the case, then those who are dead 1 Thessalonians 4:16 appear to rise after the Great Tribulation. Many Christians will not agree with this line of thinking, but I offer it for personal validation and study and not to be accepted or rejected blindly.

Reading further into Wohlberg's article, you can see how the deception was promulgated to cause the Protestant church to be asleep-at-the-wheel. Wohlberg continues and explains how, after close to 300 years, the *Jesuit Futurism* surfaced and worked its way into the Protestant Church of England. Let's narrow the focus on two individuals who played a crucial role in introducing this doctrine into the churches of America:

> … In the midst of this growing anti-Protestant climate in England, there arose a man by the name of John Nelson Darby (1800-1882). A brilliant lawyer, pastor, and theologian, he wrote more than 53 books on Bible subjects. A much-respected Christian and a man of deep piety, Darby took a strong stand in favor of the infallibility of the Bible in contrast with the liberalism of his day. He became one of the leaders of a group in Plymouth, England, which became known as the Plymouth Brethren. Darby's contribution to the development of evangelical theology has been so great that he has been called The Father of Modern Dispensationalism. Yet John Nelson Darby, like Edward Irving, also became a strong promoter of a Pre-Tribulation rapture followed by a one-man Antichrist. In fact, this teaching has become a

[119] Revelation 20:5, KJV.

hallmark of Dispensationalism. Dispensationalism is the theory that God deals with mankind in major dispensations or periods. According to Darby, we are now in the "Church Age," that is, until the rapture. After the rapture, then the seven-year period of Daniel 9:27 will supposedly kick in, and this is when the Antichrist will rise up against the Jews. In fact, John Nelson Darby laid much of the foundation for the present popular removal of Daniel's 70th week away from history and from Jesus Christ in favor of applying it to a future Tribulation after the rapture. Thus, in spite of all the positives of his ministry, Darby followed Maitland, Todd, Bellarmine, and Ribera by incorporating the teachings of Futurism into his theology. This created a link between John Nelson Darby, the Father of Dispensationalism, and the Jesuit Francisco Ribera, the Father of Futurism. Darby visited America six times between 1859-1874, preaching in all of its major cities, during which time he definitely *planted the seeds of Futurism in American soil*. The child of the Jesuits was growing up.

Futurism in America One of the most important figures in this whole drama is Cyrus Ingerson Scofield (1843- 1921), a Kansas lawyer who was greatly influenced by the writings of Darby. In 1909, Scofield published the first edition of his famous Scofield Reference Bible. In the early 1900s, this Bible became so popular in American Protestant Bible schools that it was necessary to print literally millions of copies. Yet, in the much-respected footnotes of this very Bible, Scofield injected large doses of the fluid of Futurism also found in the writings of Darby, Todd, Maitland, Bellarmine, and Ribera. Through the Scofield Bible, the Jesuit child reached young adulthood. The doctrine of an Antichrist still to come was

> becoming firmly established inside 20th-century American Protestantism. The Moody Bible Institute and the Dallas Theological Seminary have strongly supported the teachings of John Nelson Darby, and this has continued to fuel Futurism's growth. Then in the 1970s, Pastor Hal Lindsey, a graduate of Dallas Theological Seminary, released his blockbuster book The Late Great Planet Earth.[120] (Emphasis added)

I stress this topic because of the importance of knowing the origin of the pre-tribulation rapture doctrine. The question is whether this doctrine deceived the Protestant church and caused complacency to set in on spiritual growth. End-time prophecy speaks of extreme persecution of Christians. We can already see how our society is becoming more and more intolerant of people with a biblical worldview. Is this a call to stop living your lives and hide in a bunker? Of course not. We are to be found doing God's work until the return of the Lord Jesus. If your understanding of the rapture has been manipulated and has allowed your *spiritual armor* to get rusty, then it is time to become battle-ready. See Ephesians 6, which covers the parts of your spiritual armor.

Futurism has created a mentality in today's Christians to believe they will not suffer tribulation. They will be "ejected from the game" before the Great Tribulation starts and keeping the faith gets too hard. This form of spiritual complacency is dangerous. Western culture, the United States, has, for the most part, been sheltered. We have had it easy, and it has made us mentally and physically soft. We need less of the "I have my bus ticket" thinking and to take our resolve seriously.

Where we will stand when keeping the Christian faith becomes a life or death choice. It would be arrogant and unjust to

---

[120] Steve Wohlberg, "Left Behind by the Jesuits," Assembly of Yahweh, 01/22/2019 http://assemblyoftrueisrael.com/Documents/Leftbehind.htm.

think we may not be called to take a stand for our faith in Jesus. Christians past and present had their lives hanging in the balance; their decision for Jesus tipped the scale between life and death. What possible justification can we claim that would make us exempt from that same decision? There isn't one.

FUNDAMENTALISM

Fundamental Christianity today is targeted just as the early church was. When people of the early church refused to accept the Church of Rome's dogma and were labeled heretics, the Church of Rome slaughtered and tortured them by the thousands. What is a Fundamental Christian? Noah Webster's dictionary does not define a Fundamental Christian but separately defines "fundamental" and "Christian."

> FUNDAMENT'AL, *adjective* Pertaining to the foundation or basis; serving for the foundation. Hence, essential; important; as a *fundamental* truth or principle; a *fundamental* law; a *fundamental* sound or chord in music.
> FUNDAMENT'AL, *noun* A leading or primary principle, rule, law or article, which serves as the ground work of a system; essential part; as the fundamentals of the Christian faith.[121]
>
> CHRISTIAN, *noun*
> 1. A believer in the religion of Christ.
> 2. A professor of his belief in the religion of Christ.
> 3. A real disciple of Christ; one who believes in the truth of the *Christian* religion, and studies to follow the example, and obey the precepts, of Christ;

[121] Webster, *Fundamental*, http://webstersdictionary1828.com/Dictionary/fundamental.

> a believer in Christ who is characterized by real piety.... [122]

Merriam-Webster on *fundamentalism*:

> *often capitalized*: a movement in 20th century Protestantism emphasizing the literally interpreted Bible as fundamental to Christian life and teaching b: the beliefs of this movement c: adherence to such beliefs[123]

Fundamentalism is a movement beginning in the early 20th century in response to modernism, the breakdown and dilution of church doctrine. Fundamentalism holds to or stresses the infallibility[124] of the Bible in matters of faith[125], morals,[126] and historical records. It holds as foundational to Christian beliefs the doctrines of a created world[127], the birth of Christ by a virgin[128], physical resurrection[129], atonement by the sacrificial death[130] of

---

[122] Webster, *Christian*, http://webstersdictionary1828.com/Dictionary/Christian.

[123] Merriam-Webster, *Fundamentalism*, https://www.merriam-webster.com/dictionary/fundamentalism.

[124] 2 Timothy 3:16-17, 2 Peter 1:20-21, John 17:17, Hebrews 6:18, Proverbs 30:5, Psalm 119:89.

[125] John 3:16, Hebrews 11:6, Ephesians 2:8-9, 2 Corinthians 5:7,1 Corinthians 2:5, Matthew 21:21-22.

[126] 1 Corinthians 15:33, Galatians 5:19-21, 1 Corinthians 6:9-11, Exodus 20:1-17, Revelation 21:8.

[127] Genesis 1:1-31, Psalm 33:6, Colossians 1:16, Hebrews 11:3, Revelation 4:11.

[128] Isaiah 7:14, Luke 1:34, Matthew 1:18-25.

[129] 1 Corinthians 15:1-6, Philippians 3:31, John 20:19, Hosea 6:2, Luke 20:39.

[130] John 1:29, John 3:16, 1 John 2:2, Hebrews 9:12, 1 Peter 2:24, 1 John 4:10.

Jesus Christ and His return through a Second Coming.[131] Being a biblical Christian means we are in the world but not part of the world system, which is controlled by the devil.

> Wherein in time past ye walked according to the *course of this world,* according to the *prince of the power of the air,* the spirit that now *worketh in the children of disobedience*:[132] (Emphasis added)

> If ye were of the world, the world would love his own: but because ye are not of the world, but I have chosen you out of the world, therefore the world hateth you.[133]

> Love not the world, neither the things *that are* in the world. If any man love the world, the love of the Father is not in him.[134]

> And be *not conformed to this world*: but be ye transformed by the *renewing of your mind,* that ye may prove what is that good, and acceptable, and perfect, will of God.[135] (Emphasis added)

Are the above verses directing believers to hate the world, God's physical creation? I think not. But we are not to love the world's operating system, which is Luciferian. Satan has current ownership of the world, but Jesus Christ has redeemed creation,

---

[131] Revelation 1:7, Matthew 16:27, Matthew 24:27, John 14:1-3, 2 Thessalonians 2:1.

[132] Ephesians 2:2, KJV.

[133] John 15:19, KJV.

[134] 1 John 2:15, KJV.

[135] Romans 12:2, KJV.

and He will return to claim what is rightfully His. In the world, which spiritual power is the creator of dissent and in opposition to harmony? There are two spiritual powers at work—the Holy Spirit and the spirit of the antichrist (the devil).

Many religions have spiritual beings or gods as the focal point in their theology. The ecumenical movement contains rhetoric alluding to world religions serving the same God, just using different paths. This proposition is another fabricated lie. In Part 2 of the Ecumenical Trap, the focus will be to consider the origin of these gods. This information will shed light on whether the world's religions serve the God of the Bible or another god or gods?

8

Ecumenical Trap Part 2

One Way to God

If you consider the ecumenical movement, you will find an underlying theme that all religions are worshipping the same God. The only difference in the beliefs is they are taking different paths to reach God. Dr. Ravi Zacharias makes this observation on pluralism, which applies to the ecumenical movement:

> The great hazard of pluralism is the faulty deduction, in the name of tolerance, that all beliefs can be equally true. It is ultimately truth, not popularity or rights, that determines destiny.[1]

For Christianity, there is only one path. Jesus Christ Himself removed the doubt as to how many ways lead to God the Father:

[1] Zacharias, *Deliver Us From Evil*, 82.

> Jesus saith unto him, *I am the way*, the truth, and the life: *no man cometh unto the Father, but by me*.[2] (Emphasis added)

World religions outside the Christian faith will see Jesus Christ's words in the verse above as bold and arrogant—and intolerant. But when you are the Son of God, you can make such statements. Jesus Christ is God manifested in the flesh; the only way to deny the above verse is to prove that Jesus is not who He says He is. To the best of my knowledge, every attempt has failed.

For the Protestant Church to yoke itself with the ecumenical movement, it must accept other religions outside Christianity as legitimate paths to God. For these faiths to be a plausible way to God, there must be a rejection of John 14:6. Also, the deity of Jesus Christ would have to be downgraded to elevate other world religion's doctrine to that of the Holy Bible. These compromises are why a Christian cannot be a part of the ecumenical movement.

World Religious-isms

The first religious system to review is *monotheism*, which is derived from two words—*mono* meaning one and *theism* meaning god. If you consider yourself a monotheist, then you are saying that you believe in one God. Three primary world religions claim to be monotheistic. *Christianity* believes in the God of the Bible. The New Testament church, Christianity, is grafted into the commonwealth of Israel, which is also monotheistic, *Judaism*.

---

[2] John 14:6, KJV.

> Hear, O Israel: The LORD our God is one LORD: And thou shalt love the LORD thy God with all thine heart, and with all thy soul, and with all thy might.[3]

The above verse is known as the *Shema*; it is part of the Jewish morning and evening prayer and establishes the Jewish confession of faith. The third dominant religion is *Islam*, which also claims to be monotheistic. Dr. David Jeremiah states the following about Islam:

> It may come as a surprise that Islam is also monotheistic; followers believe in one god, although it is not the true God. If you have ever heard a Muslim prayer, it is addressed to one god because one of the five pillars of Islam is "There is no God but the one God, and Mohammed is His prophet."
>
> Islam rejects the doctrine of the Trinity and considers Jesus to be one of the great prophets. Allah differs from the Jewish and Christian concept of God because he is morally capricious; he declares what is good or evil, and his declaration makes it true. The Muslim has no assurance of what it takes to please Allah and be welcomed into eternal paradise.[4]

If you search for the origin of "Allah," you will find that he is not the same God of Christianity and Judaism.

> Historians, linguists, and archeologists have dug into this question for over a century. Various archeological digs in Arabia and throughout the Middle East have uncovered the answer: Islam is a modern

---

[3] Deuteronomy 6:4, KJV.

[4] David Jeremiah, with Carol C. Carlson, *Invasion of Other God: The Seduction of New Age Spirituality* (Dallas, TX: Word Publishing, 1995), 19.

> version of the ancient fertility religion of the moon god. Once this is grasped, the rise and history of Islam becomes clear.
>
> The Arab conquests were made possible because the central powers in the Middle East had exhausted themselves in wars against each other. They were not able to fight off wave after wave of Arab armies which subdued entire nations with merciless slaughter, rape and plunder.[5]

An atheist is a person who does not believe in a god. These folks will lean toward science, *theories* of evolution, and the "Big Bang." Secular humanists fall within the boundaries of atheism. Then there are the *Agnostics*; they neither believe nor disbelieve in God (middle of the road); they believe they cannot prove what is beyond the material world. Dr. Jeremiah describes Agnostics as follows:

> Agnostics do not fall in the same category as atheists because they don't know whether any deity exists. Witches, for instance, would be considered Agnostic because they practice rituals and use terminology of polytheism and pantheism, but they admit that they do not know if any "divine essence" exists. One of the girls who answers the phone at our radio ministry was startled to have a male caller identify himself as a warlock. She wasn't sure what that meant until he explained he was a male witch. For twenty minutes he gave her a lecture on the fact that there

---

[5] Robert A. Morey, "Where Did Allah Come From?" Chick Publications, 1/23/2019, https://chick.com/information/article?id=Where-Did-Allah-Come-From.

> were good witches and bad witches, and that I was bigoted in my denunciation of all witchcraft.[6]

Moving down the list of types of religion, we come to *polytheism*—the prefix *poly* meaning more than one single god. Polytheists believe in many gods. These gods may not be eternal beings, and a person can reach a state of godhood.

> Greek and Roman mythology have many kinds of gods: Zeus, Venus, Apollos, etc. People in South America and Africa who practice voodoo are polytheists. Mormonism is polytheistic because Mormons believe that God was once a man and that man can become God. If you read the Mormon literature, you will find that to be very carefully stated in what they write about themselves.[7]

The world religion of *pantheism*. *Pan* means *all,* which equates to pantheists believing that everything is a god. Pantheists gain salvation by reaching a conscious level or state which recognizes its divinity. Pantheists think this is the path, and *New Age* cults call this Christ-consciousness or self-realization.

> *Buddhism* and *New Ageism* are pantheistic, as is *Hinduism* and its sects, such as *Hare Krishnas,* even though they embrace polytheism as well. They consider all of underlying reality to be divine, with particular divine manifestations as gods and goddesses.[8]

---

[6] Jeremiah, Carlson, *Invasion of Other Gods,* 20.

[7] Ibid.

[8] Jeremiah, Carlson, *Invasion of Other Gods,* 21.

There is one final "ism" for us to review. *Transhumanism* does not fit into the traditional design of world religions; however, it carries the same motivational power. It closely parallels polytheism, where a man can become like God. It is emerging onto the world scene in disguise through science and technology.

TRANSHUMANISM

It would be a mistake to glance over the topic of transhumanism quickly—man's desire to create his salvation, his immortality. The subject of transhumanism is another tough pill to swallow, but worthy of your time to review. Humanity's deception will encompass false religious doctrine and technology, and transhumanism technology is a form of worship. As with previous topics of discussion, we'll start with a general definition. Wikipedia provides the following:

> Transhumanism (abbreviated as H+ or h+) is an international philosophical movement that advocates for the transformation of the human condition by developing and making widely available sophisticated technologies to greatly enhance human intellect and physiology.[9]

The basic definition of idolatry is the worship of anything other than God. This type of worship doesn't always mean you are bowing down before a concrete statue. We can see where humanity is praising itself for its accomplishments in science and technology. Webster's definition of idolatry:

> IDOL'ATRY, *noun* [Latin idololatria. Gr. idol, and to worship or serve.]

---

[9] Wikipedia, "Transhumanism," Wikipedia The Free Encyclopedia, 7/13/2019, https://en.wikipedia.org/wiki/Transhumanism.

1. The worship of idols, images, or any thing made by hands, or which is not God.

   Idolatry is of two kinds; the worship of images, statues, pictures, etc. made by hands; and the worship of the heavenly bodies, the sun, moon and stars, or of demons, angels, men and animals.
2. Excessive attachment or veneration for any thing, or that which borders on adoration.[10]

A more in-depth reference to Dr. Tom Horn and Cris Putnam's work with *Exo-Vaticana* in a coming chapter. Dr. Horn has written several books. In 2010, Dr. Horn and his wife Nita co-authored *Forbidden Gates: How Genetics, Robotics, Artificial Intelligence, Synthetic Biology, Nanotechnology and Human Enhancement Herald the Dawn of Techno-Dimensional Spiritual Warfare.* The title may seem long, but the Transhumanist movement incorporates all these areas of science, which blend within the transhumanist movement. This movement and scientific areas are being well-funded and supported by international bodies and governments around the world. Tom and Nita describe transhumanism as follows:

> An international, intellectual, and fast-growing cultural movement known as *transhumanism*, whose vision is supported by a growing list of U.S. military advisors, bioethicists, law professors, and academics, intends the use of genetics, robotics, artificial intelligence and nanotechnology (GRIN technologies) as tools that will radically redesign our minds, our memories, our physiology, our offspring and even

[10]Noah Webster, "Idolatry," *Webster's Dictionary* 1828-Online Edition, 7/13/2019, http://webstersdictionary1828.com/Dictionary/Idolatry.

> perhaps—as Joel Garreau, in his bestselling book *Radical Evolutions,* claims—our very souls.[11]

The *Singularity* is a point in time where technology will advance at such an exponential rate that it will reach a pivotal point in which it becomes unstoppable. Computers are building faster and smarter computers and then repeating the process. Artificial intelligence and quantum computing power make this possible. Many computer companies are competing for their share of the market. One particular company has drawn attention to itself from some influential customers; its name is *D-Wave.* On D-Wave's website under the heading *About D-Wave,* we find the following:

> Founded in 1999, D-Wave is the leader in the development and delivery of quantum computing systems, software, and services and is the world's first commercial supplier of quantum computers. Our mission is to unlock the power of quantum computing for the world. We do this by delivering customer value with practical quantum applications for problems as diverse as logistics, artificial intelligence, materials sciences, drug discovery, cyber security, fault detection and financial modeling.
>
> D-Wave's systems are being used by some of the world's most advanced organizations, including Lockheed Martin, Google, NASA Ames, Volkswagen, DENSO, USRA, USC, Los Alamos National Laboratory, and Oak Ridge National Laboratory. D-Wave has been granted over 160 U.S. patents

[11] Tom and Nita Horn, *Forbidden Gates; How Genetics, Robotics, Artificial Intelligence, Synthetic Biology, Nanotechnology, and Human Enhancement Herald the Dawn of Techno-Dimensional Spiritual Warfare* (Crane, Missouri: Defender Publishing, 2010), 125-126.

> and has published over 100 peer-reviewed papers in leading scientific journals.[12]

The transhumanist movement and the coming Singularity are not new. While these topics are decades old, there is plenty of information available in the public domain. There was a famous lecture about the Singularity given by computer scientist Verner Vinge, and Tom and Nita reference him in their book:

> In 1993, critical thinking about the timing of the Singularity concerning the emergence of strong artificial intelligence led retired San Diego State University professor and computer scientist Vernor Vinge, in his often-quoted and now-famous lecture, "The Coming Technological Singularity," (delivered at Vision-21 Symposium sponsored by NASA Lewis Research Center and the Ohio Aerospace Institute), to add that when science achieves "the technological means to create superhuman intelligence [,] shortly after, the human era will be ended."[13]

The transhumanist movement is about the next stage of evolution for humans. Science and technology are at the point where humanity is being pushed to evolve from *humankind 1.0* to *humankind 2.0*. No waiting for the failed theory of evolution. It is not about becoming "X-Men" by experiencing some form of mutation to our DNA. This movement involves the combination of science and technology with the human body; there may be upgrades for some and augmentations, enhancements, and complete transfer of human consciousness into robots for others. This

---

[12] "D-Wave, The Quantum Computing Company," About Us, 07/13/2019, https://www.dwavesys.com/our-company/meet-d-wave.

[13] Horn, *Forbidden Gates*, 132.

possibility may seem far-fetched or like science fiction, but it is not. To the international community, it is an important subject.

Individual technological and medical breakthroughs offer patient benefits. Technology provides benefits for patients with congenital disabilities, lost limbs, and other forms of disability. These breakthroughs will help our wounded warriors who have sacrificed so much for our country. The danger is there are lines and boundaries established by God that technology should not cross. If you compare biblical Scripture to today's scientific advancements, we can see what God forbade in the days before the great flood of Noah.

Today's science labs scattered around the world perform gene splicing between the species. If you are wondering whether this is real, it is. Governments are concerned that science experiments are moving too fast and have placed bans limiting how far tests can go. As was discussed earlier, it is difficult to legislate morality.

Presidential Decisions

From a White House release dated April 10, 2002, former President George W. Bush called for a ban on cloning. The following are his words:

> Science has set before us decisions of immense consequence. We can pursue medical research with a clear sense of moral purpose or we can travel without an ethical compass into a world we could live to regret. Science now presses forward the issue of human cloning. How we answer the question of human cloning will place us on one path or the other.... Human cloning is deeply troubling to me, and to most Americans. Life is a creation, not a commodity. (Applause.) Our children are gifts to be loved and protected, not products to be designed and

> manufactured. Allowing cloning would be taking a significant step toward a society in which human beings are grown for spare body parts, and children are engineered to custom specifications; and that's not acceptable.
>
> In the current debate over human cloning, two terms are being used: reproductive cloning and research cloning. Reproductive cloning involves creating a cloned embryo and implanting it into a woman with the goal of creating a child. Fortunately, nearly every American agrees that this practice should be banned. Research cloning, on the other hand, involves the creation of cloned human embryos which are then destroyed to derive stem cells.[14]

From the website *BlackListed News*, an article titled "Futurist: Genes Without Borders," published March 18, 2009, states the following concerns:

> … But the link is this: If the scientific and technological activities that concern us are occurring mostly overseas, the laws and regulations we impose in our country often have little impact.… Likewise, the genetic research that might be most troublesome to many Americans may take place in labs that are far beyond the bounds of U.S. law.
>
> The same is also true of the most promising areas of genetic investigation. President Obama alluded to that in his announcement last week overturning President George W. Bush 's 2001 limits on federal funding for human embryonic stem cell

[14] President George W. Bush, "President Bush Calls on Senate to Back Human Cloning Ban," The White House, 4/10/2002, https://georgewbush-whitehouse.archives.gov/news/releases/2002/04/20020410-4.html.

> research. "Some of our best scientists leave for other countries that will sponsor their work," he said. "And those countries may surge ahead of ours in the advances that transform our lives."[15]

As long as there are wars, countries will look for ways to gain an advantage over their enemies. The quest for the creation of a superior soldier could go back centuries, but what is known is that Hitler made his attempt at creating the "*overman.*" Nations are in a position today where they must reduce any military disadvantage. How would these upgrades change warfare and covert missions?

Scientific periodicals display limited stages of chimera growth. Our real concern is the work being done in the "black sites," classified locations without government oversight and regulation. How far will these sites push their science to gain the advantage? It is believed that the black sites have permitted chimeras to grow to maturity. If you have difficulty imagining such a creature, Hollywood is always there to promote social acceptance for what lies ahead.

In 2010, the movie "*Splice*" was released, where a chimera was allowed to grow to full maturity. If you question the reality of chimeras, let's tap into the public domain and see for ourselves. Eric Niiler, author for the website Wired, states the following in his 2016 article:

> The mighty Chimera—a single body sprouting lion, goat and snake heads—is one of the most recognizable mythological beasts. The modern chimera is not so physically striking, being a hybrid organism with organs or tissues from multiple species. But it could become an important tool for medical research.

---

[15] CQ Politics, "Futurist: Genes without Borders," BlackListed News, March 18, 2009, https://www.blacklistednews.com/?news_id=3647.

> Scientists have mixed-and-matched human and animal cells for years, hoping to one day grow replacement human organs or discover genetic pathways of human diseases.
>
> Last year, though, the National Institutes of Health banned funding of animal-human chimeras until it could figure out whether any of this work would bump against ethical boundaries. Like: Could brain scientists endow research animals with human cognitive abilities, or even consciousness, while transplanting human stem cells into the brain of a developing animal embryo? Would it be morally wrong to create animals with human feet, hands, or a face in order to study human morphology? Modern medicine thinks before it acts.
>
> After a nearly year-long ban, on August 4 the NIH said it would soon lift its moratorium and again start accepting grant applications from research labs that want to develop human-animal chimeras. "We thought it was good time to take a deep breath, pause and make sure the ethical frameworks that we have in place allows us to move forward and conduct this research responsibly," says Carrie Wolinetz, associate director for science policy at NIH.[16]

Scientists are having ethical debates about what boundaries and limitations to set over their research. Regardless of the debate's outcome, this type of research is not going away. It will be like opening Pandora's Box. Much of this text reads like a science fiction movie plot. You know the type where a lab experiment goes terribly wrong, and control is lost. Pandemics have been

---

[16] Eric Niiler, "You Can Soon Grow Human-Animal Hybrids, but You Can't Breed 'em," Wired, August 5th, 2016, https://www.wired.com/2016/08/new-nih-rules-let-grow-pigoons-cant-breed-em/.

caused in the past by infectious viruses crossing the human-animal barrier. Below are two articles from the website for *Scientific American*. The first article is by John Rennie, dated June 27, 2005, and titled *Human-Animal Chimeras*. The second article is by Andrew Joseph, dated August 4, 2016, and titled *Human-Animal Chimera Research May Resume with NIH (National Institutes of Health) Support*.

John Rennie:

> Stem cell science has become notorious for obliging society to consider again where it draws the line between human embryonic cells and human beings. Less well known is that it also pushes us to another border that can be surprisingly vague: the one that separates people from animals. Stem cells facilitate the production of advanced interspecies chimeras—organisms that are a living quilt of human and animal cells. The ethical issues raised by the very existence of such creatures could become deeply troubling.
>
> In Greek mythology, the chimera was a monster that combined the parts of a goat, a lion and a serpent....
>
> No one knows what the consequences will be as the proportion of human cells in an animal increases. Weissman and others, for example, have envisioned one day making a mouse with fully "humanised" brain tissue. The lawyer developmental programme and tiny size of this chimerical mouse fairly guarantee that its mental capacities would not differ greatly from those of normal mice. But what if human cells were instead put in the foetus of a chimpanzee? *The birth of something less beastly could not be ruled out.*
>
> The intermingling of tissues could also make it easier for infectious animal diseases to move into

> humans. *Diseases that hop species barriers can be particularly devastating because the immune systems of their new hosts are so unprepared for them (the flu pandemic of 1918 is widely believed to have sprung from an avian influenza virus).* [17] (Emphasis added)

Andrew Joseph:

> The proposed rule changes, which the National Institutes of Health announced in a blog post, would allow the agency to pay for experiments that incorporate human tissue into early-stage animal embryos, except for those of primates like monkeys and chimps.
>
> The NIH put a moratorium on funding early-stage embryonic chimeras in September because of ethical concerns. *Some bioethicists raised concerns that animals with human brain tissue might absorb some ability to think like people.*
>
> *Others were concerned about what would happen if human-animal chimeras were allowed to breed.*[18] (Emphasis added)

Two articles separated by nine years, but both with the same concern. What will happen if animals gain the ability to think as humans do? While I know God is sovereign and is ultimately in control, my imagination immediately jumped to the movie *Planet of the Apes.*

---

[17] John Rennie, "Human-Animal Chimeras," Scientific American, June 27, 2005, https://www.scientificamerican.com/article/human-animal-chimeras/.

[18] Andrew Joseph, "Human-Animal Chimera Research May Resume with NIH Support," Scientific American, August 4, 2016, https://www.scientificamerican.com/article/human-animal-chimera-research-may-resume-with-nih-support/.

Another aspect of the transhumanist movement is man's desire for an alternate path to immortality. What is meant by an alternative way? A path without God. Not only is the combining of humans with animal genetics taking place, but we also have the combining of a man with a machine. The age of the *cyborg* is upon us. Below is a simple definition for "cyborg" from Dictionary.com; with today's science, does this sound impossible?

> A person whose physiological functioning is aided by or dependent upon a mechanical or electronic device.[19]

Science has successfully mapped the human brain. The building of supercomputers and artificial intelligence (AI) is here. Again, that is what the government and private sector are willing to disclose. The rule of thumb for disclosure of what the government and the private sector reveal is you can estimate they are years, if not decades, ahead in the classified labs.

Humanity is trying to achieve immortality without God. One such attempt will be to transfer human consciousness into a synthetic brain and then house this brain in a robot. Here a person can supposedly live forever, upgrading along the way. The movie *Transcendence,* with actor Johnny Depp (2014), was about the transfer of human consciousness to a computer. This transformation is the goal of the *2045 Strategic Initiative*. You can visit www.2045.com. But a quick look at their chart displays their goals.

---

[19] "Cyborg," Dictionary.com, July 17, 2019, https://www.dictionary.com/browse/cyborg.

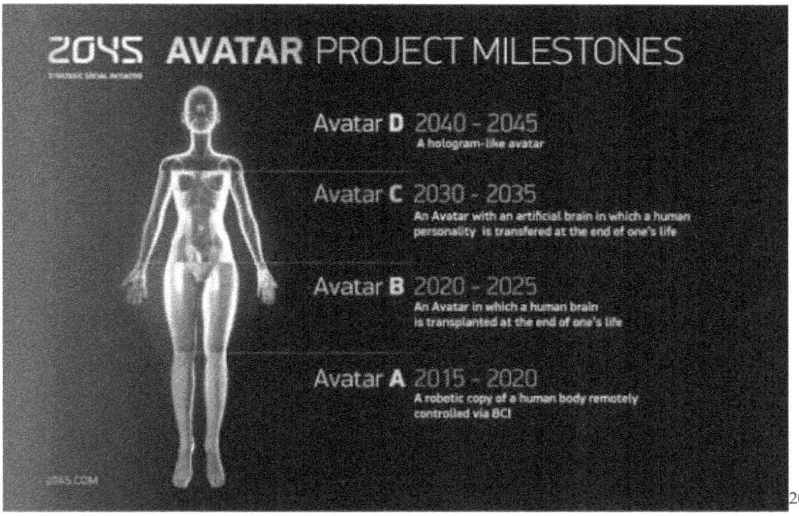

[20]

God has a plan of redemption for humanity's relationship with Him to be restored to the status before the fall in the Garden of Eden. It is not God's intention for His creation to spend eternity in our fallen state. God placed Adam and Eve outside the Garden of Eden after their fall and before they could eat from the *Tree of Life*. Eating from the Tree of Life would have permanently locked them into their fallen state because they would have become immortal.

> And the LORD God said, Behold, the man is become as one of us, to know good and evil: and now, lest he put forth his hand, and take also of the tree of life, and eat, and live for ever: Therefore the LORD God sent him forth from the garden of Eden, to till the ground from whence he was taken. So he drove out the man; and he placed at the east of the garden of

[20] www.2045.com.

> Eden Cherubims, and a flaming sword which turned every way, to keep the way of the tree of life.[21]

God chose a plan of redemption and restoration before immortality. Satan knows this. Referring to Revelation 9 again, and the locust-like creatures, in the coming Apocalypse, something happens to the people without the *seal of God*. People will seek death to escape the pain and not be able to find it.

That begs the question of why they will not be able to find death. The question that quickly comes to mind is what in the physiology of these people has changed so that they can't die, even when they seek death? Did they agree to take an upgrade from science or make a pact with the Antichrist? Has their genetic structure been modified through transhumanism?

The great flood destroyed all life on Earth. Noah's family and the animals in the ark are all that survived. The Nephilim, the offspring which resulted from mixing species, were also killed in the flood. These creatures were part human and part angelic. The flood destroyed the Nephilim's physical bodies, but what about their spiritual portion? They couldn't return to God because they did not come from God. Many speculate that these are the demon spirits that roam the earth looking for a physical body to possess, a new place to call home. From the extra-biblical text, the book *Enoch 1* offers the following explanation:

> And now, the giants who were born from body and flesh will be called Evil Spirits on the Earth, and on the Earth will be their dwelling.
>
> And evil spirits came out from their flesh, because from above they were created, from the Holy Watchers was their origin and first foundation. Evil spirits they will be on Earth and 'Spirits of the Evil Ones' they will be called.

[21] Genesis 3:22-24, KJV.

> And the dwelling of the Spirits of Heaven is Heaven, but the dwelling of the spirits of the Earth, who were born on the Earth, is Earth. And the spirits of the giants do wrong, are corrupt, attack, fight, break on the Earth, and cause sorrow. And they eat no food, do not thirst, and are not observed.
>
> And these spirits will rise against the sons of men, and against the women, because they came out of them during the days of slaughter and destruction.[22]

The New Testament shows Jesus Christ casting out demons, and note what the demons were saying when confronted by the Son of God—there appears to be a hint of a coming judgment.

> And when he was come to the other side into the country of the Gergesenes, there met him two possessed with devils, coming out of the tombs, exceeding fierce, so that no man might pass by that way. And, behold, they cried out, saying, What have we to do with thee, Jesus, thou Son of God? *art thou come hither to torment us before the time*?[23] (Emphasis added)

The book of Mark records a similar episode:

> And when he was come out of the ship, immediately there met him out of the tombs a man with an unclean spirit, Who had his dwelling among the tombs; and no man could bind him, no, not with chains: Because that he had been often bound with fetters and chains, and the chains had been plucked asunder by

---

[22] Joseph B. Lumpkin, *The Books of Enoch* (Blountsville, Alabama: Fifth Estate Publishers, 2010) 46.

[23] Matthew 8:28-29, KJV.

> him, And always, night and day, he was in the mountains, and in the tombs, crying, and cutting himself with stones. But when he saw Jesus afar off, he ran and worshipped him. And cried with a loud voice, and said, What have I to do with thee, Jesus, thou Son of the most high God? I adjure thee by God, that thou torment me not. [24]

Why all this talk about the transhumanist movement? Christian believers are becoming more of a minority in society. Like Noah, we must keep ourselves unpolluted by the world, keep ourselves redeemable in God's eyes. Noah was a godly man, and the world around him did not corrupt his gene pool.

> These are the generations of Noah: Noah was a just man and perfect in his generations, and Noah walked with God.[25]

From Jewish Historian Flavius Josephus:

> But Noah was very uneasy at what they did; and being displeased at their conduct, persuaded them to change their dispositions and their acts for the better: but seeing they did not yield to him, but were slaves to their wicked pleasures, he was afraid they would kill him, together with his wife and children, and those they had married; so he departed out of that land.[26]

---

[24] Mark 5: 2-7, KJV.

[25] Genesis 6:9, KJV.

[26] William Whiston, A.M., *The Complete Works of Flavius Josephus the Jewish Historian* (Green Forest, Arkansas: New Leaf Publishing Group, 2010) 1.3.1.

The mark of the beast was covered in the previous chapter. Christians can't take that mark, which the Antichrist will impose on the world. The world-system will push its citizens for compliance, and the system will persecute Christians and anyone else for their non-compliance.

THERE ARE DIVIDING DIFFERENCES

It is essential to know these differences in world religions because the Ecumenical rhetoric is extending its invitation outside the Christian church. The *Charisma News* website posted an article on May 24, 2016, about Pope Francis meeting with Sheikh Ahmed Mohamed el-Tayeb; he is the Egyptian Imam of al-Azhar Mosque. The piece is titled "The One World Religion Cometh: Pope Francis Warmly Welcomes Top Islamic Cleric to the Vatican." Article author Michael Snyder says the following:

> Sheikh Ahmed al-Tayeb is the Grand Imam of Cairo's Al-Azhar Mosque, and some have described him as "the highest figure in Sunni Islam." The Daily Mail said that the meeting between these two men was a "historic bid to reopen dialogue between the two churches," and as you will see below, this is yet another in a long series of attempts by Pope Francis to build bridges between Catholicism and various other faiths. In the end, what are we to make of all of this? Could it be possible that Pope Francis is laying the groundwork for the "super world church" and the coming one world religion that David Wilkerson and so many others have warned about?
>
> Today, I don't think that there is a fear of Islam as such but of ISIS and its war of conquest, which is partly drawn from Islam," he told French newspaper La Croix. "It is true that the idea of conquest is inherent in the soul of Islam, however, it is also possible

> to interpret the objective in Matthew's Gospel, where Jesus sends his disciples to all nations, in terms of the same idea of conquest.[27]

Is Pope Francis comparing the objective of Matthew's Gospel to being similar to that of military campaigns for conquest? Islam spreads Muslim belief as a military campaign. Their motto is simple, death to the unbelievers. Has this been the underlying motive for the Catholic Church's killing of millions through the centuries? What kind of message does that send to the world?

It is beneficial to have a working knowledge of Catholicism's history so you can connect past events with today's rhetoric. Pope Francis talked about ISIS as if they are evil and the Catholic Church is innocent of bloodshed. If we compare pagan Rome and the Catholic Church's historical timeline of the spilling of innocent blood, then the papacy makes today's terrorists look like preschoolers.

> Pagan Rome made sport of throwing to the lions, burning and otherwise killing thousands of Christians and not a few Jews. Yet "Christian" Rome slaughtered many times that number of both Christians and Jews. Besides those victims of the Inquisition, there were Huguenots, Albigenses, Waldenses, and other Christians who were massacred, tortured, and burned at the stake by the hundreds of thousands simply because they refused to align themselves with the Roman Catholic church and its corruption and heretical dogmas and practices. *Out of conscience they tried to follow the teachings of Christ and the apostles independent of Rome*, and for that crime

---

[27] Michael Snyder, "The One World Religion Cometh: Pope Francis Warmly Welcomes Top Islamic Cleric to the Vatican," Charisma News, 5/24/2016, https://www.charismanews.com/opinion/57367-the-one-world-religion-cometh-pope-francis-warmly-welcomes-top-islamic-cleric-to-the-vatican.

> they were maligned, hunted, imprisoned, tortured, and slain.
>
> ... Amazingly, Protestants are now embracing Rome as Christian while she insists that the "separated brethren" be reconciled to her on her unchangeable terms!
>
> Many evangelical leaders are intent upon working with Roman Catholics to evangelize the world by the year 2000. They don't want to hear any "negative" reminders of the millions of people tortured and slain by the church to which they now pay homage, or the fact that Rome has a false gospel of sacramental works.[28] (Emphasis added)

Michael Snyder continues about how Pope Francis is promoting that religions outside the Bible believe in the same God. First, this brief comment by Pope Francis and then Michael Snyder's analysis:

> I then greet and cordially thank you all, dear friends belonging to other religious traditions; first of all the Muslims, who worship the one God, ...
>
> In the video, Pope Francis explains that people all over the world are "seeking God or meeting God in different ways" and that "there is only one certainty that we have for all: We are all children of God." At about the 20-second mark, leaders from various major religions are shown declaring what they believe. First, a female Buddhist announces "I have confidence in the Buddha." Secondly, a Jewish rabbi declares "I believe in God." Thirdly, a Catholic priest tells us that "I believe in Jesus Christ," and

[28] Hunt, *A Woman Rides the Beast*, 81.

> lastly an Islamic leader is shown saying "I believe in God, Allah."
>
> If you have not seen this video, it is one of the creepiest things that I have ever seen on YouTube. [Watch the video at www.youtube.com/watch?v=-6FfTxwTX34.] It has become exceedingly clear that Pope Francis believes that all major religions are completely valid paths to the same God, and there is virtually no uproar over this.
>
> *This just shows how late in the game we really are. The one world religion that was prophesied nearly 2,000 years ago in the book of Revelation is starting to come to life, and we are witnessing the events of the last days begin to unfold right in front of our eyes.*[29] (Emphasis added.)

The primary differences in the non-Christian world religions are enough to know that these religions are not talking about the same God. Catholicism may permit compromises (to be unequally yoked) with other world religions. But it is clearly against God's Word for the body of Christ to bind itself to pagan religions. God warned Joshua about not making a covenant with the people in the land of Canaan who were not part of Israel:

> *Thou shalt make no covenant with them, nor with their gods*. They shall not dwell in thy land, lest they make thee sin against me: for if thou serve their gods, it will surely be a snare unto thee.[30] (Emphasis added)

So, what about the gods of these non-Christian religions? What is their origin, and who are they? Are these gods that have

---

[29] Michael Snyder, "The One World Religion Cometh: Pope Francis Warmly Welcomes Top Islamic Cleric to the Vatican," Charisma News, 5/24/2016, https://www.charismanews.com/opinion/57367-the-one-world-religion-cometh-pope-francis-warmly-welcomes-top-islamic-cleric-to-the-vatican.

[30] Exodus 23:32-33, KJV.

captured the minds of world religions imaginary, or were they real and commanded obedience? There is much rhetoric about how all religions are worshipping the same God. It may be true that many of the world's religions are worshipping the same god(s), but they are not the God of the Bible. If "all religions" are not praising the same God, then they cannot combine without one or more religions compromising their doctrinal beliefs.

GOD'S DIVINE COUNCIL

The Vatican has hosted conferences with world religions to promote unity and to find common ground. If common ground cannot be biblically supported, then fabricating common ground through the use of rhetoric and semantics is deceit. Our dig begins with the origin of these other gods. We will look into a book/study written by Dr. Michael S. Heiser in his book titled *The Unseen Realm.*[31]

For those readers who are not familiar with the work and creditability of Dr. Heiser's research, I provide the following public information. Dr. Heiser is an American-born Bible scholar and author. His education has its roots in the University of Wisconsin-Madison, University of Pennsylvania, and Bob Jones University. He holds the following degrees: MA in Ancient History and an MA and Ph.D. in the Hebrew Bible and Semitic Languages. He has served as a scholar-in-residence at Faithful Corporation, Liberty University, and Midwestern Baptist Theological Seminary, and his list of credentials continues and can be publicly accessed.

Chapter 14, titled "Divine Allotment," takes a more in-depth look into what happened in both the human and spiritual realm at the *Tower of Babel*. God dispersed humanity into 70 different nations, each with their language, and as we will see, their gods.

---

[31] ISBN: 978-1-57799-556-2.

It is important to note here that even though these 70 nations each had a new language, this action didn't erase their memories. They retained their knowledge of the Genesis 3:15 prophecy and of the great flood.

> And I will put enmity between thee and the woman, and between thy seed and her seed; it shall bruise thy head, and thou shalt bruise his heel.[32]

I bring this to your attention because many ancient pagan religions exhibit mother and son redeemer type figures. The subject is covered in depth by author Alexander Hislop in his book *The Two Babylons*.[33] It is helpful if you understand the existence of God's *Divine Counsel*. Outside of the Trinity, in heaven, God had a heavenly host there when He (God) created our world.

> Where wast thou when I laid the foundations of the earth? Declare, if thou hast understanding. Who hath laid the measures thereof, if thou knowest? Or who hath stretched the line upon it? Whereupon are the foundations thereof fastened? Or who laid the corner stone thereof; When the morning stars sang together, and all *the sons of God* shouted for joy? [34] (Emphasis added)

> In the ancient Semitic world, *sons of God* (Hebrew: *beney elohim*) is a phrase used to identify divine beings with higher-level responsibilities or

---

[32] Genesis 3:15, KJV.

[33] ISBN: 9781492287261.

[34] Job 38:4-7, KJV.

> jurisdictions. The term *angel* (Hebrew: *mal'ak*) describes an important still lesser task: delivering messages.[35]

Dr. Heiser emphasizes from the beginning of our world's creation that God had company. He was not alone; He created other divine beings to be members of the heavenly host. Dr. Heiser notes it is unfortunate that most commentaries omit what existed before creation. There was a heavenly family before the creation of the earthly one. From Scripture, we can see that the *"sons of God"* are divine (of the spiritual realm) and not human. These heavenly beings already existed and witnessed the creation of the world. The angelic hosts are of supernatural intelligence and abilities. When compared to humanity, these spiritual beings of supernatural abilities would be considered "god" like (little "g").

As was mentioned with transhumanism, in Genesis 6, we find the account where divine beings "sons of God" disobeyed the boundaries set by God. These actions caused corruption on the earth, and for that reason, God sent the great flood in which we find Noah and his family.

> And it came to pass, when men began to multiply on the face of the earth, and daughters were born unto them, That the sons of God saw the daughters of men that they were fair; and they took them wives of all which they chose. And the LORD said, My spirit shall not always strive with man, for that he also is flesh: yet his days shall be an hundred and twenty years. There were giants in the earth in those days; and also after that, when the sons of God came in unto the daughters of men, and they bare children to

[35] Dr. Michael S. Heiser, *The Unseen Realm* (Bellingham, Washington: Lexham Press, 2015), 24.

> them, the same became mighty men which were of old, men of renown. And GOD saw that the wickedness of man was great in the earth, and that every imagination of the thoughts of his heart was only evil continually. And it repented the LORD that he had made man on the earth, and it grieved him at his heart. And the LORD said, I will destroy man whom I have created from the face of the earth; both man, and beast, and the creeping thing, and the fowls of the air; for it repenteth me that I have made them. [36]

The New Testament gives an account of this disobedient incursion—in 1 Peter 3 and in Jude. Peter tells how Jesus spoke with the disobedient spirits who were imprisoned and awaiting judgment for their actions in Genesis 6.

> By which also he went and preached unto the spirits in prison; Which sometime were disobedient, when once the longsuffering of God waited in the days of Noah, while the ark was a preparing, wherein few, that is, eight souls were saved by water.[37]

> And the angels which kept not their first estate, but left their own habitation, he hath reserved in everlasting chains under darkness unto the judgment of the great day.[38]

For those readers who are not familiar, one-third[39] of the heavenly host rebelled with Satan against God. Satan must have used some powerful propaganda to convince one-third of the

---

[36] Genesis 6:1-7, KJV.

[37] 1 Peter 3:19-20, KJV.

[38] Jude 1:6, KJV.

[39] Revelation 12:4.

angelic hosts to oppose the Creator! A group of these fallen angels took their rebellion from the heavenly realm/dimension to our earthly realm/dimension and have been interfering with humanity from the beginning. Moving forward from Genesis 6 to 11, we come to the *Tower of Babel.* Here we find *Nimrod,* the first world leader after the *Flood,* who led the people in disobedience against God's command to spread out over the earth and complete the edict given Noah to repopulate the world.

> And God blessed Noah and his sons, and said unto them, Be fruitful, and multiply, and *replenish* the earth.[40] (Emphasis added)

Dr. Heiser's text continues with the importance of understanding what happened at the *Tower of Babel.* We know God dispersed the people into 70 different languages, dividing the people into nations with boundaries. The heavenly host inherited the management of these nations, and these angelic managers divided the Earth into territories. In Genesis, we find the story of the *Tower of Babel.*

> And the whole earth was of one language, and of one speech. And it came to pass, as they journeyed from the east, that they found a plain in the land of Shinar; and they dwelt there. And they said one to another, Go to, let us make brick, and burn them thoroughly. And they had brick for stone, and slime had they for morter. And they said, Go to, let us build us a city and a tower, whose top may reach unto heaven; and let us make us a name, lest we be scattered abroad upon the face of the whole earth.[41]

---

[40] Genesis 9:1, KJV.

[41] Genesis 11:1-5, KJV.

> And the LORD came down to see the city and the tower, which the children of men builded. And the LORD said, Behold, the people is one, and they have all one language; and this they begin to do: and now nothing will be restrained from them, which they have imagined to do. Go to, let us go down, and there confound their language, that they may not understand one another's speech. So the LORD scattered them abroad from thence upon the face of all the earth: and they left off to build the city. Therefore is the name of it called Babel; because the LORD did there confound the language of all the earth: and from thence did the LORD scatter them abroad upon the face of all the earth.[42]

In Genesis 11, the people assembled in the land of Shinar, modern-day Iraq, and God dispersed them throughout the world. Referencing Deuteronomy 32, we find written the dispersal of the nations.

> When the Most High divided to the nations their inheritance, when he separated the sons of Adam, he set the bounds of the people *according to the number of the children of Israel*. For the LORD'S portion is his people; Jacob is the lot of his inheritance.[43] (Emphasis added)

Dr. Heiser further explains that "most English Bibles do not read "according to the number of the *sons of God*" in Deuteronomy 32:8. Instead, they replace the "sons of God" with the "sons of Israel." Referencing the *Septuagint,* you will find the same interpretation that is in the *Dead Sea Scrolls*:

---

[42] Genesis 11:6-9, KJV.

[43] Deuteronomy 32:8-9, KJV.

> When the Most High divided the nations, when he separated the sons of Adam, he set the bounds of the nations according to the *number of angels of God*, And his people Jacob became the portion of the Lord, *Israel was the line of his inheritance.*[44] (Emphasis added)

This excerpt may help with the simplicity of interpreting the text:

> You just need to think a bit about the *wrong* reading, the "sons of Israel." Deuteronomy 32:8-9 harks back to the Tower of Babel, an event that occurred *before* the call of Abraham, the father of the nation of Israel. This means that the nations of the earth were divided at Babel *before Israel even existed as a people*. It would make no sense for God to divide up the nations of earth "according to the number of the sons of Israel" if there was no Israel. This point is also brought home in another way, namely by the fact that Israel is not listed in the Table of Nations.[45]
>
> So what happened to the other nations? What does it mean that they were apportioned as an inheritance according to the number of the sons of God? As odd as it sounds, the rest of the nations were placed under the authority of members of Yahweh's divine

[44] Sir Lancelot C.L. Brenton, *The Researchers Library of Ancient Texts Volume III*: The Septuagint 1851, Translation (Crane, Montana: Defense Publishers,2012), 160.

[45] Heiser, *The Unseen Realm*, 113.

council. The other nations were assigned to lesser *elohim* as a judgment from the Most High, Yahweh.[46]

A parallel passage that helps clarify and gives context to the worshipping of lesser "gods" is found in Deuteronomy.

> And lest thou lift up thine eyes unto heaven, and when thou seest the sun, and the moon, and the stars, even all the host of heaven, *shouldest be driven to worship them, and serve them, which the LORD thy God hath divided unto all nations under the whole heaven*. But the LORD hath taken you, and brought you forth out of the iron furnace, even out of Egypt, to be unto him a people of inheritance, as ye are this day.[47] (Emphasis added)

Some final thoughts from the book *Unseen Realm,* the chapter on *Divine Allotment*:

> Deuteronomy 4:19 is the other side of God's punitive coin. Whereas in Deuteronomy 32:8-9 God apportioned or handed out the nations to the sons of God, here we are told God "allotted" the gods to those nations. God decreed, in the wake of Babel, that the other nations he had forsaken would have other gods besides himself to worship. It is as though God was saying. "If you don't want to obey me, I'm not interested in being your god—I'll match you up with

---

[46] Ibid., 114., Note: 7, "It is interesting to note that the number of the nations listed in Gen 10 is seventy (see Nahum M. Sarna, Genesis [JPS Torah Commentary; Philadelphia: Jewish Publication Society, 1989],69). This is precisely the number of the sons of El in the divine council at Ugarit. This number, in the context of the disinheritance of the nations, will surface later in our discussion of the Gospels."

[47] Deuteronomy 4:19-20, KJV.

> some other god." Psalm 82, where we started our discussion, echoes this decision. That psalm has Yahweh judging other *elohim,* sons of the Most High, for their corruption in administering the nations.
>
> From the fateful decision at Babel onward, the story of the Old Testament is about Israel versus the disinherited nations, and Yahweh versus the corrupt, rebel *elohim* of those nations.[48]

Genesis 32 notes the abandonment of the disobedient peoples at the time of the Tower of Babel to the authority of divine beings (lesser gods) other than God Almighty. The title God Almighty and the *Most High* God are written to provide a distinction between God the Creator and gods, little "g," the created. These gods are of lesser power and might, which should now add clarity when reading the Bible. For there to be a Most High God, there must be a god or gods that are considered lesser in value or attribute. The Apostle Paul in the New Testament describes the heavenly host to that of a military ranking system. Note the following verses that indicate this separation; do a complete search for yourself:

> He that dwelleth in the secret place of the Most High shall abide under the shadow of the Almighty.[49]

> I have said, Ye are gods; and all of you are children of the Most High.[50]

---

[48] Heiser, *The Unseen Realm,* 114-115.

[49] Psalm 91:1, KJV.

[50] Psalm 82:6, KJV.

> I will cry unto God most high; unto God that performeth all things for me.[51]

> When the Most High divided to the nations their inheritance… [52]

> The LORD thundered from heaven, and the Most High uttered his voice.[53]

> This matter is by the decree of the watchers, and the demand by the word of the holy ones: to the intent that the living may know that the Most High ruleth in the kingdom of men, and giveth it to whomsoever he will, and setteth up over it the basest of men.[54]

Grasping this distinction removes the confusion about the function of the Divine Council. Other Bible verses support or offer proof of these heavenly rulers. These angelic rulers have authority over earthly territories. Daniel 10 provides a glimpse into the battlefield of the *heavenly realm*—the *spiritual realm,* adjacent to our physical dimension. There are indeed powerful divine beings (supernatural beings of different ranks and power) that have rulership over the nations. The prophet Daniel had been praying and fasting for 21 days about the Jews who returned from the *Babylonian Captivity* back to Jerusalem to rebuild the city. The character of the prophet Daniel is like that of Joseph, the son of Jacob.

Both Joseph and Daniel were godly men, faithful to God and above reproach. Both served in high positions of court in two of

---

[51] Psalm 57:2, KJV.

[52] Deuteronomy 32:8, KJV.

[53] 2 Samuel 22:14, KJV.

[54] Daniel 4:17, KJV.

the world's most wicked empires. However, they remained true to their faith. We find Daniel praying for an answer from God. God heard Daniel's prayer, for it had reached God's throne the same day in which Daniel offered it up. God dispatched an angelic messenger to give Daniel an answer, but the messenger was hindered in a battle for 21 days by a more powerful divine being—an angel called a prince, "principality," who is the ruling power over the Persian Empire.

So, we have an angelic being of the principality or ruler *class* who is in opposition to God's will, effecting world events in the Persian Empire, just as spoken of in Deuteronomy 32. Being in opposition to God's will is evident by the fact that this principality resisted God's messenger. The messenger-class angel lacked the power to get past the prince of Persia. The archangel Michael, whom God assigned to the nation of Israel, appeared on the scene. Michael's power exceeded that of the prince of Persia; by entering the battle, he cleared the way for the messenger to reach Daniel. Note that a prince of Greece is also mentioned—a divine being with authority over Greece, an empire that was not due to rise to power for another couple hundred years.

> And he said unto me, O Daniel, a man greatly beloved, understand the words that I speak unto thee, and stand upright: for unto thee am I now sent. And when he had spoken this word unto me, I stood trembling. Then said he unto me, Fear not, Daniel: for from the first day that thou didst set thine heart to understand, and to chasten thyself before thy God, thy words were heard, and I am come for thy words. But the prince of the kingdom of Persia withstood me one and twenty days: but, lo, Michael, one of the chief princes, came to help me; and I remained there with the kings of Persia. Now I am come to make

> thee understand what shall befall thy people in the latter days: for yet the vision is for many days.[55]
>
> Then said he, Knowest thou wherefore I come unto thee? and now will I return to fight with the *prince of Persia*: and when I am gone forth, lo, the *prince of Grecia* shall come. But I will shew thee that which is noted in the Scripture of truth: and there is none that holdeth with me in these things, but *Michael your prince*.[56] (Emphasis added)

Psalm 82 provides insight into God's judgment over the way the angelic princes misgoverned humanity. Psalm 82 notes the punishment is they *"will die like men."* References to heavenly hosts that are in the heavens between God's throne and the nations of the earth are mentioned in the New Testament as well. We find written in letters by the Apostle Paul to the church:

> For by him were all things created, that are in heaven, and that are in earth, visible and invisible, whether they be *thrones*, or *dominions*, or *principalities*, or *powers*: all things were created by him, and for him:[57] (Emphasis added)
>
> For we wrestle not against flesh and blood, but against *principalities*, against *powers*, against the *rulers* of the darkness of this world, against spiritual wickedness in *high places*.[58] (Emphasis added)

---

[55] Daniel 10:11-14, KJV.

[56] Daniel 10:20-21, KJV.

[57] Colossians 1:16, KJV.

[58] Ephesians 6:12, KJV.

> Wherein in time past ye walked according to the course of this world, according to the *prince of the power* of the air, *the spirit that now worketh in the children of disobedience*: Among whom also we all had our conversation in times past in the lusts of our flesh, fulfilling the desires of the flesh and of the mind; and were by nature the children of wrath, even as others.[59] (Emphasis added)

> As concerning therefore the eating of those things that are offered in sacrifice unto idols, we know that an idol is nothing in the world, and that there is none other God but one. For though there be that are called *gods*, whether *in heaven* or in earth, (as there be *gods many*, and lords many,)[60] (Emphasis added)

It may be of interest to know that representation of the descendants from the table of nations, the disinherited, were present at the *day of Pentecost.*[61] These people groups witnessed the work of the Holy Spirit, giving birth to the New Testament church. Peter preached, and 3,000 people joined the early church. These witnesses were able to take the gospel message of salvation back to their home countries. God is faithful to His Word in John 3:16. This event was the beginning of taking the gospel message to those disinherited nations. God made way for their reconciliation.

Psalm 82 judgment:

> I said, "You are gods, sons of the Highest, all of you; nevertheless, like men you shall die, and fall like any prince.

---

[59] Ephesians 2:2-3, KJV.

[60] 1 Corinthians 8:4-5, KJV.

[61] Acts 2:7-11.

> Arise, O God, judge the earth; For You shall inherit all nations."[62]

God *disinheriting the nations* at the Tower of Babel has been described as the *judgment of abandonment*. The Apostle Paul describes this act in Romans 1.

> For the wrath of God is revealed from heaven against all ungodliness and unrighteousness of men, who hold the truth in unrighteousness; Because that which may be known of God is manifest in them; for God hath shewed it unto them. For the invisible things of him from the creation of the world are clearly seen, being understood by the things that are made, even his eternal power and Godhead; so that they are without excuse:
>
> *Because that, when they knew God, they glorified him not as God, neither were thankful; but became vain in their imaginations, and their foolish heart was darkened.*[63] (Emphasis added)

> Professing themselves to be wise, they became fools, And changed the glory of the uncorruptible God into an image made like to corruptible man, and to birds, and fourfooted beasts, and creeping things. Wherefore *God also gave them up* to uncleanness through the lusts of their own hearts, to dishonour their own bodies between themselves: Who changed the truth of God into a lie, and *worshipped and served the creature more than the Creator,* who is blessed for ever. Amen. For this cause *God gave them up* unto vile affections: for even their women did change the

[62] Psalm 82:6-8, ESV.

[63] Romans 1:18-21, KJV.

> natural use into that which is against nature:[64] (Emphasis added)

In the very next chapter, Genesis 12, God calls Abram (Abraham) out of the land of the Chaldees. God creates a new nation (a new people) for His inheritance, separate from the people of the Tower of Babel. Through Abraham's generational seed, Jesus Christ was born, and the New Testament church and covenant are established. Several passages in the Old Testament admonish the nation of Israel not to perform or duplicate the pagan practices (doctrines) of the nations around them. These countries are outside the land of Israel. God does not change; what is an abomination to God in the Old Testament applies in the New Testament as well. Specifically, for this discussion, the first of God's Ten Commandments is *Thou shalt have no other gods before me*.[65]

THE IMMUTABILITY OF GOD

> God is not a man, that he should lie; neither the son of man, that he should repent: hath he said, and shall he not do it? or hath he spoken, and shall he not make it good?[66]

> The counsel of the LORD standeth for ever, the thoughts of his heart to *all generations*.[67] (Emphasis added)

> Of old hast thou laid the foundation of the earth: and the heavens are the work of thy hands. They shall

---

[64] Romans 1:22-26, KJV.

[65] Exodus 20:3, KJV.

[66] Numbers 23:19, KJV.

[67] Psalm 33:11, KJV.

perish, but thou shalt endure: yea, all of them shall wax old like a garment; as a vesture shalt thou change them, and they shall be changed: But thou art the same, and thy years shall have no end.[68]

For ever, O LORD, thy word is settled in heaven.[69]

The grass withereth, the flower fadeth: but the word of our God shall stand for ever.[70]

For I am the LORD, I change not; therefore ye sons of Jacob are not consumed.[71]

If we believe not, yet he abideth faithful: he cannot deny himself.[72]

Jesus Christ the same yesterday, and to day, and for ever.[73]

Every good gift and every perfect gift is from above, and cometh down from the Father of lights, with whom is no variableness, neither shadow of turning.[74]

---

[68] Psalm 102:25-27, KJV.

[69] Psalm 119:89, KJV.

[70] Isaiah 40:8, KJV.

[71] Malachi3:8, KJV.

[72] 2 Timothy 2:13, KJV.

[73] Hebrews 13:8, KJV.

[74] James 1:17, KJV.

COMMANDS NOT TO ALLOW IDOLATRY

> After the doings of the land of Egypt, wherein ye dwelt, *shall ye not do: and after the doings of the land of Canaan,* whither I bring you, shall ye not do: neither shall ye walk in their ordinances.[75] (Emphasis added)

> Ye shall not go after other gods, of the gods of the people which are round about you; For the LORD thy God is a jealous God among you) lest the anger of the LORD thy God be kindled against thee, and destroy thee from off the face of the earth.[76]

> When thou art come into the land which the LORD thy God giveth thee, *thou shalt not learn to do after the abominations of those nations*.[77] (Emphasis added)

> If my people, which are called by my name, shall humble themselves, and pray, and seek my face, and turn from their wicked ways; then will I hear from heaven, and will forgive their sin, and will heal their land.[78]

According to the ecumenical movement, the different world religions are seeking the same God, just through various forms of worship. Here is the premise for the movement's *common ground*. Jesus is God in the flesh, God incarnate. Many other religions are not in agreement with this presupposition. Recall the

---

[75] Leviticus 18:3, KJV.

[76] Deuteronomy 6:14-15, KJV.

[77] Deuteronomy 18:9, KJV.

[78] 2 Chronicles 7:14, KJV.

prophecy spoken of in the Book of Isaiah, which is often read during the Christmas holiday.

> For unto us a child is born, unto us a son is given: and the government shall be upon his shoulder: and his name shall be called Wonderful, Counsellor, The mighty God, The everlasting Father, The Prince of Peace.[79]

When you research the origin of these other gods, there is immediate disharmony. Uniting churches that claim to be of the body of Christ (the church) is one thing. But to unite in partnership the body of Christ to religions with pagan gods is in defiance of God's commandments. The above text covered the topic of other gods, so does the unifying of all these religions that claim Christianity bring today's Christian church closer or further away from the apostolic teachings of the New Testament church?

An excerpt from Dr. Donald Grey Barnhouse's book *The Invisible War* fits here. Like a lawyer's closing argument about the apostate church, I will insert it here.[80] I do this to give new food for thought. For the reader who is not familiar with Dr. Barnhouse's work, here is a brief introduction:

> The late Dr. Donald Grey Barnhouse was for many years pastor of the Tenth Presbyterian Church in Philadelphia, Pennsylvania. His outreach extended far beyond this congregation, however. He was the founder of The Evangelical Foundation and for

---

[79] Isaiah 9:6, KJV.

[80] ISBN: 978-0-310-20481-7.

many years the radio voice of Bible Study Hour and editor of Eternity magazine.[81]

Dr. Barnhouse's comments:

The Bible teaches that after the phase of the return of the Lord Jesus Christ that sees the entire church—the dead and the living—removed from this earth, there is to be a phase of His judgment connected with the false church, the apostate church. We have seen that the course of this age includes the general apostasy within the religious organizations of Christendom. The tares will grow together with the wheat until the day when He sends His angels to do the winnowing (Matthew 13:36-43). Throughout the Bible, the two movements are characterized as two women. The holy bride represents the true church, and "that woman Jezebel, which calleth herself a prophetess" and who teaches and seduces the servants of God to commit the fornication of going after strange gods (Revelation 2:20), represents the apostate church.

The marriage of the Lamb is brought into view, and the Lamb's wife has made herself ready, arrayed in fine linen, clean and white (Revelation 19:7,8). At the same time the evangelist is given a vision of "the judgment of the great whore that sitteth upon many waters … a woman seated upon a scarlet colored beast, full of names of blasphemy … having a golden cup in her hand full of abominations and filthiness of her fornication (Revelation 17:1-4).

---

[81] Donald Grey Barnhouse, *The Invisible War: The Panorama of the Continuing Conflict Between Good & Evil* (Grand Rapids, Michigan: Zondervan, 1965), Rear Cover.

Just as the bride and the bridegroom are joined at the beginning of the prophetic fulfillment, so the judgment of those who have had religion without Christ is a sure and certain thing. It is not necessary for us to expand the details. It will suffice to note that the woman—the personification of false religion—comes to power riding upon the beast—the personification of political power in the hands of the Antichrist who shall rise as Satan's last great human ally in the invisible war. Throughout the Bible, the separation of church and state, or of religion and the state, is a well-defined Scriptural principle. In the Old Testament, a man was not permitted to be both priest and king. In the New Testament, the Christian is called to such a position of witness against the world that it is hard to conceive that the world could ever voluntarily exalt to a place of leadership one whose whole calling is to stand as a witness against the course of this world and its prince, the devil. It can readily be understood that Satan seeks power through the transgression of this principle. He is primarily interested in the souls of men that he may gain their spiritual and political allegiance.

... But there are also men in the ecumenical movement whose thrust is a bid for power. They are not interested in theology as much as they are interested in fusion of organizations.[82]

DAMAGED DOCTRINE

Long before Constantine formed the Church of Rome, the apostolic church's teachings were under attack from false doctrines.

---

[82] Barnhouse, *The Invisible War*, 271-272.

The Apostle Pauls' Epistles to the New Testament churches were often for the correction of church doctrine and behavior from the false teachings of outsiders. Emperor Constantine created the state church for the Roman Empire. This action only accelerated the dilution of the Apostolic teachings.

> At the end of the second century, within a little more than one hundred and fifty years after the first preaching of the gospel, it is obvious to remark the changes already introduced into the Christian church. Christianity began already to wear the garb of heathenism. The seeds of most of those errors that afterwards so entirely overran the church, marred its beauty, and tarnished its glory, were already beginning to take root. Ministerial *parity,* which had undoubtedly existed under the ministry of the apostles, was now beginning to yield to the encroachments of ambition, and distinction of grades begun to be established that ended in the *Papal hierarchy.*[83]
>
> Ceremonies began to be added, which continued to increase, until, under papal authority, the whole of religion was made to consist of little else.[84]
>
> If the Protestant faith be true, then we can prove that it is so. *But we must not assume,* without proof, that the doctrines, beliefs, and *practices of modern*

[83] Rev. James Wharey, *Sketches of Church History* (Philadelphia: Presbyterian Board of Publication, 1840), 39.

[84] Ibid., 40.

> Protestantism constitute the religion founded by Jesus Christ, the Son of God.[85] (Emphasis added)

This chapter viewed the ecumenical movement as a possible precursor to Revelation 13. This possibility is not something that just arrived on the world stage; it has been in the works from the beginning, as far back as the Tower of Babel. Today, it has the support of influential organizations, the World Council of Churches and the Vatican. The question for Bible-believing Christians is whether or not you should "yoke" yourself with this agenda. Be wary of attaching yourself to counterfeit Christianity. Taking a "stand" for what you believe will come at a price, and only God knows what price He will ask of you. The Church of Rome goes beyond forming the apostate church to greeting with open arms the arrival of a cosmic savior—a supernatural savior that is not Jesus Christ of the Bible; this is the next topic in the plan for the Great Deception.

---

[85] Roderick C. Meredith, "The Plain Truth About the Protestant Reformation Part 1," Tomorrow's World, https://www.tomorrowsworld.org/magazines/2017/march-april/the-plain-truth-about-the-protestant-reformation-part-1.

9

Doctrines of Demons Part 1

In the previous two chapters, we considered the emerging *universal church* and how the Vatican, the papacy, is spearheading this movement. The Vatican seems to have all its "official" documents signed and in order. These events excluded the hard-core fundamental Christians. The papacy uses dual influence, one political and the other religious. When the world hears the pope speak, it assumes or makes a false connection—that he speaks for all Christians—and that is not true; he speaks for Catholicism. The ecumenical movement is just another cog in the gear wheel, which moves us closer to the delusion of 1st Timothy 4.

> Now the Spirit speaketh expressly, that in the *latter times* some shall *depart from the faith*, giving heed to *seducing spirits*, and *doctrines of devils*; Speaking lies in hypocrisy; having their conscience seared with a hot iron; ... [1] (Emphasis added)

For all practical purposes, today is the "latter times." The above verse describes the departing or falling away from the Christian faith. After identifying catalytic agents used to

[1] 1 Timothy 4:1-2, KJV.

manipulate the minds of the masses over the centuries, it is not difficult to see the setting of the prophetic stage. The Church of Rome implemented *"learning against learning,"* and our government removed the Bible from the public schools.

A large portion of Protestantism has already agreed with the ecumenical movement and joined the apostate church. The churches that remain are threatened by diluting doctrines and liberal interpretations of the Bible. Church doctrines, like ships, can drift off course if left unchecked, and its initial drift can be minute—let's say an error of one degree. As time passes—weeks, months, years, or even centuries—so does the magnitude of the gap. The gap or arc between the desired path and the path of error increases with time. Some doctrines no longer have any resemblance to the original teaching. Detection for drift can only occur by comparing today's biblical teaching to some valid point in the past.

Being human, we err; we take the wrong off-ramp when we should have stayed on the highway. Each of us most likely can recall a time in our lives when we were adrift; we went off course. Would you agree that the length of time spent drifting had a direct effect on the amount of time and energy needed to make a course correction? Imagine what it would take some churches to correct the false teaching their congregation has received over the years.

Gnostics and humanists peddle their movement as the new alternative to biblical faith. The combination of Gnosticism, humanism, and the ecumenical movement, tied with the Vatican's search for "higher beings," and you have the foundation for the delusion of the masses. Societies oscillate between spiritual revival and spiritual drought. It's a repeatable cycle. However, the *handwriting on the wall,* the prophetic markers, lean away from a church revival and real repentance. The world (humanity) believes human achievement can produce global peace and order. Man has already tried twice in the 20th century—first, with the

League of Nations after WWI and second, with the United Nations after WWII; it failed both times.

Both organizations were more about controlling the masses than establishing peace. Today's *transhumanists* believe human augmentation and genetic upgrades will elevate humans to be like God. Governments claim that humanity can make the world better through science, innovation, and by implementing more control and regulation over the masses. God's Word predicts the world's woes are going to increase in intensity before Jesus Christ's return. This line of thinking is not a doomsday mindset but an acknowledgment of God's prophetic word. Both can't be right! Many of us are familiar with the phrase that "history repeats itself because we don't learn from our mistakes." Recall the chart in chapter four, which shows the "cycle of nations," a perfect example of history repeating itself, and the pattern is detectable. The Bible has repeatable patterns also, but these patterns are for the believer's benefit, to reinforce our understanding of coming prophetic events.

> All Scripture is given by inspiration of God, and is profitable for doctrine, for reproof, for correction, for instruction in righteousness: [2]

The Bible is not a Western book; it is Eastern. It is a Hebrew book, and we cannot assign a Western view of prophecy, which can cause us to error. We like to see the biblical timeline linearly—prophecies as a single act. Upon fulfillment, we think the event will not occur again. It is not always act, completion, next prophecy, and act, completion, next prophecy. Some prophetic patterns will culminate with the final scenes of the *human/spiritual saga,* as written in the Book of Revelation. We can review two examples of this pattern, and they both involve the spirit of the antichrist working in man. The *Dynasty of the Popes* is a

---

[2] 2 Timothy 3:16, KJV.

continued succession of theocratic rulers. Some prophetic writers see the popes as the first rider in the four horsemen of the Apocalypse. This rider rides the white horse in Revelation 6.

> And I saw, and behold a white horse: and he that sat on him had a bow; and a crown was given unto him: and he went forth conquering, and to conquer.[3]

This rider, dressed in white, wears a crown and carries a bow without arrows—claiming to be a messenger of peace, yet all along in his heart, he desires to conquer. The white horse is a symbol of a conqueror in oriental imagery. There is another rider of a white horse in the Book of Revelation.

> And I saw heaven opened, and behold a white horse; and he that sat upon him was called Faithful and True, and in righteousness he doth judge and make war.[4]

The distinguishing difference between the riders is that the first one in chapter six is a counterfeit, a bow without arrows is a useless weapon. The second rider carries a sword to execute judgment on the nations of Earth. The first is an imposter, and the second is the True Victor, the Lord Jesus. Here we can see the repeated pattern through the centuries of the where the papacy claims to come in the name of peace. Acting in the name of the Prince of Peace, Jesus, yet the agenda is always domination and control. The following is from Dr. Donald Grey Barnhouse's commentary on the Book of Revelation:

> The counterfeit is revealed by a detailed comparison of the two riders. The One whose name is the Word

---

[3] Revelation 6:2, KJV.

[4] Revelation 19:11, KJV.

> of God has on His head "many crowns." The symbol is of all royalty and majesty. The Greek word is diadem. The horseman of the first seal wears no diadem. The false crown is the stephanos. Its diamonds are paste. It is the shop girl adorned with jewelry from the ten-cent counter imitating the lady born and bred who wears the rich jewels of her inheritance. All is not gold that glitters. No amount of gaudy trappings can deceive the spiritual eye. Clothes do not make the man in spite of the proverb.[5]

The second is in Daniel 8.

> And out of one of them came forth a little horn, which waxed exceeding great, toward the south, and toward the east, and toward the pleasant land. And it waxed great, even to the host of heaven; and it cast down some of the host and of the stars to the ground, and stamped upon them. Yea, he magnified himself even to the prince of the host, and by him the *daily sacrifice was taken away*, and the place of his *sanctuary was cast down*. And an host was given him against the daily sacrifice by reason of transgression, and it *cast down the truth to the ground*; and it practised, and prospered. Then I heard one saint speaking, and another saint said unto that certain saint which spake, How long shall be the vision concerning the daily sacrifice, and the *transgression of desolation*, to give both the *sanctuary and the host to be trodden under foot*?[6] (Emphasis added)

---

[5] David Jeremiah, with C.C. Carlson, *Escape the Coming Night* (Dallas, Texas: Word Publishing, 1990), 97.

[6] Daniel 8:9-13, KJV.

This prophecy points to a coming Gentile leader who profanes the temple of God in Jerusalem. It was an unfulfilled prophecy in Daniel's time. Dr. David Jeremiah explains this event in his study on the Book of Daniel titled *The Handwriting on the Wall: Secrets from the Prophecies of Daniel*.[7] Dr. Jeremiah writes how Daniel's prophetic vision was fulfilled the first time in the person of Antiochus Epiphanes, a shadow of the final fulfillment by the Antichrist spoken of in Revelation 13.

> You may never have heard of this man in your ancient history courses in school, but this prophecy was fulfilled in a person named Antiochus Epiphanes. His name means "Antiochus, God Manifest." Diabolical arrogance was his nature. After trying to conquer the world and being stopped by Roman armies, he turned his fury on Jerusalem and sacked the city. He killed some eighty thousand Jews and sold another forty into slavery.... When the Bible talks about the desecration of the temple, it is a reference to the moment when Antiochus walked into the sacred place of the Jews with a pig and slit its throat as a sacrifice on the altar of the Jewish people. Then he took the blood from that animal and sprayed it all over the inside of the temple. The Bible speaks of that as the Abomination of Desolation.[8]

Many Christian authors use Antiochus Epiphanes as an example or shadow of the coming world leader predicted for the *last days*. In the same way, Abraham offering up Isaac, his only son, as a sacrifice to the Lord was a shadow of Jesus, the only Son of God, being offered up as a *sacrifice of atonement* for the world

---

[7] ISBN: 0-8499-3365-x.

[8] David Jeremiah, with C.C. Carlson, *The Handwriting on the Wall: Secrets from the Prophecies of Daniel* (Dallas: Word Publishing, 1992), 164-165.

(John 3:16). Some events and individuals can foreshadow what the Bible predicts for the last days; this includes deceptions—some small, some grand. The workings of the spirit of the antichrist are continuous throughout our historical timeline.

> Little children, it is the last time: and as ye have heard that antichrist shall come, even now are there many antichrists; whereby we know that it is the last time.[9]

The Vatican has committed considerable resources to the search of extraterrestrial life. Why? Why would a supposed Christian church focus its resources on the search for ET? According to the Roman Catholic Church, if found, these beings would be our space brethren, and the Church of Rome is considering how to bring aliens into the Catholic fold. Authors Cris Putnam and Dr. Thomas Horn completed an investigation into this matter in their book *Exo-Vaticana: Petrus Romanus, Project L.U.C.I.F.E.R and the Vatican's Astonishing Plan for the Arrival of an Alien Savior*.[10]

Exo-Vaticana exposes several vital topics that could solidify the Church of Rome's connection to the coming cosmic deception. Excerpts from Cris Putnam and Dr. Horn's book show the Vatican's intentions and projected responses to extraterrestrial visitation. The Church of Rome gives the impression that the Bible's authority, and the gospel message, may require reevaluation and modification to fit the coming *cosmic paradigm*. Can you hear the *watchman's* horn? From a Christian perspective, our circumstances are filtered through the Bible when we seek godly direction. It is not the reverse. We do not sift the Bible through our situations or world events to see if it is relevant in deciding the best course of action.

---

[9] 1 John 2:18, KJV.

[10] ISBN: 978-0-9848256-3-9.

Dr. Horn and Cris Putnam were permitted access to the Mt. Graham facility and given a tour and untethered access to speak with the staff. They conducted interviews with astronomers and directors to get their view on the project of extraterrestrial contact.

It may be helpful to have a visual of the Mt. Graham facility. Brief descriptions of site telescopes and staff will be covered first. You can also visit the Mt. Graham International Observatory website for additional technical information at https://mgio.arizona.edu.

VATICAN ADVANCED TECHNOLOGY TELESCOPE (VATT)

[11]

> The Vatican Advanced Technology Telescope (VATT) truly lives up to its name. Its heart is a 1.8-m f/1.0 honeycombed construction, borosilicate primary mirror. This was manufactured at the University of Arizona Mirror Laboratory, and it pioneered both the spin-casting techniques and the stressed-lap polishing techniques of that Laboratory which are being used for telescope mirrors up to 8.4-m in

[11] "VATT," Vatican Observatory,01/29/2019, http://www.vaticanobservatory.va/content/specolavaticana/en/research/facilities/vatt.html.

diameter. The primary mirror is so deeply-dished that the focus of the telescope is only as far above the mirror as the mirror is wide, thus allowing a structure that is about three times as compact as the previous generation of telescope designs.... The building in which the telescope is housed is designed to isolate thermally the ambient temperature in the dome from the heated observing room and living quarters. This isolation is achieved by using the section between the dome and the main facility as a thermal barrier and by exhausting air from this section and from the dome out from the north and mainly downwind side of the building.[12]

LARGE BINOCULAR TELESCOPE (LBT)

... LBTO is headquartered on the Tucson campus of the University of Arizona.

The binocular design of the Large Binocular Telescope (LBT) has two identical 8.4m telescopes mounted side-by-side on a common altitude-

[12] Ibid.

azimuth mounting for a combined collecting area of a single 11.8m telescope. The entire telescope and enclosure are very compact by virtue of the fast focal ratio (F/1.14) of the primary mirrors.

The two primary mirrors are separated by 14.4m center-to-center and provide an interferometric baseline of 22.8m edge-to-edge. The binocular design, combined with integrated adaptive optics utilizing adaptive Gregorian secondary mirrors to compensate for atmospheric phase errors, provides a large effective aperture, high angular resolution, low thermal background, and exceptional sensitivity for the detection of faint objects.[13]

L.U.C.I.F.E.R. Device

LUCI1 - LUCI2

LUCI 1 and LUCI2 are a pair of infrared multi-mode instruments. In seeing-limited mode, each has a 4 arc-minute square field of view and will be capable of long-slit and multi-slit spectroscopy as well as

[13] "Overview," Large Binocular Telescope Observatory, 01/29/2019, http://www.lbto.org/overview.html.

imaging in the near infrared zJHK bands from 0.89 (LUCI1) or 0.96 (LUCI2) to 2.44 microns. Each instrument includes diffraction-limited optics covering a 30-arcsecond field of view for use with the adaptive secondary mirrors. In seeing limited mode, the image scale is 0.12"/pix (N3.75 camera) for imaging and 0.25 "/pix (N1.8 camera) for spectroscopy. With the N30 camera in AO mode, it is 0.015 "/pixel. Laser-cut slit masks reside in a jukebox inside the instrument cryostat. Various gratings provide resolutions from ~2000 for H+K to 6500-8500 in single band z, j, H, K in the basic modes.[14]

SUBMILLIMETER TELESCOPE (SMT)

[15]

The Arizona Radio Observatory (ARO) owns and operates two radio telescopes in southern Arizona: A 12 Meter Alma Prototype Telescope located 50 miles South-West of Tucson on Kitt Peak and the

[14] "Instruments," Large Binocular Telescope Observatory, 01/29/2019, http://www.lbto.org/instruments.html.

[15] "Home Page," Arizona Radio Observatory, 01/29/2019, http://aro.as.arizona.edu/index.htm.

Submillimeter Telescope (SMT) located on Mt. Graham near Safford, Arizona.

Combined, the two telescopes routinely cover the entire millimeter and submillimeter windows from about 4.6 mm to about 0.6 mm, and at the SMT observations can be made all the way to 0.3 mm with PI instruments.[16]

Jesuit Astronomers of the Vatican Observatory Research Group (VORG)

VORG Staff as found in the book:

1. Jesuit Priest Guy Consolmagno, lead Astronomer.

   Note Update: "On September 18, 2015, Brother Guy Consolmagno SJ has become the new director of the Vatican Observatory. He succeeds Fr. José Funes SJ, who is ending the second of his five-year terms. Fr. Funes's tenure included successfully guiding the Observatory to new modern headquarters in the Papal Summer Gardens, and beginning the ongoing program of upgrading the Vatican Advanced Technology Telescope in Arizona. We all wish Fr. Funes, SJ great success in his new assignment, returning to his home to teach at the Jesuit University in Córdoba, Argentina."[17]

---

[16] Ibid.

[17] "New Director of Vatican Observatory," Vatican Observatory, http://www.vaticanobservatory.va/content/specolavaticana/en.html.

2. Father Jose Funes, director of Vatican Observatory (at the time of interview)

3. Dr. Christopher Corbally, vice director, (at the time of interview)

4. Father Giuseppe Tanzella-Nitti, an Opus Dei Theologian of the Pontifical University of the Holy Cross in Rome.

5. Jesuit George V. Coyne, director of Vatican Observatory in 1978.

6. Malachi Martin: "Malachi Brendan Martin (Irish: Maolsheachlainn Breandán Ó Máirtín; July 23, 1921 – July 27, 1999), occasionally writing under the pseudonym Michael Serafian, was an Irish Catholic priest and writer on the Catholic Church. Originally ordained as a Jesuit priest, he became Professor of Paleography at the Vatican's Pontifical Biblical Institute."[18]

The Mt. Graham staff are very open about their search for extraterrestrial life.

> This was confirmed minutes later by the Jesuit father on duty that day (whom we got on film), who told us that among the most important research occurring with the site's Vatican astronomers is the search for extrasolar planets and advanced alien intelligence.... While we were given complete and unrestricted opportunity to question how the devices are used and what distinctively sets each of the

[18] "Malachi Martin," Wikipedia: The Free Encyclopedia, 01/29/2019, en.wikipedia.org/wiki/Malachi Martin.

> telescopes on Mt. Graham apart, we had not expected the ease with which the astronomers and technicians would also speak of UFOs! This was especially true when we walked up the gravel road from the VATT to the LBT, where we spent most of the day with a systems engineer who not only took us to all seven levels of that mighty machine—pointing out the LUCIFER device (which he lovingly referred to as "Lucy" several times and elsewhere as "Lucifer") and what it is used for, as well as every other aspect of the telescope we tried to wrap our minds around.[19]

There have been media announcements coming from, as the authors put it, high-level Vatican astronomers about how the proof of *extraterrestrials may affect religious faith*. Horn and Putnam's primary reason for journeying to the Mt. Graham facility was to inquire about this very question and to ask questions directly from those sources, lead astronomer Guy Consolmagno, and others. *Exo-Vaticana* contains excerpts from Guy Consolmagno's book that, once published and in stores, was quickly pulled back off the shelves.

[19] Thomas Horn, Cris Putnam, *Exo-Vaticana: Petrus Romanus, Project L.U.C.I.F.E.R. and the Vatican's Astonishing Plan for the Arrival of an Alien Savior* (Crane, Montana: Defender Publishing, 2013), 14-15.

... Jesuit priest like Guy Consolmagno, a leading astronomer who often turns up as a spokesman for the Vatican. He has worked at NASA and taught at Harvard and MIT, and currently splits his time between the Vatican observatory and laboratory (Specola Vaticana) headquartered at the summer residence of the pope in Castel Gandolfo, Italy, and Mt. Graham in Arizona. Over the last few years, Consolmagno has focused so much time and effort in an attempt to reconcile science and religion in public forums, specifically as it relates to the subject of extraterrestrial life and its potential impact on the future of faith, that we decided to contact him.... he authored entitled *Intelligent Life in the Universe: Catholic Belief and the Search for Extraterrestrial Intelligent Life*, which had been pulled by the publisher shortly after it was authorized by Rome in 2005 and is no longer available anywhere. It is a gold mine of what he and the Vatican are considering regarding the ramifications of astrobiology and specifically the discovery of

> advanced extraterrestrials (this is perhaps the reason it was pulled).[20]

During the initial selling of *Exo-Vaticana,* there was a limited offer of Guy Consolmagno's book in PDF form. I was able to obtain a copy and will reference it. Dr. Horn and Cris Putnam continue:

> In it, he admits how contemporary societies will "look to The Aliens to be the Saviours of humankind."[21]
>
> To illustrate the theological soundness of this possibility, Consolmagno argues that humans are not the only intelligent beings God created in the universe, and these non-human life forms are described in the Bible. He starts by pointing to angels, then surprises us by actually referencing the Nephilim:[22]

Nephilim are the offspring between angles (fallen) and human women. Their corruption upon man and the earth are the main reason God cast the judgment of the great flood. Dr. I. D. E. Thomas wrote a small but informative book that precedes *Exo-Vaticana* and looks specifically into the relationship between UFOs and Nephilim. Dr. Thomas' book is titled *The Omega Conspiracy; Satan's Last Assault on God's Kingdom.* For the reader who may not be familiar with Dr. Thomas' work, the following description is from the information section located at the end of his book:

---

[20] Ibid., 17.

[21] Guy Consolmagno, *Intelligent Life in the Universe: Catholic Belief and the Search for Extraterrestrial Life* (London: Catholic Truth Society, 2005), 5.

[22] Thomas Horn, Cris Putnam, *Exo-Vaticana,* 17.

I.D.E. Thomas is one of a long line of Welsh preachers, and he has traveled extensively in Europe, the Orient, and on the American continent. His sermons have been described in the press as "powerful and passionate," "intellectually articulate" and "spiritually probing." A native of Wales in the United Kingdom, Dr. Thomas has held three pastorates in that country: the Amman Valley, Caernarvon and Llanelli, where he succeeded the Reverend Jubilee Young. For ten years he conducted special preaching missions in the United Kingdom and the United States. He also served as Commentator for the BBC (British Broadcasting Corporation).

The following excerpt is from Dr. Thomas on the Nephilim:

> So far so good. But the question is: Does our salvation lie with visitors from outer space? Is our redemption in the hands of extraterrestrial who supposedly man and operate UFOs? Are the creatures who sired the Nephilim in the days of Genesis returning as "Saviors from the Skies" or "Brethren from Space"? [23]
>
> The return of the Nephilim, a super race sired by beings from another dimension, is the only viable explanation for what is happening. As incredible as this sounds, let us regard the ancient saying of Heracleitus who, 500 years before Christ said, "*Because it*

[23] Dr. I.D.E. Thomas, *The Omega Conspiracy; Satan's Last Assault on God's Kingdom* (Crane, Missouri: Anomalos Publishing House, 2008), 183, 7.

> *is sometimes so unbelievable the truth escapes becoming known."* [24] (Emphasis added)

Guy Consolmagno early on in his text makes this declaration of uncertainty:

> But the first and most important fact we have to confront in the whole question of "extraterrestrial intelligence" is this: we don't know. Of all the planets we've found orbiting other stars, it's not clear if any of them are suitable places for life as we know it. On none of them, nor indeed anywhere closer to us in our own Sun's system of planets, have we ever found evidence that completely, uncontrovertibly, proves life originated in some place other than just here on Earth. As far as we know for sure, we could be alone. And so that means that everything else we can say about extraterrestrial life, indeed almost everything in this booklet, is speculation and guess-work.[25]

If Consolmagno's book was just speculation at that point, why broadcast it and create seeds of doubt on the sovereignty of God's Word? It is easy to understand Dr. Horn and Cris Putnam's interest in the investigation. Is Satan using the Catholic Church to plant seeds of deception that he will harvest later? Consolmagno made another comment that immediately brought to mind past research. Just as Dr. Horn and Cris Putnam noted in their book the segment about aliens being our saviors, the sentences that came prior caught my *mind's eye.*

> I have to recognize that there is another reason why a *lot of people are hungry to be visited by alien beings.*

---

[24] Ibid., 8.

[25] Guy Consolmagno, *Intelligent Life in the Universe,* 3-4.

> Seeing a world full of pain, full of disease and warfare, injustice and poverty, they hope that somehow any race advanced enough to cross the vast distances between the stars and visit us must also be *advanced enough to know how to overcome all those human problems*. They look to The Aliens to be the saviours of humankind.[26] (Emphasis added)

Chapter two of this book provided a look into how *propaganda* can precondition people's minds to accept the governing minority's next mass template. Our children are a prime target, their minds are pliable, and their mental defenses are weak. The current culture has lost faith and trust in the political system and its representatives, and justifiably so.

The world is hungry for solutions; people want deliverance from the chaos of violence and the instability of world economies, and people want to feel safe and secure. However, there are dangers in expecting too much from our governments in the way of solving society's problems. On the "Cycle of Nations" chart, located on the second page in chapter four, the *Dependency* stage is the last step before a nation returns to *Bondage*. Part of personal freedom is being responsible for yourself and your well-being.

We all need help at times, which is not the same as surrendering or offloading your responsibilities to the state. Governments are administrative agencies. How we manage our households determines collectively the culture we have. The citizens determine a nation's character, not its governmental agencies. As previously shown, the doctrines a nation permits determine its nature. Faith in humankind's ability to solve its problems continues to grow weaker.

The world is hungry for a heavenly savior, but not the supernatural savior of the Bible, Jesus Christ. Persecution of biblical

---

[26] Ibid., 5.

Christianity is again on the rise. The humanist movement and Gnosticism attack faith in God as being archaic. Over the last ten years, the entertainment industry has produced dozens of superhero movies. Superheroes are either humans with advanced augmentation or extraterrestrials with superpowers. Hollywood portrays these people as the only solution to protecting humankind from itself and alien invasion. Our worldview is affected by what we experience and consider to be true. These movies condition the masses to think about what lies just beyond the fringe of what is currently possible. All that is needed is the lies and wonders spoken of in prophecy to build doubt and weaken a person's beliefs.

> Even him, whose coming is after the working of Satan with all power and signs and lying wonders, and with all deceivableness of unrighteousness in them that perish; because they received not the love of the truth, that they might be saved.[27]

The devil's tactics have not changed. Planting the seed of doubt worked with Eve, and she was in the perfect environment. Hollywood can make fiction look realistic to the human mind. We can say it is only entertainment. Recall a statement made by Edward Bernays about the power of motion pictures on the human psyche:

> The American motion picture is *the greatest unconscious carrier* of propaganda in the world today. It is a great distributor for ideas and opinions. The motion picture can standardize the ideas and habits of a nation.[28]

---

[27] 2 Thessalonians 2:9-10, KJV.

[28] Bernays, *Propaganda*, 156.

Movies, entertainment or not, affect the human psyche. One powerful example of demonic influence was the movie the *Exorcist*. Note the following excerpt from Dr. Thomas' *Omega Conspiracy*:

> From the movie *The Exorcist*, with the Ouija Board, Paul Scott, the syndicated columnist, called this motion picture the most dangerous film ever produced in the United States. He cited 80 documented cases where persons, after reading the book, themselves became possessed.[29]

There is more to say about the Nephilim (human-hybrids) later in this chapter, but first, let us return to Guy Consolmagno's conclusion about the increasing desire for an alien savior. This desire brings us to the potential reaction of our youth, who are said to be hungry for the arrival of an alien or Nephilim savior. In Dr. David Jeremiah's book *Invasion of Other Gods,*[30] Dr. Jeremiah spotlights the minds of our children and how the entertainment industry is manipulating them. History has shown that you can usurp a nation's society without firing a shot. An enemy will use the youth (unknowingly) of a country as a *fifth column*. Chapter five of the *Invasion of Other Gods* is titled "Rescue Our Captive Children." Dr. Jeremiah wrote his book in 1995. Note whether any of the following excerpts have a prophetic tone. Let us take a quick detour to express this point.

> "Mommy ... Mommy ... Mommeee ..." Those shrieks of terror coming from the next room at 1 A.M. hit Mom and Dad like an electric shock. "I'll go," said Mom, stumbling out of bed as if an earthquake had hit. Four-year-old Trudy's wailing was reaching

---

[29] Thomas, *The Omega Conspiracy*, 20.

[30] ISBN 0-8499-1195-8.

another crescendo by this time. Dad rolled over, remembering his seven o'clock breakfast date with a client. *Just one good night's sleep is all I want. Why does that child have so many nightmares*?

"Now, now, Trudy, it's all right," Mother murmured, hugging the trembling little figure close.

"He was in my room ... he ... he was coming to get me," she sobbed.

"There's no one here except you and me, Honey. Now cuddle up and go back to sleep."

As Trudy began to quiet down, she hugged her favorite stuffed animal. No, it's not a teddy bear or a soft doll but a vivid green dragon with black wings and a huge tail with red scales along the sides. It has a lion's mouth, pointy teeth and claws, two glowing red eyes, and a third large green eye in the center of its forehead.

Can you imagine taking your child to bed and saying prayers with him or her, then tucking the little one in to sleep with a dragon? Children have grown to want these ugly, hybrid, mutant, supernaturals on their wallpaper, curtains, lunchboxes, and T-shirts.... Whatever happened to Christopher Robin and Winnie the Pooh?

But that's only a small part of what is captivating and capturing the minds and souls of our children today. The world of evil spirits is establishing a beachhead in the toy box.

On television (including cartoons), in movies, and in current children's fiction, occult references are mentioned in spells, magic, pantheism, polytheism, reincarnation, psychic powers, and supernatural forces. These are not like the bad witch and good fairy godmother within the pages of the Brothers Grimm or Hans Christian Anderson. As Bob and

> Gretchen Passantino wrote in their excellent book, *When the Devil Dares Your Kids*,[31] They differ qualitatively from the supernaturalism of classic fairy tales, where good and evil are distinguishable, morality is rewarded, and evil ultimately is vanquished by good. Instead, the typical supernaturalism of children's programming promotes relativism, a neutral force or power that can be used either for good or evil.[32] (Bold emphasis added)

In the same chapter, Dr. Jeremiah inserts an article by John Dvorak, a writer for the *San Francisco Examiner*. I found this to be an interesting way to gauge a country's moral compass and thought it worthy of inserting into the text:

> When trying to understand the mood of the country, its future and its direction, where do you turn?
>
> Many journalists follow the annals of Congress. Others have deep discussion with learned professors. You know where I go? I'll tell you. I go to Toys "R" Us. Here's where the coming generations are molded. Let me tell you, the future die is cast, and the image is a sick one.
>
> It is not that the toy business hasn't always been fraught with weird fads, tasteless imagery and warped symbols that have little value, but now it's worse than ever. One is simply overwhelmed by the

---

[31] David Jeremiah, with C. C. Carlson, *Invasion of Other Gods: The Seduction of New Age Spirituality* (Dallas: Word Publishing, 1995), 73-74.

[32] Bob and Gretchen Passantino, "When the Devil Dares Your Kids," in *Invasion of Other Gods*, ed. David Jeremiah, 74. Dallas: Word Publishing, 1995.

plethora of toys best described as gruesome, gory and irresponsible.[33]

Larry McCain, who authored a book called *Early Earth*, compares today's grotesque toys to the gods of the ancients.

> *These creatures that show up in archaeology and mythology are not just figments of the imagination. They were literal, physical demonic entities that appeared in civilizations of the past. These types of demagogues, or demonic beings, were represented as part human and part animal in their characteristics like this bird-human of the Assyrians*. They can be horse and human-like creatures, fish and human like the god Dagon of the Philistines, part Jaguar part human, but the tongue hanging out over the chin is the universal symbol of demonic possession. And one of the most popular combinations is human and serpent. You can find them on the toy shelves. It is not surprising that pagan religions worshipped serpents and dragons, for the Bible tells us that is exactly what Satan is. He is the Old Serpent and the Dragon.[34] (Emphasis added)

The creatures out of the pit are like the toys in the store I visited! Those people left on earth during the Tribulation will meet those monsters face to face. I have often wondered, as I studied the book of Revelation, how in the world people would see these creatures and not realize something was terribly wrong. Perhaps by the time the world gets to that point, *people on earth will be so desensitized to the gruesome images*

---

[33] Berit Kjos, "Your Child and the New Age," in *Invasion of Other Gods*, ed. David Jeremiah, 76. Dallas: Word Publishing, 1995.

[34] Ibid.

> *being foisted on them and their children that they won't even get their attention. If you play with the toy all your life then see the real thing, the crossover from imagination to reality is a very small step.* This is only conjecture, of course, but no less absurd than what we are seeing in the toy boxes of America. (Emphasis added)

> Larry McCain expressed it this way:[35]
>
> Our generation won't be shocked by *demonic invasion*. They are actually anticipating that extraterrestrial intelligent beings who look very different from us will someday contact the earth and help us with ecological, monetary and political problems.[36] (Emphasis added)

Dr. Jeremiah mentioned the creatures coming *"out of the pit."* You can find that scene in Revelation 9:1-10.

> And the fifth angel sounded, and I saw a star fall from heaven unto the earth: and to him was given the key of the bottomless pit. And he opened the bottomless pit; and there arose a smoke out of the pit, as the smoke of a great furnace; and the sun and the air were darkened by reason of the smoke of the pit. And there came out of the smoke locusts upon the earth: and unto them was given power, as the scorpions of the earth have power. And it was commanded them that they should not hurt the grass of the earth, neither any green thing, neither any tree; but only those men which have not the seal of God in their foreheads. And to them it was given that they

---

[35] David Jeremiah, with C. C. Carlson, *Invasion of Other Gods*, 77.

[36] Berit Kjos, "Your Child and the New Age," in *Invasion of Other Gods*, ed. David Jeremiah, 77-78. Dallas: Word Publishing, 1995.

> should not kill them, but that they should be tormented five months: and their torment was as the torment of a scorpion, when he striketh a man. And in those days shall men seek death, and shall not find it; and shall desire to die, and death shall flee from them. And the shapes of the locusts were like unto horses prepared unto battle; and on *their heads* were as it were *crowns like gold,* and their *faces were as the faces of men.* And they had *hair as the hair of women,* and their *teeth were as the teeth of lions.* And they had breastplates, as it were *breastplates of iron;* and the sound of their wings was as the sound of chariots of many horses running to battle. And they had *tails like unto scorpions,* and there were stings in their tails: and their power was to hurt men five months.[37] (Emphasis added)

The above lengthy segments from Dr. Jeremiah's book give insight into how our children are being preconditioned and desensitized to the appearance of aliens and Nephilim entering the world stage. The movie industry portrays these creatures as potential saviors of humankind instead of focusing on the real Savior, Jesus Christ. Now let's return to the Vatican's plans for greeting our long-lost space brothers.

> Read that again, then ask yourself: Did the Vatican's top astronomer actually mean to use the story of the Nephilim from the Bible as an example of the kind of "space saviors" man could soon look to for salvation? This incredible assertion is only topped by what he says next. In quoting John 10:16, which says, "And other sheep I have, which are not of this fold: them also I must bring, and they shall hear my voice;

[37] Revelation 9:1-10, KJV.

> and there shall be one fold, and one shepherd," Consolmango writes: "Perhaps it's not so far-fetched to see the Second Person of the Trinity, the Word, Who was present 'In the beginning' (John 1:1), coming to lay down His life and take it up again (John 10:18) not only as the Son of Man but also as a Child of other races?[38]

When I consider John 10:16, my understanding is that the "*other sheep*" are the Gentile nations, which were disinherited at the Tower of Babel. They are outside the commonwealth of Israel but are now able to be grafted into the "*True Vine*" (Jesus Christ) because of the New Covenant established by the blood of Jesus. Does Scripture support this interpretation?

> I say then, Have they stumbled that they should fall? God forbid: but rather through their fall *salvation is come unto the Gentiles*, for to provoke them to jealousy. ... And if some of the branches be broken off, and thou, being a wild olive *tree, wert graffed in* among them, and with them partakest of the root and fatness of the olive tree[39] (Emphasis added)

> ... remember that you were at that time separated from Christ, alienated from the *commonwealth of Israel and strangers to the covenants of promise, having no hope* and without God in the world.[40] (Emphasis added)

Dr. Horn and Putnam continue:

---

[38] Guy Consolmagno, "*Intelligent Life in the Universe*," in *Exo-Vaticana*, ed. Cris Putnam and Thomas Horn, 18. Crane, Montana: Defender Publishing, 2013.

[39] Romans 11:11, 17, KJV.

[40] Ephesians 2:12, KJV.

Do Vatican scholars actually believe Jesus might have been the Star-Child of an alien race? Do Consolmango and/or other Jesuits secretly hold that the virgin birth was in reality an abduction scenario in which Mary was impregnated by ET, giving birth to the hybrid Jesus?

All this would seem impossible theology if not for the fact that other high-ranking Vatican spokespersons—those who routinely study from the "Star Base" (as local Indians call it) on Mt Graham—have been saying the same in recent years. This includes Dr. Christopher Corbally, vice director for the Vatican Observatory Research Group on Mt. Graham until 2012, who believes our image of God will have to change if evidence of alien life is confirmed by scientists (including the need to evolve from the concept of an "anthropocentric" God into a "broader entity"), and the current Vatican Observatory director, Father Jose Funes, who has gone equally far, suggesting that alien life not only exists in the universe and is "our brother," but will, if discovered, confirm the "true" faith of Christianity and the dominion of Rome. When the *L'Osservatore Romano* newspaper (which only publishes what the Vatican approves) asked him what this meant, he replied:[41] "How can we rule out that life may have developed elsewhere? Just as we consider earthly creatures as 'a brother,' and 'sister', why should we not talk about an 'extraterrestrial brother,' It would still be part of creation,"[42] ... and

---

[41] Putnam and Horn, *Exo-Vaticana,* 19.

[42] "Vatican Astronomer Says it's OK to Think Aliens Exist," *USA Today*, May 14, 2008, http://www.usatoday.com/news/religion/2008-05-14-vatican-aliens_N.htm," in *Exo-Vaticana,* ed. Cris Putnam and Thomas Horn, 19. Crane, Montana: Defender Publishing, 2013.

> believing in the existence of such is not contradictory to *Catholic doctrine*.[43]

The Roman Catholic Church drowned or burned people at the stake for speaking such things. They were considered to be having communication or relationships with *familiar spirits*. Further in this chapter, research suggests these *extraterrestrial brethren* are the demons of old in disguise. Communication with such entities was considered demonic. Note the Old Testament Laws for the Hebrews would be to execute these individuals by stoning.

> Regard not them that have familiar spirits, neither seek after wizards, to be defiled by them: I [am] the LORD your God.[44]

> And the soul that turneth after such as have familiar spirits, and after wizards, to go a whoring after them, I will even set my face against that soul, and will cut him off from among his people.[45]

> A man also or woman that hath a familiar spirit, or that is a wizard, shall surely be put to death: they shall stone them with stones: their blood [shall be] upon them.[46]

---

[43] Father Jose' Gabriel Funes, S.J., "Believing in Aliens Not Opposed to Christianity, Vatican's Top Astronomer Says," Catholic News Agency, May 13, 2008, in *Exo-Vaticana*, ed. Cris Putnam and Thomas Horn, 19. Crane, Montana: Defender Publishing, 2013. http://www.catholicnewsagency.com/news/believing_in_aliens_not_opposed_to_christianity_vaticans_top_astronomer_says/.

[44] Leviticus 19:31, KJV.

[45] Leviticus 20:6, KJV.

[46] Leviticus 20:27, KJV.

> So Saul died for his transgression which he committed against the LORD, [even] against the word of the LORD, which he kept not, and also for asking [counsel] of [one that had] a familiar spirit, to enquire [of it];[47]

> And it came to pass, as we went to prayer, a certain damsel possessed with a spirit of divination met us, which brought her masters much gain by soothsaying:[48]

Is the Church of Rome exhibiting missionary adaptation by changing its dogma toward extraterrestrials and familiar spirits? Could the finger which points to the heretic be turning 180 degrees back on itself?

> From the '70s through the '90s, it was Monsignor Corrado Balducci—an exorcist, theologian, member of the Vatican Curia (governing body at Rome), and friend of the pope—who went perhaps furthest, appearing on Italian national television numerous times to state that ETs were not only possible, *but were already interacting with Earth and that the Vatican's leaders were aware of it.* ...at a forum concerning the enormous UFO flap in Mexico, he stated,[49] I always wish to be the spokesman for these star peoples who also are part of God's glory, and I will continue to bring it to the attention of the Holy Mother Church.[50]

---

[47] 1 Chronicles 10:13, KJV.

[48] Acts 16:16, KJV.

[49] Cris Putnam and Thomas Horn, *Exo-Vaticana,* 20.

[50] Paola Leopizzi Harris, "Monsignor Corrado Balducci Says Mexico Blessed with UFO Sightings," *MUFON [Mutual UFO Network] Journal,* March 28,

Whatever you make of his claims, Balducci was a member of a special group of consultants to the Vatican, a public spokesperson for Rome on the matter of extraterrestrial life as well as UFO and abduction phenomenon, and his assertions have never been contradicted by the Catholic church.

Perhaps most intriguing was Catholic theologian Father Malachi Martin who, before his death in 1999, hinted at something like imminent extraterrestrial contact more than once. While on Coast to Coast AM radio in 1997, Art Bell asked Malachi why the Vatican was heavily invested in the study of deep space at the Mt. Graham Observatory we visited. As a retired professor of the Pontifical Biblical Institute, Malachi was uniquely qualified to hold secret information pertaining to VATT. His answer ignited a firestorm of interest among Christian and secular ufologists when he replied,[51] Because the mentality ... amongst those who [are] at the ... highest levels of Vatican administration and geopolitics, know ... what's going on in space, and *what's approaching us,* could be of great import in the next five years, ten years (emphasis added)[52]

2006, http://www.mufon.com, in *Exo-Vaticana,* ed. Cris Putnam and Thomas Horn, 20. Crane, Montana: Defender Publishing, 2013.

[51] Cris Putnam and Thomas Horn, *Exo-Vaticana,* 21.

[52] "Comet and Father Malachi Martin" (ART BELL INTERVIEWS FATHER MALACHI MARTIN: Transcript of the April 5th, 1997 interview with late Father Malachi Martin by Art Bell), Godlike Productions, January 7, 2007, http://www.godlikeproductions.com/forum1/message326615/pg1. in *Exo-Vaticana,* ed. Cris Putnam and Thomas Horn, 21. Crane, Montana: Defender Publishing, 2013.

Consider the following verse from the Gospel of Luke and see if it parallels Malachi Martin's comment, *"what's approaching us."*

> Men's hearts failing them for fear, and for looking after those things which are coming on the earth: for the powers of heaven shall be shaken.[53]

> When we asked Father Guy Consolmango what he thought of Malachi's claims, he actually seemed miffed by the man, saying, "I have heard stories about the late Malachi Martin which make me rather suspicious of statements that come from him. I was at the observatory in the 1990s, and he never visited us nor had anything to do with us."[54] "This reaction seems consistent with how many other Catholic priests despised Malachi's willingness to disclose what Rome otherwise wanted buried, especially the satanic cabal within the Jesuit order Malachi wrote about in his best-selling books.[55]

We cannot accuse the Vatican of trying to hide where they stand on the "ET" agenda because it is public knowledge. But this doesn't mean the public should openly accept Rome's news, which it is forming into doctrine, which the Bible proves to be both non-biblical and deceptive. The Bible has already given advanced notice of this enemy's arrival. Why would a church that claims to be Christian even consider the *Theory* of Evolution?

---

[53] Luke 21:26, KJV.

[54] This quote came from a personal interview in an email correspondence between Thomas Horn and Guy Consolmagno on November 7, 2012, in *Exo-Vaticana:* ed. Cris Putnam and Thomas Horn, 21. Crane, Montana: Defender Publishing, 2013.

[55] Cris Putnam and Thomas Horn, *Exo-Vaticana,* 21.

Note the following excerpt from *Exo-Vaticana,* an article from *Newsweek* writer Sharon Begley:[56]

> Writing for *Newsweek* on May 15, 2008, article, "The Vatican And Little Green Men," journalists Sharon Begley noted that "[this] might be part of a push to demonstrate the Vatican's embrace of science … Interestingly, the Vatican has plans to host a conference in Rome next spring to mark the 150th anniversary of the Origin of Species, Charles Darwin's seminal work on the theory of evolution. Conference organizers say it will look beyond entrenched ideological positions—including misconstrued creationism. The Vatican says it wants to reconsider the problem of evolution "with a broader perspective" and says an "appropriate consideration in needed more than ever before."[57]
>
> The "appropriate consideration" Begley mentioned may have been something alluded to buy Guy Consolmagno three years earlier in an interview with the *Sunday Herald*. That article pointed out how Consolmagno's job included reconciling "the wildest reaches of science fiction with the flint-eyed dogma of the Holy-See" and that his latest mental meander was about "the Jesus Seed," described as "a brain-warp-intelligent, self-aware life may also have had a Christ walk across its methane seas, just as Jesus did

---

[56] (updated link: https://www.newsweek.com/vatican-and-little-green-men-221558).

[57] Sharon Begley, "The Vatican and Little Green Men," *Newsweek,* May 15, 2008, http://www.newsweek.com/blogs/lab-notes/2008/05/15/the-vatican-and-little-green-men.html, in *Exo-Vaticana,* ed. Cris Putnam and Thomas Horn, 22. Crane, Montana: Defender Publishing, 2013.

here on Earth in Galilee. The salvation of the Earthlings."[58]

This sounds like a sanctified version of panspermia—the idea that life on Earth was "seeded" by something a long time ago, such as an asteroid impact—but in this case, "the seed" was divinely appointed and reconciled to Christ.[59]

ET & SALVATION

No shortage of propaganda is coming out of the Vatican:

> May 2008 L'Osservatore Romano interview with Father Funes, an article titled "The Extraterrestrial Is My Brother." In the English translation of the Italian feature, Funes responds to the question of whether extraterrestrials would need to be redeemed, which he believes should not be assumed. "God was made man in Jesus to save us," he says. "If other intelligent beings exist, it is not said that they would have need of redemption. They could remain in full friendship with their Creator.[60]

---

[58] Neil Mackay, "And On the Eighth Day—Did God Create Aliens?" Sunday Herald—Scotland, November 28, 2005, http://www.sundayherald.com/53020 (site discontinued: see alternatively, from Signs of the Times: http://www.scott.net/articles/show/106410-And-on-the-eighth-day-did-God-create-aliens-).

[59] Cris Putnam and Thomas Horn, *Exo-Vaticana*, 22.

[60] Father Jose' Funes, "The Extraterrestrial Is My Brother," *L'Osservatore Romano*, May 14, 2008 (English translation of article viewable here: http://padrefunes.blogspot.com/.) in *Exo-Vaticana*, ed. Cris Putnam and Thomas Horn, 22-23. Crane, Montana: Defender Publishing, 2013.

> By "full friendship,' Funes reflected how some Vatican theologians accept the possibility that an extraterrestrial species may exist that is *morally superior to men*—closer to God than we fallen humans are—and that, as a consequence, they may come here to evangelize us. Father Guy Consolmagno took up this same line of thinking when he wrote in his book, Brother Astronomer: Adventures of a Vatican Scientist:[61] (Emphasis added)

> So the question of whether or not one should evangelize is really a moot point. Any alien we find will learn and change from contact with us, just as we will learn and change from contact with them. It's inevitable. And they'll be evangelizing us, too.[62]

Earth has already experienced "non-human" visitations. These beings (extraterrestrials) were both superior in power and intelligence when compared to humanity. However, as speculated above, they were not morally superior! And closer to God? The Holy Spirit puts His *seal* on true Christians. How much closer to God can you get when God's Spirit takes up residence inside of you?

> Now he which stablisheth us with you in Christ, and hath anointed us, is God; Who hath also *sealed* us,

---

[61] Cris Putnam and Thomas Horn, *Exo-Vaticana,*23.

[62] As quoted by the article: Brother Guy Consolmagno, "Would You Baptize an Extraterrestrial?: A Jesuit Priest Says the Discovery of Life Elsewhere in the Universe Would Pose No Problem for Religion," *Beliefnet,* last accessed December 4, 2012, http://www.beliefnet.com/News/Science-Religion/2000/08/Would-You-Baptize-An-Extraterrestrial.aspx?p=2. in *Exo-Vaticana,* ed. Cris Putnam and Thomas Horn, 23. Crane, Montana: Defender Publishing, 2013.

> and given the earnest of the Spirit in our hearts.[63] (Emphasis added)

> In whom ye also trusted, after that ye heard the word of truth, the Gospel of your salvation: in whom also after that ye believed, ye were *sealed* with that holy Spirit of promise, [64] (Emphasis added)

> And grieve not the holy Spirit of God, whereby ye are *sealed* unto the day of redemption.[65] (Emphasis added)

One-third of the angels in heaven rebelled against God, their Creator, and disobeyed His will. That is the foundation of the whole Genesis 6 incursion. They are guilty of sin by disobeying God. It blows the whole "morally superior" idea out of the water. The Apostle Paul warns us against accepting another gospel, whether from man or angel—which in this case can appear as an alien visitor and deceive many.

> But though we, or an *angel from heaven*, preach any other gospel unto you than that which we have preached unto you, let him be accursed.[66] (Emphasis added)

The Catholic church's priests move closer to the dark side when Father Giuseppe Tanzella-Nitti, an Opus Dei theologian of the Pontifical University of the Holy Cross in Rome, states that our space brothers would evangelize humanity.

---

[63] 2 Corinthians 1:21-22, KJV.

[64] "Which is the earnest of our inheritance until the redemption of the purchased possession, unto the praise of his glory." Ephesians 1:13-14, KJV.

[65] Ephesians 4:30, KJV.

[66] Galatians 1:8, KJV.

> Giuseppe states this would *not immediately oblige the Christian "to renounce his own faith in God*_simply on the basis of the reception of new, unexpected information of a religious character from extraterrestrial civilizations,"[67] but that *such a renunciation could come soon after as the new "religious content"* originating from outside the Earth is *confirmed as reasonable and credible.* "Once the trustworthiness of the information had been verified," the believer would have to "reconcile such new information with the truth that he or she already knows and believes on the basis of the revelation of the One Triune God, conducting a re-reading [of the Gospel] inclusive of the new data.[68]

The Catholic Church had requested and forced people to *"renounce their faith"* before during the *Roman Catholic Inquisitions,* where millions were tortured and killed for holding to their Christian faith. Could we be looking at another Inquisition? Will Christians who refuse to exchange their faith in God's Word for some extraterrestrial's gospel be persecuted or shunned by the world? It is foolish to insinuate that God did not foresee this projected alien visitation coming, *real or manufactured,* and that He is not sovereign.

The Bible gives forewarning in its prophecies of the coming deception. We are told not to accept any new gospel from man or angel (alien); I cannot stress this point enough. The fact that the Vatican is even considering any of this should raise red flags throughout the Christian world. Who is the heretic now? These

---

[67] Giuseppe Tanzella-Nitti, "EXTRATERRESTRIAL LIFE," Interdisciplinary Encyclopedia of Religion and Science, last accessed December 4, 2012, http://www.disf.org/en/Voci/65.asp, in *Exo-Vaticana,* ed. Cris Putnam and Thomas Horn, 23. Crane, Montana: Defender Publishing, 2013.

[68] Ibid.

Catholic theologians are speculating the rejection of apostolic teaching only to accept doctrine from demons.

We don't have to wait for the projected alien gospel's verification. God's Word verified it 2,000 years ago, and we are told not to accept the lie. The dimension of time does not restrain God. Therefore, He knows the future and has already orchestrated any future issues into His written Word in the form of prophetic warnings.

Former Vatican observatory Vice Director Christopher Corbally made this statement about the possibility of other inhabited worlds:

> While Christ is the First and Last Word (the Alpha and the Omega) spoken to humanity, he is not necessarily the only word spoke to the universe ... For, the Word spoken to us does not seem to exclude and equivalent "Word" spoken to aliens. They, too, could have had their "Logos-event." Whatever that event might have been, it does not have to be a repeated death-and-resurrection, if we allow God more imagination than some religious thinkers seem to have had. For God, as omnipotent, is not restricted to one form of language, the human.[69]

Corbally's above statement sounds very similar to how the serpent spoke to Eve, using semantics to twist the Scripture. All this speculation is propaganda and is following the devil's plan by planting seeds of doubt in the form of a retrovirus, only to be activated later.

---

[69] J. Antonio Huneeus, "The Vatican Extraterrestrial Question," *Open Minds Magazine*, June/July 2010, Issue 2, 59. in *Exo-Vaticana*, ed. Cris Putnam and Thomas Horn, 24. Crane, Montana: Defender Publishing, 2013.

THE DAYS OF NOAH

Do extraterrestrials come from the far reaches of space? As with any information that is received, it is helpful to determine its origin and truthfulness. Historical evidence supports an alternative view. UFOs and aliens are said to be extraterrestrial. The alternate view is they are interdimensional. They are from the spiritual realm. The fallen angelic host that rebelled with Satan against God is part of the end-time deception. Before continuing the evaluation of Roman Catholic church doctrine that spans centuries, from the *Church Age* to the *Space Age*, we must detour again. Are there any historical records that will shed light on the real character of UFOs?

The probability that "extraterrestrials" are from the spirit realm rather than some distant galaxy is high. Fallen angels and demons change their technological appearance to meet the current human paradigm, but they are the same false gods that have been visiting Earth for thousands of years. Their interference with human history is not new. Recall that there are divine beings who rebelled against God. And some of this fallen heavenly host further disobeyed by intermixing with humankind. A more in-depth look into the Genesis 6 incursion is our starting point for the benefit of the readers who are not familiar with the biblical text.

> And it came to pass, when men began to multiply on the face of the earth, and daughters were born unto them, that the *sons of God* saw the *daughters of men* that they were fair; and they took them wives of all which they chose. And the LORD said, My spirit shall not always strive with man, for that he also is flesh: yet his days shall be an hundred and twenty years. There were *giants* in the earth in those days; and *also after* that, when the *sons of God came in unto* the *daughters of men*, and they *bare children to them*, the

> same became *mighty men* which were of old, men of renown.[70]

Let's identify the players involved in the four verses listed above. We have the *"daughters of men,"* or *daughters of Adam* in some translations. Human women. There are the divine beings again that were covered earlier, *"sons of God."* And a new group of players, the offspring from the merging of spiritual beings with humans, resulting in *"giants"* the *"mighty men"* of old—Greek mythology called them titans. The Hebrew word is (nephiyl, נְפִל H5307), which is the origin of the word *Nephilim.* The Old Testament contains several passages about the Israelites doing battle with these Nephilim (giants). The Nephilim were smaller than the Titans but mighty in size when compared to a man.

---

[70] Genesis 6:1-4, KJV.

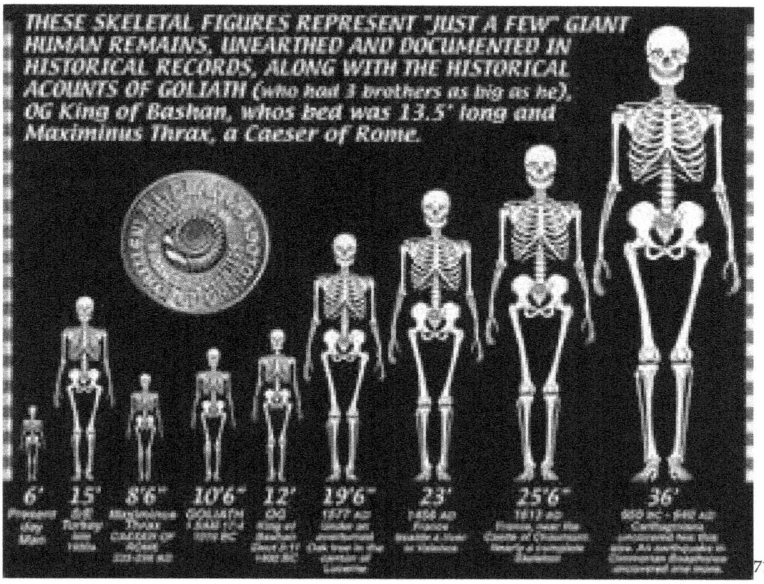
THESE SKELETAL FIGURES REPRESENT "JUST A FEW" GIANT HUMAN REMAINS, UNEARTHED AND DOCUMENTED IN HISTORICAL RECORDS, ALONG WITH THE HISTORICAL ACOUNTS OF GOLIATH (who had 3 brothers as big as he), OG King of Bashan, whos bed was 13.5' long and Maximinus Thrax, a Caeser of Rome.
6'
15'
8'6"
10'6"
12'
19'6"
23'
25'6"
36'
[71]

Nephilim populated the land of Canaan, which was promised to the Israelites by God through Abraham. Egypt enslaved the Israelites for 400 years; during that time, the Nephilim population increased. God claimed the Canaan territory as His inheritance after the incident at the Tower of Babel. (*Goliath,* who young David slew, was a Nephilim.)

> And there we saw the giants, the sons of Anak, *which come* of the giants: and we were in our own sight as grasshoppers, and so we were in their sight.[72]

---

[71] "History Corner Where are all those Giant Nephilim Bones that Were Sent to the Smithsonian?" Coeur d'Alene Post Falls, 08/19/2018, https://cdapress.com/syd_albright/20180819/history_corner_where_are_all_those_giant_Nephilim_bones_that_were_sent_to_the_smithsonian.

[72] Numbers 13:33, KJV.

> Yet destroyed I the Amorite before them, whose height *was* like the height of the cedars, and he *was* strong as the oaks; yet I destroyed his fruit from above, and his roots from beneath.[73] (Bold emphasis added)

Plenty of other verses mention these offspring, but that is not the point of interest with the alien and fallen angel connection. As in chapter eight of this book under the subheading *"Other Gods,"* we find the "sons of God." "Sons of God" in ancient Hebrew is "ben 'elohiym" as listed in Strong's Concordance.[74] These creatures are the divine beings that are part of the heavenly host. Here we are told that these beings have entered our dimension (earthly realm) and taken human women and created offspring. The Bible identifies these offspring as "giants" and "mighty men." Recalling Dr. Heiser's definition of "sons of God":

> In the ancient Semitic world, *sons of God* (Hebrew: *beney elohim*) is a phrase used to identify divine beings with higher-level responsibilities or jurisdictions. The term *angel* (Hebrew: *mal'ak*) describes an important still lesser task: delivering messages.[75]

It is essential to understand who these divine beings are and who their hybrid (demigods) offspring are. Here are the results of having these Nephilim offspring inhabiting the Earth:

---

[73] Amos 2:9, KJV.

[74] Under, H1121 and H430. James Strong, LL.D., S.T.D., *Strong's Exhaustive Concordance of the Bible: Hebrew and Chaldee Dictionary* (Nashville, Tennessee: Thomas Nelson Publishers, 1990), 21, 12.

[75] Dr. Michael S. Heiser, *The Unseen Realm* (Bellingham, Washington: Lexham Press, 2015), 24.

> And GOD saw that the wickedness of man was great in the earth, and that every imagination of the thoughts of his heart was only evil continually.[76]

According to the interviews found in Horn and Putnam's book *Exo-Vaticana,* the public media and the Vatican's speculations of an extraterrestrial contact is expected to be a benevolent one—some cosmic family reunion. This premise is where people who are not informed about man's previous encounters with non-human intelligent beings need to stop. Stop and ask yourself whether recorded history supports a different view.

Ancient records and modern scientific research offer the belief that any impending extraterrestrial visitations are deceptive and not benevolent. A humorous example that makes the point is the big difference between the movies *ET* and *Alien*. We have reviewed the Church of Rome's stand on an alien encounter. Now we will walk through recorded history in search of non-human and supernatural visitations. The Days of Noah refer to a particular period. Noah lived 600 years before the great flood and 350 years afterward. In the Gospel of Matthew, Jesus answers the question of what signs to look for before His return.

> But as the days of Noe were, so shall also the coming of the Son of man be. For as in the days that were before the flood they were eating and drinking, marrying and giving in marriage, until the day that Noe entered into the ark, and knew not until the flood came, and took them all away; so shall also the coming of the Son of man be."[77]

The interpretation is simple if you read it literally. Humanity will be so busy with itself—its desires, its will, and its needs—

---

[76] Genesis 6:5, KJV.

[77] Matthew 24:37-39, KJV.

that people will be ignorant of the prophetic signs. If we were asking for scriptural support for literal interpretation, we could look to the following verses:

> Watch therefore: for ye know not what hour your Lord doth come. But know this, that if the goodman of the house had known in what watch the thief would come, he would have watched, and would not have suffered his house to be broken up.[78]

> For yourselves know perfectly that the day of the Lord so cometh as a thief in the night. For when they shall say, Peace and safety; then sudden destruction cometh upon them, as travail upon a woman with child; and they shall not escape. But ye, brethren, are not in darkness, that that day should overtake you as a thief.[79]

> Behold, I come as a thief. Blessed is he that watcheth, and keepeth his garments, lest he walk naked, and they see his shame.[80]

ANCIENT RECORDS

The Book of Genesis records that before the flood of Noah, humankind had become very wicked, and all its thoughts and imaginations focused on doing evil. The ancient text tells of wickedness, of hybrid beings, of idolatry, and the mixing of genetic material (the species). Jewish Historian Flavius Josephus records in his works the Genesis 6 incursion:

---

[78] Mathew 24:42-43, KJV.

[79] 1 Thessalonians 5:2-4, KJV.

[80] Revelation 16:15, KJV.

> … For many angels of God companied with women, and begat sons that proved unjust, and despisers of all that was good, on account of the confidence they had in their own strength; for the tradition is, that these men did what resembled the acts of those whom the Grecians call giants. But Noah was very uneasy at what they did; and being displeased at their conduct, persuaded them to change their dispositions and their acts for the better: but seeing they did not yield to him, but were slaves to their wicked pleasures, he was afraid they would kill him, together with his wife and children, and those they had married; so he departed out of that land.[81]

Centuries later, Daniel 2:43 gives this intriguing verse. This may simply be breeding people of a weak nation (clay) with people of a strong nation (iron). Option two may be the mixing of man's genetics with something non-human, as they did in Genesis 6.

> And whereas thou sawest iron mixed with miry clay, *they* shall mingle themselves with the seed of men: but they shall not cleave one to another, even as iron is not mixed with clay.[82] (Emphasis added)

Today we would consider the antediluvian world's genetic violations part of ancient history. However, the Book of Daniel predicts these sins to repeat in the future. You and I are living in those future times.

We are seeing a repeat of these forbidden acts today. Related to the topic of transhumanism, these creatures are known as

---

[81] William Whiston, *The Complete Works of Flavius Josephus; The Antiquities of the Jews* (Green Forest: Arkansas, 2010), 3.

[82] Daniel 2:43, KJV.

chimeras. These acts are part of what caused God to bring the great flood. As we read above in Father Consolmagno's interviews, he even considered the Nephilim (hybrid offspring) as a possible cosmic messiah to humanity. The fallen angels and Nephilim have walked among humans throughout history. This fact allows us to investigate the results of their involvement with understanding. Let's take a closer look at the characteristics of the Nephilim and the disobedient watcher-class angels.

EXTRA-BIBLICAL TEXT

Why was God's judgment on the world so harsh that He would bring the flood to cleanse the Earth? A portion of the angelic host crossed the dimensional boundaries established by God the Creator. To gain a better understanding of these events, we'll look at books of historical relevance that are outside the Bible. These books are considered extra-biblical text, not part of the Bible but contextually significant. The Bible supersedes these books when there is a conflict.

Why should we consider these books at all? During the early church period before the writing of the Gospels and Epistles of the apostles were compiled into the biblical canon, the apostles had the Old Testament in Greek known as the Septuagint, and these other books—specifically, the book of Enoch 1, the book of Jasher, and the book of Jubilees. The Apostles Jude, James, Paul, and Peter referenced these texts in their writings. It would be beneficial to review these texts that were part of the apostle's *worldview.*

> The First Book of Enoch was discovered in the 18th century. It was assumed to have been penned after beginning of the Christian era. This theory was based upon the fact that it had quotes and paraphrases as well as concepts found in the New Testament. Thus,

> it was assumed that it was heavily influenced by writers such as Jude and Peter.
>
> However, recent discoveries of copies of the book among the Dead Sea Scrolls found at Qumran prove the book was in existence long before the time of Jesus Christ. These scrolls force a closer look and reconsideration. It becomes obvious that the New Testament did not influence the Book of Enoch; on the contrary, the Book of Enoch influenced the New Testament.[83]

In the Book of Jude, we can see where Jude copies directly from the Book of Enoch.

Jude 1:14-15, KJV (biblical text)

> ... Behold, the Lord cometh with ten thousands of his saints, To execute judgment upon all, and to convince all that are ungodly among them of all their ungodly deeds which they have ungodly committed, and of all their hard speeches which ungodly sinners have spoken against him.

Enoch 1:9 (referenced text)

> And behold! He comes with ten thousand of His holy ones (saints) to execute judgment on all, and to destroy all the ungodly (wicked); and to convict all flesh of all the works of their ungodliness which they

[83] Joseph B. Lumpkin, *The Books of Enoch: The Complete Volume Containing: 1 Enoch; 2 Enoch; 3 Enoch* (Blountsville, Alabama: Fifth Estate Publishers, 2009), 11.

> have ungodly committed, and of all the hard things which ungodly sinners have spoken against Him.[84]

Jude 1:5-6, KJV (biblical text)

> I will therefore put you in remembrance, though ye once knew this, how that the Lord, having saved the people out of the land of Egypt, afterward destroyed them that believed not. And the angels which kept not their first estate, but left their own habitation, he hath reserved in everlasting chains under darkness unto the judgment of the great day.

Enoch 6:6 (referenced text)

> And they were in all two hundred who descended in the days of Jared in the summit of Mount Hermon, and they called it Mount Hermon, because they had sworn and bound themselves by mutual curses on the act.[85]

The Apostle Peter also made use of the books available to him in the first century.

2 Peter 2:4, KJV (biblical text)

> For if God spared not the angels that sinned, but cast them down to hell, and delivered them into chains of darkness, to be reserved unto judgment;

---

[84] Ibid., 22.

[85] Ibid., 27.

Enoch 88:1 (referenced text)

> And I saw one of those four who had come out first, and he seized that first star which had fallen from heaven, and bound it hand and foot and cast it into an abyss; now that abyss was narrow and deep, and horrible and dark.[86]

Apostle Paul's letter to Timothy, 2 Timothy 3:8, KJV

> Now as Jannes and Jambres withstood Moses, so do these also resist the truth: men of corrupt minds, reprobate concerning the faith.

If you search the Book of Genesis, you will not find a mention of Jannes and Jambres, so where did the Apostle Paul find their names?

Jasher 79:27 (referenced text)

> And when they had gone Pharaoh sent for Balaam the magician and to *Jannes* and *Jambres* his sons, and to all the magicians and conjurors and counsellors which belonged to the king, and they all came and sat before the king.[87] (Emphasis added)

In the Old Testament, we find mention of the Book of Jasher.

Joshua 10:13, KJV

> And the sun stood still, and the moon stayed, until the people had avenged themselves upon their

---

[86] Ibid., 157.

[87] *Book of Jasher* (Springfield, Utah: Cedar Fort Inc., 2010), 222.

> enemies. Is not this written in the book of *Jasher*? So the sun stood still in the midst of heaven, and hasted not to go down about a whole day.

2 Samuel 1:18, KJV

> Also he bade them teach the children of Judah the use of the bow: behold, it is written in the book of *Jasher*.

The above excerpts help provide historical value to these extra-biblical books.

The Bible lists fourteen other books, which the academic world considers to be lost:

1. *The Book of Wars of the Lord* – Numbers 21:14.
2. *The Annals of Jehu* – 2 Chronicles 20:34.
3. *The Treatise of the Book of the Kings* – 2 Chronicles 24:27
4. *The Book of Records, Book of the Chronicles of Ahasuerus* – Esther 2:23, 6:1.
5. *The Acts of Solomon* – 1 Kings 11:41.
6. *The Sayings of Hozai* – 2 Chronicles 33:19.
7. *The Chronicles of David* – 1 Chronicles 27:24.
8. *The Chronicles of Samuel, Nathan, Gad* – 1 Chronicles 29:29.
9. *Samuel's book* – 1 Samuel 10:25
10. *The Records of Nathan the Prophet* – 2 Chronicles 9:29.
11. *The Prophecy of Ahijah the Shilonite* – 2 Chronicles 9:29.
12. *The Treatise of the Prophet Iddo* – 2 Chronicles 13:22.

The Book of Enoch 1 gives the 200 watcher-class angel leaders (chiefs) names. These are the angels who came down on Mt. Hermon in the days of Jared. They taught humanity forbidden knowledge. This teaching may be why their punishment was so severe.

> And they were in all two hundred who descended in the days of Jared in the summit of Mount Hermon, and they called in Mount Hermon, because they had sworn and bound themselves by mutual curses on the act. And these are the names of their leaders: Samlaza, their leader, Araklba, Rameel, Kokablel, Tamlel, Ramlel, Danel, Ezeqeel, Baraqijal, Asael, Armaros, Batarel, Ananel, Zaqiel, Samsapeel, Satarel, Turel, Jomjael, These are their chiefs of tens.
> (Enoch 6:6-8)[88]

Now you have the watcher chief's names. What the watchers taught humanity is listed below. Their teaching increased humanity's wickedness and sinful nature. It was not God's plan for humanity to have this knowledge.

MT. HERMON TEACHERS

> And the angels taught them charms and spells, and the cutting of roots, and made them acquainted with plants. (Enoch 7:2)[89]

> And Azazel taught men to make swords, and knives, and shields, and breastplates, and taught them about metals of the earth and the art of working them, and

[88] Joseph B. Lumpkin, *The Books of Enoch*, 27.

[89] Ibid., 28.

> bracelets, and ornaments, and the use of antimony, and the beautifying of the eyelids, and all kinds of precious stones, and all coloring and dyes.
> (Enoch 8:1)[90]

> And there was great impiety, they turned away from God, and committed fornication, and they were led astray, and became corrupt in all their ways.
> (Enoch 8:2)[91]

> Semjaza taught the casting of spells, and root-cuttings, Armaros taught counter-spells (release from spells), Baraqijal taught astrology, Kokabel taught the constellations (portents), Ezeqeel the knowledge of the clouds, Araqiel the signs of the earth, Shamsiel the signs of the sun, and Sariel the course of the moon. And as men perished, they cried, and their cry went up to heaven. (Enoch 8:3)[92]

The wickedness on the Earth at that time was so full of bloodshed. God cast judgment on both the watchers who committed fornication with human women and their offspring. We know from the Epistles of Peter and Jude that God imprisoned these watchers in *Tartarus*.

> Tartarus, the infernal regions of ancient Greek mythology. The name was originally used for the deepest region of the world, the lower of the two parts of the underworld, where the gods locked up their

---

[90] Ibid., 29.

[91] Lumpkin, *The Books of Enoch*, 28.

[92] Ibid., 29-30.

enemies. It gradually came to mean the entire underworld ... [93]

Book of Jasher

But in the latter days of Methuselah, the sons of men turned from the Lord, they corrupted the earth, they robbed and plundered each other, and they rebelled against God and they transgressed, and they corrupted their ways, and would not hearken to the voice of Methuselah, but rebelled against him.[94] (Jasher 4:4)

And their judges and rulers went to the daughters of men and took their wives by force from their husbands according to their choice, and the sons of men in those days took from the cattle of the earth, the beasts of the field and the fowls of the air, and taught the mixture of animals of one species with the other, in order therewith to provoke the Lord; and God saw the whole earth and it was corrupt, for all flesh had corrupted its ways upon earth, all men and all animals.[95] (Jasher 4:18)

Book of Jubilees

For owing to these three things came the flood upon the earth, namely, owing to the fornication wherein

---

93 "Tartarus," Encyclopedia Britannica, 02/01/2019, https://www.britannica.com/topic/Tartarus.

94 The Book of Jasher (Springfield, Utah: CFI, 2010; originally published by J. H. Parry and Company, 1887), 8.

95 Ibid., 9.

> the Watchers against the law of their ordinances went a whoring after the daughters of men, and took themselves wives of all which they chose: and they made the beginning of uncleanness. (Jubilees 7:21)
>
> And they begat sons the Naphidim, and they were all unlike, and they devoured one another: and the Giants slew the Naphil, and the Naphil slew the Eljo, and the Eljo mankind, and one man another. (Jubilees 7:22)
>
> And every one sold himself to work iniquity and to shed much blood, and the earth was filled with iniquity. (Jubilees 7:23)
>
> And after this they sinned against the beasts and birds, and all that moveth and walketh on the earth: and much blood was shed on the earth, and every imagination and desire of men imagined vanity and evil continually. (Jubilees 7:24)
>
> And the Lord destroyed everything from off the face of the earth; because of the wickedness of their deeds, and because of the blood which they had shed in the midst of the earth He destroyed everything.[96] (Jubilees 7:25)

The extra-biblical text provides greater detail of the wickedness that came from the rebellious watchers and their offspring, and this may explain why Dr. Horn was surprised when Father Consolmagno suggested that the Nephilim could be a sort of savior. Once you understand the wickedness of the antediluvian

---

[96] The Book of Jubilees, Translated by R. H. Charles (Mineola, New York: Dover Publications, 2010), 68-69.

world, the possible repeat of such acts should send chills down your back.

In this chapter, there is a great deal of discussion about supernatural beings and the invisible realm (spiritual realm), which included non-human entities—angles, demons, extraterrestrials, etc. It is natural for people to add mystical attributes to what they don't fully understand. To attempt removing the mystical aura, let's look at the word *invisible* and *supernatural*. The simple meaning of *invisible* is "not visible; not perceptible by the (human) eye": [97]

The human eye works as follows:

> In a normal eye, the light rays come to a sharp focusing point on the retina. The retina functions much like the film in a camera. ... The retina receives the image that the cornea focuses through the eye's internal lens and transforms this image into electrical impulses that are carried by the optic nerve to the brain.[98]

> The human eye can detect the visible spectrum of the *electromagnetic spectrum*—a range of wavelengths between 390 to 700 nanometers. This is why scientists have always assumed that infrared light, a type of electromagnetic radiation with longer wavelengths

---

[97] "Invisible," Dictionary.com, 2/24/2019, https://www.dictionary.com/browse/invisible.

[98] "How Does The Human Eye Work?" National Keratoconus Foundation, 02/24/2019, https://www.nkcf.org/about-keratoconus/how-the-human-eye-works/.

than visible light, has been "invisible" to the human eye.[99] (Emphasis added)

So, the human eye is like a radio receiver, and it can receive electromagnetic waves that are within the frequency range of light waves the normal eye can see.

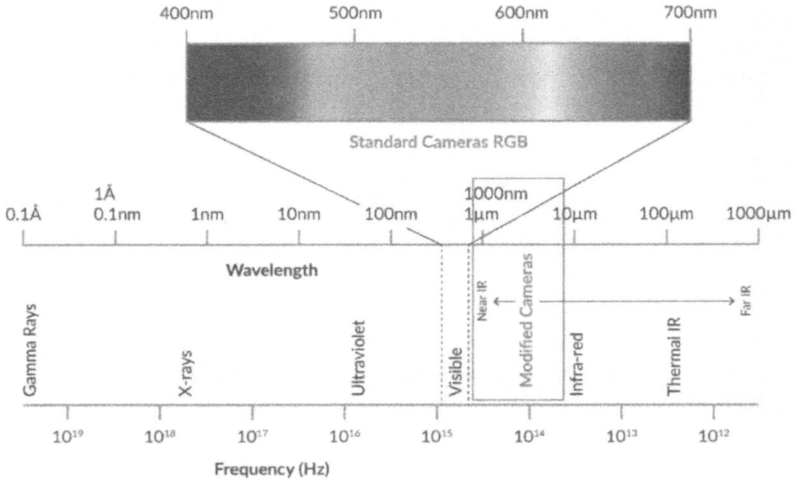

But our eyes have limitations just as any radio receiver has a beginning and end to its range of reception. Some animal species can see the ultra-violet frequency range, which is above the high end of the visible light spectrum. And other animals can see the infrared frequency range, which is below the low end of the visible light spectrum. Why the science class?

Usually, humans cannot see into the spiritual realm. This is not mystical—it's outside the functional range of the human eye (electromagnetic receiver). So when something is considered invisible, it is outside our frequency range. The Bible provides a

[99] Lecia Bushak, "The Human Eye Can See Infrared Light, Plus 5 Other Things You Had No Idea Eyes Can Do," Medical Daily, 02/24/2019, https://www.medicaldaily.com/human-eye-can-see-infrared-light-plus-5-other-things-you-had-no-idea-eyes-can-do-312946.

few accounts where both men and animals can see into the spiritual (unseen) realm. The first account we will look at is Balaam's donkey. Balaam was a prophet traveling to the Moabite king, and the Lord wanted him to stop. Balaam couldn't see the angel that was sent to stop him until the angel made himself visible, but his donkey saw the angel immediately.

> And the ass saw the angel of the LORD standing in the way, and his sword drawn in his hand: and the ass turned aside out of the way, and went into the field: and Balaam smote the ass, to turn her into the way.[100]

The next verse is about Elisha, the Lord's prophet. The king of Syria was at war with Israel. Each time the king of Syria planned an ambush for the Israelites, the Israelites were given advanced notice by Elisha. The Syrian king suspected he had a traitor in his camp, but his servants said no, it is the man Elisha the prophet. So, the king has him tracked down to the town of Dothan. The next morning the town is surrounded by Syrian troops, Elisha's servant goes out in the morning to perform his duties and freaks out.

> And when the servant of the man of God was risen early, and gone forth, behold, an host compassed the city both with horses and chariots. And his servant said unto him, Alas, my master! how shall we do? And he answered, Fear not: for they that be with us are more than they that be with them. And Elisha prayed, and said, LORD, I pray thee, open his eyes, that he may see. And the LORD opened the eyes of the young man; and he saw: and, behold, the

[100] Numbers 22:23, KJV.

> mountain was full of horses and chariots of fire round about Elisha.[101]

The science lesson on light waves and the biblical accounts of being able to see into the spiritual realm is to make a point. Much of the UFO sightings, demons, and fallen angels (extraterrestrials) are in the form of energy or light. These UFOs can materialize and disappear quickly; the term is *transmogrification.* They can change their physical state from a solid mass to energy, thereby entering and leaving our realm (our dimension). The human eye cannot fully see in those frequency ranges. The Mt. Graham Observatory has spent considerable money to have both the SMT Telescope (radio-below visible light) and the LBT Telescope (infrared-below visible light). What are they seeing? The second term in which we add mystical attributes is the word *super*natural.

> Words formed with super- have the following general senses: "to place or be placed above or over" (superimpose; supersede), "a thing placed over or added to another" (superscript; superstructure; supertax), "situated over" (superficial; superlunary) and, more figuratively, "an individual, thing, or property that ...[102]

This definition means something is above what is natural. This attribute could be in intelligence and strength. We know from reviewing the accounts of the watchers that came down on Mt. Hermon in the days before the great flood that they were both superior in intelligence and strength. In the book of Kings, one angel is sent to slay Sennacherib's Assyrian army (185,000

---

[101] 2 Kings 6:15-17, KJV.

[102] "Super," Dictionary.com, 02/24/2019, https://www.dictionary.com/browse/super.

soldiers) and prevent the destruction of King Hezekiah and Jerusalem.

> And it came to pass that night, that the angel of the LORD went out, and smote in the camp of the Assyrians an hundred fourscore and five thousand: and when they arose early in the morning, behold, they were all dead corpses.[103]

What is the importance of all this? Angels, with all their superior intelligence and strength, and the Nephilim, with their superhuman abilities, are still creatures. They are created beings and not God the Creator. Therefore, they are nothing in comparison to the power and sovereignty of Jesus Christ, who holds the universe together.

> For by him were all things created, that are *in heaven*, and that are in *earth, visible and invisible*, whether they be *thrones*, or *dominions*, or *principalities*, or *powers*: all things were created by him, and for him: And he is before all things, and by him *all things consist*.[104] (Emphasis added)

The coming cosmic deception may include the arrival of a real or manufactured extraterrestrial. Regardless of the aliens' abilities, it is foolishness to put your faith in what is biblically predicted to be *deception*. In the next chapter, Part 2 of Doctrines of Demons, we will look at the UFO phenomenon from a non-biblical approach by using the scientific viewpoint and analysis. We will find that scientific research draws a similar conclusion that UFOs have deceit and evil intentions.

---

[103] 2 Kings 19:35, KJV.

[104] Colossians 1:16-17, KJV.

10

Doctrines of Demons Part 2

Chapter nine laid the foundation with the Vatican's proposal to have open arms toward extraterrestrial visitors. Whether this visitation is real or fabricated, the assumption is such visitation would be benevolent. This chapter will focus on connecting UFOs to the spiritual realm.

Individuals of high rank within the Catholic Church have made comments that leave vague impressions that the Vatican is more concerned about who will baptize who and how the gospel of Jesus Christ may have to be altered to fit the impending alien revelation. The Church of Rome has not forgotten the teaching of Ignatius Loyola always to be the mediator of power when an opportunity arises, in this case, between humankind and extraterrestrials. Recall Ignatius Loyola's instructions:

> Nor will it contribute a little to our advantage, if, with caution and secrecy, we foment and heighten the animosities that arise among princes and great men, even to such a degree that they may weaken each other. But if there appear any likelihood of

> reconciliation, then as soon as possible let us endeavor to be the mediators, lest others prevent us."[1]

Willingness to alter the gospel should raise the red flag of warning. Any changes to God's Word is in defiance to His command (not a suggestion).

> Ye shall not add unto the word which I command you, neither shall ye diminish ought from it, that ye may keep the commandments of the LORD your God which I command you.[2]

The Genesis 6 event and afterward prove that humanity has experienced visitations by "extraterrestrials" before. The difference now is today's extraterrestrials were called gods, angels, and demons in the days of antiquity. The proposed responses of Rome ignore the warnings given by Jesus Christ and His Apostles, forewarnings that are close to 2,000 years old.

Ancient history, as recorded in Genesis 6 and the extra-biblical text, indicates that extraterrestrial beings (non-human) will have abilities above that of the natural man. The antichrist and false prophet will have advanced capabilities to perform the signs and wonders prophesied in the Bible. However, as previously noted, these superior abilities in power and intellect are not a guarantee of their moral superiority. Consider what Jesus said:

> For there shall arise false Christs, and false prophets, and shall shew *great signs* and *wonders;* insomuch that, if it were possible, they shall *deceive* the very elect. *Behold, I have told you before.*[3] (Emphasis added)

---

[1] Brownlee, *Secret Instructions of the Jesuits,* 141.

[2] Deuteronomy 4:2, KJV.

[3] Matthew 24-24-25, KJV.

In the following pages, I intend to consider the existence of the connection between UFOs and the demons of old. Documented reports from witnesses, along with the analysis from men of science, will be used to look at the UFO question as rationally as possible. If today's UFOs are the same entities that have visited Earth for thousands of years, then history should offer insight to their real agenda. It isn't tourism. Could it be a continuation of sowing the seeds of deceit and change that are in opposition to God's biblical narrative for humanity's redemption? To look at the UFO phenomenon rationally, it would seem natural first to ask what our scientists have to say about it. While early on, the consensus was leaning toward denial and rationalization. As more information became available, the views changed. Dr. Thomas makes a note of how the scientific community struggled with making sense of the UFO problem. There is a certain stigma attached to a person who says they believe in UFOs. From Dr. Thomas' book, *The Omega Conspiracy*, we have the following evaluation:

> While multitudes are convinced that we are being visited by cosmic travelers, millions of others view UFOs as nothing more than a hoax. To them, the evidence offered by people around the world is too incredible to believe. Even on the official level, doubt prevails. Despite skepticism, the UFO controversy has proven one thing—neither the state nor the science can explain the phenomenon.[4]

Scientists try to rationalize the phenomenon by saying witnesses see optical illusions, plasma discharges, reflection from the sun, swamp gas, etc. However, as the evidence continues to come in, there is a change of mind developing within the scientific community:

---

[4] Thomas, *Omega Conspiracy*, 27.

> Others have experienced a similar change of mind. When the prestigious American Astronomical Society conducted a survey of its members, an impressive 53 percent said that UFOs "certainly" or "probably" should be investigated further. When a simple poll of U.S. Citizens was taken in the 50s, only 3.4 percent believed in UFOs and that they were manned by extraterrestrial beings. By 1978 that percentage had risen to 57 percent.
>
> What happened was undoubtedly this: millions began with outright disbelief, then as the data increased and more evidence became available, the disbelief dissolved into doubt. Later, as the data kept increasing, and the evidence simply would not go away, the doubt turned to wonder. That seems to be the stage that multitudes have reached today; unable on one hand to fully explain the evidence, and unable on the other hand to explain it away, they are left suspended in a state of wonderment.[5]

Author Jacques Vallee is a French-born astronomer and mathematician. Vallee received his education in France and the United States as follows: BSc Mathematics (University of Paris); M.S. Astrophysics (University of Lille Nord de France); Ph.D. Computer Science (Northwestern University, USA). Dr. Vallee migrated to the United States in the 1960s and worked with Dr. J. Allen Hynek, who headed the U.S. Air Force's *Project Blue Book Report No. 14*.

---

[5] Ibid., 29.

Dr. J. Allen Hynek (left) and Jacques Vallee (right).

Jacques Vallee authored several books—*The Invisible College, Messengers of Deception,* and *Passport to Magonia*—which delve into the UFO phenomenon. They offer analysis to move the origin of these mysterious objects from extraterrestrial to a higher dimension that encompasses our own, just as its 3-D surroundings contain a 2-D picture—a dimension Christians refer to as the spiritual realm. Is there a link between the behavior of creatures from folklore, demons, and UFOs? You can find stories of folklore and demons throughout history. Today's media portray UFOs as a recent phenomenon and didn't make the front page until the Roswell crash.

The year was 1947, and the location, Roswell, New Mexico. The original news report speculated that an alien ship crashed. The United States Government recanted the statement and made a weak attempt to cover it up with a story about a weather balloon crash. From that point forward, for decades, there have been millions of reported UFO sightings and contacts. Some were nothing more than hoaxes, but others were legitimate reports made by honest, respectable Americans who tried to explain what they had seen and experienced.

The variety of occupations and backgrounds vary within every stratum of the American population, by men and women who held respectable positions in our communities—Air traffic controllers, aeronautical engineers, weather bureau observers, astronomers, FBI agents, and police officials were at all different levels; state, county, and city commercial airplane pilots from American, United, Eastern, Pan American, etc. There were vast numbers of military personnel, men and women from all the branches of our armed forces—guided-missile trackers, radar operators, and troops in the field. The number of UFO witnesses is large. Combining the variety of cultural backgrounds and human imagination brings Vallee to write the following in his preface to *Passport to Magonia:*

> Thus the only angle from which the total phenomenon could have been viewed in its true perspective has been neglected: the investigators have never recognized the fact that *beliefs identical to those held today have recurred throughout recorded history and under forms best adapted to the believer's country, race, and social regime.*[6] (Emphasis added)

Vallee goes on to say that there is a central theme. Aerial beings are visiting humanity, but what is the real origin of these visitors? Do they come from places of legend? Regardless, it is a place that man seems to be unable to reach.

> Emissaries from these supernatural abodes come to earth, sometimes under human form and sometimes

[6] Jacques Vallee, *Passport to Magonia* (Brisbane, Australia: Daily Grail Publishing, 2014), 11.

> as monsters. They perform wonders. They serve man or fight him. They influence civilizations through mystical revelation. They seduce earth women, and the few heroes who dare seek their friendship find the girls from Elfland endowed with desires that betray a carnal, rather than purely aerial, nature.[7]

> It aims only at the documentation of a recurrent myth; namely the myth of contact between mankind and an intelligent race endowed with apparently supernatural powers. In the pursuit of this goal, I have had to take great liberties with many current beliefs, with scientific conformity, and with some matters of faith.[8]

Both Jacques Vallee and author John Keel compare UFO visitations to supernatural events of the Bible. This brings back the question of whether they are from the same place and point of origin. To the Christian, Heaven is the abode of angelic hosts. Vallee and Keel, for the most part, have views that are sterile of personal religious faith. If the facts establish that UFOs and angels have a common origin, then the proposal that UFOs (fallen angels) have intruded into human affairs for thousands of years is true, and the UFO guise is part of stage setting for some evil agenda, possibly the turning of the masses to the final Antichrist.

Before proceeding, it may be necessary to clarify the premise and purpose. This information is not to pull the Christian reader into mystical areas of legend, occult, and folklore, or to weaken their beliefs in God's Word. The primary focus is validating the origin of UFOs with the spiritual realm. I include myths and legends because they fall into the same supernatural arena that affects human cultures.

---

[7] Ibid., 12.

[8] Ibid.

Humanity has a history of paranormal visitations, and these visitations are associated with the fallen angels. Recall the delegation of the disinherited nations at the Tower of Babel to *lesser gods.* The more you study this phenomenon and the human encounters with creatures of folklore and UFOs, the view that these beings are from some far-off galaxy quickly diminishes. Scripture is clear that man contends with the supernatural. The Apostle Paul makes it known is his epistles:

> For we wrestle not against flesh and blood, but against principalities, against powers, against the rulers of the darkness of this world, against spiritual wickedness in high places.[9]

Also, note that traditions and folklore have a direct effect on what a culture accepts or rejects to be a possibility. To these creators of deception, the human mind must be shaped and molded to produce the desired response. The world has experienced supernatural events in the past. Understanding these events help with clarity for future events because their origin is the same.

Jacques Vallee links a direct effect on human consciousness with UFO contact in the foreword of *The Invisible College.*

> At Northwestern University, the team around Professor J. Allen Hynek, of which I was a part, had access to the files of the U.S. Air Force Project Blue Book. They were augmented by the collections of sighting data I had brought from Europe when I emigrated from France in 1962. These files did support the notion that UFOs were physical objects with all the characteristics of an advanced technology, but they also posed some intriguing challenges of a different kind: *witnesses described an alteration of*

[9] Ephesians 6:12, KJV.

> *consciousness in the presence of the phenomenon, and even some unexplained physiological effects.*[10] (Emphasis added)

In chapter one of this book, we reviewed two views of how history is formed, either by the Accidental or the Conspiratorial Theory. The Conspiratorial Theory has small, powerful groups (minority) controlling a large group (majority) by manipulating nations and cultures. We can assign Accidental and Conspiratorial Theories to the human element. The Bible provides us with the supernatural element. Here the minority group steering humanity are angels who govern distinct regions of the Earth. Refer to Dr. Michael Heiser's book *The Unseen Realm,* for a peek behind the spiritual veil and how spiritual beings are influencing humanity. Angelic *principalities* rule over the world's empires. This interference in the affairs of man by angels can be seen through UFO activities as well. Note Vallee's comment:

> The UFO phenomenon is a direct challenge to this arbitrary dichotomy *between physical reality and spiritual reality.*[11]
>
> In this sense the UFO phenomenon is undoubtedly real. What does it mean, then, to say that it may *represent a control system*? And what is the quantity that is being controlled? I will try to show that what takes place through close encounters with UFOs is *control of human beliefs,* control of the relationship *between our consciousness and physical reality,* that this control has been in force throughout history, and that it is of

---

[10] Jacques Vallee, *The Invisible College; What a Group of Scientists Has Discovered About UFO Influence on the Human Race* (San Antonio, Texas: Anomalist Books, 2014), xi.

[11] Vallee, *The Invisible College,* 2.

> secondary importance that it should now assume the form of sightings of space visitors. [12] (Emphasis added)

> No theory of UFOs can be deemed acceptable if it does not account for the reported psychic effects produced by these objects. By "psychic effects" I refer to the space-time distortions experienced by percipients of craft-like devices which appear of "fade away" on the spot, in ways, that are reminiscent of descriptions of "materializations" in the spiritualist literature.[13]

To link UFOs and the Earth's supernatural events to spiritual powers, we can compare known angelic characteristics described in the Bible and that of UFOs solely for the commonality of origin. The spiritual battle described in the Bible has not ended; there is no time-out. The fallen angels and demons mask themselves to hide their deception. It is clear from 2 Corinthians 11:14 that Satan and his angels can appear as ministers of light. Outside the Bible, we have extra-biblical text available for profiling angelic characteristics.

In Acts 12:7-10, we find the Apostle Peter locked up in prison by King Herod. The Apostle James, the brother of John (the sons of thunder), had already been killed by Herod. Peter is locked up in the most secure area of the prison, with guards shackled to him. An angel of the Lord came upon Peter, and *a bright light shined* all around. The angel woke Peter, his chains fell off, and the angel guided Peter out of prison. They moved past guards and locked gates without hindrance. What man considers to be a physical barrier, a spirit being would see as no problem. *Peter wasn't sure if he was dreaming or if it was real*. When the angel had

---

[12] Ibid., 3.

[13] Ibid., 6.

Peter safely outside the prison, and on a side street, the *angel vanished,* and Peter came to his senses, realizing that it wasn't a dream. Angels have supernatural powers. Determining if an angel is friend or foe depends on whom the angel is obeying, God or Satan. This allegiance decides the purpose of the interaction, to either assist or deceive humanity.

Many witnesses of UFO encounters describe their experience as being in a dreamlike state. Many UFO encounters are explained away by man's scientific limitations. Investigating officials tell witnesses they have experienced what is called a *hypnopompic* episode—a dream that overlaps into a person's waking state. If this is true, there have been thousands of people with no previous medical history of these episodes to be experiencing them. So if the UFO encounters are not real, then what is causing this mass hypnopompic outbreak? While the scientist may wish to redirect the phenomenon, the witnesses are telling a different story:

> Since 1959, there has been an accumulating mountain of evidence that would place UFO activity within a spiritual and religious framework. Many of the contactees when asked to describe what happened to them, referred to *occult mysticism, psychic manifestations* and *telepathic communications.* So pronounced have been the religious and cultic references, that a number of religious and semi-religious groups have crystallized around these alleged UFO sightings and communications.[14] (Emphasis added)

What is the purpose of the bright light that shines when spiritual beings and UFOs appear? Is this the result of a spiritual being crossing over into our dimension? That light appears to have a paralyzing effect on the human body. Note none of the guards

---

[14] Thomas, *Omega Conspiracy,* 52-53.

were woken up or disturbed. Light is an electromagnetic wave. Received through the eye, it is a direct electrical connection to the brain. If hacking into the human mind is the goal, then connecting to the brain's cerebral network through the eye is the portal of choice. The human eye is a high-speed electrical interface; it allows the bypassing of cognitive barriers. Advertisement and marketing companies have proved the effectiveness of using the human eye as a visual interface. They have successfully reached the human subconscious through subliminal messaging. The portal for this process was the human eye. John Keel makes a note of electromagnetic waves in *Operation Trojan Horse*:

> The contactee's real experience is in his or her mind as some powerful beam of electromagnetic energy is broadcasting to that mind, bypassing the biological sensory channels.[15]

> They constitute the real phenomenon. And there are other objects, invisible to human eyes, but discernible, on occasion, to radar and to those people who are more attuned to receiving the signals from those unknown electromagnetic radiations around us.[16]

It is not uncommon for a person of religious orientation who has a supernatural encounter to immediately categorize it as either being from God or the devil. The Christian's discernment between friend or foe is crucial at this point; *prior* knowledge of the biblical text will be the deciding factor. Author Jessie Penne-Lewis wrote her book, *War on the Saints,* during the Great Welsh revival of 1904. In it, she says where our knowledge is weak is where we are vulnerable to deception.

---

[15] Keel, *Operation Trojan Horse,* 294.

[16] Ibid., 324.

> Deception has to do with the mind. It means a wrong thought admitted to the mind, under the deception that it is truth. Since the deception is based on ignorance, and not on a person's moral character, a Christian who is true and faithful in the knowledge he has, is open to deception in the sphere where he is ignorant of the 'devices' of the devil (2 Corinthians 2:11) and what he is able to do. A 'true' and 'faithful' Christian is liable to be deceived by the devil because of his ignorance.[17]

Satan the deceiver is well aware of this human response and uses it to his advantage. Scripture tells us that the devil can appear as a messenger of light rather than who he, is a messenger of darkness.

> For such are false apostles, deceitful workers, transforming themselves into the apostles of Christ. And no marvel; for Satan himself is transformed into an angel of light. Therefore it is no great thing if his ministers also be transformed as the ministers of righteousness; whose end shall be according to their works.[18]

The Apostle Paul's encounter with Jesus on the Damascus road left him temporarily blinded. The priest Zacharias, the father of John the Baptist, was made mute, unable to speak by the angel who informed him that his wife Elizabeth was to have a child.

The Apostle Paul's experience:

---

[17] Jessie Penn Lewis, *War on the Saints* (Fort Washington, Pennsylvania: Christian-Literature-Crusade, 1995), 45.

[18] 2 Corinthians 11:13-15, KJV.

> And as he journeyed, he came near Damascus: and suddenly *there shined round about him* a light from heaven: ... And the men which journeyed with him stood speechless, hearing a voice, *but seeing no* man. ...but they led him by the hand, and brought him into Damascus.[19] (Emphasis added)

The priest Zacharias:

> And Zacharias said unto the angel, Whereby shall I know this? For I am an old man, and my wife well stricken in years. ...And, behold, thou shalt be dumb, and *not able to speak*, until the day that these things shall be performed, because thou believest not my words, which shall be fulfilled in their season.[20] (Emphasis added)

Many of our world's religions and folklore derive their origins from a superior race that arrived from the sky. The biblical text makes it clear who has the authority over Earth's atmosphere:

> Wherein in time past ye walked according to the course of this world, according to the *prince of the power of the air*, the spirit that now worketh in the children of disobedience:[21] (Emphasis added)

> The visitors have the power to fly through the air using luminous craft, sometimes called "celestial chariots." With these manifestations are associated impressive physical and meteorological displays,

[19] Acts 9:3,7,8, KJV.

[20] Luke 1:18,20, KJV.

[21] Ephesians 2:2, KJV.

which the primitive authors call "whirlwind," "pillar of fire," etc. The occupants of these craft, to whom popular imagery will later ascribe wings and luminosity, are similar to man and communicate with him. They are organized under a strict military system:[22]

TIMELINE

The Documented history of UFO visitation extends back centuries.

> In Japan, on August 3, 989, during a period of great social unrest, three round objects of unusual brilliance were observed; *later they joined together*.
>
> The date was September 24, 1235, seven centuries before our time, and General Yoritsume was camping his army. Suddenly, a curious phenomenon was observed: mysterious sources of light were seen to swing and circle in the southwest, moving in loops until the early morning. General Yoritsume ordered what we would now term a "full-scale scientific investigation," and his consultants set to work. Fairly soon they made their report. "The whole thing is completely natural, General," they said in substance. "It is only the wind making the stars sway."[23] (Emphasis added)
>
> September 12, 1271, the famous priest Nichiren was about to be beheaded at Tatsunokuchi, Kamakura,

---

[22] Vallee, *Passport to Magonia,* 17.

[23] Ibid., 18.

> when there appeared in the sky an object like a full moon, shiny and bright.
>
> In 1361, a flying object described as being "shaped like a drum, about twenty feet in diameter" emerged from the inland sea off western Japan.
>
> On January 2, 1458, a bright object resembling the full moon was seen in the sky, and this apparition was followed by "curious signs" in heaven and earth.
>
> On January 3, 1569, in the evening, a flaming star appeared in the sky. It was regarded as an omen of serious changes, announcing the fall of the Chu Dynasty. Such phenomena continued during the seventeenth and eighteenth centuries. For instance, in *May, 1606, fireballs* were continuously reported over Kyoto, and one night a *whirling ball of fire resembling a red wheel* hovered near the Nijo Castle and was observed by many of the samurai. The next morning the city was filled with rumors and the people muttered: "This must be a portent." (Emphasis added)

Are the fireballs recorded above in the year 1606 the same type of fireballs that swept across the United States in 1871, causing the great Chicago fire?

> One noon in September, 1702, the sun took on a bloody color several days in succession and cotton-like threads fell down, apparently falling from the sun itself—phenomena reminiscent of the 1917 observations in Fatima, Portugal.[24]

> A brief examination of legendary elements in Western Europe in the Middle Ages will show that a

[24] Vallee, *Passport to Magonia*, 19.

similar rumor about strange flying objects and supernatural manifestations was spreading there, too. Indeed, Pierre Boaistuau, in 1575, remarked:

The face of heaven has been so often disfigured by bearded, hairy comets, torches, flames, columns, spears, shields, dragons, duplicate moons, suns, and other similar things, that if one wanted to tell in an orderly fashion those that have happened since the birth of Jesus Christ only, and inquire about the causes of their origin, the lifetime of a single man would not be enough.[25]

Between the years 1937 and 1945, an entity who identified herself as the Queen of the Universe appeared more than 100 times to four young girls in the tiny hamlet of Heeded, Germany. The girls, aged twelve through fourteen, were Anna Schultz. Greta and Maria Ganseforth, and Susanna Bruns. These visions began in November 1937 and continued throughout the war, with the Lady urging the world to "pray, pray much, especially for the conversions of sinners."[26]

On Sunday, June 18, 1961, four young girls were playing marbles outside the little village of Garabandal, Spain, when they suddenly saw an "angel." The girls Mary Cruz Gonzalez, eleven, Conchita Gonzalez, twelve, Jacinta Gonzalez, twelve and Mary Loly Mazon, twelve (none of the Gonzalez girls were directly related), said that he appeared to be about nine years old, was dressed in a long, seamless

---

[25] Vallee, *Passport to Magonia,* 20.

[26] Keel, *Operation Trojan Horse,* 286-287.

> blue robe, had a small face with black eyes, and "fine hands and short fingernails." For some reason, he gave the impression of being very strong. This figure was surrounded by a dazzling glow and faded into thin air without saying a word.[27]

A Wanaque, New Jersey, police officer, Sergeant Benjamin Thompson, was not only temporarily blinded by a UFO in 1966, but he said, "It took away my voice, and I was hoarse for two weeks after that."[28]

UFOs exist, and they are considered a mystery. These supernatural intrusions are affecting and altering human behavior. These intrusions into our space-time are changing our culture's collective mind. Jacques Vallee makes the following related remark:

> What matters here is the link between certain unusual phenomena—observed or imagined—and the alteration of the witnesses' behavior. In other words, these accounts show that it is possible to affect the lives of many people by showing them displays that are beyond their comprehension, or by convincing them that they have observed such phenomena, or by keeping alive the belief that their destiny is somehow controlled by occult forces.[29]

Recorded history documented UFO sightings, sightings of luminous objects that appear in the skies above. UFO imagery and design take on the appearance of advanced technology, which is always superior for the recorded period. The Wright Brothers were still on the ground floor with their airplane at the

---

[27] Ibid., 287.

[28] Ibid., 292.

[29] Vallee, *Passport to Magonia*, 20.

end of the 19th century, yet many witnesses reported seeing magnificent airships.

In a courtroom of law, it only takes a handful of witnesses to determine the verdict in a case. UFO investigators have written many books numbering in the hundreds or thousands. The witnesses documented through the centuries number in the millions. While the mystery of what these people experienced is perplexing to pin down, the probability is high that supernatural entities are involved. The UFOs' agenda is what is on trial, not the witnesses who can only explain what they experienced, whether it was real or imposed on their memories.

Author and journalist John Keel wrote several books, and the one of interest for this study is titled *Operation Trojan Horse,* published in 1970. John Keel spent four years investigating and researching UFO events. He did this, as he puts it, full time, seven days a week, for four years without a vacation. The enigma of UFOs hasn't changed; Hollywood puts its twist on the subject to sell movies.

What is the significance of conducting a serious-minded study on the origin of UFOs? They appear to be part of a cosmic deception. People would benefit from knowing who or what is affecting the minds of witnesses. This interference in the human psyche is collectively changing our culture. What could create the following human response?

> Men's hearts failing them for fear, and for looking after those things which are coming on the earth: for the powers of heaven shall be shaken.[30]

Author John Keel begins in the first few pages of his book with this statement:

---

[30] Luke 21:26, KJV.

> The phenomenon of unidentified flying objects is a gigantic iceberg, and the truly important aspects are hidden far beneath the surface. Nearly all of the UFO literature of the past twenty years has leaned toward the trivia, the random sightings which are actually irrelevant to the whole, and to the meaningless side issues of government policy, dissection of personalities, and the conflicts which have arisen within the various factions of the UFO cultists.[31]
>
> *History, psychiatry, religion, and the occult have proven to be far more important* to an understanding of the whole than the many books which simply recount the endless sightings of aerial anomalies.[32] (Emphasis added)
>
> Cunning techniques of deception and psychological warfare have been employed by the UFO source to keep us confused and skeptical. Man's tendency to create a deep and inflexible belief on the basis of little or no evidence has been exploited. These beliefs have created tunnel vision and blinded many to the real nature of the phenomenon, making it necessary for me to examine and analyze many of these beliefs in this text.[33]

It is not a question of whether UFOs are real—they have been tracked on radar and seen by witnesses with credible reputations through the years.

---

[31] John A. Keel, *Operation Trojan Horse: The Classic Breakthrough Study of* UFOs, 3rd ed. (San Antonio, Texas: Anomalist Books, 2013), 1.

[32] Ibid., 2-3.

[33] Keel, *Operation Trojan Horse,* 2.

> There have been frequent radar sightings of UFOs for the past twenty years, not only on military radar but on the sets of weather bureaus and airports. Often in these cases ground witnesses have also reported seeing the objects visually. When the Federal Aviation Agency tower at the Greensboro-High Point Airport in Greensboro, North Carolina, picked up an unidentified flying object early on the morning of July 27, 1966, several police officers in the High Point-Randolph County area also reported seeing unidentifiable objects buzzing the vicinity. They said the objects appeared to be at an altitude of 500 feet and described them as being round, brilliant red-green, and appeared to be emitting flashes of light.[34]

In 1966, there was a large number of UFO sightings scattered all over. At the time, the Secretary of Defense was Robert S. McNamara. The Air Force briefed Secretary McNamara, and the House of Foreign Affairs Committee followed with a meeting on March 30, 1966. News reporters asked Secretary McNamara if there was anything to these flying saucer mysteries. He replied:

> "I think not … " I have talked to the Secretary of the Air Force and the Air Force Director of Research and Engineering, and neither of them places any credence in the reports we have received to date."[35]

Now, this was back in 1966. It is easier for our government to deny the truth or to ignore the problem if it will keep panic from developing in the American population. Keel took a statistical approach to his investigation. His research was not about denying the witnesses' claims. His method uses the witnesses'

---

[34] Ibid., 6.

[35] Ibid., 7.

reports to determine the UFOs' actual nature. The Air Force attempted in the early 1950s to gather useful data but gave up on the project. John Keel's book lists the details of many UFO sightings for comparison of circumstances, dates, times, and geographic locations to establish patterns. Interestingly, Wednesdays and Saturday nights have a high count of sightings. Why are Wednesdays and Saturdays a high point for activity?

> In *Myth and Legend of Ancient Israel* by Angelo S. Rapport, the following statement appears: "*Concerning 'demons*:' They lodge in trees, caper bushes, in gardens, vineyards, in ruined and desolate houses, and the eves of Wednesday and Saturday were considered dangerous times. [36] (Emphasis added)

Early on, John Keel makes this analysis:

> Already we can arrive at one disturbing conclusion based upon these basic factors of behavior. If these lights are actually machines operated by intelligent entities, they obviously don't want to be caught. They come in the dead of night, operating in areas where the risks of being observed are slight. They pick the middle of the week for their peak activities, and they confine themselves rather methodically to the political boundaries of specific states at specific times. All of this smacks uneasily of a covert military operation, a secret build-up in remote areas.[37]

Keel immediately follows with the thought that, unfortunately, it is not that simple. In the United States in the Midwest, there was a major "flap," a large number of sightings in 1897. We

---

[36] Keel, *Operation Trojan Horse*, 109.

[37] Ibid., 20.

know non-humans visited ancient civilizations and were thought to be gods. Ancient cultures around the world have recorded these visitors in their history. Dr. Thomas provides this short review in *The Omega Conspiracy*:

> Most people are aquatinted with the mythologies of ancient Greece and Rome. The gods or semi-gods in these traditions go under different names, but their behavior has a common denominator. Whether these gods are called Zeus or Jupiter, Poseidon or Neptune, Aphrodite or Venus, Eros, Cupid ... their sex orgies, promiscuities, cruelties, and violence are all of the same cloth. And so are their offspring.[38]

> Ancient Sumerian records tell of gods descending from the stars and fertilizing their ancestors. This interbreeding of gods from heaven and women from earth is supposed to have produced the first men upon the earth.
>
> The native inhabitants of Malekula, in New Hebrides believe that the first race of men were direct descendants of the sons of heaven.
>
> The Incas held that they were the descendants of the "sons of the Sun."
>
> The Teutons claimed that their ancestors came with the flying Wanen.
>
> Some of the South Sea Islanders trace their ancestry to one of the gods of heaven, who visited them in an enormous gleaming egg.
>
> The Koreans believed that a heavenly king, "Hwanin," sent his son, "Hwanung," to earth, married an earth woman who gave birth to Tangun

[38] Dr. Thomas. *The Omega Conspiracy*, 89.

> Waggom. It was he who was supposed to have welded all the primitive tribes together into one kingdom.
>
> The ancient tradition Tango-Fudoki in Japan tells the story of the Island Child. The only difference here is that it was a man from earth and a maiden from heaven that came together in marriage, and spent their time together in heaven and not on earth.
>
> From India comes the Mahabharata and other ancient Sanskrit texts, which tell of "gods" begetting children with women of earth, and how these children inherited the "supernatural" skills and learning of their fathers.
>
> A similar mythology is found in the Epic of Gilgamesh, where we read of "watchers" from outer space coming to planet Earth, and producing giants.
>
> An early Persian myth tells that before the coming of Zoroaster, demons had corrupted the Earth, and allied themselves with women.
>
> A further convincing element in this string of samples, is that these myths and legends belong to people so far removed from each other by time, space, and language that collaboration or conspiracy is out of the question. How then does one explain this phenomenon?[39]

With a timeline to reveal a long history of visitations, several authors conclude that these beings are local in origin. Keel asked how long this has been going on. You may find his response to censored history interesting:

> History prefers fantasy to fact. Legend endures while truth coughs up blood, which dries and fades. We

[39] Ibid., 91.

> prefer to teach our children that Christopher Columbus was a hero and have buried his glaring faults. We choose to pass on the nonsense that the Great Chicago Fire of October 8, 1871, was ignited when Mrs. O'Leary's discontented cow kicked over a lantern, and we forget that the fire was actually caused by a gigantic, still unexplained fireball that swept low across the skies of several states, destroying dozens of communities and creating a kind of death and havoc which would not be seen again until the great fire raids of World War II.

The footnotes reference the "fireball." This reference creates curiosity about the great fire of London in 1666. Little nuggets of information like this expose missing pieces of the grand puzzle and motivate the desire to dig deeper, beyond the veil of propaganda. The footnote:

> In Chapter Four of his book *Mysterious Fires and Lights*, researcher Vincent H. Gaddis documented the spectacular and disastrous fires that swept across Iowa, Minnesota, Indiana, Illinois, Wisconsin, and the Dakotas. Wisconsin suffered the greatest loss of life, with 1,500 deaths recorded in Green Bay alone on that horrible night. Four times as many were killed in Peshtigo, Wisconsin, as in Chicago.[40]

Keel gives his opinion of how history is revised until it satisfies the powers-that-be.

> *We are more enthralled with our interpretations of great events than with the events themselves, and we gingerly alter the facts generation after generation until history*

---

[40] Keel, *Operation Trojan Horse*, 25.

> *reads the way we think it should read.*[41] (Emphasis added)

Late in the 19th century, there were large numbers of flaps across the United States, close to 50 years before the Roswell Incident. Then, as now, witnesses did their best to explain what happened. Then, as now, when a witness attempts to describe their experience, they are met with resistance. Their neighbor's reality is disturbed by these testimonies. The default or defensive response is to ridicule and discredit the witness rather than face the possibilities.

The first photograph of a UFO was on August 12, 1883. Jose Bonilla, a Mexican astronomer, was the photographer. Professor Bonilla compiled his report, which contained pictures from a camera mounted to telescope and calculations that estimated that the UFOs, 143 cigar-shaped objects, were about 200,000 miles away. He submitted his report to the French journal *L'Astronomie. The authorities couldn't explain the photograph, so the event was forgotten.*[42]

Five years prior, a Texas farmer named John Martin reported his sighting, which took place on Thursday, January 24, 1878. It made the Dennison, Texas, news, and *the farmer became known by his neighbors as "Crazy John."* The book contains plenty of records about eyewitness sightings. But here is where it gets interesting—the UFOs are not spaceships, but, as you will see, advanced technology in comparison to the period.[43]

> In April 1897, thousands of people throughout the United States were seeing huge "airships" over their towns and farms. Scores of witnesses even claimed to have met and talked with the pilots. According to

---

[41] Ibid.

[42] Ibid., 26-27.

[43] Ibid., 27.

> the New York Herald, Monday, April 12, 1897, a news dealer in Rogers Park, Illinois, took two photographs of a cigar-shaped craft. "I had read for some days about the airship," the news dealer, Walter McCann, was quoted as saying. "But I thought it must be a fake."[44]

Jules Verne, a French author, wrote the book *Masters of the World* in 1903 only six years after the great airship flap of 1897. The book's story was about an advanced airship with military capabilities. As the events increased, the news media at the time turned to whom they considered a man of scientific authority, Thomas Alva Edison. Thomas Edison had this to say on April 22, 1897:

> "You can take it from me that it is a pure fake," ... "I have no doubt that airships will be successfully constructed in the near future but ... it is absolutely impossible to imagine that a man could construct a successful airship and keep the matter a secret[45]

DIFFERENT TYPES OF UFO MACHINES

UFOs in the luminous form don't appear to have mass or to be solid matter. Witnesses were making reports across the United States about unidentifiable aircraft with advanced technology compared to the time.

On Tuesday, December 12, 1967, Mrs. Malley was driving her car when she saw an illuminated flying object shaped like a boxcar and with a domed top containing red and green windows. The bright object was pacing Mrs. Malley's car.

---

[44] Ibid., 27.

[45] Ibid., 28.

On the morning of June 12, 1790, in Alencon, France, there was a report of an enormous globe that had crashed: "The eye-witnesses of this event were two mayors, a physician and three other local authorities who confirm my report,"[46] stated police Inspector Liabeuf.

Thanksgiving week in 1896 is when the great "airship mystery" started in the United States. The San Francisco *Call*, San Francisco *Chronicle*, and other journals published these reports. It is important to note the description is an "airship." Witnesses claimed to have spoken with the pilots.

> Crews on ships were seeing, glowing spheres and saucer-shaped machines rising out of the water and flying away while the Wright brothers were still fussing with gliders.[47]

In the spring of 1897, reports of these airships began to spread and were mainly in the Midwest, from Texas to Michigan.

> In 1897, when people saw actual objects they described them as being cigar-shaped or being large dark forms with lights attached. No flying saucers turned up in the reports I have collected. But the night-time observations then were exactly the same as they are now: bright lights with colored lights flashing around them, often moving in an erratic fashion but apparently controlled. It is possible that the airship was nothing more than a decoy—a cover for the real activity that was taking place in 1897.

---

[46] Ibid., 74.

[47] Ibid., 79.

> Certainly these objects did not consist of one or two clumsy balloons shuffling across the country.[48]

There were plenty of reports about the airships worldwide during the late 19th century and early 20th century. There were sightings in Russia, Sweden, and New Zealand. The Wright Brothers' airplane was still in its infancy stages. There were reports of strange aircraft that didn't seem to fit into the technological capabilities of the times. On June 30, 1908, there was the "meteor explosion in Siberia. The following year there were several reports about cigar-shaped objects in the night skies, exhibiting their flashing lights. A new machine was seen flying in the night skies with its powerful beams of light.

> At 1 A.M. people around the harbor of Boston, Massachusetts, saw "a bright light passing over." "Immigration Inspector Hoe ... came to the conclusion that is was an airship of some kind" (*New York Tribune*, December 21, 1909).[49]

The newspapers printed several more sightings in late December of 1909. The next year followed with reports of a biplane flying over the island of Manhattan. At 8:45 p.m. on Tuesday, August 30, 1910, "a long black object" flew low over the Island of Manhattan. Like the airship flap of 1897, there were several sightings of strange airplanes that were dual in color, gray or black, and had no identifiable markings. By law, active aircraft require identification markings. These became looked upon as some type of private aircraft. The mysterious delta-shaped UFOs make their appearance on the scene:

---

48 Ibid., 95.

49 Ibid., 120.

> Whole formations of unidentified delta-winged craft have been seen over the United States. At least one case was given careful study by the U.S. Air Force. *Project Blue Book Report No. 14* lists as "unidentified" the following incident: "A naval aviation student, his wife, and several others were at a drive-in movie from 2115 to 2240 hours [9:15 to 10:40 P.M.] on Sunday, April 20, 1952, during which time they saw nine objects in a group, and there were about twenty groups.

Until researching data for this book, I was not aware of the mystery flying machines of the 19th and 20th centuries. Those machines were something we could conceive as possibly being built by man and kept secret from the public eye. The critical factor to take away from these sightings is the impact it had on the minds of the masses. Flying machines did not entirely create panic; it was more human curiosity than anything. The public responded differently to Orson Welles' *War of the Worlds* radio broadcast in 1938. The statistics were that 1 in 12 people believed the show to be real.

> The great majority of all sightings throughout history have been of "soft" luminous objects, or objects that were transparent, translucent, changed size and shape, or appeared and disappeared suddenly. Sightings of seemingly solid metallic objects have always been rare. The "soft" sightings, being more numerous, comprise the real phenomenon and deserve the most study.[50]

The difficulty is determining what people are actually seeing. The behavior of UFOs, luminous objects, indicates they are

---

[50] Keel, *Operation Trojan Horse*, 30.

not completely solid; they are paraphysical. Their aerial maneuvers defy the laws of inertia, as we understand it. In our dimension, a physical object has weight and, therefore, has mass. An object attempting to make a sharp right turn at 16,000 miles per hour is going to complete the maneuver in the form of a curve as opposed to a right angle due to the law of inertia. But UFOs have done just that, at incredible speeds, making right-angle turns and disappearing.

The fact that UFOs have been tracked on radar making high-speed right-angle turns forms a hypothesis that UFOs change from a solid object to a massless object along their path of trajectory—returning to their hyper-dimensional origin, above our three-dimensional world, four dimensions if you consider "time." Keel uses the term *transmogrification* to describe this ability to change its physical characteristics rapidly. Transmogrification is the ability to make a change in appearance or form. This change will be a common occurrence with legends and folklore.

The Bible supports this rapid change with spiritual beings. Angels have taken on a human form to communicate with man. In the 1950s, the number of UFO sightings was in the thousands, and the media outlets were asking questions. The U.S. Government could no longer ignore the problem. None of the armed forces wanted to touch the issue because of the stigma associated with it. By default, it fell to the U.S. Air Force because the problem was in the air, and that is the Air Force's domain.

> The U.S. Air Force made its major contribution to the subject in 1955 with the publication of *Project Blue Book Special Report No. 14*. This was undoubtedly the most important single contribution to the UFO problem. It was a statistical survey and computer study prepared for Air Force by the Battelle Memorial Institute, containing 240 charts and graphs detailing the geographical distribution of sightings and other vital data. It was the only quantitative study ever

> produced by anyone. Many dismissed *Special Report No. 14* as "another whitewash," because the basic conclusion of the study was that there was no evidence of extraterrestrial origin and no suggestion that an advanced technology was involved. When I carried out my own statistical studies using thousands of reports from the 1960s, I was startled to discover that my findings merely verified the material in *Special Report No. 14*. It was embarrassing, at first, to realize that an objective examination of the evidence proved that the UFO enthusiasts were wrong and the Air Force was right.
>
> Sensible research must be dictated by this basic precept: Any acceptable theory must offer an explanation for all the data. The paraphysical hypothesis meets this criterion. The extraterrestrial hypothesis does not.[51] (Bold emphasis added)

What does a person do when they see something they cannot explain and are asked to describe it? They do the best they can with their current level of knowledge (available reference points).

> Dr. Donald Menzel, a Harvard astronomer, recognized that people were seeing something and had tried to explain the phenomenon within the restrictions of their own scientific disciplines.[52]

When I read Dr. Menzel's opinion, I immediately thought about the Apostle John. The Roman emperor Domitian exiled John to the island of Patmos. The Apostle's John's background was from an agricultural society. When John was young, he was

---

[51] Ibid., 34-35.

[52] Ibid., 39.

a fisherman by trade. There on that island, he received prophetic visions from the Lord Jesus, which were written down and are known as the final book of the Bible, the *Book of Revelation*. I suspect it must have been a mind-blowing experience, if not terrifying for the apostle, and then he described in words what he was seeing. The Apostle John provided a written report of his supernatural experience. Like the UFO witnesses, he had to explain what he had seen without any personal experience for comparison. Let's return to locust-type creatures from the abyss as an example; the Lord gives the Apostle John a vision:

> And the shapes of the locusts were like unto horses prepared unto battle; and on their heads were as it were crowns like gold, and their faces were as the faces of men. And they had hair as the hair of women, and their teeth were as the teeth of lions. And they had breastplates, as it were breastplates of iron; and the sound of their wings was as the sound of chariots of many horses running to battle. And they had tails like unto scorpions, and there were stings in their tails: and their power was to hurt men five months.[53]

Above, the Apostle John uses the adjective "like" eight times to compare what he is seeing. He used descriptive words to express his vision—words like heads with gold crowns, faces of men, hair of women, teeth of a lion, breastplates of iron, wings that created the sound of horses pulling chariots, and, finally, tails of scorpions. John described what he saw with words from the time he lived. Witnesses of UFOs are doing the same thing. With their current knowledge, they possess of the world around them and attempt to describe a supernatural event; this adds to the difficulty in determining what the UFOs are. You have just

[53] Revelation 9:7-10, KJV.

read about how a witness can have challenges identifying what they have seen without a point of reference for comparison. Below is an example of a person who is familiar with biblical Scripture. She quickly identifies UFO activity as demonic based on her knowledge from studying the Bible. The gaps in our knowledge base are where we will be vulnerable to deceit.

> Recently the U.S. Government Printing Office issued a publication compiled by the Library of Congress for the Air Force Office of Scientific Research: UFOs and Related Subjects: An Annotated Bibliography. In preparing this work, the senior bibliographer, Miss Lynn E. Catoe, actually read thousands of UFO articles, books and publications. In her preface to this 400-page book she states:
>
> *"A large part of the available UFO literature is closely linked with mysticism and metaphysical. It deals with subjects like mental telepathy, automatic writing, and invisible entities, as well as phenomena like poltergeist manifestations and possession … Many of the UFO reports now being published in the popular press recount alleged incidents that are strikingly similar to demoniac possession and psychic phenomena which has* long been known to theologians and parapsychologists."[54] (Emphasis added)

What the secular world calls hyper-dimension, Christians refer to as the spiritual realm—the domain where angelic beings, the supernatural exist, both obedient and disobedient to God. This hyper-dimension encompasses ours. The Bible gives many accounts where angels enter our dimension to conduct God's will with man and others (fallen angels) to interact with humanity on behalf of the devil. Men and women of antiquity were

[54] Ibid., 40.

aware that angels traversed across the heavens. Note the following scriptural references, the first from the Book of Genesis, where Jacob has a dream, and the second from the Book of Job. Both describe the movement of spiritual beings between Heaven and Earth:

> And he dreamed, and behold a ladder set up on the earth, and the top of it reached to heaven: and behold the *angels of God ascending and descending on it.*[55] (Emphasis added)

> Now there was a day when the *sons of God* came to present themselves before the LORD, and Satan came also among them. And the LORD said unto Satan, Whence comest thou? Then Satan answered the LORD, and said, *From going to and fro in the earth, and from walking up and down in it.*[56] (Emphasis added, especially for, the "sons of God"—*ben 'elohiym*).

The Book of Job is considered a book of antiquity, and the above verse was written after Lucifer's fall. Before his rebellion, he was called Lucifer, but Job refers to Lucifer as Satan. From that verse, we know that fallen angels were traveling back and forth between the spiritual realm and the world of humankind since ancient days. This detail is a factor when making the connection between UFOs and demonic spiritual forces. John Keel makes a secular conclusion about UFO interdimensional travel between our Earthly realm and an adjacent realm.

> Thus, by all the standards of our sciences (and our common sense), the UFOs do not really exist as solid objects. They may be a constant part of our

[55] Genesis 28:12, KJV.

[56] Job 1:6-7, KJV.

> environment, but they are not an actual part of our reality. We cannot, therefore, catalog them as manufactured products of some extraterrestrial civilization sharing our own dimensions of time and space. They are extradimensional, able to move through our spatial coordinates at will but also able to enter and leave our three-dimensional world.[57]

There is deception at work and has been for centuries. From the Garden of Eden, the devil's goal has been to deceive humanity and draw us away from God. The desire for a cosmic savior is on the rise due to the lack of knowledge, due to ignorance of the world's true supernatural Savior, Jesus Christ.

Conclusion

I'll begin summarizing this book with the initial purpose and premise, to motivate the reader to look into the origin of why you believe what you believe to be the truth. Hopefully, enough evidence has been presented to show the existence of active agendas to hide the truth from the masses, the reality of what is, the reality of humanity's history. The goal is to prompt you to verify your beliefs, some of which you may have questioned—opinions with which you may use to function daily, beliefs that perhaps, by tradition, you have accepted without question and are now passing on to the next generation.

A few tools in the enemies' arsenal are used to launch their deceptive plans, which have been identified. Our enemy uses propaganda, false flags, learning-against-learning, indoctrination, and Hegelian-Dielectric, etc. Key factors that develop our worldviews are our education, the doctrine we receive, religious or humanistic, and our programming both as an individual and

---

[57] Ibid., 58.

as a nation. It is openly clear that our public schools, which started as centers of education with high scholastic and moral standards, have become centers of indoctrination for our children.

As parents, how do we compete with the influence of an eight-hour school day, our children's peers, the Hollywood agenda, and messaging from the music industry? All these inputs are part of the foundation of the "New Morality," a morality that is being imposed on our children. For parents, it seems almost impossible to counteract so many hours of programming and mind-bending doctrine. We may only see our child for a couple of hours a day.

It is not my place to dictate the answer to your life's scenario. Personal and cultural boundaries are needed to reduce or block these harmful inputs, especially for our children. We must keep the indoctrination out and implement some form of the first line of defense for the minds of our youth because they are the primary target of the onslaught for control. We are responsible for protecting them and preparing them for what they will have to face in their coming years. Consider this comment by Dr. Ravi Zacharias about not removing barriers without first questioning why they were erected to begin with.

> It has been rightly said that before any fence is removed, one should always pause long enough to find out why it was placed there in the first place. The moral law God gave Moses at Mount Sinai was just that. It not only revealed the nature of God and His purpose for His creation, it also served as a boundary line for the people, a line that could not be crossed with impunity.[58]

---

[58] Zacharias, *Deliver Us From Evil*, 131.

The battlefield for humanity has always been the mind. If this were not true, the enemy would not invest so much time and resources to shape what we believe and how we think. History reveals to us that men and women before us have faced similar challenges and problems, some with life-threatening circumstances. The Pilgrims and Puritans fled Europe to escape the Church of Rome and the church of England. They endured the hardships of settling in the New World. These men and women gave our country its Christian foundation and a public-school system that taught the knowledge of God, high moral standards, and the value of quality education.

History also reveals the existence of watchmen who did their best to sound the alarm, to warn their neighbors and fellow citizens that they were under attack. The attack wasn't always with guns and bullets but from clandestine organizations that desired to bring the free world under their control. These organizations wanted to remove our freedom to hear God's Word in our public schools. To take away our freedom of choice, take away our freedom to hold to the religious faith of our choosing. And take our Republic in which we live—built by men and women who believed in absolutes and Godly morals.

All along, the battle for power and control marched on through Inquisitions, wars, political intrigue, and the shedding of the innocent blood of millions of men, women, and children by the hands of the Church of Rome and the papacy's militia, the Jesuits. This culminated, from the Church Age to the Space Age, in the final Great Deception that Jesus Christ and the apostles warned us about over 2,000 years ago. It created a desire for the masses to hunger for a savior who would solve all the world's problems. This supernatural savior, which the masses hope for, is not the supernatural Savior of the Bible, Jesus Christ, the Son of God, but a cosmic savior who is a counterfeit with supernatural abilities that will deceive the masses. Note the following verse from the Book of Revelation:

> And the great dragon was cast out, that old serpent, called the devil, and Satan, which deceiveth the whole world: he was cast out into the earth, and his angels were cast out with him.[59]

For those of you that believe in a literal Judgement Day, you know that each of us must stand alone and answer for ourselves. Can we genuinely claim ignorance as an excuse? The Christian who believes in Jesus Christ as Savior has an Advocate, a Savior that will intercede on their behalf before God, the *Most High*. Have you taken the time to know Him, to understand what the Bible has to say before you make an intelligent conscience decision of what is the truth? It is my hope that everyone comes to the knowledge of salvation through Jesus Christ, and I wish you the best in your pursuit of the Truth.

[59] Revelation 12:9, KJV.

Appendix

Scripture that Supports Salvation Through Jesus Christ

- Jesus answered and said to him, "Most assuredly, I say to you, unless one is born *again*, he cannot see the kingdom of God." (John 3:3)
- Jesus answered, "Most assuredly, I say to you, unless one is born of water and the Spirit, he cannot enter the kingdom of God." (John 3:5)
- For God so loved the world that He gave His only begotten Son, that whoever believes in Him should not perish but have everlasting life. (John 3:16)
- He who believes in the Son has everlasting life; and he who does not believe the Son shall not see life, but the wrath of God abides on him. (John 3:36)
- So they said, "Believe on the Lord Jesus Christ, and you will be saved, you and your household." (Acts 16:31)
- For all have sinned and fall short of the glory of God … (Romans 3:23)
- Being justified freely by His grace through the redemption that is in Christ Jesus … (Romans 3:24)
- But God demonstrates His own love toward us, in that while we were still sinners, Christ died for us. (Romans 5:8)

- Much more then, having now been justified by His blood, we shall be saved from wrath through Him. (Romans 5:9)
  - ***Salvation:*** *The act of saving, preserving from or deliverance from destruction, danger, or great calamity.*
  - *Atheist:* Denies the existence of God, heaven, or hell, … yet fears death.
    "There is a God-shaped vacuum in the heart of every man that cannot be filled by any created thing but only by God, the Creator, made known through Jesus." (French Mathematician Blaise Pascal, 1623-1662)
  - *All men sin, some to a greater or lesser degree.*
  - Our pride makes us want to participate in the act of being saved. Being saved means being saved. You don't save yourself from drowning. There will be sinners in heaven because they repented and received the gift of salvation that God offers through the acceptance of Jesus.

- For the wages of sin [is] death, but the gift of God [is] eternal life in Christ Jesus our Lord. (Romans 6:23)
  Note: The word "death" means separation. Applying this definition to the verse above, you have separation from God. This is spiritual death (the second death), not our physical death. That happens at an appointed time.

- If we confess our sins, he is faithful and just to forgive us [our] sins, and to cleanse us from all unrighteousness. (1 John 1:9)

- That if you confess with your mouth the Lord Jesus and believe in your heart that God has raised Him from the dead, you will be saved. For with the heart one believes unto righteousness, and with the mouth confession is made unto salvation. For the Scripture says, "Whoever believes on Him will not be put to shame." For there is no distinction between Jew and Greek, for the same Lord over all is rich to all who call upon Him. For "whoever calls on the name of the LORD shall be saved." (Romans 10:9-13)

- For by grace you have been saved through faith, and that not of yourselves; [it is] the gift of God, not of works, lest anyone should boast. (Ephesians 2:8,9)

- And this is the testimony: that God has given us eternal life, and this life is in His Son. (1 John 5:11)

Bibliography

A. Souter, D.LITT. *Tertullian Concerning the Resurrection of the Flesh.* New York: The Macmillian Company, 1922.

Agency, Catholic News. "Believing in aliens not opposed to Christianity, Vatican's top astronomer says." *Catholic News Agency.* May 13, 2008. https://www.catholicnewsagency.com/news/believing_in_aliens_not_opposed_to_christianity_vaticans_top_astronomer_says (accessed January 24, 2019).

Allen, James. "As A Man Thinketh." In *Motivational Classics:Three Renowned Books In One Volume*, by James Allen. ExecutiveBooks, n.d.

Allix, Peter. *The Ecclesiastical History of the Ancient Churches of the Albigenses.* Oxford: Claredon Press, 1821.

Andelin, Dr. Aubrey P. *Man of Steel and Velvet: A Guide to Masculine Development.* Pierce City, Missouri: Pacific Press Santa Barbara, 1972.

Anderson, Scott, and Jon Lee Anderson. *Inside the League: The Shocking Expose' of How Terrorists, Nazis, and Latin American Death Squads Have Infiltrated the World Anti-Communist League.* New York: Dodd, Mead and Company, 1986.

"Archives." *International Journal of Humanities and Social Sciences.* January 1, 2017. http://www.ijhssnet.com/view.php?u=https://www.ijhssnet.com/journals/Vol_7_No_1_January_2017/7.pdf (accessed November 11, 2019).

Arizona Radio Observatory. n.d. http://aro.as.arizona.edu/index.htm (accessed January 29, 2019).

Association, American Historical. *American Historical Association: Story of Propaganda.* n.d. https://www.historians.org/about-aha-and-membership/aha-history-and-archives/gi-roundtable-series/pamphlets/em-2-what-is-propaganda-(1944)/the-story-of-propaganda (accessed August 21, 2018).

Barnhouse, Donald Grey. *The Invisible War: The Panorama of the Continuing Conflict Between Good & Evil.* Grand Rapids, Michigan: Zondervan, 1965.

Becker, Gavin De. *The Gift of Fear.* New York: Dell Publishing, 1997.

Beecher, Edward. *The Papal Conspiracy Exposed.* Boston: Stearns and Company, 1855.

Begley, Sharon. "Newsweek." *Newsweek.* 05 15, 2008. www.http://newsweek.com/blogs/lab-notes/2008/05/15/the-vatican-and-little-green-men.html (accessed January 25, 2019).

Beliefnet. "Would You Baptize an Extraterrestrial." *Beliefnet: Inspire Your Everyday.* August 2000. https://www.beliefnet.com/news/science-religion/2000/08/would-you-baptize-an-extraterrestrial (accessed January 26, 2019).

Bernays, Edward L. *Propaganda.* New York: Liveright Publishing Corp., 1928.

Berry, Dr. Susan. *Breitbart.* n.d. https://www.breitbart.com/politics/2017/10/23/camille-paglia-public-schools-creating-students-know-nothing/#disqus_thread. (accessed 12 3, 2018).

Bessel A. Van der Kolk, MD. *The Body Keeps Score: Brain, Mind, and Body in the Healing of Trauma.* New York: Viking; the Penguin Group, 2014.

Bible Reasons. n.d. https://biblereasons.com/being-set-apart/ (accessed November 12, 2018).

Billington, James H. *Fire in the Minds of Men.* New Brunswick, New Jersey: Transaction Publishers, 2007.

Book of Jasher. Springfield, Utah: Cedar Fort Inc., 2010, Originally published by J.H. Parry & Company, 1887.

Brenton, Sir Lancelot C.L. *The Researchers Library of Ancient Texts Volume III.* Crane, Montana: Defense Publishers, 2012.

Brittanica, Encyclopedia. *Encyclopedia Brittanica.* August 1, 2016. https://www.britannica.com/topic/Mayflower-Compact (accessed November 14, 2018).

Broadbent, E. H. *The Pilgrim Church.* London: Pickering and Inglis LTD, 1931.

Brownlee, W.C. *Secret Instructions of the Jesuits.* New York: American and Foreign Christian Union, 1857.

Bunker, Micahel. *Swarms of Locusts: The Jesuit Attack On the Faith.* New York: Writers Club Press, 2002.

Bush, President George W. *The White House.* April 10, 2002. https://georgewbush-whitehouse.archives.gov/news/releases/2002/04/20020410-4.html (accessed 07 13, 2019).

Bushak, Lecia. "The Human Eye Can See Infrared Light, Plus 5 Other Things You Had No Idea Eyes Can Do." *Medical Daily.* December 3, 2014. https://www.medicaldaily.com/human-eye-can-see-infrared-light-plus-5-other-things-you-had-no-idea-eyes-can-do-312946 (accessed February 24, 2019).

Cardinal Gibbons, Bishop Keane, Edwin D. Mead and Honorable John Jay. *Denominational Schools.* Boston: Committe of One Hundred, 1889.

Cashin, Edward J. "Trustee Georgia." *New Georgia Encyclopedia.* September 2, 2015. https://www.georgiaencyclopedia.org/articles/history-archaeology/trustee-georgia-1732-1752#The-Georgia-Charter (accessed November 2, 2019).

"Catholics in British America." *The American Revolution.* n.d. http://www.ouramericanrevolution.org/index.cfm/page/view/p0155 (accessed November 2, 2019).

Chapman, James L. *Americanism versus Romanism: or the cis-Atlantic battle between Sam and the Pope.* Nashville, Tennessee, 1856.

Charles, Translated by R.H. *The Book of Jubilees.* Mineola, New York: Dover Publications, 2010.

Cheever, George B. *Right of the Bible in Our Public Schools.* New York: Robert Carter & Brothers, 1859.

Chery, Fritz. *Bible Reasons.* March 9, 2018. https://biblereasons.com/being-set-apart/ (accessed 01 15, 2019).

Chick, Jack. *Alberto.* Chino, California: Chick Publications, 1979.

Chiniquy, Charles. *Fifty Years in the Church of Rome.* Chicago: Adam Craig, 1891.

Chiniquy, Father. *Fifty Years in the Church of Rome.* Chicago: Adam Craig; 77and 79 Jackson St., 1891.

Church, Catholic. *The Great Encyclical Letters of Pope Leo XIII.* New York: Benziger Brothers, 1903.

"Comet and Father Malachi Martin." *Godlike Productions.* April 5, 1997.

http://www.godlikeproductions.com/forum1/message326615/pg1 (accessed February 24, 2019).

Consolmagno, Guy. *Intelligent Life in the Universe: Catholic Belief and the Search for Extraterrestrial Life.* London: Catholic Truth Society, 2005.

contributors, Wikiquote. *Paul Harvey.* n.d. https://en.wikiquote.org/w/index.php?title=Paul_Harvey&oldid=2445220 (accessed August 16, 2018).

Conway, Moncure D. *Addresses and Reprints.* Boston: Houghton Mifflin Co., 1909.

Cusak, Mary Frances. *The Black Pope: A History of the Jesuits.* London: Marshall, Russell & Co. Ltd., 1896.

De Rosa, Peter. *Vicars of Christ: The Darkside of the Papacy.* New York: Crown Publishers, 1988.

Desanctis, Luigi. *Popery, Puseyism and Jesuitism.* London: D.Catt, translated from original Roma Papale, 1865, 1905.

Dictionary.com. n.d. https://www.dictionary.com/ (accessed February 24, 2019).

Dollinger, J.H. Ignaz Von. *The Pope and the Council.* London: Rivington, 1869.

Donovan, Colin B. "Fasting and Abstinence." *Catholic Online.* n.d. https://www.catholic.org/lent/abfast.php (accessed February 27, 2019).

Durant, Will. *THE AGE OF FAITH: A History of Medieval Civilization--Christain, Islamic, and Judaic--from Constantine to Dante: A.D. 325-1300.* New York: Simon and Shuster, 1950.

D-Wave; TheQuantum Computing Company. n.d. https://www.dwavesys.com/our-company/meet-d-wave (accessed 07 13, 2019).

Edmond Paris, A. Robson, tr.,. *Teh Vatican Against Europe.* London: P. R. MacMillan, Ltd., 1961.

Elliot, Edward B. *Commentary on the Apocalypse, Volume 1.* London: Seeley, Burnside and Seeley, 1847.

Extraterrestrial Life. n.d. http://www.disf.org/en/Voci/65.asp (accessed February 24, 2019).

Family, Focus On The. "The Truth Project." *The Truth Project.* Greer, SC: Focus on the Family, 2004.

Fresenborg, Bernard. *Thirty Years in Hell or "From Darkness to Light".* Saint Louis, Missouri : North American Book House, 1904.

Fulton, Justin Dewey. *The Roman Catholic Element in American History.* Cincinnati: Moore, Wilstach, Keys & Overend, 1856.

G. T. Bettany, M.A, BSc. *A Popualr History of the Reformation and Modern Protestantism.* London: Ward, Lock, Bowden, 1895.

Goodreads. n.d. https://www.goodreads.com/quotes/33-men-occasionally-stumble-over-the-truth-but-most-of-them (accessed August 16, 2018).

Got Questions. n.d. https://www.gotquestions.org/ecumenism-ecumenical.html (accessed November 11, 2018).

Griesinger, Theodor. *The Jesuits: Their Complete History.* London: W.H. Allen & Co., 1903; originally published in 1873.

Gruen, Erich S. *Oxford Classical Dictionary.* December 22, 2016. https://oxfordre.com/classics/view/10.1093/acrefore/9780199381135.001.0001/acrefore-9780199381135-e-8134 (accessed October 31, 2019).

Guinness, H. Grattan. *Romanism and the Reformation.* Toronto: S. R. Briggs, 1887.

Harcourt, Richard. *The Great Conspiracy Against Our Public Schools.* San Francisco, California: California News Company, 1890.

Harris, General Thomas M. *Rome's Responsibility for the Assassination of Abraham Lincoln.* 1897. http://www.antichristconspiracy.com/HTML%20Pages/Rome%27s%20Responsibility%20for%20the%20Assassination%20of%20Lincoln.htm (accessed September 25, 2018).

Heiser, Dr. Michael S. *Unseen Realm.* Bellingham, WA: Lexham Press, 2015.

Herbermann, Charles G. "The Catholic Encyclopedia, Vol. 12: Philip II- Reuss." *Christian Classics Etheral Library.* n.d. http://www.ccel.org/ccel/herbermann/cathen12.html. (accessed November 12, 2019).

Hillman, Os. *Crosswalk.* n.d. https://www.crosswalk.com/family/homeschool/high-school/did-you-know-that-education-in-america-was-once-very-christian.html (accessed November 16, 2018).

—. *Crosswalk.com.* n.d. https://www.crosswalk.com/family/homeschool/high-school/did-you-know-that-education-in-america-was-once-very-christian.html (accessed August 28, 2018).

Horn, Tom and Nita. *Forbidden Gates; How Genetics, Robotics, Artificial Intelligence, Synthetic Biology, Nanotechnology, and Human Enhancement Herald the Dawn of Techno-Dimensional Spiritual Warfare.* Crane, Missouri: Defender Publishing, 2010.

Horton, Geoff. n.d. http://www.geoffhorton.com/PapalClaims.html (accessed July 3, 2019).

"How Does The Human Eye Work?" *National Keratoconus Foundation.* n.d. https://www.nkcf.org/about-keratoconus/how-the-human-eye-works/ (accessed February 24, 2019).

Huneeus, J. Antonio. "The Vatican Extraterestrial Question." *Open Minds Magazine,* June/July 2010: 59.

Hunt, Dave. *A Woman Rides the Beast.* Eugene, Oregon: Harvest House, 1994.

James Strong, LL.D., S.T.D. *Strongs Exhaustive Concordance of the Bible.* Nashville, Tenessee: Thomas Nelson Publishers, 1990.

Jeremiah, David. *The Handwriting on the Wall: Secrets From The Prophecies of Daniel.* Dallas: Word Publishing, 1992.

Jeremiah, David, and C.C. Carlson. *Escape the Coming Night.* Dallas, Texas: Word Publishing, 1990.

Jeremiah, David, and Carol C. Carlson. *Invasion of Other Gods: Teh Seduction of New Age Spirituality.* Dallas, TX: Word Publishing, 1995.

Joseph, Andrew. *Human--Animal Chimer Research May Resume with NIH Support.* August 4, 2016. https://www.scientificamerican.com/article/human-animal-chimera-research-may-resume-with-nih-support/ (accessed July 13, 2019).

Keel, John A. *Operation Trojan Horse: The classic Breakthrough Study of UFOs.* San Antonio, Texas: Anomalist Books, 2013.

Keller, Timothy J. *Counterfeit gods: the empty promises of money, sex and power, and the only hope that matters.* New York, New York: Dutton, member of the Penguin Group, 2009.

Kensit, John Alfred. *The Jesuits: Their History and Crimes.* London: Protestant Truth Society, 1918.

Kepler, Johannes. *The Staddon Family.* n.d. https://www.staddonfamily.com/2010/07/01/keplers-quote/. (accessed January 17, 2019).

Kjos, Berit. "Reinvent the World." *Kjos Ministries.* 2001. https://www.crossroad.to/articles2/Reinvent1.htm (accessed December 5, 2018).

—. *Your Child and the New Age.* Wheaton, Illinois : Victor, 1990.

Klett, Leah Marieann. *Gospel Herald.* March 16, 2015. http://www.gospelherald.com/articles/55719/20150526/pope-francis-calls-for-unity-between-evangelicals-catholics-division-the-work-of-devil.htm (accessed January 18, 2019).

—. *The Gospel Herald Church.* May 26, 2015. https://www.gospelherald.com/articles/55719/20150526/pope-francis-calls-for-unity-between-evangelicals-catholics-division-the-work-of-devil.htm (accessed November 11, 2018).

Large Binocular Telescope Observatory. n.d. http://www.lbto.org/overview.html (accessed January 29, 2019).

Laurens, J. Wayne. *The Crisis: Or, the Enemies of America Unmasked.* Philadelphia, Pennsylvania: G. D. Miller, 1855.

Leone, Jacopo. *The Jesuit Conspiracy: The Secret Plan of the Order.* London: Chapman and Hall, 1848.

Leopizzi, Paola. "Monsignor Corrado Balducci Says Mexico Blessed with UFO Sightings." *MUFON [Mutual UFO Network],* March 28, 2006.

Lewis, Jesse Penn. *War the Saints.* Fort Washington, Pennsylvania: Christian-Literature-Crusade, 1995.

Lewy, Guenter. *The Catholic Church and Nazi Germany.* Da Capo Press, 2000.

Liguori, Saint Alphonsus De. *Dignity and Duties of the Priest or Selva.* New York : Benziger Brothers, 1889.

Long, Phillip J. "Why did Paul go to Arabia?" *Reading Acts.* September 8, 2017. https://readingacts.com/2017/09/08/why-did-paul-go-to-arabia/ (accessed July 22, 2019).

Lumpkin, Joseph B. *The Books of Enoch.* Blountsville, AL: Fifth Estate Publishers, 2010.

Mackay, Neil. "And On the Eighth Day--Did God Create Aliens?" *Sunday Herald--Scotland,* November 28, 2005.

Macpherson, Hector. *The Jesuits in History.* Springfield, Missouri: Ozark Book Publishers, 1997; originally published in Edinburgh 1914.

Maltz, Maxwell. *Psycho-Cybernetics.* New York: Pocket Books, 1960.

Manhattan, Avro. *The Vatican Billions.* Chino, California: Chick Publications, 1983.

—. *The Vatican in World Politics.* New York: Gaer Associates, 1949.

—. *The Vatican's Holocaust.* Huntsville, Arkansas : Ozark Books, 1986.

Meredith, Roderick C. "500 Years of The Protestant Reformation." *Tomorrow's World,* May-June 2018.

Merriam-Webster. n.d. https://www.merriam-webster.com/ (accessed 12 27, 2018).

Michael Muller, C.S.S.R. *The Catholic Priest.* Baltimore: Kreuzer Brothers, 1872.

Morey, Robert A. "Where Did Allah Come From?" *Chick Publications.* n.d. https://chick.com/information/article?id=Where-Did-Allah-Come-From (accessed January 23, 2019).

Muse'e. n.d. https://www.museeprotestant.org/en/notice/the-catholic-reformation-or-counter-reformation/ (accessed January 18, 2019).

Office of the Historian. n.d. https://history.state.gov/milestones/1866-1898/yellow-journalism (accessed September 16, 2018).

Ostling, Richard N. "Keeper of the Straight and Narrow. Joseph Cardinal Ratzinger." *Time Magazine.* December 6, 1993. http://content.time.com/time/magazine/article/0,9171,979775,00.html (accessed March 7, 2019).

Owings, Hank. "What religions in the world require chastity or celibacy by their religious leaders/priests?" *Quora.* July 5, 2012. https://www.quora.com/What-religions-in-the-world-require-chastity-or-celibacy-by-their-religious-leaders-priests (accessed February 27, 2019).

Paine, Thomas. "The AGE OF REASON - Welcome To The Deism Site!" n.d. www.deism.com/images/theageofreason1794.pdf (accessed September 4, 2018).

Paris, Edmond. *The Secret History of theJesuits.* Chino, California: Chick Publications, ; originally published in 1965, 1975.

—. *The Vatican Against Europe.* Springfield , Missouri: Ozark Book Publishers, 1993.

Parkman, Frances. *France and England in North America.* New York: The Viking Press, ; originally published in 1865, 1983.

Passantino, Bob, and Gretchen Passantino. *When the Devil Dares Your Kids.* Ann Arbor, Michigan: Servant, 1991.

Perrin, J. Paul. *History of the Waldenses: Anterior to the Reformation.* Philadelphia: Griffith and Simon, 1846.

Philosophy, All About. *Absolute Truth - New Worldview.* n.d. https://www.allaboutphilosophy.org/absolute-truth.htm (accessed August 15, 2018).

Productions, God Like. "Comet and Father Malachi Martin." *godlikeproductions.* January 7, 2007. www.godlikeproductions.com/forum1/message326615/pg1. (accessed January 24, 2019).

Putnam, Cris, and Thomas Horn. *Exo-Vaticana: Petrus Romanus, Project L.U.C.I.F.E.R. and the VAtican's Astonishing Plan for the Arrival of an Alien Savior.* Crane, Montana: Defender Publishing, 2013.

Rauschning, Hermann. *The Voice of Destruction.* New York: G. P. Putman's Sons, 1940.

Remsburg, J.E. *Six Historic Americans.* Crown Right Book Company, 2001.

Rennie, John. *Human-Animal Chimeras.* June 27, 2005. https://www.scientificamerican.com/article/human-animal-chimeras/ (accessed July 13, 2019).

Rev. L. Giustiniani, D.D. *Papal Rome As It Is.* Baltimore: Printed at Publication Rooms No. 7, 1843.

Riemer, George. *The New Jesuits.* Boston, Massachusetts: Little, Brown & Co.,, 1971.

Rome, G. B. Nicolini of. *History of the Jesuits: Their Origin, Progress, Doctrines, and Designs.* London: Henry G. Bohn, 1854.

Rufus W. Clark, D. D. *Question of the Hour: The Bible and The School Fund.* Boston: Lee and Shepard, 1870.

Ryan, Danielle. *RT Question More.* n.d. https://www.rt.com/op-ed/424298-false-flag-syria-attack/ (accessed August 21, 2018).

S.C.L., Rev. J.H.Macguire. *The Catholic Handbook or Every Protestant His Own Controversialist.* London: Seeley & Co.; Hatchard & Son; Wertheim & Mackintosh: Nibbet & and at The British Reformation Society's Office, 1860.

Samuel F. B. Morse, A. M.,. *Foreign Conspiracy Against The Liberties of The United States.* New York: American and Foreign Christian Union, 1855.

Saussy, F. Tupper. *Rulers of Evil.* Reno: Ospray Bookmakers, 1999.

Schaff, Philip. "History of the Christian Church, Volume VIII: Modern Chrisianity. The Swiss Reformation." *Christian Classics Ethereal Library.* November 27, 2002. http://www.ccel.org/ccel/schaff/hcc8.html (accessed March 18, 2019).

Science, Interdisciplinary Encyclopedia of Religion and. "Extraterrestrial Life." *Interdisciplinary Encyclopedia of Religion & Science.* 2008. http://inters.org/extraterrestrial-life (accessed January 26, 2019).

Shaeffer, Francis A. *A Christian Manifesto.* Wheaton, Illinois: Crossway Books, 1981.

Shepard, J. E. C. *The Babington Plot.* Toronto, Canada: Wittenburg Publications, 1987.

Smietana, Bob. "LifeWay Research." *LifeWay.* 04 25, 2017. https://lifewayresearch.com/2017/04/25/lifeway-research-americans-are-fond-of-the-bible-dont-actually-read-it/ (accessed 12 15, 2018).

Snyder, Michael. "The One World Religion Cometh: Pope Francis Warmly Welcomes Top Islamic Cleric to the Vatican ." *Charisma News.* May 24, 2016. https://www.charismanews.com/opinion/57367-the-one-world-religion-cometh-pope-francis-warmly-welcomes-top-islamic-cleric-to-the-vatican (accessed January 22, 2019).

Sparknotes: Yellow Journalism and the Rise of American Anger: 1895-1897. n.d. http://www.sparknotes.com/history/american/spanishamerican/section2/ (accessed August 21, 2018).

Spurgeon, Charles Haddon. *Geese in their Hoods: Selected Writings on Roman Catholicism.* 1873.

Stetzer, Ed. "Charisma." *Charisma Magazine.* 10 9, 2014. www.charismamag.com/life/culture/21076-dumb-and-dumber-how-biblical-illiteracy-is-killing-our-nation?showall=1&start=0 (accessed 12 5, 2018).

—. "The Exchange." *Christianity Today.* 10 17, 2014. https://www.christianitytoday.com/edstetzer/2014/october/biblical-illiteracy-by-numbers.html (accessed 12 5, 2018).

Steve Feazel, Dr. Carol M. Swain. *Abduction: How Liberalism Steals Our Children's Hearts and Minds.* Meadville, Pennsylvania: Christian Faith Publishing, Inc., 2016.

Strong, James. *Strong's Exhaustive Concordance of the Bible: Hebrew and Chadee Dictionary.* Nashville: Thomas Nelson Publishers, 1990.

Terry, Brother. *God and America.* n.d. http://www.angelfire.com/la2/prophet1/america.html (accessed August 22, 2018).

Tertullian, Translated by Peter Holmes, Editied by Alexander Roberts, James Donaldson, and A. Cleveland Coxe. *The*

Ante-Nicene Fathers Vol. 3,: Translations of the Writings fo the Fathers down to A.D. 325. Buffalo, New York: Christian Literature Publishing Co., 1885.

"The Maryland Toleration Act of 1649." *American History; From Revolution to Reconstruction and Beyond.* n.d. http://www.let.rug.nl/usa/documents/1600-1650/the-maryland-toleration-act-1649.php (accessed 2019 2, November).

Thoams, I.D.E. *The Omega Conspiracy; Satan's Last Assault on God's Kingdom.* Crane, Missouri: Anomalos Publishing House, 2008.

Thompson, Glen L. *St. Paul's Lutheran Church and School.* n.d. https://www.stpls.com/uploads/4/4/8/0/44802893/augsburg-confession.pdf (accessed January 20, 2019).

Thompson, R. W. *The Footprints of the Jesuits.* New York: Hunt & Eaton, 1894.

—. *The Papacy and The Civil Power.* New York: Harper & Brothers Publishers, 1876.

Thomson, Secretary Charles. *Journals of the Continental Congress 1774-1789.* Washington: Government Printing Office, 1904.

Today, USA. "Vatican Astronomer Says it's OK to Think Aliens Exist." *USA Today.* May 14, 2008. www.usatoday.com/news/religion/2008-05-14-vatican-aliens_N.htm (accessed January 24, 2019).

Tryon Edwards, D.D. *A Dictionary of Thoughts.* Cassell Publishing Company, 1908.

Under the Radar Nedia. July 19, 2012. https://undertheradarmedia.wordpress.com/2012/07/19/bill-clintons-mentor-carroll-quigley-reveals-fraud-of-the-two-party-system/ (accessed January 18, 2019).

University, Princeton. "The London Magazine, Or, Gentleman's Monthly Intelligencer, Volume 43." 1774.

Vallee, Jacques. *Passport to Magonia: From Folklore to Flying Saucers.* Brisbane, Australia: Daily Grail Publishing, 2014.

—. *The Invisble College; What a Group of Scientist Has Discovered About UFO Influence on the Human Race.* San Antonio, Texas: Anomalist Books, 2014.

Vatican Observatory. n.d. http://www.vaticanobservatory.va/content/specolavaticana/en/research/facilities/vatt.html (accessed January 29, 2019).

Vladimir Lenin Quotes. n.d. https://www.brainyquote.com/quotes/vladimir_lenin_132031 (accessed August 10, 2019).

Webster, Noah. *American Dictionary of the English Language: Noah Webster 1828.* Chespeake, Virgina: Foundation for American Christian Education, 2010.

—. *Webster's Dictionary 1828 - Online Edtion.* n.d. http://webstersdictionary1828.com/.

West, Mick. *Metabunk.org.* December 11, 2011. https://www.metabunk.org/debunked-a-conspiracy-so-monstrous-he-cannot-believe-it-exists-hoover.t330/ (accessed January 18, 2019).

Wharey, Rev. James. *Sketches of Church History.* Philadelphia, PA: Presbyterian Board of Publication, 1840.

White, Ellen G. *The Great Controversy.* Deland, Florida: Laymen for Religious Liberty, 1990, originally published in 1888, 1990.

Wikimedia Commons. n.d. https://commons.wikimedia.org/w/index.php?curid=14634426 (accessed November 22, 2018).

Wikipedia. *WikipediA The Free Encyclopedia.* n.d. https://en.wikipedia.org/wiki/Pilgrims_(Plymouth_Colony) (accessed August 31, 2018).

Willaim Whiston, A.M. *The Complete Works of Flavius Josephus the Jewish Historian.* Green Forest, Arkansas: New Leaf Publishing, 2010.

Wohlberg, Steve. "Left Behind by the Jesuits." *Assembly of Yahweh.* n.d. http://assemblyoftrueisrael.com/Documents/Leftbehind.htm (accessed January 22, 2019).

World Council of Churches. n.d. https://www.oikoumene.org/en/about-us (accessed 01 15, 2019).

"Would You Baptize an Extraterrestrial?" *beliefnet:Inspire Your Everyday.* n.d. https://www.beliefnet.com/news/science-religion/2000/08/would-you-baptize-an-extraterrestrial?p=2 (accessed February 24, 2019).

www.ingramcontent.com/pod-product-compliance
Lightning Source LLC
Chambersburg PA
CBHW032037090426
42744CB00004B/41
9781946615473